W9-BTM-005

BEFORE

&

AFTER

ALEXANDER

BEFORE

&

AFTER

ALEXANDER

THE LEGEND AND LEGACY OF ALEXANDER THE GREAT

RICHARD A. BILLOWS

OVERLOOK DUCKWORTH
NEW YORK • LONDON

This edition first published in hardcover in the United States in 2018 by
The Overlook Press, Peter Mayer Publishers, Inc.

NEW YORK
141 Wooster Street
New York, NY 10012
www.overlookpress.com
For bulk and special sales, please contact sales@overlookny.com
or write to us at the above address.

LONDON
30 Calvin Street
London E1 6NW
info@duckworth-publishers.co.uk
www.ducknet.co.uk

Cataloging-in-Publication Data is available from the Library of Congress
A catalog record for this book is available from the British Library

Book design and type formatting by Bernard Schleifer
Manufactured in the United States of America
FIRST EDITION
1 3 5 7 9 10 8 6 4 2
ISBN 978-1-59020-740-6 (US)
ISBN: 978-0-7156-5281-7 (UK)

For Clare, at last . . .

CONTENTS

INTRODUCTION

I N June 323 BCE, in a palace in Babylon, a young man lay dying. Around his bed were a host of attendants, doctors, and generals, concerned about the imminent death of the ruler of their world. The young man was Alexander the Great, and though he was just thirty-two years old, he had already conquered one of the largest empires in history and made himself forever famous as one of history's greatest military leaders. For the generals gathered at his bedside, however, Alexander's death presented a huge problem: he had no clear successor. There was a vast empire to be organized and ruled, and no one knew how it was to be done or by whom. In the end, it took forty years of rivalry and warfare among Alexander's generals to sort out the succession to his power.

One hundred and fifty years later a new power, the young Roman state, began to expand into and take over the lands that Alexander had conquered and ruled so briefly, and they found in the eastern Mediterranean region a civilization based on the Greek language, Greek cities, and Greek culture, established there by the work of Alexander's Successors. That Greek-based civilization is known today as the Hellenistic civilization, and though taken over by the Romans it endured as the civilization of the eastern Mediterranean world for another five hundred years or so, until the triumph of Christianity and, eventually, Islam brought about radical changes. As the conqueror who made this great era of Hellenistic civilization possible, Alexander the Great's life, career, and achievements have been studied over and over by historians, giving rise to literally hundreds of books and probably thousands of detailed articles about the great conqueror. Much less studied, however, are the development of the Macedonian state and army under Alexander's father Philip II, which made Alexander's career possible, and the activities and policies of Alexander's Successors, which created the organizational framework in which Hellenistic civilization developed and flourished.

The aim of this book is, first, to offer a detailed study of the career of Philip II (Chapters 1–4). The state of Macedonia before Philip's succession to the throne was a disorganized and disunited backwater, peripheral to the local great powers of Athens, Sparta, and Persia. Philip II built up an entirely new type of army with a new style of warfare, and through this army united Macedonia, expanded its borders, and turned it into the greatest power in the ancient world by his death at the age of forty-seven, assassinated by a disgruntled officer in his own bodyguard. It was the state and army built by Philip that provided Alexander with the tools to undertake his career of conquest.

After a relatively brief review of Alexander's conquests (Chapter 5), the book treats in some detail the forty years after Alexander's death, showing how his greatest generals—men who, like Alexander, had been trained in the army and wars of Philip II—took control of Alexander's conquests and built the three great Hellenistic empires in those lands: the Antigonid Empire in the Balkan region, the Seleucid Empire in western Asia, and the Ptolemaic Empire in Egypt and Libya. By settling tens, if not hundreds of thousands of Greek colonists, for whom they built hundreds of new Greek cities in western Asia and Egypt, and by encouraging many natives to settle in these new cities too, adopting Greek names, the Greek language, and Greek culture as their own, these rulers helped to establish Hellenistic civilization as the culture of the eastern Mediterranean world for over half a millennium (Chapters 6–7).

This book thus covers a topic of enormous interest and importance to the history of western civilization, that of the establishment of Greek culture as a universal culture from the rivers of Iraq to the Adriatic Sea, and from the Black and Caspian Seas to the deserts of Arabia and the border of the Sudan. Everywhere within this vast and diverse territory, between 300 BCE and 300 CE (and later) there were to be found Greek cities with Greek citizens, speaking and reading the Greek language, and living their lives according to the social, cultural, and political patterns established in Classical Greece in the sixth, fifth, and fourth centuries BCE. This remarkable civilization left, as is well known, a rich cultural heritage that has deeply influenced western (and indeed Muslim) culture and civilization ever since. It is as the facilitators who made possible this spread of Greek culture, and its establishment throughout the eastern Mediterranean and western Asia as the dominant culture, that Philip II of Macedonia, his son Alexander, and Alexander's Successors remain an important and fascinating topic of study.

MAPS

MAP 1: Greece - 5th century

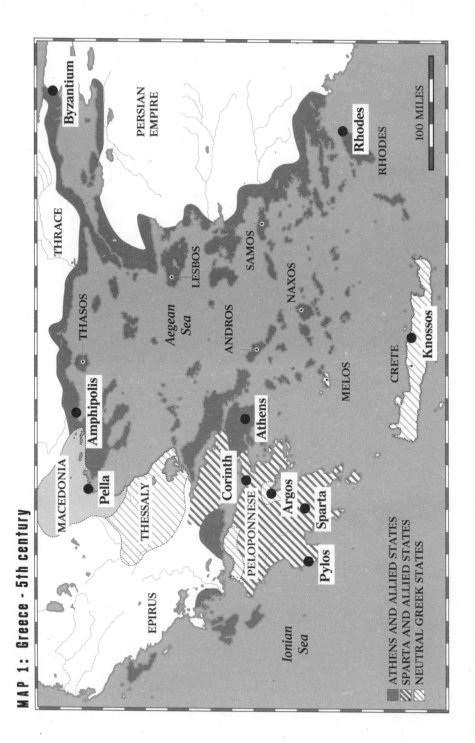

THRACE

Byzantium

PERSIAN EMPIRE

RHODES

Rhodes

THASOS

LESBOS

SAMOS

Aegean Sea

NAXOS

ANDROS

MACEDONIA

Amphipolis

Pella

MELOS

CRETE

Knossos

THESSALY

Athens

Corinth

PELOPONNESE

Argos

Sparta

Pylos

EPIRUS

Ionian Sea

100 MILES

ATHENS AND ALLIED STATES
SPARTA AND ALLIED STATES
NEUTRAL GREEK STATES

MAP 2: Macadonia

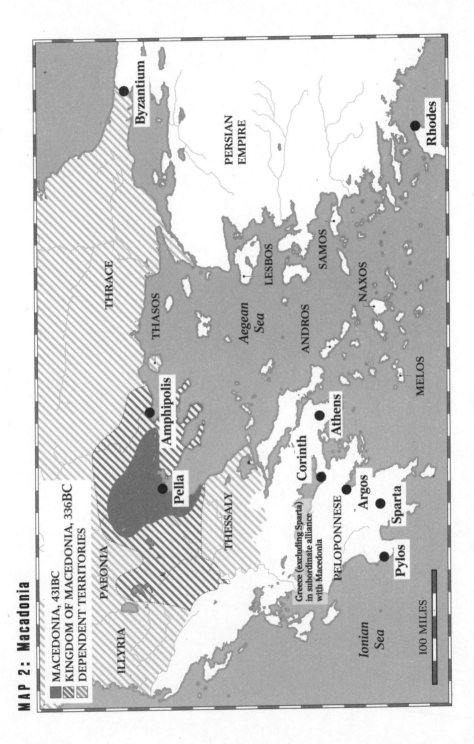

■ MACADONIA, 431BC
▨ KINGDOM OF MACEDONIA, 336BC
▩ DEPENDENT TERRITORIES

ILLYRIA

PAEONIA

THRACE

Byzantium

THASOS

Amphipolis

Pella

THESSALY

Aegean Sea

LESBOS

SAMOS

PERSIAN EMPIRE

ANDROS

NAXOS

Rhodes

Greece (excluding Sparta) in subordinate alliance with Macedonia

Corinth

Athens

PELOPONNESE

Argos

Sparta

MELOS

Pylos

Ionian Sea

100 MILES

MAP 3: Alexander

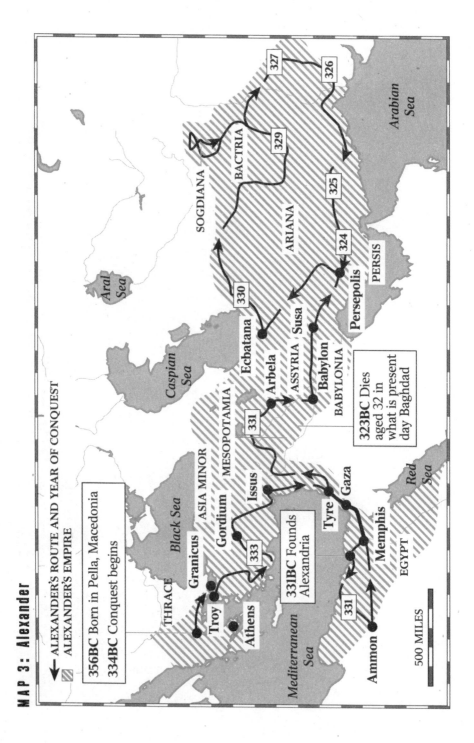

→ ALEXANDER'S ROUTE AND YEAR OF CONQUEST

▨ ALEXANDER'S EMPIRE

356BC Born in Pella, Macedonia
334BC Conquest begins

331BC Founds Alexandria

323BC Dies aged 32 in what is present day Baghdad

THRACE

Black Sea

Granicus

Troy

ASIA MINOR

Athens

Gordium

MESOPOTAMIA

Issus

333

331

Arbela

ASSYRIA

Tyre

Gaza

Susa

Babylon

BABYLONIA

Memphis

331

EGYPT

Mediterranean Sea

Red Sea

Ammon

500 MILES

Ecbatana

330

Caspian Sea

Aral Sea

SOGDIANA

BACTRIA

329

ARIANA

Persepolis

PERSIS

324

325

326

327

Arabian Sea

MAP 4: Diadoche

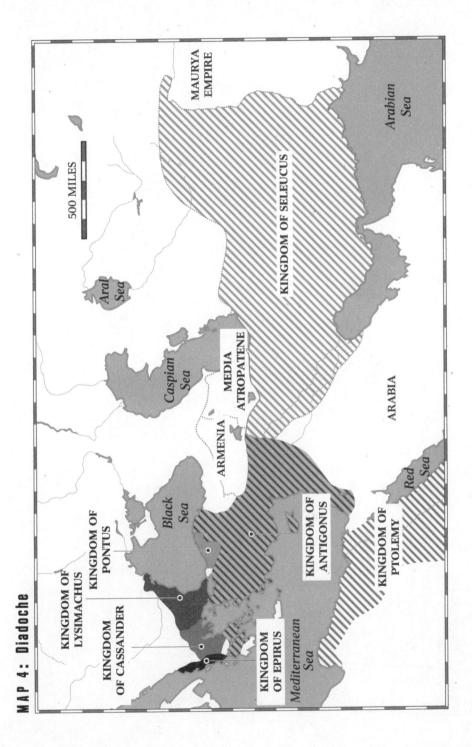

MAP 5: Helenistic

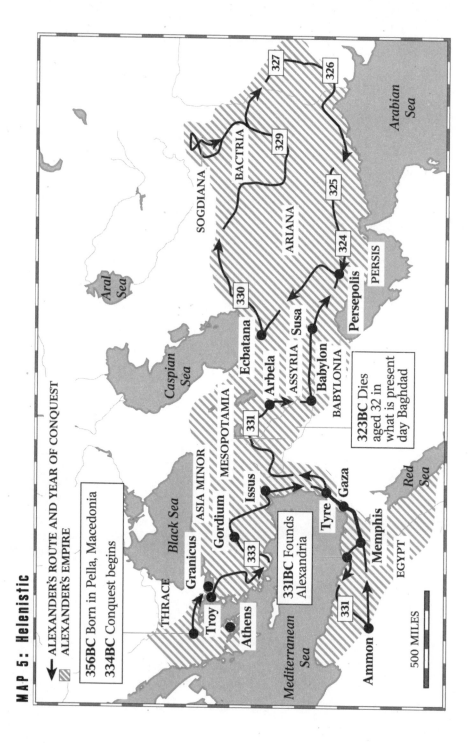

→ ALEXANDER'S ROUTE AND YEAR OF CONQUEST
▨ ALEXANDER'S EMPIRE

356BC Born in Pella, Macedonia
334BC Conquest begins

331BC Founds Alexandria

323BC Dies aged 32 in what is present day Baghdad

THRACE
Black Sea
Granicus
Troy
Athens
Gordium
333
Issus
ASIA MINOR
MESOPOTAMIA
331
Ecbatana
Arbela
ASSYRIA
Susa
Babylon
BABYLONIA
330
Caspian Sea
Aral Sea
SOGDIANA
BACTRIA
329
330
ARIANA
324
Persepolis
PERSIS
325
326
327
Arabian Sea
Tyre
Gaza
Memphis
EGYPT
331
Ammon
Red Sea
Mediterranean Sea

500 MILES

CHAPTER 1

Macedonia before Philip II

T HE NORTH-WEST BEND OF THE AEGEAN SEA FORMS A GREAT GULF— the Thermaic Gulf—enclosed by land on three sides. To the west, sweeping northwards from the foothills of majestic Mount Olympus, lie the gently rolling plains of Pieria and Emathia; to the north the rich Amphaxitis plain, on either side of the broad Axius River, extends upward from the coast to the hills of Almopia and Messapion; and to the east the Chalcidice peninsula projects into the Aegean like a squat, three-tined fork (see map 1). In the fourth century BCE these lands were occupied by one of the most remarkable people in western history: the Macedonians.

1. WERE THE MACEDONIANS GREEK?

Who were the Macedonians? The question is simple, but it is anything but simple to answer, since the issue of the ethnic and linguistic identity of the ancient Macedonians has been caught up in the identity politics of the modern peoples and states of the southern Balkan peninsula. As the great Ottoman Empire slowly decayed and crumbled away in the second half of the nineteenth century, in the southern Balkan region four key local peoples sought to establish nation-states encompassing as much territory as possible, and their respective claims collided in Macedonia: the Greeks to the south, the Albanians to the north-west, the Serbs to the north, and the Bulgars to the north-east. In this territorial rivalry, the Greeks used history to bolster their claim to Macedonian lands, making the following argument: the ancient Macedonians were Greek; Macedonia is thus a historically Greek land; Macedonia should therefore, like other historically Greek lands, be part of the modern Greek state. The response to this argument from the Serbs and the Bulgars was, in great part, built around denying the Greekness of the ancient Macedonians, and they found some strong evidence and notable scholars to support that part at least (the non-Greek identity of the ancient

Macedonians) of their claims. Thus arose the "Macedonian question" which still arouses partisan passions in the southern Balkan region: were the ancient Macedonians Greek or were they not?

One of the approaches scholars have made to try to answer this question is through archaeological data. If it could be somehow proved archaeologically that the ancient Macedonians belonged to the Greek peoples of archaic and classical times (the eighth to the fifth centuries BCE), or that they did not, the Macedonian question would be answered. As a result, a good deal of time and effort has been spent on studying the Macedonian region and its surroundings, in an attempt to show the origin of the ancient Macedonian people. Much has been learned from this archaeological exploration but, despite some confident claims, nothing has been proved about Macedonian origins. In order to establish such proof, we would need to find some clear markers in the archaeological record that could be tied to Macedonian identity: a distinctive style of pottery, for example, or method of disposing of the dead, or technique of house-building. Any such thing that could be traced in archaeological explorations, shown to be distinctively Macedonian, and then linked to other peoples or regions, would make possible a tracing of Macedonian origins and (perhaps) identity. But no distinctive Macedonian marker of this sort exists.

In the fifth and fourth centuries BCE, the Macedonians did, we know, have some very distinctive features. There was a peculiar, beret-like Macedonian hat called the *kausia* (ill. 1). There was a distinctive Macedonian shield: small and round, and decorated with medallion-like elements around its rim (ill. 2). Unfortunately, though archaeologists have found images of these Macedonian features on gravestones, coins, and the like from the fourth century and later, there is no trace of them before the fifth century. It would be even better if we could find inscriptions mentioning the presence of Macedonians, either in Greek or in a non-Greek language. But again, archaeology has not found such inscriptions earlier than the late fifth century. The results of archaeological exploration, full of interest as they are, do not help settle the Macedonian question. What we see is that the southern Balkan region was, in the first half of the first millennium BCE, home to various groups of people who had similar material culture, no doubt learning from and influencing each other, moving about the Pindus and Rhodopi

1. Coin of Bactrian-Greek ruler Antimachus wearing a Macedonian *kausia*
(*Author's photo, taken at Metropolitan Museum, NY*)

2. Coin of Macedonian king Antigonus II Gonatas showing Macedonian shield with head of Pan (*Wikimedia Commons from cgb.fr*)

ranges and their upland plateaus, or down into their neighboring coastal plains. Who these people or peoples were can only be determined, however, when we start to get written records. And those written records were produced by Greeks, beginning about 750 BCE.

The earliest surviving Greek inscriptions, mostly very brief groups of letters, date from the middle and second half of the eighth century; and the earliest surviving works of Greek literature, the Homeric epics, also date from the second half of the eighth century, by most scholars' reckoning. Nowhere in these early inscriptions do we find mention of Macedonians: as already mentioned, Macedonians are not mentioned in any inscriptions earlier than the fifth century. Nowhere in Homer's two great epics, the *Iliad* and the *Odyssey*, are Macedonians mentioned either. That is especially notable for the *Iliad*, because in its second book there is to be found a kind of geography of Greece: the so-called Catalogue of Ships. Ostensibly a list of the "heroes" and peoples who fought in the Trojan War, the Catalogue is in fact a kind of survey of Greek communities and peoples, first of central and southern Greece, and then of northern Greece. It probably derives from the oracle of Apollo at Delphi, since its pattern shows two itineraries around Greece, both starting from the region of the oracle; and it probably reflects the state of Greece around the end of the eighth century, when the oracle was first becoming important. The survey of northern Greece is basically limited to Thessaly and its immediate surroundings; it does not extend as far north as Macedonia, but then neither does it extend west into Epirus or Acarnania. Similarly, a small appendix, as it were, mentions a few of the Aegean islands, but leaves out most of the Cyclades and all of the Sporades. In other words, the author of the Homeric epics ignores Macedonia, but his geography of Greece is certainly incomplete, however you look at it, so the absence of Macedonia need not imply anything about Macedonian identity.

The first literary reference to Macedonia comes in one of the texts belonging to what is known as the Hesiodic corpus, the so-called *Catalogue of Women*. Though there is broad consensus among most scholars dating Hesiod around 700, there is considerable uncertainty about the date of this *Catalogue*, because we cannot be sure whether it was really composed by Hesiod, that is, by the author of the two surviving epic poems that come to us under the name of Hesiod—the *Theogony* and the *Works and Days*. The *Catalogue of Women* survives only in fragments, and while it is attributed to Hesiod in ancient sources, it may in fact have been composed up to 150 years later by an anonymous poet. But whether we call it Hesiod's work and date it ca. 700, or place it around 550, or somewhere in between, it contains the earliest surviving reference to Macedonia either way.

The first fragments of this *Catalogue of Women* deal with the origins of the Greek people, specifically with the "eponymous ancestors" of the Greek people. Ancient (and modern) Greeks called themselves "Hellenes" and considered themselves to be descended from a common ancestor named Hellen son of Deucalion (not to be confused with the infamous Helen of Troy, whose name was properly Helene). This kind of genealogical expression of identity is not familiar to us today, except perhaps to readers of the Bible. For there, in the book of Genesis, is to be found a very similar sort of account of the origin of the Israelite people. The patriarch of this people was—we are told—Jacob son of Isaac, who had another name: Israel, after which his descendants were called Israelites. Jacob Israel was the father of twelve sons, the eponymous ancestors of the twelve tribes of Israel: the Levites, named for Jacob's son Levi; the Judaeans, named for his son Judah, and so on. Just so, Hellen was the ancestor of the Hellenes (Greeks), through his children: his son Aeolus was the ancestor of one great branch of the Greek people, the Aeolians; his son Dorus was the ancestor of the Dorians; and his son Xouthus was the father of Ion, ancestor of the Ionians.

> And the war-loving ruler Hellen engendered
> Dorus and Xouthus and horse-loving Aeolus.
> The sons of Aeolus, law-setting rulers,
> Were Cretheus and Athamas and clever Sisyphus,
> Unjust Salmoneus and overbold Perieres.
> (*Catalogue of Women* Fragment 4)

Such is the Hesiodic genealogy of the Greek people, or rather a small fragment of it. And it is in this context that we first meet with the name Macedon. Fragments 1 and 3 of the *Catalogue of Women* offer the following:

> Hesiod in the first book of the Catalogue says that Deucalion was the son of Prometheus and Pronoea, and that Hellen was the son of Deucalion and Pyrrha.
> (Scholiast to Apollonius Rhodius 3.1086)

and:

> The land of Macedonia was named after Macedon, the son of Zeus and Thyia, daughter of Deucalion, as Hesiod tells:
> She conceived and bore to thunderbolt-loving Zeus
> Two sons, Magnes and horse-loving Macedon,
> Who established their home around Pieria and Olympus.
> Magnes again [was father of] Dictys and god-like Polydectes.
> (Constantine Porphyrogenitus *De Thematibus* 2.48a)

What emerges from this, then, is that according to this author, be it Hesiod or another archaic poet, the ancestor of the Macedonian people was the brother of the ancestor of the Magnesian people, both nephews of Hellen, the ancestor of the Greeks; and he lived in the region of Pieria and Olympos where the historical Macedonians lived. To this early poet, then, the Macedonians were not descendants of Hellen, but closely linked genealogically to them, coming from the same familial background of Deucalion and his children. Did he think of the Macedonians as Greeks? There is, arguably, some ambivalence about this; but it is worth noting that the Magnesians who lived, in the fifth and fourth centuries, among the mountains east of Thessaly, between the Thessalian plain and the sea, were never considered anything other than Greeks, though sharing the same descent as the Macedonians in the *Catalogue of Women*.

So far the Macedonians are seen, in the only early source that mentions them, as at the very least closely linked to the Greek people by genealogy. The next writers to mention the Macedonians were the two great fifth-century historians, founders of history writing, Herodotus and Thucydides. Basically, such information as we have about the Macedonians before the fourth century comes from these two writers, and it does not add up to a great deal. Neither of them directly addresses the question of Macedonian ethnicity. Herodotus mentions contacts between the Macedonian ruler Amyntas and the deposed Athenian tyrant Hippias about the year 510; tells of the establishment of Persian domination over Macedonia ca. 500; and tells a number of stories about Amyntas' son and successor as ruler of Macedonia, Alexander I. Several stories have to do with Alexander's involvement in the great war between the Persians and the Greeks in 480/79, in which Alexander is presented as a Persian vassal, but a friend of the southern Greeks, and especially of the Athenians. Most interesting, though, is a story about the origin of the Macedonian ruling family or clan, called the Argeadae.

As Herodotus tells the story (8.137–38), three brothers from the ruling family of Argos, the Temenids, were sent into exile and, after certain adventures, settled in Macedonia and became rulers of that land. The youngest of the three, Perdiccas, was the ancestor of the Macedonian rulers of the fifth century, Alexander I and his successors. The Temenids, in turn, were supposed to be descended from the greatest of all Greek heroes, Heracles; so according to this story, the Macedonian ruling family came from the southern Greek city most famed in mythic stories and legends, Argos, and were descendants of the most highly regarded hero of Greek myth, Heracles—just as were the two royal fam-

ilies of the Spartans. And Herodotus further alleges that this Argive
Temenid descent of the Macedonian ruling family was accepted as true
by the judges of the Olympic games, who allowed the young Alexander
to compete in the sprint race there based on this account of his Hellenic
ancestry (5.22). Left in question in all this is the identity of the other
Macedonians. Were they Hellenes? Herodotus doesn't say, though the
apparent need of Alexander to prove himself Greek by alleging Argive
descent may seem to imply that Macedonians were not regarded as
Greeks. This alleged Argive Temenid descent, by the way, has been accepted as true by some scholars, though it is surely clear that it is merely
a self-serving story put about by Alexander—for whom descent from
Heracles and Argos would give greatly improved status among the
Greeks—based on the similarity between the name of his family
(Argeadae) and the name Argos.

Thucydides tells of the expansion of Macedonian power from
Pieria northwards and eastwards, through Bottiaea and Almopia to the
Amphaxitis and beyond into the northern Chalcidice, and westwards
into the upland plateaus of the eastern Pindus (2.99). Interestingly, he
accepts the story that the Macedonian rulers were originally Temenids
from Argos, and alleges that they and their followers drove out the original inhabitants of the regions they conquered: Pierians were displaced
from Pieria, Almopians from Almopia, Bottiaeans from Bottiaea, and
so on. That might seem to imply that the Macedonians were mostly
Hellenes, who invaded and conquered their later homeland from southern Greece. Later he tells of a joint expedition conducted by the Macedonian ruler Perdiccas II and the Spartan commander Brasidas in 422
(4.124–25). Perdiccas' forces are said to be composed of "the Macedonians over whom he ruled and hoplites (heavily armed infantry) of the
Hellenes who lived there" (4.124); later there is mention of a Macedonian and Chalcidian cavalry force nearly a thousand strong and "a
great crowd of *barbaroi*"; and then, when the arrival of Illyrian warriors to join their opponents frightened Perdiccas' army into flight
(4.125), we hear of "the Macedonians and the mass of *barbaroi*" fleeing. What is thus left unclear is whether Thucydides counted the Macedonians as *barbaroi* (foreigners) or not.

Clear statements about the identity of the Macedonians first
emerge in fourth-century sources, like the Athenian politician and ora-

tor Demosthenes, where the Macedonians were presented as *barbaroi*. However, such statements occur in the context of enmity between southern Greeks and the Macedonians, in which the Macedonians tend to be likened to the Persians of old, and the war of the southern Greeks against them to the resistance of the southern Greeks, in the days of Miltiades, Leonidas, and Themistocles, to the Persian invasions. Presenting the Macedonians, therefore, as *barbaroi* just like the Persians, is propaganda and not necessarily to be trusted. There were cultural, social, and political differences between the northern Macedonians, and the southern city-state Greeks, that justified use of the term "barbarian" (in its original meaning, non-Greek-speaking) in the eyes of southern Greek (mostly Athenian) writers. But whether this was an expression of real ethnic/linguistic difference or propagandistic prejudice remains to be decided.

The argument against counting the ancient Macedonians as Greek really hinges on some remarks made in various sources about the language spoken by the Macedonians. In sources dealing with the reign of Alexander the Great, or with the time of his Successors, we hear several times of persons speaking (or not being able to speak) *Makedonisti*—that is, in the Macedonian manner—or more specifically speaking in the Macedonian *phone* (language or dialect). Some scholars interpret these passages to mean that there was a Macedonian language, separate and distinct from Greek. Support for this view is offered by a few words quoted in later sources as being "Macedonian": the first-century BCE geographer Strabo (7 fr. 2) offers the word *peligones* as Macedonian for "those holding positions of honor"; and the fifth-century CE lexicographer Hesychius tells us that *gotan* was the Macedonian word for pig (*hus* in standard Greek). But are these words really the remnants of a distinct Macedonian language? Living on the northern fringe of the Greek world, cheek by jowl with (and often intermingled with) non-Greek Illyrians, Paeonians, Thracians, and others, it would not be surprising for the Macedonians to use "loan-words" derived from those languages; and Strabo in fact goes on to say that Spartans and Massilians (Greek colonists of Marseilles in southern France) also used the word *peligones* with the meaning *gerontes* (that is, members of the Council of Elders). And as for a Macedonian *phone*, this could perfectly well mean a Macedonian dialect of Greek: compare Plato's reference (in his *Cratylus* 398d) to "the old Attic *phone*," that is, the old dialect spoken by the Athenians.

In order to decide what is really meant by references to a Macedonian *phone*, or to Macedonians as *barbaroi*, we need to begin by understanding what standard of "Greekness" is being applied. Because although some very able historians—most famously Ernst Badian—have argued strongly that our ancient sources regarded the Macedonians as non-Greek, what those sources—all written by inhabitants of Greek city-states, and mostly by Athenians—are really saying is that the Macedonians were not *city-state Greeks*. The standard being applied is that of Greeks who lived in a certain way: in cities that were at the same time autonomous small states, where political decisions were taken collectively in councils and assemblies of citizens, where citizens practiced a culture and way of life revolving around the *agora* (town square and/or market place), the *gymnasion* (meeting place to exercise, bathe, and socialize), and the *theatron* (viewing space to attend dramatic and/or musical performances). Macedonia, in the fifth and fourth centuries, was governed by a tribal monarchy and landowning aristocracy: there were no councils and assemblies; Macedonia had very few cities; those it did have were newly built in the late fifth and fourth centuries and were not autonomous states; and in Macedonia the culture of the *agora*, the gymnasium, and the theater had not yet taken hold. Macedonians, therefore, from the city-state Greek perspective, looked foreign and lived their lives in a foreign way.

Well, we can stipulate that the Macedonians were not southern Greeks, not city-state Greeks; but does that mean that they were not Greeks? The proper approach to answering this question finally has been shown by scholars working at the Research Center for Greek and Roman Antiquity in Athens, above all Miltiades Hatzopoulos and Argyro Tataki: they have focused attention on the nomenclature of the Macedonians, that is on the names attested to have been used by Macedonians. Names carry meaning, and are clear indicators of the linguistic background and heritage of the people using them; and in pre-modern times people were typically rather conservative in their naming habits. Study of names attested to have been used by fifth- and fourth-century Macedonians is highly revealing: the names are overwhelmingly Greek in their etymology, that is, they are based on Greek words. For example, many Macedonians used names based on the Greek word *hippos* (horse): *Philippos* (horse-lover), *Hippolochos* (horse regiment), *Hipponikos* (horse victor), *Hipparchos* (horse ruler), *Hippias* (horsey), and so on. Names based on the Greek word *nike* (victory) were in common use: *Nikanor* (victor), *Andronikos* and *Nikandros* (man-victor), *Nikomachos* (victor in battle), *Nikarchos* (victorious ruler), *Nikippos* (horse victor), *Nikodemos* (victor for the people), and the like. Particularly popular too, were names built from the Greek word for war, *polemos*: *Eupolemos* (good at war), *Polemaios* or *Ptolemaios* (warlike), *Tlepolemos* (daring in war), *Polemokrates* (powerful in war), *Polemon* (warrior) and so on. Further, the Macedonians are attested as using names drawn from Homer, the archetypal Greek poet: *Alexandros, Menelaos, Hektor, Kassandros, Neoptolemos,* to name a few. The vast majority of known Macedonian names are in fact Greek names, based on Greek words, and found more or less frequently elsewhere in Greece too. The obvious conclusion would be that the Macedonians were, linguistically speaking, Greeks.

Equally revealing, to my mind, is the history of the Macedonian Empire conquered and established by Alexander the Great and his Successors, especially when compared with the Roman Empire. The Romans had very little high culture of their own when they first began to encounter the Greeks in the third and second centuries BCE; and as is well known, they learned eagerly from the Greeks, adopting their literary forms, their philosophies, their theater and bathing culture, and so on. But in the lands they conquered, the Romans spread a language of their own (Latin); the Romans used names derived from their own Latin language; the Romans produced works of literature and philosophy based on and in some cases copying Greek literature and philosophy, but written in their own Latin language. By contrast, the Macedonians in their empire spread, not a Macedonian language and Macedonian culture, but the Greek language and Greek culture. One will look in vain throughout the revealingly-called Hellenistic (that is, Greek-based) civilization created by the Macedonians through their conquests and empires for any sign of a Macedonian language, or any distinctively Macedonian (and non-Greek) form of culture. As spreaders of the Greek language and Greek culture, therefore, the Macedonians must be counted as Greeks.

The whole "Macedonian question" is thus a modern red herring, based on modern notions of nationality and ethnicity. So far as we can tell, the ancient Macedonians were speakers of a dialect of Greek: their names make this clear. Though other Greeks evidently found the Macedonian dialect hard to understand and harder to speak, and found the Macedonian way of life "foreign" and in some ways uncongenial, that does not make the Macedonians non-Greek: it merely makes them different, peripheral, perhaps from a certain point of view "backward" Greeks. At most, the difference between the Macedonians and their language, and other Greeks and their language, may have been akin to the difference one may see today between Dutch—a language that is Germanic in structure and etymology, deriving from old Germanic roots— and German itself, which comes from the same linguistic roots. More likely, the difference is merely one of dialect, akin to the difference between the kind of English spoken in (for example) such places as Scotland and Louisiana: inhabitants of Glasgow and of the rural parts of Louisiana will almost certainly find it very hard to understand one another, but they both speak the English language.

2. THE EARLY HISTORY OF MACEDONIA

Though Herodotus and Thucydides claimed to know of a whole lineage of kings ruling Macedonia before the fifth century, these rulers are merely names to us, with at best one or two legendary tales attached. The history of Macedonia, in the sense that we have written historical source materials to go on, begins with the reign of Alexander I, ruler of Macedonia during the first decades of the fifth century, down to his death ca. 454. As we have seen, Herodotus had a number of stories to tell about this ruler—specifically about his relations with the Persians, and with the Athenians and other southern Greeks—and he emerges as a key figure in the earliest growth of what came to be, eventually, the Macedonian state. It was apparently during the reign of Alexander that, taking advantage of the weakness and disorder left behind in the wake of the retreat of Persian power from the Balkan region after 479, the Macedonians seized control of neighboring regions to their east and west. In the east, they advanced beyond the Axius River to the Strymon, and along with the broad lands between the rivers also took much of the northern Chalcidice. To the west, Alexander established a form of domination over the peoples and dynasts dwelling in the upland plateaus on the eastern side of the Pindus: Eordaea, Elimea, Orestis, Lyncus, and perhaps also Tymphaea and Pelagonia (see map 1). During this time, if not before, the peoples dwelling in these regions came to be considered, and perhaps to consider themselves, as Macedonians akin to the Macedonians of the coastal plains. In the fourth century, as a result, when Macedonia emerges more fully into history, we hear of a basic division between "lower" Macedonia—the original heartland of Pieria and the coastal plains to the north and north-east of it as far as the Axius valley—and "upper" Macedonia, meaning the upland plateaus of the Pindus, just listed. The unifying factor was the rule of the Argead dynasty, which came from "lower" Macedonia and had its seat in the town of Aegae (modern Vergina) in Pieria.

After the death of the foundational ruler Alexander I about 454, the history of Macedonia became for nearly a hundred years rather unstable and at times chaotic. Alexander had at least five sons—Perdiccas, Philip, Alcetas, Menelaus, and Amyntas—several of whom vied with each other for power during the 440s and 430s, and whose sons and descendants competed for rule of Macedonia thereafter (see genealogical table 1). Since later Macedonian rulers are known to have been polygamous, and such hostility and rivalry between brothers is a common feature in polygamous dynasties, these brothers may well have been Alexander's sons by different wives.

By the late 430s or early 420s Perdiccas, apparently the oldest of Alexander's sons, had seemingly established himself as the ruler of Macedonia, at least according to Athenian sources. The Athenians were much interested in Macedonia as a crucial source of timber for building their fleet, and interfered freely in the Macedonian region, dominating the coastal cities and their ports, and making alliances with and/or against Perdiccas, whichever seemed most likely to further Athenian influence in the region. Perdiccas, struggling to cope with the countervailing ambitions of his brothers and nephews, of local dynastic rulers in "upper" Macedonia, of the Athenians, and of powerful neighboring Illyrian and Thracian rulers, is presented in the Athenian sources as weak, vacillating, and chronically untrustworthy. But the fact that he managed, in the face of all these difficulties, to maintain himself as the ruler of Macedonia and pass on his rule to his son Archelaus, who succeeded on Perdiccas' death in 413, shows rather that Perdiccas must have been a shrewd man of considerable ability.

Archelaus appears to have been a stronger character than his shrewd father. According to Thucydides, he managed to unify Macedonia effectively, and to strengthen its military preparedness:

> but Archelaus the son of Perdiccas . . . later built the ones (i.e. forts) that are now in the country (Macedonia), and he set out straight roads and for the rest prepared things for war with horses and weapons and other equipment in a better way than all the other eight kings who ruled before him. (Thucydides 2.100).

Archelaus also built a new capital city for Macedonia at Pella, in those days a coastal city at the head of the Thermaic Gulf (it now lies some miles inland as a result of silting); and he strengthened relations between Macedonia and southern Greece by forming a strong alliance with the Athenians, and inviting important cultural leaders like the painter Zeuxis and the tragedian Euripides to spend time at his court, fostering "city-state" culture there. Archelaus was, however, assassinated unexpectedly in 399, ushering in a forty-year period of chronic instability in Macedonia that undid all his good work.

Archelaus was immediately succeeded by his son Orestes, but since Orestes was a child he needed a regent. It was his regent Aeropus—some sort of relative, perhaps his uncle—who actually ruled, until in about 396 Orestes died (or was killed?) and Aeropus assumed power in his own right. His rule only lasted for another three years or so, however, before he died, probably late in 394 and reputedly of disease. Macedonia then descended into a chaotic situation. Aeropus had a son, Pausanias, who claimed the throne, but that claim was disputed by a certain Amyntas "the Little" who may have been another son of Archelaus, or more plausibly of Perdiccas' brother Menelaus. He seized power and ruled briefly in 393 as Amyntas II, but in that year it seems Aeropus' son Pausanias was also ruling part of Macedonia: both men issued coins, which have a remarkably similar look. Both rulers were soon killed: Amyntas the Little was assassinated by the Elimiote dynast Derdas; Pausanias was killed by another Amyntas, who became the new ruler of Macedonia. Known to history as Amyntas III, his claim to rule Macedonia came through the fact that his father Arrhidaeus was a grandson of Alexander I via the latter's fifth son Amyntas. Having killed Pausanias and seized the throne, Amyntas III nominally ruled Macedonia for about twenty-four years, until his death in 370.

In hard reality, Amyntas III's rule was precarious at best as he faced challenges from rival claimants to power—a certain Argaeus and another Pausanias are specifically named—and was driven out of all or most of Macedonia on apparently two separate occasions. In order to cling to what power in Macedonia he could, he was forced to make a series of pacts with other strong powers: the dynast Derdas in Elimea, the Illyrians, the powerful city-state of Olynthus in the Chalcidice, the Spartans, and the Athenians. By such pacts, he at times ceded effective control of large parts of his kingdom. Though some thoughtful and excellent attempts have been made to reconstruct the detailed history of Macedonia during these chaotic years—Eugene Borza's *In the Shadow of Olympus* is probably the best—the plain truth is that our knowledge of precise reigns, relationships, events, and chronology of Macedonia before the rule of Philip II is as spotty and insecure as Macedonia was unstable. Even after the death of Amyntas III, Macedonia saw three brief and weak rulers during the next decade—Alexander II (ca. 370/69), Ptolemy "of Aloros" (ca. 368–366), and Perdiccas III (366–360)— before Philip II brought stability at last.

3. THE NATURE OF MACEDONIAN SOCIETY

Macedonia, then, was a tribal kingdom or chiefdom—it is unclear whether Macedonian rulers used the title *basileus* (king) before the time of Alexander the Great, though southern Greek writers certainly gave them that title—ruled by members of a dynastic family called the Argeadae. At one time, there was a widespread belief among ancient historians that Macedonia was a constitutional monarchy: the theory was that the Macedonian people under arms (that is, the adult males of the military class or caste) were the sovereign element in the state, and had the right to freely elect their monarchs, and to try cases of treason. This notion was based on some episodes during the reign of Alexander the Great (336–323) and the time of his Successors. On several occasions when he was proposing to execute important Macedonian leaders, Alexander summoned meetings of his army to inform them of the basis for considering the leaders in question guilty of treason, and to gauge the army's reaction to these charges. After Alexander's death, the Macedonian soldiery involved themselves in the disputes among the leading officers as to how the succession should be settled, and the final compromise arrangement that was agreed on was approved by the army by acclamation. These events were worked up by scholars writing in the early twentieth century into a constitutional right for the "Macedonians under arms" to settle the succession and conduct treason trials.

Unfortunately, no example of such a treason trial, or of the Macedonian army choosing a new king, can be pointed to in Macedonian history prior to Alexander the Great. Instead, we hear of plenty of executions and assassinations, and of frequent usurpations of the throne from existing kings by rival claimants of the Argead family, quite often by assassination: rulers who were assassinated included Archelaus, probably Orestes, Amyntas the Little, Pausanias, Alexander II, Ptolemy of Aloros, and perhaps others. The notion of any Macedonian constitution was called into question in a series of important articles in the 1970s and 1980s, and is now no longer much believed in, though it has still a few defenders. What we see instead, in Macedonia, is a region and people loosely held together by allegiance to a ruling family or clan, and a certain sense of common identity. The Argead family was, though, more of a "first among equals" for much of its history. Local regions of Macedonia, especially upper Macedonia, had powerful dynastic families of their own—a family frequently using the name Derdas in Elimea, for example, and a family using the name Arrhabaeus in Lyncus—who were as often rivals and opponents of the ruling Argead family as they were allies or subordinates.

Macedonia was, in effect, a country of large landowners who formed a powerful aristocracy over whom only the strongest rulers could exercise meaningful control. In order to be able to govern, the Argead ruler needed to win the backing of a significant portion of this powerful aristocracy. Those aristocratic landowners who backed the ruler would be designated his *hetairoi* (companions), and formed an advising council of state (*synedrion*) helping him to govern. Crucially, they also expressed their backing by riding to the ruler's support in times of conflict (which was frequent!) with bands of mounted retainers. Before the time of Philip II, Macedonian military power was overwhelmingly based on cavalry, and besides the few hundred cavalrymen a strong ruler could raise himself, he needed the mounted retainers of leading aristocrats in order to field a sizable cavalry army. Equipped with breast-plates and stout lances, Macedonian cavalry were of excellent fighting quality, as Thucydides informs us (2.100). But even strong Macedonian rulers could seldom put more than six or seven hundred cavalry in the field—only with allied forces from neighboring Elimea or the Chalcidice could forces over a thousand strong be mobilized—and the plain truth is that cavalry did not rule the battlefields of ancient Greece: heavily armed infantry did.

Ancient cavalry, before the time of the later Roman Empire, lacked the built-up saddles and stirrups that gave medieval and early modern cavalry a secure seat on their mounts, enabling them to function as shock troops. Ancient cavalrymen, the Macedonians included, rode either bareback, or with at most a blanket between them and their horses. Their seat on their horses therefore depended on their ability to grip with their thighs, and was always rather insecure at best. Any major impact was liable to unseat the rider, so it was not possible for ancient cavalrymen to charge into enemies with "couched lances" in the style of medieval jousters: thrusts at the enemy were made by swinging the arm, and had only the force of the cavalryman's arm and upper-body strength behind them; and even such thrusts carried the danger of unseating. Furthermore, horses will not charge into a stationary obstacle they can see no way over or around. Disciplined infantry able to present and maintain a solid and unflinching formation in the face of a cavalry charge would thus see the impetus of the charge falter and dissipate as the horses got close enough to see that they could not leap over the mass of men confronting them, nor pass through gaps that did not exist. As their horses pulled up, cavalry were limited to riding along the front of the disciplined infantry formation, hurling insults and, if equipped with them, javelins, but doing little damage. Disciplined phalanxes of southern Greek hoplites (heavily armored infantry: see ill. 3) knew this very well, and were consequently little troubled by cavalry charges.

What this means for Macedonia is that even strong rulers who could reliably mobilize relatively large cavalry forces of six to eight hundred could not compete when confronted by large and well-disciplined infantry forces, especially the hoplite phalanxes of the city-state Greeks.

3. Greek hoplites on Attic vase in Athens Archaeological Museum
(*Wikimedia Commons photo by Grant Mitchell*)

Athenians, Spartans, and Thebans were thus able to intervene effectively in Macedonia almost at will; and when sufficiently unified (as in the Olynthian League of the early fourth century) even the colonial city-states of the Chalcidice could be more than a match for the rulers of Macedonia. Macedonian cavalry were very effective in the open, hit-and-run style of warfare of northern Greece and the southern Balkan region, where the large plains and plateaus gave ample room to maneuver and infantry forces tended to be lightly armed and poorly disciplined. In this style of warfare, the cavalry dominated the field of battle, and the infantry were present largely to provide support to the free-wheeling cavalry. Macedonian rulers could mobilize thousands of light infantry of this sort, but we can see from the descriptions of Macedonian campaigning provided by Thucydides and Xenophon that they were ill disciplined and ineffective when confronted by southern Greek heavy infantry, or even by more numerous and motivated Illyrian or Thracian armies. This explains the basic features of Macedonian history as we know it: strong rulers like Alexander I and Archelaus, who could establish their authority over the Macedonian aristocracy, were able to dominate Macedonia and compete very effectively against neighboring tribes and peoples, but were no match for the Persians or the southern Greek powers; weaker rulers, however, faced chronic instability due to their inability to enforce the submission of local Macedonian dynastic families, and that domestic weakness made them almost helpless in the face of outside interventions, not only by southern Greek hoplite armies, but even by Illyrian and Thracian forces.

With its dominant class of aristocratic families owning most of the land, Macedonia was a highly stratified society, with a rather small elite class of wealthy landowners, a large population of poor people dependent in various ways on the rich, and only a very small "middling" element between the two. Cities had not developed down to 400 BCE, and people lived in a few smallish towns and—for the most part—villages in the countryside. In the late fifth and early fourth centuries at any rate, when we start to have some evidence, we see the wealthy landowning class living in a style that resembles that of the heroes of Homeric epic. That may to some degree have been a matter of imitation: Homer was very popular in Macedonia, as the names drawn from the Homeric epics, referred to above, indicate. Macedonian rulers and other great leaders were surrounded by bands of retainers called *hetairoi* or companions, just like Homeric heroes. And like Homeric heroes they spent a great part of their time and energy on fighting, hunting, and feasting. Hunting helped to provide the meat for the feasts the Macedonian aristocrats enjoyed: boar, deer, hare, fowl of various sorts, and other game animals were abundant in the marshes, woods, and hills of Macedonia, and a man's worth in this society was in large part measured by his hunting skills. The few remains of elaborate art surviving from this period of Macedonia often depict the hunt, and there are numerous anecdotes of leading Macedonians hunting. Together with the prevalence of herding in the economy, this meant that meat-eating was much more common in Macedonia than in southern Greece, at least among the wealthy, and the meat-rich diet may help to explain a feature often commented on by southern Greek writers: many of the Macedonian elite were particularly large and beefy men. Philip II's marshal Parmenio was a big man, as was Alexander the Great's beloved companion Hephaestion. Among Alexander's Successors, Lysimachus was strong enough to have once won a "cage fight" against a lion; in later life he liked to show off his scars from the fight. Seleucus, we are told, once stopped a rampaging bull with his bare hands. Demetrius was heroically tall. Biggest of all, Antigonus the One-Eyed was a huge and intimidating figure, bulky and scarred as well as immensely tall.

These men were heavy drinkers at their feasts too. Stories of drunkenness at the feasts abound, and with drunkenness went disorder and not infrequent violence. Philip II's assassination was, according to the stories we have, in part at least motivated by insults and violence inflicted on one of his guard officers during a drunken feast; at the feast for Philip's last (seventh) wedding a drunken brawl erupted between the uncle of the bride, Alexander, and Philip himself; and Alexander once killed one of his officers at a feast in a fit of drunken rage. To the Macedonian aristocracy all of this was just manly exuberance: after all, Homer's heroes had behaved very similarly. To southern Greeks in their city-states, who had long left behind the kind of life depicted in Homer, the manners and lifestyle of the Macedonians seemed primitive and uncivilized. Some of the Macedonian elite recognized this themselves: the Macedonian rulers Archelaus and Philip II strove to introduce Athenian culture and manners at their courts, and Alexander once commented to southern Greek intellectuals at a feast that they must feel as if they were surrounded by beasts in the company of the boisterous Macedonians.

The lifestyle of poor Macedonians was, of course, very different, but it has gone largely unrecorded by our sources, who themselves came exclusively from the elite class. There is one relatively late source that does have a few words to say about it: the historian Arrian in his account of the reign of Alexander the Great.

> "When Philip came to power over you, you were indigent wanderers, most of you wearing animal hides and herding a few sheep in the mountains, and fighting in defense of them poorly against neighboring Illyrians and Triballians and Thracians; but he gave you cloaks to wear instead of hides, brought you down from the mountains into the plains, made you a match in battle for the foreigners along your borders . . . he made you city-dwellers and organized you with proper laws and customs . . ." (Arrian *Anabasis* 7.9.2).

These words are said to have been spoken by Alexander in a harangue to his rebellious Macedonian soldiers at Opis in 325/4. Though we can't be sure that Alexander said just this, the words at the very least represent the view of Macedonian conditions held by Arrian, a well-educated and well-informed Greek historian writing in the second century CE, based on sources (now lost) that were contemporary or near contemporary to Philip and Alexander, such as the fourth-century BCE historians Marsyas of Pella and Theopompus of Chios. The lifestyle of the poor depicted here does make sense: shepherding on a seasonal transhumance basis—that is, moving the flocks between highland pastures in summer and lowland in winter—has been a very common way of life in central and northern Greece all the way into the twentieth century. So the notion that a large part, perhaps even a majority of poor Macedonians made a living by animal husbandry, focused especially on sheep and goats, seems quite plausible. The seasonal movements between different regions made the building of cities unnecessary as well as impossible with the limited resources available. This kind of movement helps to explain the links between the otherwise separate regions of "upper" and "lower" Macedonia. And a population of poor pastoralists, dressed in skins, lacking permanent settlements, and living largely hand to mouth, the prey of stronger and more settled neighboring peoples, accords with what we know of early Macedonian history.

Herein lay the weakness of Macedonia: it was not that resources were lacking, it was that the socio-economic conditions of Macedonia did not permit the diffusion of wealth down the social scale to produce a well-to-do middle class, to enable the development of cities, to allow for a disciplined army of well-equipped infantry to be raised. Macedonia was rich, but most Macedonians were poor. Most Macedonians were dependent serfs, and so Macedonia itself was often at the mercy of stronger neighboring powers. The Macedonian aristocracy was strong, but the Macedonian rulers and people were correspondingly weak, and so Macedonia was weak. But for all that, the resources of Macedonia, human and material, created the potential for strength under the right conditions.

4. THE NATURAL RESOURCES OF MACEDONIA

The inability of Macedonian rulers to mobilize effective infantry armies was not due to any lack of manpower. Macedonia was, by the standards of classical Greece, a large country, with expansive and well-watered agricultural plains and plateaus, capable of sustaining a substantial population. Estimating that population is difficult for any period of Macedonian history, due to the absence of reliable statistics of any sort, but especially so for early Macedonia—before the reign of Philip II, that is—since we don't even know where exactly the boundaries of Macedonia were at any given time. The territory of the greater Macedonia created by Philip II covered at least over 30,000 km², which at a standard population density for the ancient world of some 40 persons per km² would give a population of some 1.2 million. If we reduce that territory by half, and assume a rather low population density of 30 per km², we arrive at a figure of some 450,000 as a conservative estimate for the population of pre-Philip Macedonia. A ruler strong enough to impose his authority over even this "smaller Macedonia" would thus have had ample manpower resources in principle: by comparison, the population of Athens at the height of her power and success in around 440 BCE has never been suggested to have been greater than 250,000.

With a relatively large territory and population (compared to the city-states of southern Greece), Macedonia had the potential to be a strong power, and it had other important resources besides land and people. As mentioned above, the land of Macedonia was well-watered. Water was a scarce and important commodity in ancient Greece, because Greece is a rather arid country with relatively low annual rainfall, providing barely enough water resources to make agriculture viable in an average rainfall year. The famous older civilizations of the ancient world, in Mesopotamia (Iraq) and Egypt, relied on very large and perennially flowing rivers—the Tigris and Euphrates in Mesopotamia, the Nile in Egypt—to provide plentiful water for agriculture via irrigation. In most of Greece, the small rivers and streams dry up completely after the winter/spring rains, leaving the country dry and parched in summer and autumn. Agriculture by irrigation was not possible, therefore, leaving farmers to practice "dry-farming," in which the crops are dependent on rainfall for watering, and the growing season is during the winter/spring rainy season. But in northern Greece, rainfall was more abundant than in southern Greece, and more importantly winter snows covered the heights of the Pindus and Rhodopi massifs, providing a summer melt run-off that kept northern rivers flowing year round. Macedonia was particularly favored in this regard, with the large rivers Haliacmon, Axius, and Strymon providing year-round water, and several smaller rivers—the Loudias and the Echedorus (modern Gallicus)—supplementing them, as well as numerous streams and springs. So not only did Macedonia have, along with Thessaly, the largest agricultural plains in Greece, but these plains were well watered all year round. Consequently, Macedonia was one of the two regions of ancient Greece (along with Thessaly again) that was not only invariably self-sufficient in its grain supply, but was capable of producing a surplus available for export.

Most of Greece was severely lacking in forestation in antiquity, as Plato for example noted; and yet the cities of Greece required large supplies of timber for their building activities, and especially for their crucial ship-building. Here again Macedonia was particularly favored: the slopes of the Pindus and Rhodopi foothills, and of the Cholomon range in the northern Chalcidice, were heavily forested, particularly in the varieties of evergreens suited to ship-building purposes. Macedonia was, thus, one of the most important suppliers of timber to classical Greece, and the only one in Greece itself. The timber resources of Macedonia were by tradition a monopoly of the ruler, who determined what timber might be extracted and by whom, and who derived a potentially large income from this. Under strong rulers, then, timber was a source of wealth and strength. But timber could also be a curse: it was the timber resources of Macedonia that led the Athenians to intervene constantly in the internal affairs of Macedonia, and to seek to control (often very effectively) the ports along the Macedonian coast. These ports—Pydna and Methone on the western shore of the Thermaic Gulf, and Therme on the eastern side—were in any case not strictly Macedonian cities, but colonies founded from southern Greece, in part no doubt with access to timber in mind. Thus the very timber that was a valuable resource to the Macedonians, was also a contributing cause of the weakness of most Macedonian rulers and their inability to control Macedonia's coast and ports.

Another important natural resource of Macedonia was metals: iron and copper, silver and gold were all mined in various parts of Macedonia and its immediate environs, offering a significant source of wealth to the ruler strong enough to assert control. The utilitarian metals iron and copper were mined in a number of places throughout Greece. In the Macedonian region, mining in the Cholomon range of the northern Chalcidice was particularly significant for these metals, but not much is known about it, unfortunately. We are better informed about the sources of the precious metals which, in the form of coinage, played a crucial role in the economic life of ancient Greece. Mining silver and gold was, like the extraction of timber, controlled by the ruler of Macedonia, and was a key source of wealth (and thus potentially of power). The suggestively named Echedorus (literally "gift-holder") River was a significant source of gold, which was panned from its sandy bed. Important silver mines were located in the nearby Dysoron mountain range from which Alexander I drew an income, as Herodotus tells us (5.17), of one silver talent per day. The Cholomon range in the northern Chalcidice was an important source of silver and gold: mining there seems to have been begun by the mid-fourth century, though it is not clear whether it pre-dated the reign of Philip II. Silver was also mined extensively in the region of Mount Pangaeum, between the rivers Strymon and Nestus, where the Thasians had founded a colony named Crenides. Philip II later re-founded this city as Philippi and began extensive and highly remunerative gold-mining operations in the region in addition to the silver. Access to, and ideally control of these mines and the wealth they produced would enable a strong Macedonian ruler to fund a variety of projects, such as building forts and cities, and building up his military forces. It was clearly this wealth which helped Alexander I to extend the boundaries of Macedonia during his reign, and enabled Archelaus to build fortifications and roads, and to better equip his army.

Macedonia, then, had the potential in manpower, in agricultural resources, and in wealth derived from timber and mining, to be a powerful state; and yet it remained until the advent of Philip II a weak and unimportant backwater, peripheral to the history of the Greek and near-eastern great powers. The cause of this weakness was clearly the Macedonian way of life: like their neighbors to the south, the Thessalians, the Macedonians never developed large cities and the city-state way of life that was found elsewhere in Greece. Instead, as we have seen, a traditional landed aristocracy maintained dominance over the region—socially, economically, and politically—with a way of life that centered around horse rearing and riding, hunting, and warfare: hence the popularity noted above of names associated with horses, victory, and war. We are told, for example, that though the Macedonian aristocracy adopted the city-state Greek custom of reclining on couches at dinner, only men who had achieved the feat of killing a wild boar without using a hunting net were permitted to recline. Those who had not achieved this feat had to sit at dinner, as women and children did (Athenaeus 18a). Since we know that the symposium—the upper-class drinking party with groups of men reclining on couches after dinner, drinking wine and entertaining each other with talk, song, and party games— was a key part of Macedonian social life, men whose hunting skills were deficient had this fact rubbed in their faces at every social occasion, with the couches debarred to them. Further, Aristotle informs us (*Politics* 1324b) that in early Macedonia a man was not permitted to wear a belt until he had killed an enemy in war. In this emphasis on riding, drinking, hunting, and fighting, the Macedonian aristocracy was similar, to be sure, to many other aristocracies known to us: in classical Greece, the Spartiates had the same interests, for example; in more modern times, the English aristocracy of the eighteenth and early nineteenth centuries could be pointed to.

Most similar to the Macedonians, though, were clearly their contemporary neighbors, the Thessalians. There too the landowning aristocracy were great riders of horses, great cavalry fighters, keen hunters and symposiasts. There too, cities developed only late (in the fifth and fourth centuries) and never achieved the autonomous status of city-*states*. And in Thessaly too, warfare centered around the aristocratic cavalry, with the heavy infantry hoplite phalanx failing to develop. Which meant that Thessaly, like Macedonia, was weak compared to the southern Greek city-states, despite its size and wealth. In the city-states of southern Greece and the eastern Aegean, economic and social advances in the sixth and fifth centuries produced a large and well-to-do middle class of independent small farmers, tradesmen, and artisans. These men could afford to equip themselves with the expensive panoply of the hoplite (heavy infantryman), and had free time to devote to military training and warfare on an intermittent basis. For the Greek hoplite was a citizen militiaman who served his community as a warrior at his own expense and only when needed; and this duty of military service was intimately bound up with his rights as a participating citizen in his community. Such an independent and well-to-do middle class was lacking in Thessaly and Macedonia; and it is for this reason that these regions lacked hoplite phalanxes. We know that in Thessaly the majority of the population lived on the landed estates of the aristocracy, farming those lands for their aristocratic lords, and existing in a slave-like status akin to that of the helots of Sparta or the serfs of medieval Europe: these Thessalian serfs were known as *penestai*. It seems clear that the majority of the Macedonian population, too, lived in a serf-like condition, as dependants on the estates of the aristocracy: it has been estimated that as many as three in five Macedonians were essentially serfs like the Thessalian *penestai*, and that may even be an underestimate. Even those Macedonians outside the aristocracy who were free and independent were for the most part not well-to-do, if we can believe our sources.

This, then, was the land over which Philip II became ruler in the winter of 360/59, and the task he set himself was to raise Macedonia out of this weakness, and to realize at last the potential strength and power that the size and resources of Macedonia had always promised. He was to succeed in this task more spectacularly than even the wildest hopes of his supporters can have imagined, with incalculable consequences for subsequent Greek and western history, as we shall see.

CHAPTER 2

Philip's Childhood

HIS FULL NAME WAS *PHILIPPOS AMYNTA MAKEDON*, THAT IS, PHILIP, son of Amyntas, the Macedonian. He was born in the year 383, and became famous as king Philip II of Macedonia, the king who re-organized his country and built it into a great power dominating Greece and the Balkan region. Yet he can have had little expectation, when growing up, of ever ruling his native land. His father Amyntas was ruler of Macedonia for some twenty-four years (393–370), but Philip was only the youngest of three sons of Amyntas by his wife Eurydice: his two older brothers, Alexander and Perdiccas, had prior claims to succeed to their father's power. In addition, in the polygamous tradition of Macedonian rulers, Amyntas also had three more sons by another wife named Gygaea: Archelaus, Menelaus, and Arrhidaeus. The likelihood of the young Philip ever succeeding to the position of ruler must have seemed remote—but not impossible. For during the opening decades of the fourth century, as we have already seen, Macedonia went through a series of succession crises and disputes, during which any descendant of the foundational ruler Alexander I could— and many did—make a claim to the rulership. As a member of the Argead ruling clan, then, and a descendant of Alexander I, the position of ruler was always a possibility for Philip; but as the youngest of three brothers, and to all appearances a loyal brother at that, he must have expected to play a secondary role. And the weakness and instability of Macedonia, and of his father's rule, can have done little to encourage high expectations.

1. THE REIGN OF AMYNTAS III

Amyntas' rule of Macedonia was interrupted on at least two occasions: around 392, shortly after he came to power, and around 383/2, just about the time of Philip's birth. The details are sketchy and murky, like

almost all of Macedonia's history before the reign of Philip, and historians have debated endlessly whether and when and by whom Amyntas
was driven from power and restored to power. The key evidence comes
from the historians Diodorus and Xenophon, and while those two often
disagree about the course of events, in this case their accounts are most
likely complementary.

Diodorus tells us that shortly after Amyntas came to power, Macedonia suffered an Illyrian invasion which drove him out of the country
entirely (Diodorus 14.92.3–4). He reports that, in an evidently futile
attempt to gather enough support to hold onto his kingdom, Amyntas
ceded border territories in the east to the Olynthian League. This is generally assumed to refer to the region of Anthemous in the north-west
Chalcidice, though some scholars think rather of the Lake Bolbe region
to the east (see map 1). Either way, it seems the grant was intended to
be temporary, in return for some sort of aid. If the aid materialized, it
did not work. Amyntas was forced to leave Macedonia, and was only
restored to power some time later thanks to Thessalian help, presumably from the Aleuadae of Larissa in northern Thessaly, long-time allies
of the Argead kings. Further Diodorus states that some sources alleged
that another ruler named Argaeus held power in Macedonia for two
years at this time: we are perhaps to imagine that he was installed with
Illyrian support, since the Illyrians apparently dominated Macedonia
at this time.

Who exactly this Argaeus was is unclear, except that he must have
been an Argead descendant of Alexander I to be able to claim power.
The name Argaeus is attested earlier in the list of Argead kings: the second ruler, after the founder Perdiccas, in Herodotus' king-list was so
named. Indeed, the clan name *Argeadai* presumably derives from the
name Argaeus, meaning descendants of Argaeus—rather than the
meaning "men from Argos" as implied by Herodotus' story of Argive
origins for the clan. Since Argaeus was to make another attempt on the
Macedonian throne nearly thirty-five years later, in 359 (as we shall
see), he must have been rather a young man at the time of his first period in power, or pretending to power as the case may be. Perhaps we
should see in him a younger brother or son of Amyntas the Little, descending from Alexander I via Menelaus. The fact that he evidently
ruled, to the extent that he did rule, under Illyrian patronage, will

hardly have endeared him to the Macedonian aristocracy and people, however.

The Illyrians normally constituted more of a threat to raid and pillage upper Macedonia, rather than to occupy and dominate the realm. A loose agglomeration of separate, and at times mutually hostile, tribes inhabiting roughly what is now central and northern Albania, Montenegro, and parts of coastal Croatia, the Illyrians are little known to history: they produced no records of themselves, and are mentioned by our Greek sources only rarely and tangentially. Usually, split into numerous tribes and clans, they were no more than a nuisance to their Greek-speaking neighbors to the south. But at times a tribal leader of more than usual ability might succeed in uniting behind him enough of the tribes to become a regional power, and that is what happened in the 390s as a remarkable leader named Bardylis won control of much of Illyria. Bardylis ruled over the Illyrians for nearly forty years, from the 390s until the early 350s, and was powerful enough to pose a serious threat to Macedonia on a number of occasions. The first such occasion was his invasion of Macedonia in about 392, driving Amyntas III out and allowing Argaeus to rule at least part of Macedonia for a year or two.

When his Thessalian allies finally enabled Amyntas to recover the core part of his kingdom, probably in late 391 or early 390, he was able to drive out Argaeus and win back the support of most Macedonians: the Macedonians certainly objected strongly to Illyrian domination, and so to a ruler supported by Illyrian power. But he was left with two intractable problems: how to maintain himself against further Illyrian pressure, and what to do about the Olynthian League which now controlled part of Macedonia. On his own, Amyntas lacked the power to deal with these two threatening neighbors effectively, and his Thessalian allies had preoccupations within Thessaly. Amyntas was forced to negotiate with the Illyrians: in order to prevent another Illyrian invasion he was obliged to pay tribute to the Illyrian ruler. Buying off foreign enemies in this way is known to historians of early England as "paying the Danegeld," after the tribute moneys sent by Saxon rulers to buy off their all-too-powerful Danish neighbors in northern Britain. As the Saxons discovered, the problem with "paying the Danegeld" is that the Danes always come back for more: it is not a satisfactory solution, and Amyntas was to find the same. But he had, in his weakness, little choice. To cement his agreement, most likely, Amyntas married an Illyrian wife, the daughter of an Illyrian chief named Sirrhas. Her original Illyrian name is unknown: she adopted a Macedonian name, Eurydice, and became the mother of Amyntas' sons and successors. The oldest son of this marriage, Alexander, must have been born by 388 at the latest, as he was an adult able to assume rule of Macedonia at his father's death in late 370.

Having, for the time being, successfully bought off the Illyrians with tribute money and a marriage alliance, Amyntas needed to bolster his support within Macedonia. One of the most powerful men in Macedonia at this time was the head of the dynastic family which dominated the upper Macedonian canton of Elimea, Derdas. Known to us from southern Greek sources, Derdas controlled a cavalry force as large and of as good quality as that of Amyntas, and interacted with southern Greek powers at times as an essentially independent ruler. It has been suggested that it was Derdas' support that helped Amyntas III seize power in the first place, that is, that the assassinations of Amyntas the Little by Derdas and of Pausanias by Amyntas III Arrhidaeou were part of a concerted plan to make Amyntas Arrhidaeou ruler. At any rate, good relations between Amyntas and Derdas are attested in this period, and with Derdas behind him, Amyntas had at least one solid base of support for his power. But he likely felt the need for more.

It may well have been at this time, then, that Amyntas entered into his second marriage, with the intriguingly named Gygaea. The name is attested as being used in the Argead clan: a sister of the foundational ruler Alexander I was named Gygaea, suggesting that Amyntas' new wife may also have belonged to the clan. Indeed it has been suggested that she was the granddaughter of Alexander I's son Menelaus, though it is not clear on what basis. If correct though, she may have been a daughter or niece of Amyntas the Little; and the marriage was likely intended to heal the breach between rival branches of the Argead line, shoring up Amyntas' support within Macedonia. That the marriage belongs to the period of the early to mid-380s seems likely based on the likely time of birth of the oldest son of the marriage, Archelaus. Since Alexander, son of Eurydice, was able to succeed his father Amyntas in late 370 without opposition, he seems likely to have been the oldest son. Gygaea's son Archelaus did eventually seek the rulership, but not until after the death of Eurydice's second son Perdiccas in 360, as a rival to Eurydice's third son Philip. Perdiccas was likely born about 385. It seems plausible that Archelaus was born about the same time, perhaps slightly later than Perdiccas, and so was old enough to mount an attempt at the rulership only after Perdiccas' demise. That would likely place his parents' marriage around 387 to 385, and would make sense in light of Amyntas' need to win internal support in Macedonia at that time. For having settled matters, for the time being, with the Illyrians, he needed to deal with the threat posed by the Olynthians.

We have seen that under the threat of the Illyrian invasion ca. 392, Amyntas had ceded borderlands in the northern Chalcidice to the Olynthians in the hope or expectation of Olynthian aid, which either failed to materialize or was ineffective, as Amyntas was in fact driven out of Macedonia by the Illyrians. Restored to power in Macedonia by his Thessalian allies, Amyntas made a treaty with the Olynthian League, part of which survives in an inscription: both parties agreed to help each other against future attacks, and both agreed not to make any deals with three named Greek cities in the region (Acanthus, Mende, Amphipolis) or the Bottiaeans, without the other party's consent; in addition the Chalcidians of the League received certain rights to import timber and pitch from Macedonia. The treaty seemed to favor the Olynthian League, and the Olynthians continued, as Diodorus tells us, to control and enjoy the revenues of the land that Amyntas had ceded under Illyrian pressure back in 392. When Amyntas now, in about 384/3, feeling more secure in Macedonia, attempted to redress the balance of power with the Olynthians and win back the ceded territory, the Olynthians responded by driving Amyntas out of eastern Macedonia and capturing various Macedonian towns including the new capital Pella, already the largest city in Macedonia. All this is reported by Xenophon, who alleges that by late 383 Amyntas had effectively lost control of his kingdom (*Hellenica* 5.2.12–13; 5.2.38).

It was at this low point in Amyntas' career, then, that Philip was born, the third of Amyntas' sons by Eurydice, but probably his fourth or fifth son overall. Amyntas in fact survived the Olynthian threat that confronted him at the time of Philip's birth by appealing to the Spartans. In 386 a general or common peace had been agreed to throughout the Greek world, under pressure from the Persian king Artaxerxes II and overseen by the Spartans. By this so-called King's Peace, all Greek city-states were to be mutually free and autonomous, and the Spartans saw to the enforcement of this condition. In 383, the Olynthians as leaders of the alliance of city-states in the Chalcidice generally known as the Olynthian League were pressuring as yet unaffiliated cities in the region to join. Two of these cities, Acanthus and Apollonia, sent embassies to Sparta protesting this Olynthian pressure, and calling on the Spartans to enforce their right to freedom and autonomy by forcing the Olynthians to leave them in peace. The Acanthian envoy, according to Xenophon, illustrated Olynthian ambitions and the danger to the King's Peace (and Spartan predominance in Greece), by describing how the Olynthians had virtually driven Amyntas from his kingdom and seized control of Macedonia, and alleging that Sparta's perennial rivals the Athenians and Thebans were preparing to ally with the Olynthians. The Spartans decided to act, and in 382 war ensued between the Spartans and the Olynthian League.

This war was a godsend to Amyntas, who sent an embassy of his own to Sparta, according to Diodorus (15.19.3), further urging the Spartans to action. To prosecute the war, the Spartans sent a large infantry force to the Chalcidice, and allied with Amyntas and his friend Derdas in order to obtain cavalry. Derdas' cavalry, in particular, gave an excellent account of themselves and, though the war proved more difficult than at first anticipated, the Spartans did in the end win: in 379 the Olynthians were forced to capitulate. They had to disband their alliance system, and Amyntas gained back his lost territories. Of course, freedom from the threat posed by the Olynthian League might have been off set by uncomfortable pressure from the new power in the region, the Spartans. But Amyntas was spared this by a new development in southern Greece.

Between 379 and 377 the Athenians, encouraged by their allies the Thebans, founded a new alliance system aimed at forcing the Spartans to stop meddling in the affairs of other Greeks, that is, to reduce Spartan predominance in Greece. This Second Athenian Confederacy, together with the Thebans, was soon at war with the Spartans. As a result the Spartans spent the 370s campaigning on land in Boeotia against the Thebans, and at sea against the Athenians, leaving them unable and unwilling to interfere further in the north. However, Amyntas was not to be left entirely in peace. The renewal of Athenian naval power led to renewed Athenian demand for Macedonian timber for ship-building, and renewed Athenian pressure to control the ports on Macedonia's coast, in particular Methone and Pydna. Thus the demise of one threat to Amyntas led to the rise of another.

Amyntas responded in the only way he could: he abandoned his alliance with the Spartans and instead negotiated a treaty with the Athenians, seeking at least to control the Athenian threat by making concessions. Macedonian interest in Amphipolis—the crucial former Athenian colony at the mouth of the River Strymon—was ended, and in 371, at a general Greek peace conference, Amyntas went so far as to recognize formally the Athenians' claim to that city. Amyntas adopted the great Athenian general Iphicrates, a man whose strong connections in Thrace could help Amyntas in that quarter, as well as in his native Athens. The adoption was purely *pro forma*, but it illustrated Amyntas' need to placate the Athenians. So too did the sending of a large consignment of ship-building timber to the Athenian statesman Timotheos in the late 370s. Diodorus also reports that, abandoning his long-time alliance with the Aleuadae of Thessalian Larissa, Amyntas agreed to a treaty with the rising new power in Thessaly, Jason of Pherae, in this same period of the late 370s (Diodorus 15.60.2). It is likely also in this period of the mid to late 370s that Amyntas formed a marriage alliance with another important Macedonian baron, Ptolemy of Aloros, who received as his bride Amyntas' daughter Eurynoe. The need to shore up his support within Macedonia was still strong.

In late 370, finally, Amyntas died, apparently of natural causes, since no source alleges any violence, and his oldest son Alexander succeeded peacefully to his power, initially at least. Philip was about thirteen years old at this time. Amyntas was probably no more than sixty when he died, by no means an old man, given that his sons were (all six of them, it seems) under twenty. His reign had been a study in survival over weakness. Threatened several times with expulsion from his power, he had clung to his position as ruler thanks to the support of powerful but potentially threatening Macedonian barons such as Derdas and Ptolemy, to tribute payments sent regularly to keep the Illyrians away, and to alliances from a position of weakness with outside powers such as the Olynthians, the Spartans, the Athenians, and the Thessalian Aleuadae and Jason. Amyntas was clearly a clever and versatile man, and when necessary a persuasive one, but he was never able to muster the strength to begin to rebuild the improvements within Macedonia begun under Archelaus, let alone to advance Macedonia from its long-time role as a second- or third-rate power dominated by its neighbors.

2. YOUNG PHILIP

This chapter is entitled "Philip's Childhood," yet it may have been noticed that so far very little has been said in it directly about Philip himself: there has been much contextual discussion of the reign of Philip's father and of conditions within Macedonia in particular and in the broader Greek world, but no description or anecdotes about Philip's own life and experiences growing up. This reflects, it must be said, the state of our sources, unlike in the case of Philip's son Alexander, of whose childhood ancient writers preserved a considerable amount of descriptive material. Philip's experience growing up in Amyntas' Macedonia was, on the one hand, one of privilege as a son of Macedonia's ruler, but on the other, one of chronic weakness and insecurity as Amyntas clung to power only by a series of agreements with stronger outside powers. But though we have hardly any direct testimony regarding Philip's childhood, we can say in a general way what it will have been like. In all probability, Philip was born in exile, but the family was soon able to return to Macedonia, and it was in the new capital of Pella, built under Archelaus, that he grew up during the 370s. As the son of Macedonia's ruler, however precarious that rule may have been, Philip certainly experienced luxury, receiving the best that was to be had in Macedonia by way of upbringing and education.

It was standard in ancient Greece for children to spend the first seven or so years of their lives in the charge of their mothers, and in the case of the wealthy and high-born also of nurse-maids and other servants. The real education of boy children began at about the age of seven, and involved their introduction into the world and concerns of men. In ancient Macedonia, that meant—for upper-class boys at any rate—a training in horse riding, hunting, and fighting; for upper-class Macedonians were hunters and cavalry warriors before all else. The hunting culture of the Macedonians is abundantly attested in literary

4. Lion hunt mosaic from Pella, Macedonia (in Pella Museum)
Wikimedia Commons public domain photo)

and artistic media (see ill. 4), with the most dangerous animals being the most prized game, because to kill a dangerous animal was to show off one's manly courage (*andreia*). So, for example, a Macedonian man had to prove himself by killing a wild boar without the use of a hunting net before he was permitted to recline on a couch at the traditional male dining and drinking parties. In the fourth century BCE, deer and boar were plentiful in Macedonia, and frequently hunted; but bear, panther, and lion were also to be found. The European lion (*Panthera leo europaea*) did not die out in the Balkan region until the first century BCE; lions and lion hunting are frequently shown in ancient Greek paintings and mosaics (see ill. 4). To hunt and kill a lion was of course the ultimate test of manliness. The great popularity of hunting at the Macedonian court is well attested in the time of Philip and his son Alexander, and it is clear that Philip grew up learning to hunt. The most notable depiction of this is perhaps from the royal tomb at Aegae that may actually be the tomb of Philip himself (though more probably of his son Arrhidaeus, also known as Philip III), on the facade of which is a magnificent painting depicting a hunt in which deer, a boar, a lion, and a bear are shown.

More important even than hunting was warfare, and the core of a young Macedonian noble's upbringing was learning to ride and to fight from horse-back. Upper-class Macedonian youths were taught to ride from a young age, and learned also the skills of using the sword

5. Macedonian cavalryman (Antigonus the One-Eyed?) from the Alexander Sarcophagus (Istanbul Archaeological Museum)   (*Wikimedia Commons photo by Marsyas*)

and the spear. Weapons drill included, in Macedonia, participation in special warrior dances, during which the dancers would twirl their weapons and engage in mock fighting. These armed dances of the Macedonians, mostly in honor of gods such as Heracles and Athena Promachos (Athena the "front-fighter"), patron deities of the Macedonian elites, are well attested: it was in fact at a performance of such dancing that Philip's oldest brother Alexander was to be assassinated. As to horse-riding skills, ancient Greek horses were smaller than modern horses, and were ridden bareback (see ill. 5), using the thighs to grip the horse and maintain a seat on it. Thrusting with the spear or hacking with the sword required excellent grip and balance on the horse: a Macedonian rider needed strong legs, especially thighs. This training in hunting and fighting, then, was physically demanding and promoted a high degree of fitness and strength. Trained in this way, Philip enjoyed excellent health throughout his life, engaging constantly in extremely physically demanding pursuits and campaigns, and overcoming several life-threatening wounds.

Besides riding, hunting, and fighting, the upper-class Macedonian lifestyle revolved around the *symposium*, the male dining and drinking party. Upper-class Macedonian men were notoriously heavy drinkers (in the eyes of southern Greeks, that is), and like his son Alexander, Philip was no exception to this, as various stories tell us. Macedonian youths would first be introduced to the manners and customs of the *symposium* in their early teens, when they would act as servers and pourers (when slaves were not performing these tasks), and otherwise sit and observe. As we have seen, only when they had proved themselves in the hunting field did Macedonian youths graduate to full participants in the *symposium*. Since the *symposium* involved a great deal of singing, with the singer accompanying himself on the lyre, and conversation on many topics, including literature and philosophy (at the more high-class *symposia* at least), the young Macedonian noble was necessarily taught music—how to sing and play the lyre—and learned some of the classic songs of Greek culture by such greats as Alcaeus, Ibycus, Simonides, Anacreon, and others. And at the top level of society Philip inhabited, as a member of the ruling family, a basic education not just in literacy, but in the great literature of the Greek city-states—Homer, Hesiod, the great Athenian dramatists, history, philosophy, and rhetoric—will certainly have been provided. Philip famously hired the great philosopher Aristotle to educate his own son Alexander. As the younger son of a much less powerful and wealthy ruler, Philip himself was likely not educated at quite such a high level; but as an adult and a ruler we find that he was not just a well-informed man and a good speaker, but a patron of the arts welcoming philosophers, historians, dramatists, actors, and other notable cultural figures at his court, so it should not be doubted that he received a top-quality education.

All of this training and education did not happen in isolation: princes of the ruling family were normally provided with entourages of boys of their own age, drawn from the Macedonian *hetairos* class and called *syntrophoi* (literally, those reared along with one). We know of this practice specifically from the boyhood of Alexander, whose *syntrophoi* included various notable Macedonian nobles such as Ptolemy son of Lagos, Harpalus son of Machatas, Marsyas son of Philip, and most famously Hephaestion. These *syntrophoi* were educated alongside Alexander, also enjoying the teaching of Aristotle as a result. Just so Philip himself will have had his entourage of *syntrophoi* while growing up, providing him not only with companions, but crucially with a network of contacts within the Macedonian nobility. We can in fact guess at the identity of one of these *syntrophoi*: an exact coeval of Philip, born in 383/2, was Antigonus son of Philip, known to history as Antigonus the One-Eyed, founder (after Alexander's premature death) of the Antigonid dynasty of Macedonian kings. Like Philip, Antigonus grew up in Pella, and he is reported to have been a companion of Philip throughout Philip's career. Just as Antigonus' much younger half-brother Marsyas was later a *syntrophos* of Alexander, so is Antigonus likely to have been of Philip. For all of his father's difficulties, then, Philip evidently enjoyed a comfortable and excellent childhood and education.

Only one ancient source preserves an anecdote about the childhood of Philip, and unfortunately it only illustrates the historian's problem in treating Philip's youth. In a speech to the Athenian people about an embassy he had served on to Philip as king in 347, the orator Aeschines told how he had reminded the Macedonian king of the various benefits he, his family, and Macedonia in general had received from the Athenian people. Among these benefits, he says, was an occasion when the Athenian general Iphicrates saved the family of Philip from a rival Argead and would-be ruler of Macedonia named Pausanias. Amyntas and his oldest son Alexander II had recently died, Aeschines tells us, and Pausanias took this opportunity to try to return from exile to seize power, with most Macedonians supporting him. Taking advantage of the disorder in the region, the Athenians sent out Iphicrates with a small force to try to seize control of their former colony Amphipolis. When he arrived in the area, Philip's mother Eurydice sent for him to plead for his help. This is how Aeschines painted the scene:

> Then, I said, your mother Eurydice sent for him (Iphicrates) and, as all those present say, she placed your brother Perdiccas in Iphicrates' arms, and set you—a small child still—on his knees, and said, "Amyntas the father of these little boys, when alive, made you his son and treated the city of the Athenians kindly, so it is proper for you both privately to treat these boys as a brother, and publicly to be our friend." And she went on to make a strong entreaty both for your sakes and for her own, concerning the rule (of Macedonia) and concerning your safety in general. And hearing this, Iphicrates drove Pausanias out of Macedonia and saved the rulership for you. (Aeschines *On the Embassy* 28–29)

A very affecting scene, to be sure; but this anecdote cannot be true as it stands, despite the fact that Aeschines was a contemporary witness and alleges that he spoke these words to Philip himself. Quite simply, Amyntas died in 370, and Alexander II was assassinated in 369/8. That would place this scene most likely in the middle of 368. Philip, born about 383, was no small child then, but a youth of fourteen or fifteen, and his brother Perdiccas was at least a year older, sixteen or seventeen years old. Aeschines uses the word *paidion* to refer to the boys, meaning a child under seven years of age, according to the Greek Lexicon of Liddell and Scott. But Perdiccas and Philip were in fact not *paidia* at this time but teenagers, and the mind boggles at the image of Iphicrates with a sixteen-year-old youth in his arms, and another fourteen-year-old on his knees. In the homoerotic and pederastic culture of classical Greece, and classical Athens in particular, Eurydice's reported action would have been tantamount to offering her sons for Iphicrates' sexual enjoyment. In point of fact, at the time of Pausanias' attempt to seize power, Philip was not present in Macedonia at all: he had been handed over by his brother Alexander to the Theban general Pelopidas as a hostage in 369, as we shall see below, and was living in Thebes.

One wonders what Philip made of these words, if Aeschines really spoke to him as he told the Athenians that he had. He must have been inwardly laughing at the claims made here, and at the fool that Aeschines was making of himself. We are left to wonder what to make of this story. Is any of it true? Iphicrates likely did in fact intervene to help Eurydice against Pausanias, but not in the manner or for the reasons Aeschines alleged. And if a man like Aeschines could so misstate things when speaking to Philip himself, and to a contemporary audience of Athenian citizens, what does that say about the rest of our sources? If the reader has been irritated at the frequency of conditionals, of such constructions as "may have" or "could have," and use of the terms "perhaps" or "maybe" in this chapter, and at the lack of information about Philip himself, I trust that he or she will now understand.

3. The Reigns of Alexander II and Perdiccas III

Amyntas' death, and the succession of his son Alexander II, came at a time of profound change in the power relations within the Greek world. In 371, the Athenians and Spartans, exhausted by war, had summoned a general peace conference in an attempt to arrange a "common peace" after the model of the King's Peace of 386: a peace for all Greek states at once, guaranteeing all of them freedom and autonomy. The peace was agreed upon, but then came the process of swearing to abide by it.

The Spartan king Agesilaus presided; the representative from Thebes, Epaminondas, attempted to swear on behalf of the Boeotian federation set up under Theban leadership (not to say under Theban pressure) during the 370s. Agesilaus refused to permit this: as in 386, he demanded that the Boeotian federation be disbanded, making each Boeotian community free and autonomous, and insisted that each Boeotian community must swear to the peace separately. Epaminondas (unlike the Theban representative in 386) refused this demand and left the conference without swearing. This meant a continuation of war between the Spartans and the Thebans, a war for which the Spartans were ready: an army some ten thousand strong, including around fifteen hundred Spartiates, was waiting in central Greece under the other Spartan king Cleombrotus. As soon as they had news of the outcome of the peace conference, Cleombrotus and his men invaded Boeotia from the north and marched to attack Thebes.

The Thebans too were ready. They mobilized an army in excess of eight thousand men and marched out under the command of Epaminondas to face the Spartans. The two armies met at a small town in Theban territory named Leuctra, and there occurred one of the most shocking upsets in military history. For more than two hundred years the Spartans had been invincible in any large-scale infantry battle: their expertise, prowess, indomitable courage, and unbeatable determination to conquer or die were legendary. Yet at the battle of Leuctra the Spartans were decisively defeated by Epaminondas' Thebans, to the stunned surprise of the Greek world. After the battle, about seven hundred of the fifteen hundred Spartiate (that is, full Spartan citizen) warriors present lay dead, which was shocking enough. But far more shocking was that nearly eight hundred of them survived the battle, defeated and in flight. Spartans were not supposed to flee, to survive defeat: everyone knew the tale of the Spartan wives and mothers who handed their men, as they left for war, their shields with the words "come back with this, or on it". Returning with one's shield meant victorious; returning on one's shield meant dead: the laconic words meant "conquer or die".

What was the Spartan state to do with eight hundred men who had saved themselves in defeat by flight? According to Spartan law, they were now non-persons, stripped of citizen rights, denied access to their lands, their homes, to the sacred spaces of the Spartan communities, to be rejected and ignored by their families. But these eight hundred now represented more than half of all surviving Spartiates, for the number of Spartiates had dwindled over a hundred years of non-stop war to little more than two thousand before the disaster of Leuctra. The Spartan authorities were in a quandary: to follow the law would reduce the number of full Spartiates to just over than five hundred, not enough to think of sustaining the Spartan system and Spartan power; but how could they ignore the law they had lived by for two centuries and more? King Agesilaus, appealed to for his advice, solved the problem: the law was to remain in effect, from the next day. The disgraced eight hundred got a one-day moratorium, and were saved, to themselves and to the Spartan state. But Spartan power had taken a hammer-blow: the mystique of Spartan invincibility, of Spartan refusal to survive defeat, was gone. Over the next few years, the victorious Thebans, led by Epaminondas, dismantled Spartan power in the Peloponnese, reducing Sparta to second-rate status and making themselves the dominant military power in Greece.

It was in the midst of this radical upheaval, then, that Amyntas died, and his son Alexander, about twenty years old at this time, succeeded as Alexander II. He took up the rulership of Macedonia apparently peacefully and without opposition, evidently backed by the powerful barons who had supported his father, including perhaps Derdas and Ptolemy. Like his father, Alexander was obliged to buy off the threat of the Illyrians with tribute payments. Nonetheless, he was full of confidence in himself. The young ruler soon received an appeal from his father's old allies, the Aleuadae clan of Larissa: there was trouble in Thessaly after the assassination of the great tyrant Jason of Pherae, and the Aleuadae had been driven from their Larissan base and were in danger of losing their dominant position in northern Thessaly. Alexander gladly mobilized a Macedonian force and entered Thessaly, quickly capturing Larissa and surrounding towns. But he did not restore the Aleuadae to power: instead he sought to retain control of northern Thessaly for himself. That proved a grave error of judgment.

Just as many Peloponnesian cities, long oppressed by the Spartans, had appealed to the Thebans, as the new power in Greece, for help, so the Aleuadae and their allies in Thessaly now appealed to Thebes too. And just as Epaminondas led a large Theban force into the

Peloponnese to dismantle Spartan power there, so Pelopidas—the other great Theban leader of this time—led a substantial Theban force north, to intervene in Thessaly. Pelopidas' force was far too strong for Alexander to tangle with: his Macedonian forces were sent back to Macedonia like naughty children, the Aleuadae were restored to power in northern Thessaly, Jason's successor in Pherae—another Alexander—was confined to his home city, and Thessaly was brought under Theban patronage.

This episode seems to have fatally damaged young Alexander's standing: when he returned to Macedonia he had to face a rebellion of powerful aristocratic interests led by his own brother-in-law Ptolemy, who rumor had it was conducting an affair with Alexander's mother (and his own mother-in-law) Eurydice. One party or the other, perhaps in fact Alexander himself, appealed to the Theban Pelopidas to arbitrate, and in 368 Pelopidas entered Macedonia with a substantial entourage and settled the dispute. Alexander was to retain the throne; Ptolemy's position as powerful baron and adviser to the king was likewise assured; the Macedonians were to be clients of the Thebans; and to assure their future good behavior a number of prominent Macedonians were secured and sent to Thebes as hostages. Among these hostages was Alexander's youngest full brother, Philip. Aged about fourteen at this time, the young Philip thus came to live in Thebes for three formative years in his mid-teens. In a highly romanticized account, Diodorus has Philip lodge at the house of Epaminondas' father, there to be educated along with the future star Epaminondas himself. In reality, of course, Epaminondas was at this time already a mature adult, the victor of Leuctra, and was away in the Peloponnesos combating the Spartans. Plutarch tells us that Philip lodged at the house of Pammenes, an associate of Epaminondas and Pelopidas, and a notable leader in his own right.

The point of Diodorus' fictionalized account of Philip's time in Thebes is to emphasize the notion that Philip learned about military leadership and governing from and with the great Thebans who dominated Greece in the 360s, and though his details are not true, the general point is universally conceded. Philip certainly absorbed some of the key ideas and strategies of the great Theban leaders during his years as a hostage at Thebes, which were thus a crucial turning point in his life and career.

Epaminondas, Pelopidas, and their associates had begun a revolution in Greek warfare, which Philip was to complete. The standard and dominant style of Greek warfare, that of the heavy infantry hoplite stationed in a phalanx formation several thousand strong, had been developed in the seventh and sixth centuries, and had remained largely unchanged since. The hoplite was a citizen militia soldier, who served in his free time and at his own expense. Most importantly, he provided his own military equipment at his own expense: the standard hoplite panoply included bronze greaves, or shin protectors; a cuirass or corslet to protect the torso; a large bronze helmet covering the entire head, with cut-outs for the eyes and mouth; and a large, heavy, round shield, about one meter in diameter, made of solid wood with extensive bronze reinforcement on the rim and outer face (see ill. 3). This equipment made the hoplite relatively invulnerable to frontal attack, but slow and cumbersome. Several thousand such hoplites drawn up in neat lines and files—usually about eight lines made a standard phalanx—created a fearsome formation. In the narrow plains and valleys of Greece, it was easy to position such a phalanx in a place where its flanks could not be turned: an enemy had to confront it frontally, and try to push it backwards and force it into flight by sheer pressure.

The Spartans had made themselves the undisputed masters of this style of warfare by devoting themselves exclusively to hoplite training and pursuits emphasizing physical fitness: sports and hunting, mostly. The full Spartiate owned an estate worked by helot serfs which provided a living. Freed from such concerns, the Spartiate entered the appalling Spartan training system—the *agoge*—at the age of seven, and spent his life from then on as a hoplite warrior pure and simple. In essence, the Spartiates were professional soldiers, while the citizen militia warriors of the rest of Greece were amateurs. A Spartan army would normally consist of thousands of allied soldiers, and an elite force of Spartiates generally no more than two or three thousand strong. By the early fourth century, as we have seen, demographic decline had reduced the Spartiate caste to only a little over two thousand, but they were still able to dominate the battlefields of Greece. The elite Spartiate unit would be drawn up, in battle, on the right flank of the army, their allies making up the center and left. As they marched forward to engage, the Spartiates, fitter and better disciplined than their allies, would invariably draw slightly ahead and be the first to engage. Their unique skill and discipline in the art of hoplite infighting and concerted shoving would enable them to drive back the force opposing them on the enemy left very rapidly, whereupon they would turn leftwards and proceed to roll up the rest of the enemy formation from left to right.

In this simple and effective way, the Spartans ruled Greek battle-fields for over two hundred years, and the usually so inventive Greeks accepted the traditional way of fighting, accepted the advantage this gave to Spartan collective training and discipline, and let a few thousand Spartiates dominate Greece. The Thebans under Epaminondas and Pelopidas did not end this Spartan dominance by trying to beat the Spartans at their own game, as numerous Greek leaders and armies had failed to do. Epaminondas re-thought the basic strategy and formation of Greek warfare. Normally the best troops in any army were stationed on the right, and the aim when confronted by the Spartans was to use one's superior right wing to drive away the allies on the Spartans' left before the Spartiates could win the battle from their own right wing. No one ever succeeded: the Spartans were too good and too quick at their task of driving back their opponents. Epaminondas decided to confront the Spartans head-on, stationing his best troops on his left, opposite the Spartiates, at Leuctra. But he realized that even his best troops could not match the iron discipline and cohesion of the Spartiates, the fruit of their decades of training. He had to find a solution to this, and he found it in a tactical formation of remarkable simplicity. Instead of drawing up his phalanx a standard and uniform eight ranks deep, he thinned out and held back the part of his formation facing Sparta's allies, and vastly increased the depth of his formation on the left, facing the Spartiates: he knew that if the Spartans themselves were beaten, the Spartan allies would not stay to fight. Forming up his left wing some thirty lines deep, he created a weight of troops that the Spartans simply could not overcome. Though they fought with their usual determination and discipline, the Spartiates were inevitably driven backwards, and Epaminondas used cavalry to harass them from the right as they gave ground. And seeing the Spartiates, to their wonder, being driven back, the rest of the Spartan army gave ground too and turned to flight.

Thus, by applying some careful rational analysis to the process of hoplite fighting, and the reasons for Spartan dominance, Epaminondas and his associates found a simple and elegant solution that ended the myth of Spartan invincibility. During Philip's stay in Thebes, Epaminondas was mostly away in the Peloponnese, where he dismantled Sparta's age-old alliance system, known as the Peloponnesian League, whereby the Spartans had successfully kept the Peloponnese subordinated; and he ringed Sparta with two newly created and inherently hostile city-states: Messenia and Megalopolis. Meanwhile Pelopidas was busy during these years campaigning in Thessaly and building Theban dominance in northern Greece. Witnessing this from within Thebes, staying at the house of one of the most important associates of Epaminondas and Pelopidas, Philip too was brought to reflect on the nature of warfare, the weakness of his father and brother as rulers, the inability of Macedonia to compete in hoplite warfare with her southern Greek neighbors, and what might be done to create a military system that would enable the Macedonians to do what the Thebans were doing: break the balance of power in Greece and change it to Macedonia's advantage. For Philip, when his time came, did not attempt merely to copy what the great Theban leaders had done: he went much further and invented a whole new style of warfare, as we shall see.

In Macedonia, while Philip was at Thebes, things went from bad to worse for Alexander II. Ptolemy had gauged his real weakness, and not long after the agreement brokered by Pelopidas, Alexander was killed—still in the year 368 it seems—while watching a performance of a Macedonian war dance called the *telesias*. The assassination was evidently carried out on Ptolemy's orders, and it was he who seized power, ruling nominally as regent for Perdiccas, the next son of Amyntas, and jointly with the queen mother Eurydice. But Ptolemy proved no stronger than Alexander. His power was at once challenged by a rival claimant to the throne, an Argead pretender named Pausanias. It is not clear who this Pausanias was: at a guess perhaps a son of the Pausanias son of Aeropus who had ruled briefly in 393. Such a son would have been in his mid-twenties in 368: an appropriate age to seek power. He apparently enjoyed considerable support in Macedonia, and it was only thanks to a fortuitous intervention by the Athenian commander Iphicrates, old friend and ally (and adopted son) of Amyntas, who happened to be in the northern Aegean with a force on Athenian business, that the challenge of Pausanias was seen off. In 367, however, Pelopidas invaded Macedonia again: he was angered by the upsetting of the settlement he had proposed, and Ptolemy had to buy him off with presents, reassurances, and the handing over of further hostages.

Perceiving Ptolemy's weakness, Perdiccas began to lay plans to assert himself, take power, and rule in his own right. Born by 384 at the latest, and likely a year or two earlier, he was now at least eighteen years old, and naturally impatient of having a regent ruling for him, particularly perhaps since the regent was co-habiting with his (Perdiccas') mother. In 366 or early 365 Ptolemy was assassinated and Perdiccas became the ruler of Macedonia as Perdiccas III. Like his older brother Alexander, he felt full confidence in his abilities as ruler and took a number of steps to bolster his position in preparation for a major move to end Macedonia's humiliating subordination to the Illyrians. Perdiccas re-affirmed Macedonia's relationship with Thebes, and negotiated the return of his bother Philip after three years. Epaminondas was planning to develop a Theban fleet and challenge the Athenians at sea, and for that he would need Macedonian ship-building timber. Athenian power in the north Aegean, especially her control of the Macedonian ports Pydna and Methone, was irksome, and Perdiccas sought ways to counter this. Athenian pressure on her rebellious former colony Amphipolis provided this: appealed to by the Amphipolitans for help, Perdiccas established a Macedonian garrison in Amphipolis, keeping that crucial city out of Athenian hands and in the Macedonian orbit.

To further shore up his power within Macedonia, Perdiccas established young Philip, in his late teens now, in control of some substantial territory within Macedonia. Unfortunately, our sources do not specify where, nor whether this amounted merely to some estates for Philip to manage, or to governorship of some province or region. But there are some grounds on which to speculate. Philip, notoriously, married many times during his reign, in the usual polygamous manner of Argead rulers. One of his first wives, probably in fact his first, was named Phila and came from the dynastic house of the south-western "canton" in upper Macedonia named Elimea: she was the daughter of Amyntas' old ally Derdas, and sister of his like-named son, the younger Derdas. It has been speculated that the older Derdas had died, and that in effect, through this marriage, Philip was made by Perdiccas the governor of Elimea, displacing the younger Derdas, who is later met with living in exile. Elimea was an important region, which could be a crucial source of support to an ambitious Macedonian king if it was loyally governed. And its position in the south-west meant it was far enough away from the major barbarian threats to Macedonian security—from the Illyrians, Paeonians, and Thracians in the north—to serve as a secure source of supplies and support to a Macedonian ruler combating those threats.

It is evident that Perdiccas had spent his years as ruler down to 360 building up the Macedonian army. Exactly how he went about this is unclear, though revenues from timber sales to the Thebans and Athenians will likely have helped. What we know is that by 360 he had at his disposal an infantry force many thousands strong, substantially more than four thousand in fact, likely on the order of seven or eight thousand at least. No previous Macedonian ruler is attested to have commanded an infantry force of this size: it was clearly a new development in Macedonia, an infantry force raised by means on which we can only speculate, armed and trained in a manner of which we know nothing. But its purpose at least was clear. Perdiccas ended the tribute payments to the Illyrians, who were still ruled by old Bardylis. When Bardylis responded by leading a major Illyrian invasion of northern Macedonia, Perdiccas marched forth to meet him with his large new infantry army, leaving Philip behind in control of his province—likely, as we have suggested, Elimea.

The outcome of this campaign was disastrous for Perdiccas and Macedonia. In a great battle fought somewhere in north-west Macedonia, likely in Pelagonia, and perhaps not far from Lake Ohrid, Perdiccas and his army were disastrously defeated. The young king Perdiccas III was killed in the fighting, along with, we are told, some four thousand of his men: it is this number of dead that reveals how large Perdiccas' army had been. Much of the army must certainly have survived: it is rare in warfare for as much as half of an army to die in battle. But the thousands of survivors, leaderless and defeated, could do nothing but flee. Many of them were no doubt captured, but many likely got away, to disperse back to their homes or to whatever other refuge they could find. The Macedonian army effectively ceased to exist, and north-west Macedonia lay wide open to the invading Illyrians, who occupied a large portion of it, the cantons of Pelagonia and Lyncus at the least.

Once again, as so often in these years, Macedonia needed a new ruler. Perdiccas had married some years earlier and left a son named Amyntas, but the boy was not more than two or three years old and could not possibly take up the rulership of Macedonia at this time. That left Perdiccas' brother Philip, now (late 360) about twenty-four years old; his half-brothers Archelaus, Menelaus, and Arrhidaeus, and two former pretenders still living in exile—Argaeus and Pausanias—to compete for power. It was of course Philip who stepped in, took control of Macedonia, and proceeded over the course of a remarkable twenty-four-year reign to transform Macedonia, and with it the history of the eastern Mediterranean world. Until 360, as we have seen, our knowledge of Macedonia and its history is sparse and sketchy, but the accession to power of Philip as king changed that: for the first time the focus of Greek historians turned northward and centered on Macedonia and a Macedonian ruler. The real history of Macedonia, therefore, begins with the reign of Philip II.

CHAPTER 3

The Reign of Philip

6. Medallion of Emperor Alexander Severus showing portrait of Philip II of Macedonia   (*Wikimedia Commons public domain image by Jastrow*)

This man [Philip] ruled over the Macedonians for twenty-four years, and starting with the weakest of resources he built his kingdom into the greatest of the powers in Europe; taking over Macedonia when it was a slave to the Illyrians he made it the master of many great peoples and cities. Through his own excellence he received the leadership of all of Greece, the cities willingly subordinating themselves . . . Conquering in war the Illyrians, the Paeonians, the Thracians, the Scythians, and all the peoples neighboring on these, he took it upon himself to overthrow the kingdom of the Persians, and having sent forces ahead into Asia was in the act of freeing the Greek cities there when he was cut short in the midst of it all by fate. But he left behind so many and such great forces that his son Alexander required no further allies to bring about the destruction of Persian power. And Philip achieved all of this not by luck, but through his own excellence. For this king excelled in military shrewdness, in courage, and in brilliance of mind.   (Diodorus 16.1.3–6)

FEW IF ANY RULERS IN WORLD HISTORY CAN EVER HAVE TAKEN UP POWER under circumstances as difficult, indeed as outright disastrous, as those confronting Philip when he assumed the rule of Macedonia in the winter of 360/59. The defeat of his brother Perdiccas in battle against Bardylis and his Illyrians did not just result in Perdiccas' death:

it brought about the near total destruction of the Macedonian army. As we have seen, as many as four thousand Macedonian soldiers are reported to have died along with Perdiccas in this battle; many of the survivors were doubtless captured by the victorious Illyrians; and those who got away simply dispersed to their homes or some other refuge. The main army of the Macedonian state thereby ceased to exist in any useful sense, and the northwestern portion of Macedonia—Pelagonia and Lyncus at least, and likely some portions of Eordaea and Orestis, perhaps as much as a quarter of Macedonian territory in all—was occupied by the Illyrians and ceased temporarily to be part of Macedonia. That in itself constituted a major problem for the new ruler of Macedonia, but it was only a part of the difficulties Philip had to confront.

The defeat and death of the Macedonian ruler, and destruction of his army, was taken as an opportunity by various other neighbors and rivals of the Macedonians to extend their power at Macedonia's expense, or to gain influence over Macedonia, or simply to loot and pillage in Macedonia to their hearts' content. From the upper Axius valley to the north of Macedonia, Paeonian tribesmen invaded the Amphaxitis plain, looting, killing, and destroying as they came. From the south, an Athenian expedition of thirty ships and three thousand hoplites under the general Mantias appeared at Methone, convoying the Macedonian pretender Argaeus with a force of exiles and mercenaries, with the aim of installing Argaeus as a pro-Athenian puppet ruler over Macedonia. The Athenian goal was to control the Macedonian coast, ensuring access to Macedonian timber, and especially to win back control of the strategic former Athenian colony of Amphipolis, which was occupied at the time by a Macedonian garrison installed by Perdiccas. From the east, a large Thracian army gathered, probably commanded by the great Thracian ruler Cotys and accompanied by another Macedonian pretender named Pausanias, preparing to invade Macedonia to install Pausanias as a pro-Thracian puppet ruler. With the army destroyed, and enemy forces invading Macedonia from the north-west, north, east, and south, it looked as if Macedonia was simply falling apart, to survive at best as a partitioned region ruled by outsiders or by puppet rulers installed by outsiders. The prospects facing Philip seemed bleak indeed.

One must recall that at this time Philip was a young man of just twenty-four and untried in command, the son of a ruler who had been weak at best, and the younger brother of rulers who had been outright failures. There was nothing in the situation he faced or in his immediate past history to suggest that he had any prospect of being a successful ruler. Yet the task Philip set himself was not merely to deal with these immediate threats to Macedonia's integrity and security, but to raise Macedonia to the position of a major regional power able to over-match its regional rivals and threaten their security and integrity, rather than merely struggling to preserve itself against their attacks. And over the course of his twenty-four-year reign he was to succeed spectacularly in this self-imposed task; so spectacularly that it is a wonder he is not remembered as one of the great rulers in western history.

1. DEFUSING THE INITIAL CRISIS

Before Philip could even begin to work towards his major aims and goals, however, he had to deal with the immediate problems con-fronting his rule in particular and Macedonia in general: how he man-aged to deal with the multi-faceted and drastic crisis brought about by Perdiccas' defeat would determine whether he would ever have the chance to strengthen Macedonia at all. In the event, it must be said that, his youth and inexperience notwithstanding, Philip's analysis and as-sessment of the problems confronting him and the means available to him for coping with them was brilliant. In one short year he defused the crises and established himself firmly as Macedonia's unquestioned ruler. How did he go about this?

The greatest difficulty limiting Philip's possibilities was the lack of military force. The destruction of Perdiccas' main Macedonian army did not leave Macedonia denuded of military manpower, by any means; but it gave Macedonians little incentive to join up with and serve under a ruler—Philip—whose prospects of success seemed bleak at best. What probably saved Philip in the beginning was having a secure base of power with some military force of his own, in the region of Macedonia—possibly Elimea as we have seen—over which his brother had placed him. He realized immediately, however, that he lacked the military force to confront Bardylis and his Illyrians in the north-west or the Thracian army approaching from the east. He correctly drew the conclusion that he must try to deal with these two threats by diplomacy and, if possible, bribery. Before he could do so, he had to establish himself as ruler of

Macedonia, which presumably involved occupation of the new capital city established by Archelaus, Pella. At Pella, Philip would be at the center of things, controlling the Macedonian court and such administrative institutions as there might be. More importantly, it was no doubt at Pella that the royal treasury was located. That Philip seized and controlled this is nowhere stated; but in his first moves against Macedonia's enemies he was able to engage in extensive "bribery" (giving of presents, to put it more neutrally), showing that he had significant funds at his disposal from the start. Where else but from the royal treasury could such funds have come?

Though our sources unfortunately offer little detail, it is clear that Philip initiated negotiations with Bardylis which resulted in some sort of truce at a minimum, perhaps an outright peace agreement. Bardylis was, perforce, left in control of the portions of upper Macedonia he had already occupied, since there was nothing to be done about it as things stood. In return for acknowledging Bardylis' occupation, Philip got a respite from further Illyrian attacks. It seems likely that he also sent some sort of tribute payment and/or a promise to resume the tribute payments his father Amyntas had made to keep the Illyrians out of Macedonia. It is likely too that Philip's marriage to the Illyrian Audata, probably a daughter or niece of Bardylis, occurred at this time, and as part of this negotiation. By Audata, his second wife, Philip eventually had a daughter named Cynnane. This shrewd but humiliating diplomacy, then, secured Philip's north-western flank and bought him a period of quiet from that quarter in which to act.

The second great issue facing Philip was the threatened Thracian invasion from the east, led by Cotys with the aim of installing Pausanias as puppet ruler. Here again Philip was too weak to respond other than by diplomacy. Philip apparently met with Cotys in person, and by a mixture of promises and bribes persuaded the aged Thracian ruler to abandon his project. Cotys was no doubt promised that Philip would be a suitably friendly and humble Macedonian ruler, so that there was no need to install Pausanias; and cash gifts from Philip took the place of loot extracted by force. Pausanias was thus abandoned and, since nothing further is ever heard of him, likely either killed outright or handed over to Philip for execution. Very fortunately for Philip, Cotys died soon after this agreement was reached and his great Thracian realm was divided into three parts, each ruled by one of his three sons. These three much smaller and weaker Thracian realms offered a much lesser threat to Macedonia and Philip, particularly as Cotys' three sons immediately entered into rivalries against each other, rivalries which Philip was eventually able to exploit effectively to his advantage.

The two gravest threats to Philip's position as Macedonian ruler, and to the stability of Macedonia, were thus dealt with for the immediate time being by a mixture of diplomacy and bribery that was, while humiliating, effective and necessary. But such humiliating diplomacy could hardly help to ensure Philip's position within Macedonia, as Macedonian ruler. He needed a show of strength to persuade the Macedonians that he could be more than a weak puppet of stronger outside powers. There remained two threats to be dealt with: the Athenians and their would-be puppet ruler Argaeus, and the Paeonians. Success in whichever threat he first confronted was absolutely necessary, and Philip therefore assessed which of these was the weaker and therefore the easier to deal with. He decided to confront Argaeus and the Athenians first, no doubt also in part because, in marching on the ancient capital Aegae and seeking to occupy it, Argaeus represented the more existential threat to Philip himself as Macedonian ruler. Consequently, he sent messengers to the Paeonian ruler Agis, to buy him and his raiders off for the time being with gifts and promises.

One thing Philip could not afford to do at this time was get embroiled in a major war with the Athenians: they were too powerful and he lacked the resources. His problem thus was to eliminate Argaeus without antagonizing the man's Athenian backers too much. He quickly found the solution. The guiding principle to Athenian policy in the north Aegean for more than half a century had been to recover control of their former colony Amphipolis at the mouth of the River Strymon. They had founded this colony in 438/7 to give them a secure base from which to import the Macedonian and Thracian timber which was vital to their ship-building; but they lost control of it in 424 when the Spartan commander Brasidas induced the population to rebel and ally with Sparta. Since then the Athenians had made numerous unsuccessful attempts to recover control, and the installation of a Macedonian garrison in Amphipolis by Perdiccas was a key cause of Athenian hostility to Perdiccas and his brother Philip. Philip was so short of military manpower that he could not afford to maintain this garrison in any case: he needed those troops for other purposes. However, upon withdrawing the garrison from Amphipolis he made a virtue of necessity by letting the Athenians know that he supported their claim to Amphipolis, words that cost him nothing but won him the beginning of good will among the Athenians. He followed up by seeking a formal declaration of peace.

As a result of this, the Athenian commander in the north, Mantias, who had been sent to Methone with thirty ships and three thousand hoplite warriors, kept his Athenian hoplites at Methone and sent Argaeus to Aegae with only a small force of mercenaries and exiles, but with very few Athenians. The people of Aegae correctly assessed Argaeus' chances of making himself ruler of Macedonia as negligible and refused to back him: they were perhaps angered too by Argaeus' foreign backing. As a result Argaeus was obliged to retreat back towards the coast, and here—along the route between Aegae and Methone—Philip and his forces lay in wait. In a sharp battle, Argaeus' force was decisively defeated. Most of the mercenaries were killed, as almost certainly was Argaeus himself (he is never heard of again). The surviving Macedonian exiles were arrested, but the Athenians among Argaeus' force were carefully separated out and released without ransom and even with compensation for their losses. They presumably returned to Mantias at Methone and strengthened the impression that Philip was well disposed to Athens. Thus Philip had brought an end to the Athenian threat to his power by showing careful good will to the Athenians at little cost; had eliminated his rival Argaeus once and for all; and had shown himself a promising military leader by winning his first military engagement with decisive ease.

Now that the Macedonians saw reason to believe in Philip, he was able to begin recruiting further soldiers and prepare to deal with the remaining threat of the Paeonians. Here he again had some good luck: the Paeonian ruler Agis apparently died at this time, leaving the Paeonians with much weaker leadership. Philip launched a swift expedition up the Axius valley and inflicted a sharp defeat on the Paeonian tribesmen, who thereafter troubled Macedonia very little, and in fact came under Macedonian suzerainty. As the campaigning season of 359 drew to a close, Philip could congratulate himself on his achievements. He was now firmly established as ruler of Macedonia. By an astute, and as it was to prove highly characteristic mix of diplomacy, bribery, and victorious military engagement, he had calmed or seen off the various threats to Macedonia. The two pretenders Pausanias and Argaeus were no more; the Paeonians were cowed; the Athenians were considering a formal peace; the Thracians were quiet; and the Illyrian threat was contained by tribute and marriage alliance. The Macedonian people were duly impressed by their astute young ruler; but Philip knew that his achievements to date were only temporary. To win true security for Macedonia, and for his own rule of Macedonia, he needed a far greater military force than he could as yet command. Only a strong military force could truly secure Macedonia against the Illyrian threat, overawe the Athenians into staying out of Macedonian affairs, and keep the Paeonians and Thracians cowed. Having won himself a breathing space, therefore, Philip devoted the fall of 359 and the winter and spring of 358 to military recruitment, and to the creation of a new Macedonian army.

The process is described by Diodorus at 16.1–2: Philip traveled around Macedonia summoning the people to assemblies where he built up their morale and explained his plans. He recruited men, and re-organized the training and equipment of the Macedonian infantry. He himself, as ruler, provided his recruits with their new-style equipment and led them in a series of competitive training drills and maneuvers. He taught them a new style of close-order fighting he had devised, and he thereby "first established the Macedonian phalanx". The exact meaning of Diodorus' words, the kind of equipment and fighting Philip introduced, and the claim that he originated the Macedonian phalanx, are all controversial and have been the source of much scholarly debate. All of this will be examined in detail in the next chapter. But whatever the details of Philip's work, one clear result is not in dispute: by the summer of 358 Philip was able to dispose of an army of ten thousand well trained infantry and in excess of six hundred cavalry. Such a military force is without precedent in recorded Macedonian history, except perhaps in the force Perdiccas had led to confront the Illyrians two years earlier. But Philip's force seems to have been better trained and equipped than his brother's had been, though its purpose was the same: to confront the Illyrians.

In the summer of 358 Philip invaded north-western Macedonia

at the head of this army: he had never had any intention of allowing the Illyrians to control the north-western cantons of Macedonia permanently, the peace he had negotiated in 359 being merely an expedient to earn a respite in which to rebuild Macedonia's army. Now that the army was ready, the peace was abandoned: when Bardylis sent messengers to Philip to protest his action and demand he adhere to the terms of the peace, Philip demanded that all Illyrian forces should withdraw from Macedonian territory. That meant a military confrontation, and Bardylis summoned his forces, which matched those of Philip almost exactly: ten thousand infantry and five hundred cavalry, according to Diodorus (16.4.4). The battle that occurred somewhere in north-western Macedonia was hard-fought. Philip himself commanded a picked force of elite infantry on the right of his phalanx, and instructed his cavalry stationed on the far right wing to charge around the Illyrians' left flank and attack them from the rear. The Illyrians responded by forming themselves into a square, and put up a desperate fight. But Philip's newly trained and organized infantry proved irresistible: the Illyrian resistance was overcome, and when they broke and ran Philip's cavalry kept up a determined pursuit to kill as many fleeing Illyrians as possible and make the victory decisive. Some seven thousand Illyrians perished, we are told, a full two-thirds of the army engaged; and the Illyrians had no choice but to withdraw entirely from Macedonian territory.

Thus Philip had triumphantly overcome all the problems confronting Macedonia at his accession, and shown himself to be already the strongest Macedonian ruler since the founding ruler, Alexander I. At about this same time the Athenians agreed to a peace treaty with Philip, leaving him in full control of Macedonia and free from any external threat. He had at his disposal a victorious army that was the largest in Macedonia's history, and the good will of his people whom he had saved from foreign invasion and occupation and the seeming dissolution of their state. As a result of this great victory, Philip could now embark on the process of state-building by which he hoped to turn Macedonia into the strongest state in Greece and the Balkan region, instead of one of the weakest.

The problems initially confronting Philip can be separated into three major sets of issues: there were the internal issues of Macedonia's political and military weakness, its characteristic disunity and regional rivalries, and the disloyalty of members of the ruling Argead family and of other dynastic and aristocratic families; there were the constant threats of invasion and harassment posed by the barbarian peoples to Macedonia's north and east—the Illyrians, Dardanians, Paeonians, and Thracians above all; and there was the issue of relations, often hostile relations, with the various Greek states and communities to the south of Macedonia, in the first place the Olynthian League and the Thessalians, and beyond them the stronger states dominating the rest of the Greek mainland—Thebans and Athenians most prominently.

The historical sources on which we have to rely for information were almost exclusively written by southern city-state Greeks (especially Athenians), and were overwhelmingly interested in relations between Philip and the city-states of Greece (especially Athens). This seriously distorts a basic historical reality: it is made to seem that Philip's main preoccupation throughout his reign was relations with the Athenians and other city-state Greeks, when in point of fact Philip's main concerns were rather with solving Macedonia's internal problems, creating a properly unified state, and establishing Macedonian dominance over its barbarian neighbors, rather than the other way around. While we can trace the history of Philip's relations with southern Greece, and especially the Athenians, in considerable detail, we get only occasional glimpses into how he dealt with the more crucial issues of internal weakness and barbarian foes. It seems most useful to treat each of these issues separately in turn, gathering all the information we can to present the best possible picture of how Philip went about dealing with each of these three sets of issues.

2. BUILDING A MACEDONIAN STATE

Undoubtedly the primary issue confronting Philip was that of establishing his rule over Macedonia, of unifying it into a coherent state under his control, and of strengthening it militarily, politically, socially, and economically. He began this project with an enormous source of strength: the large infantry army he had built and led to victory over the Illyrians gave him a secure power base no previous Macedonian ruler had at his disposal. The army was indeed the key to Philip's state-building success, and to the nature of the Macedonian state he brought into being. I will defer detailed discussion of Philip's military reforms, and of the Macedonian army, to the next chapter. Here, I shall discuss the unification of Macedonia, the proper subordination of the Macedonian aristocracy, the improvement of the Macedonian economy, and the creation of a Macedonian warrior "middle class" that formed the backbone of the Macedonian state and Macedonian power for several centuries to come.

One of the difficulties Macedonian rulers had faced throughout Macedonia's history was the lack of unity of the country. As already described in Chapter 1, the core lands of Macedonia comprised two broad regions, generally referred to as lower and upper Macedonia; upper Macedonia was itself divided by mountain ranges into a series of sub-regions, each of which had its own local traditions and dominant families or clans. Within these upland sub-regions, or cantons as they are often called, local dynastic families had a tendency to take power and set themselves up as rivals or outright enemies of whatever Argead prince was ruling Macedonia at the time. Members of a dynastic family in Lyncus, for example, using the name Arrhabaeus and claiming descent from the old Bachhiad ruling clan of early Corinth, set themselves up at times as independent rulers of their region: the first Arrhabaeus was an enemy of Perdiccas II in the 420s (Thucydides 4.74–78 and 124–28); the second Arrhabaeus was an enemy of Archelaus (Aristotle *Politics* 1311b). The same is the case with the princely Derdas family of Elimea. We know of at least three princes of this name: the first was an enemy of Perdiccas II (Thucydides 1.57.3); the second probably assassinated the ruler Amyntas II (the Little), as we have seen, but was subsequently an ally of Amyntas III (Xenophon *Hellenica* 5.2.38–41); the third was an enemy of Philip, captured and killed at the sack of Olynthus in 347 (Athenaeus 10.436c, 13.557b). Further, Thucydides (2.80) tells us of a king of Orestis named Antiochus. Indeed, in an early treaty between Athens and Perdiccas II from ca. 440, preserved in an inscription (*Inscriptiones Graecae* I³.89), we find among those who swear to the treaty, along with Perdiccas himself and members of his family, four men with the title *basileus* (king) from upper Macedonia: Arrhabaeus, Derdas, Antiochus, and a fourth whose name is unfortunately lost.

To make Macedonia strong, Philip needed to fully integrate the upper Macedonian cantons into the Macedonian state, and to subordinate the dynastic families there once and for all. Derdas of Elimea was driven out of his territory and forced into exile: as we have seen, he fled to Olynthus and was there captured by Philip (and fairly certainly executed). Members of his family stayed in Elimea, but now as subordinates of the Argead ruler: we find an Elimiote Harpalus son of Machatas (a name used by the Derdas family) serving loyally under Alexander some years later. The princely dynasty of Lyncus had Philip to thank for driving out the Illyrian occupiers in 358: they perforce had to accept subjection to Philip. Three sons of Arrhabaeus II named Arrhabaeus, Heromenes, and Alexander remained quietly subordinate during Philip's reign. The first two were executed by Alexander on suspicion of complicity in the plot to murder Philip; but we may suspect that they were really guilty of being perceived as potential threats to Alexander's succession to his father's power. The plain fact is that Philip's new army, his victory over the Illyrians, and the many further victories that followed, made him far too formidable for the dynasts of upper Macedonia to challenge. They had to be content with subordination to Philip, and seek advancement in his service, or face being exiled and/or executed. The manpower of upper Macedonia was mobilized in Philip's service: in the fully developed Macedonian army at the end of Philip's reign and the beginning of Alexander's, we find large battalions of infantry drawn from the regions of upper Macedonia as established segments of the Macedonian heavy infantry phalanx (see further Chapter 4, below). Their experience of successful military service, and the rewards they won as a result, made them loyal to Philip and his successor rather than to the old local dynastic families.

Thus a mixture of threats and rewards brought the dynastic houses of upper Macedonia to heel, and successful military service in Philip's army and wars transferred the loyalty of the men of upper Macedonia to Philip, and integrated them into the Macedonian identity. The other great threat to Macedonian unity came from the Argead ruling family itself. For almost a hundred years, since the death of Alexander I in about 454, Macedonia was plagued by rivalries between competing branches of the Argead family descending from Alexander's many sons. Members of the Argead family had not scrupled to ally themselves with great Macedonian aristocrats, with members of the upper Macedonian dynastic houses, or even with foreign powers such as the Olynthians, the Thracians, and the Athenians, in their quests to overthrow the ruling Argead and take his place. Not only for his own sake, but to create a stable and unified Macedonia, Philip could not allow that. He ruthlessly eliminated all members of the Argead family, therefore, except his own immediate heirs.

Right at the start of his reign, Philip eliminated the representatives of two rival branches of the Argead clan who were trying to make themselves ruler with foreign backing: Argaeus with Athenian support, and Pausanias with Thracian support. We have seen how Philip bought off their foreign support and ended these threats to his position. So far as we can tell, what remained of the Argead family after the deaths of these two pretenders, were Philip's three half-brothers, Archelaus, Menelaus, and Arrhidaeus, and his nephew Amyntas son of Perdiccas. His three half-brothers were direct rivals to Philip for rule of Macedonia, and the eldest, Archelaus, seems already to have made a play for power in 359. What exactly happened is not known, but Archelaus met a violent end. The other two brothers fled and eventually found refuge in Olynthus, like Derdas; and like Derdas they perished at the sack of Olynthus in 347 (Justin 8.3.10). That left, besides Philip himself, only Amyntas alive of the Argead family. As his dead brother's young son, Amyntas was Philip's ward and, until he had sons of his own, his heir presumptive. Philip brought Amyntas into his own household and had him carefully brought up there, eventually along with his (Philip's) own sons Arrhidaeus and Alexander. After all, Philip could not know whether his sons would survive childhood and prove to be suitable heirs. When Amyntas reached adulthood, Philip showed that Amyntas was very much in his thoughts as part of his family by marrying his own daughter Cynnane (by his Illyrian wife Audata) to Amyntas. At the same time, of course, this kept Amyntas firmly under his control and within his own immediate family circle; and Amyntas remained loyal as long as Philip was alive.

With potential Argead pretenders eliminated, the dynastic upper Macedonian houses thoroughly subjected, and upper Macedonia firmly integrated into the Macedonian state, the most dangerous obstacles to Macedonian unity had been dealt with. But there was also the problem of the Macedonian aristocracy more generally. The Macedonian aristocracy were primarily big landowners, who lived a life centered around horse-rearing, hunting, warfare, and the symposium (drinking party). Their estates were apparently worked by a kind of serf class, freeing them from the need to do any productive work. Besides the serfs, they had tenants and retainers who, in periods of warfare (endemic during most of Macedonian history) served their lords as cavalry (the retainers) and light infantry (the tenants). The Macedonian army before the time of Philip was, indeed, made up of the personal followings of various aristocrats added to the personal following of the ruler himself, who was a great landowner like the aristocrats. The military power of the ruler thus depended on the degree to which he was able to persuade members of the aristocracy to back him. Those aristocrats who did support a given ruler became his *hetairoi* (companions, a term going back to Homeric times), and served as his *synedrion* (governing/advisory council). The importance of the aristocratic role as *hetairoi* of the ruler is illustrated by the existence of a major annual festival celebrating it, named the *hetairidia*. One should also note the naming of a set of "barons from lower Macedonia" (Errington 1990 p. 15) as guarantors of the peace treaty with Athens preserved in *Inscriptiones Graecae* I³.89.

Strong rulers were those who succeeded in uniting the vast majority of the aristocracy behind them; weak rulers were those who failed to do this. And there was a clear tendency in early Macedonian history (before Philip II, that is) for aristocrats to rally behind rival pretenders to the throne (that is, those opposing the sitting ruler), or even, as in the case of Ptolemy of Aloros in the early 360s, to set themselves up as rivals to the ruler. A stable and successful Macedonia required bringing the aristocracy to heel and ending their divisive ways. Philip's creation of a new and powerful infantry army beginning in 358 gave him an unprecedented position of strength from which to deal with the aristocracy: no aristocratic landowner, no matter how wealthy and powerful, could compete militarily with Philip's army. Any aristocrat, or even coalition of aristocrats, who set themselves up against Philip faced the prospect of a visit by Philip's new Macedonian phalanx, and possible annihilation. That intrinsically gave the Macedonian aristocracy a strong incentive to demonstrate loyalty to Philip; but this was a negative incentive. Philip gave them a positive incentive too. As Philip's new army campaigned around the southern Balkan region, winning battles and wars, Philip seized lands from defeated enemies and incorporated them into Macedonia. By traditional notions of "spear-won land," these conquered lands belonged to the ruler and were his to dispose of. Philip granted to favored aristocrats additional estates of conquered land, vastly increasing their wealth. But they did not own these additional estates outright: instead they had revocable possession, and the condition of maintaining possession was to continue demonstrating loyalty to the ruler, to Philip that is. According to the contemporary historian Theopompus, Philip's eight hundred or so *hetairoi* at the height of his reign held, thanks to this policy, as much landed wealth as the ten thousand wealthiest men from the rest of Greece combined.

The aristocracy were thus firmly subordinated to Philip's rule by a carrot and stick approach: the carrot was the gaining of vast new estates to increase their wealth; the stick was the threat of losing those estates and, in the extreme, of being annihilated by Philip's army. But Philip was not satisfied with just this: he pursued two further policies to increase his control of the aristocracy. In the first place, Philip invited leading men from all the rest of Greece to move to Macedonia and enter his service, becoming his *hetairoi*, and like the native aristocrats being rewarded with large revocable estates of conquered land. These new, immigrant *hetairoi* owed their wealth and status entirely to Philip's favor, and were self-interestedly loyal to Philip as a result; they thus formed a powerful block of support that Philip could use against any disaffected Macedonian aristocrats. Some famous examples of such new *hetairoi* are Eumenes of Cardia, the Cretan Nearchus, Erigyius of Mitylene, and Medeius of Larissa.

In addition, and very importantly, Philip was interested in binding the sons and grandsons of the aristocracy to his service, making them not only loyal followers, but *useful* ones. To this end he established a school at Pella and invited the aristocracy of Macedonia to send their sons there, to receive the best education available (essentially an Athenian education) at Philip's expense. Naturally, the invitation could not be refused: an aristocrat who declined to send his son(s) would signal thereby his lack of trust in Philip and be suspected of disloyal designs, perhaps of outright plans to rebel. While this genuinely offered the aristocracy an excellent free education for their sons, and of course fostered mutual familiarity and relationships among the sons of the aristocracy, no one was unaware that this school also meant that the sons of the aristocracy were now under Philip's control. They served effectively as hostages for the good behavior of their fathers, and were educated in the way Philip judged best. This latter is a crucial point: Philip needed the aristocracy to feel true loyalty and commitment to the Macedonia he was building; and he also, crucially, needed capable officers for the army and military system he was developing. While literacy skills, and a grounding in literature, music, and rhetoric were doubtless the basics of the education provided, physical training, and especially military training, obviously played a major role too, especially in a special system of what might be called higher education.

When the boys being educated reached their late teens, roughly their eighteenth year, they were inducted into a group called the *paides* (literally youths, in this context) who served for some two years a kind of military apprenticeship in the immediate entourage of the ruler, in this case Philip himself. They waited on Philip, provided personal service and attendance, and fought directly with and under him in battle, as a kind of guard in addition to the regular royal bodyguard. Though we never hear of it before the time of Philip, the institution of the *paides* may have been an old and traditional part of Macedonian society: it will no doubt have been normal for the teenage sons of the ruler's *hetairoi* to serve him in this way. But Philip certainly placed a new and more thorough emphasis on the *paides*, making service in this group an integral part of the passage from youth to manhood for the Macedonian aristocracy. For by having the sons of the aristocracy in his personal service and entourage, he could inculcate loyalty to himself and personally train them in the business of serving as officers in his new-style army and military system. The success of this training system is well seen in the officers of Alexander's army, all of whom had, like Alexander himself, grown up in service to Philip and in Philip's training system. It is no coincidence that so many of Alexander's officers—the likes of Ptolemy, Craterus, Seleucus, Cassander, Lysimachus, and others—proved to be highly capable and successful generals: they had learned the necessary skills in the same school as Alexander himself, under Philip.

Another matter that required development and improvement under Philip was the Macedonian economy: a state is at bottom only as strong as its economy allows it to be. As I pointed out in Chapter 1, Macedonia had the potential in land, manpower, and natural resources such as timber and metals to be a wealthy and powerful society. This potential had never been fulfilled, in part due to the constant pressure on Macedonia by invading forces from the Balkan region, looting and pillaging and at times occupying swathes of Macedonian territory; in part due to the occupation of the Macedonian coast and harbors by southern Greek colonies which came to be dominated by the Athenians, giving Athens control over Macedonian trade; and in part due to the archaic social system of aristocratic dominance and the concomitant disunity. Philip's successful military activity drove invaders out of Macedonia and, by extending Macedonian control over neighboring territories, provided an era of peace and security hitherto unknown for the Macedonians themselves. It also enabled Philip to seize control of the harbors on the Macedonian coast—Pydna, Methone, Therme—and assert his own control over trade between Macedonia and the Aegean and eastern Mediterranean world. And of course Philip had fully unified Macedonia and brought the aristocracy to heel, creating the conditions for socio-economic advancement within Macedonia.

Before the time of Philip Macedonia had virtually no cities: there was the old seat of the Argead clan, Aegae, though it seems to have been little urbanized; and there was the new capital Pella, founded by Archelaus. Philip fostered the development of cities, both within Macedonia proper and in the extended borderlands he added to Macedonia. In Macedonia, cities were developed around such settlements as Dion, Beroea, Edessa, Europus, Heracleia Lyncestis, and Argos Oresticon, while existing cities like Pella, Pydna, Therme, and eventually also Amphipolis were strengthened. When Philip extended the border of Macedonia westward, annexing western Thrace as far as the River Nestus, he refounded the settlement of Crenides as Philippi and strengthened it with Macedonian colonists. When he further annexed south-central Thrace up to the Hebrus valley, he founded the city of Philippopolis (modern Plovdiv) and established fortified military settlements at Beroi (modern Stara Zagora), Kabyle (Kabile, near Yambol), and Bine. To strengthen his southern expansion into Thessaly he established a Macedonian colony at Gonnoi on the Thessalian side of the Vale of Tempe, and he may have established Macedonian garrison-settlers elsewhere in Thessaly too, for example at Oloosson. These are the foundations we know of: there may well have been more. As we have seen, Alexander was later to claim that Philip "made you (i.e. the Macedonians) city-dwellers and organized you with proper laws and customs" (Arrian *Anabasis* 7.9.2).

An effect of this urbanization was, of course, economic development. We learn further that Philip had marshes drained and lowland forests cleared for agriculture. He extended and improved Macedonian mining operations, for example making the gold and silver mining in the Pangaeum region around Philippi much more thorough and efficient, eventually deriving an annual income of a thousand talents (a stupendous sum: the Athenians at the height of their power in the fifth century received less than half of that in tribute payments from their subject-allies) from mining operations there. This enabled him to produce an abundant, well-made silver coinage to fund his activities (see ill. 7). Since our sources are simply not interested in economic policy and development, there is not much to be added to this in detail. But overall it is clear that Philip revolutionized Macedonian economic life. The establishment of internal peace and security, the process of urbanization, the development of trade through properly controlled and improved harbors, the more thorough and efficient exploitation of timber and metals, above all the clearing and draining of land and extension of agriculture: all of this made Macedonia a far wealthier land and the Macedonians for the first time a prosperous people. Again to quote the words attributed to Alexander: "When Philip came to power over you, you were indigent wanderers, most of you wearing animal hides and herding a few sheep in the mountains . . . he gave you cloaks to wear instead of hides, brought you down from the mountains into the plains . . ." (Arrian *Anabasis* 7.9.2). It is for these reasons that Philip was fondly remembered by the Macedonians for generations afterward as the father of his people.

That brings us to Macedonia's most important resource: the Macedonian people. In some sense everything Philip did was in service to the Macedonian people, but not to all of them evenly. The impression we get of the Macedonians before Philip is of a powerful aristocracy, a large serf class working for the aristocrats, and not much in between. This is why Macedonian military strength had always been based on cavalry supplied by the aristocracy, with infantry forces few in number: usually not more than perhaps four or five thousand, who were ill-trained, ill-equipped, and undisciplined. In realizing that a strong and

7. Tetradrachm coin of Philip II from Amphipolis mint
(Wikimedia Commons public domain image by Jastrow)

secure Macedonia required a large and effective infantry army, Philip knew that he needed a free warrior class of "citizens." Much of his reforming activity was aimed in large part at bringing that warrior class into existence. That he succeeded is made clear by the following army statistics. At the beginning of his reign, in 358, absolutely needing a victory over the Illyrians and therefore mobilizing the largest force he could muster, Philip managed to gather an army of ten thousand infantry and six hundred cavalry. Just after the end of Philip's rule, when his son Alexander invaded the Persian Empire in 334 with what was still Philip's army, we learn that twelve thousand Macedonian infantry and eighteen hundred cavalry marched with Alexander, while another twelve thousand infantry and fifteen hundred cavalry were left behind in Macedonia for home defense. The number of available infantry was thus twenty-four thousand—two and a half times those available in 358—while the number of the Macedonian cavalry had multiplied more than fivefold, from six hundred to three thousand three hundred. Moreover, despite the fact that Alexander did nothing during his thirteen-year reign to supplement Macedonian manpower—instead siphoning it off constantly for his wars of conquest—we find that at the end of Alexander's reign there were more than fifty thousand Macedonians under arms, another near doubling of the number. This growth seems to have been entirely due to the policies put in place by Philip.

How did Philip achieve this spectacular growth in military manpower? To some extent this was an effect of the social and economic policies outlined above: the establishment of peace and security, the development of cities and trade, the expansion of agriculture and consequent growth of wealth, will all have had beneficial demographic effects, raising the birth rate and the survival rate of infants, and thus increasing the Macedonian population. But there was clearly more to it than that: Philip had specific policies aimed at developing the "warrior class" I have spoken of. It is not at all clear how much of a population of free farmers, herders, and small craftsmen, suitable for mobilization and training as a close-order infantry phalanx, there may have been in Macedonia before the time of Philip. Our accounts of Macedonian warfare, with its lack of any well trained infantry formations, suggest that any such class of free men cannot have been very large, or much motivated to fight for Macedonia's rulers. By various means Philip extended this segment of the population and established in them a warrior spirit and pride in Macedonian identity. One of his policies was population movement, or resettlement. Within Macedonia, it appears, settlers were moved from lower Macedonia to upper Macedonia, and vice versa, partly no doubt with the aim of further unifying Macedonia. But one suspects, given Philip's need for military manpower, that some at least of these settlers may have been taken from the serf population, becoming free men eligible for military recruitment in the act of being resettled. More significantly, as new territories were added to Macedonia—for example the Chalcidice, and western Thrace between the rivers Strymon and Nestus—Macedonians were settled within these territories, becoming well-to-do farmers and serving as a permanent garrison and Macedonianizing element; but also, themselves and their sons, becoming eligible for recruitment into infantry service.

In such ways Philip clearly enormously expanded the segment of the population available for military service, as the army numbers presented above prove beyond doubt. Most crucial were the land clearing and consequent expansion of agriculture, the urbanization, and the resettlement program, particularly in the newly conquered territories. All of this gave Macedonia for the first time, so far as we can tell from our sources, a large class of men suitable for service in an infantry phalanx. Calling these men up for repeated spells of infantry training and service; teaching them through weapons drills and route marches; leading them on successful campaigns in which they won battles, conquered lands, and acquired booty; all of this fostered in this newly well-to-do and independent class of men the requisite warrior spirit and a fierce pride in their Macedonian identity that simply had not existed before. And it is worth noting that not all of these men were ethnically Macedonian to begin with: Philip certainly welcomed southern Greeks into Macedonia and into his service; it is quite likely that no small number of Paeonians, Thracians, even Illyrians living in the border territories absorbed into Macedonia were Macedonianized by the resettlement process and became part of Philip's warrior class.

The overall effect of Philip's reforms on the Macedonian people is well illustrated by a characteristic anecdote revealing how Philip was remembered by his people. Plutarch in his "Sayings of Kings and Commanders" (*Moralia* 179d) reports that an old lady was importuning Philip to deal with a problem she had, and when Philip replied that he had no time to look at her case just then she responded, "Then you should stop being king!" Instead of being angry at this, Philip accepted the rebuke and dealt right then not only with her issue, but with those of other petitioners too. The point of the story is not that it actually happened just so, but that it was a story told about Philip by his people; that is, that this story reveals how the Macedonians viewed Philip, as a ruler who genuinely cared about his people, was approachable, and had their best interests at heart. By way of contrast, Plutarch tells another story of a later Macedonian ruler, Demetrius the Besieger, who instead of dealing with his people's petitions properly threw them away, not wanting to be bothered (Plutarch *Life of Demetrios* 42). Plutarch says that, seeing this, the Macedonians were infuriated and reflected on "how accessible Philip had been and how considerate in such matters." Thus Philip was fondly remembered by the Macedonians for many generations as a true father to his people, the epitome of what a good ruler should be.

3. SUBDUING THE BARBARIAN BALKAN REGION

If properly unifying and strengthening Macedonia internally was Philip's number one priority, the second without a doubt was securing Macedonia against invasion, raiding, and even conquest by its barbarian neighbors to the north-west, north, and east. Throughout his reign, from his first days in power until almost his last, he campaigned again and again against Illyrian, Dardanian, Paeonian, Agrianian, Triballian, and Thracian peoples living in the Balkan region, roughly in modern-day Albania, Montenegro, Serbia, and Bulgaria. His ultimate success in this project of securing Macedonia is illustrated in maps 2 and 3, showing the extent of Macedonian power and control at the beginning and end of his rule. We have already seen above that two of Philip's earliest campaigns, in 359/8, were against invading Paeonian and Illyrian forces in northern and north-western Macedonia, giving him two crucial early victories. He continued as he had begun.

To start with the Illyrian front, the defeat of Bardylis and his Dardanian Illyrians changed the balance of power among the Illyrian tribes: we hear of a certain Grabus becoming the strongest Illyrian ruler, and extending his power all the way to the Macedonian border. Grabus is perhaps a title rather than a name: he apparently ruled over a tribe called the Grabaei. Grabus recognized a serious threat in the rising power of Macedonia, and in 357 to 356 joined up with a northern coalition aimed at defeating Philip. The initiative seems to have come from a Thracian ruler: Cetriporis, son of Berisades and grandson of the great Thracian ruler Cotys, ruled over the westernmost of the three chieftaincies into which Cotys' great kingdom had been divided at his death, sharing thus a border with Macedonia. He persuaded the Paeonian Lyppeius, son of Agis, and the Illyrian Grabus to form a grand northern alliance. While Philip himself moved east in 356, marching up to the River Nestus, founding Philippi, and then going to aid his allies the Chalcidians in the capture of Potidaea, he sent a large Macedonian force under Parmenio to deal with Grabus and his Illyrians.

Parmenio was from a great upper Macedonian family, most likely from Pelagonia, and so knew the Illyrians and their style of fighting well. He was some fifteen years older than Philip, and was one of Philip's earliest supporters—impressed no doubt by Philip's victory over Bardylis—and most important aides. The Athenians every year elected ten magistrates named *strategoi*, that is generals: Philip supposedly once jokingly congratulated them on finding ten generals every year, when he himself had only ever found one general in his lifetime: Parmenio. The point is that Parmenio was a capable and loyal general on whom Philip could rely to take command in campaigns he himself could not oversee: usually facing multiple threats in different regions, Philip needed reliable and loyal generals, and Parmenio was the best of them. In the summer of 356, Parmenio and his forces inflicted a serious defeat on Grabus' Illyrians, news of which reached Philip just after he captured Potidaea in (it seems) early August.

The defeats inflicted on Bardylis and Grabus enabled Philip to annex to Macedonia Illyrian borderlands to the north and west of Lake Lychnitis (Ohrid), in the territories of the Dassaretae and the Deuriopi, perhaps also the Bryges further north (see map 3). This gave upper Macedonia a secure buffer zone against future Illyrian attacks, as well as opening up lands for Macedonian settlement. The expanded and enhanced Macedonian border, at Illyrian expense, did not of course end Illyrian hostility. Our sources unfortunately tell us little about Philip's Illyrian warfare, but we do hear of further campaigning by Philip against Illyrians in 350, in 345 against the Illyrian dynast Pleuratus, and in 337 against another Illyrian dynast named Pleurias. The last was Philip's last major campaign before his sudden assassination in 336, so that Philip ended his rule as he began it, with successful warfare against the Illyrians. It is noteworthy that whereas down to 358 warfare between Illyrians and Macedonians invariably occurred in Macedonia, as a result of Illyrian invasions, after 358 it was Philip's Macedonian forces that invaded Illyrian lands, campaigned successfully there, and annexed Illyrian territories.

Whereas the Illyrians were a serious threat to Macedonian security, the Paeonians were more of a nuisance: inveterate raiders and looters, but nothing more. Our sources tell us even less about Philip's pacification of Paeonia than of his Illyrian campaigns, but the result is clear. The campaign in late 359 (or possibly early 358?), shortly after the death of the Paeonian ruler Agis, ended any threat to Macedonia in that region for some years. In 356, however, Agis's son and successor Lyppeius joined—as we have seen—with Cetriporis and Grabus in the northern coalition against Philip. How he was dealt with we are not told, but it appears that he once again became a problem to Philip in 353, after Philip's defeat in Thessaly by the Phocian army of Onomarchus. Once again, we hear nothing of how Lyppeius and his Paeonians were dealt with, but four years later Isocrates (5.21) remarked that Philip had subjected the Paeonians. It appears that Paeonia was annexed as a tributary territory and settled with a few Macedonian fortress-colonies for security; but Lyppeius was seemingly allowed to remain as ruler, for we hear of his successor Patraus still ruling the Paeonians under Alexander in the late 330s (Demosthenes 1.13). In 340 Alexander, then sixteen years old and serving as regent of Macedonia during Philip's absence in eastern Thrace, led an army west of Paeonia to engage the Maedi in the upper Strymon valley, whom he defeated and where he founded a fortress-colony named Alexandropolis after himself. Thus the boundary of Macedonia to the north was extended up the Axios and Strymon valleys to defensible and fortified mountain frontiers.

The Thracians represented a threat similar to that of the Illyrians: major Thracian incursions led by kings such as Sitalces in the time of Perdiccas II and Cotys at the start of Philip's reign showed how unsatisfactory Macedonia's eastern frontier was. It is no surprise, therefore, that as soon as Philip had established his rule over Macedonia securely, he began to extend his power eastwards into Thrace, at the expense of the Thracian successors of Cotys. At the death of Cotys, his kingdom had been divided among his three sons Berisades (western Thrace), Amadocus (central Thrace), and Cersebleptes (eastern Thrace). This created a weakness Philip was quick to exploit. It also helped that Berisades, whose westernmost Thracian realm bordered on Macedonia, only ruled for a year or two before dying and being replaced by his son Cetriporis, obviously a younger and less experienced ruler. It was Cetriporis who, by organizing the anti-Macedonian "northern Alliance" with the Paeonian Lyppeius and the Illyrian Grabus about 357/6, provided the occasion for Philip to begin his decades-long series of interventions in Thrace.

Philip's first move was along the coast of the Aegean, crossing the River Strymon and marching east. He had received an appeal from the Thasian colony of Crenides in the rich Pangaeum mining district. The people of Thasos had for generations had an interest in the mineral resources on the mainland across from their island, founding the colony of Neapolis (modern Kavala) on the Aegean coast and, much later around 360, the colony of Crenides inland in the Drama plain. The aim was to exploit the silver and gold mines of the region, but the Thasians lacked the resources to support the colony, which came under immediate pressure from the surrounding Thracians. Philip now provided the support the Thasians could not, taking over Crenides and refounding it with an addition of Macedonian settlers and the new name Philippi, after himself. The new settlement was fortified with strong walls, and the surrounding Drama plain was drained for agriculture, enabling the Philippians to feed and defend themselves. The silver and gold mines of Pangaeum were then exploited with vastly greater thoroughness and efficiency than ever before, bringing Philip a huge annual income and enabling him to strike a plentiful and attractive new coinage (see ill. x). Meanwhile Cetriporis saw his northern allies, the Illyrians and Paeonians, soundly defeated, leaving him powerless to deal with Philip. An alliance with the Athenians, always interested in controlling the north Aegean coast as much as possible, proved no help, and he had to acquiesce in Philip's takeover of the Drama plain and the Thracian coast as far as the River Nestus.

In subsequent years, 355 and 354, Philip further extended his power along the north Aegean coast, more at the expense of the Athenians than of the Thracians. He had already seized Amphipolis at the mouth of the Strymon in 357, despite his earlier promise to the Athenians to regard it as theirs. The city was reinforced with a large contingent of Macedonian colonists and rapidly Macedonianized. The founding of Philippi posed a threat to Neapolis on the coast: it was clearly desirable for whoever controlled the Drama plain also to control Neapolis, the region's outlet to the sea. Neapolis was seized by Philip in 355, apparently, and in 354 he moved further east to capture the southern Greek colonies of Abdera and Maroneia (see map x). In taking these coastal cities, Philip was posing a potential threat to Amadocus, the ruler of central Thrace whose territories lay immediately inland. Amadocus fortified the passes leading inland from the coast and barred Philip's further progress. All the same, Philip was able to negotiate an agreement with Cerseobleptes, the easternmost and strongest of the three Thracian rulers who had succeeded Cotys. That represented a threat sufficient to keep Amadocus quiet for the time being.

This agreement did not last long: in 353 Philip suffered an unexpected defeat in Thessaly, as we shall see, and that led Cerseobleptes to transfer his allegiance to the Athenians, Philip's enemies since his annexation of Amphipolis. Busy in Thessaly, Philip was not able to respond in Thrace until the fall of 352; but then a near two-year campaign beginning in October or November of 352 saw him considerably strengthen his position in Thrace. Allying himself now with Cersebleptes' rival Amadocus and the Athenians' enemies Perinthus and Byzantium, he marched along the coast to the fortress of Heraion Teichos, which he began to besiege. The siege lasted into 351, but eventually Philip captured the place, and apparently handed it over to the Perinthians. Philip had demonstrated that neither the Athenians nor the Thracian rulers could prevent him invading Thrace and operating there at his will. For now, that was enough, and he returned to Macedonia where much other business awaited him. He controlled the Thracian coast now almost as far as the Thracian Chersonnese, which was held by the Athenians, and the Thracian rulers inland were cowed. With that, Philip was satisfied for several years. It was not until 346 that he campaigned in Thrace again, and then only briefly. It was perhaps at that time that the sons of Berisades were removed from power and western Thrace up to the Nestos fully annexed to Macedonia. The aim of the campaign, however, was to weaken Cersebleptes, which was achieved by a resounding victory at Hieron Oros in early summer. Cersebleptes was obliged to make a subordinate alliance with Philip, but left in command of his realm. The central Thracian ruler Amadocus had apparently died, to be succeeded by a son named Teres, who was also now allied to Philip. In just a few months, any potential threat from Thrace was neutralized.

The final move in Philip's long series of interventions in Thrace took place in the years 342 to 339, when for reasons left rather obscure—perhaps Cersebleptes was again intriguing with the Athenians—Philip decided to annex Thrace once and for all. A series of campaigns in 342 and 341 culminated in a crushing victory by Philip's army over the joint forces of Cersebleptes and Teres in summer of 341, with both rulers now being deposed from power. Philip founded a series of Macedonian colonies in the Hebrus valley (see above, p. 79), including most famously Philippopolis (modern Plovdiv). He made contact with a tribe called the Getae in the Danube valley and established an alliance with them, cemented by marrying the Getan king's daughter Meda. He consolidated Macedonian control of the Thracian coast on the Black Sea, but met with setbacks when he attacked and besieged his former allies Perinthus and Byzantium which, thanks to Persian and Athenian help, he failed to capture. Giving up there, he decided to return to Macedonia via the Danube. There he fought briefly against some Scythians north of the Danube and, feeling that his control of Thrace was now securely established, marched south towards Macedonia. Crossing through the mountain passes of Triballia, however, he was ambushed by local Triballian tribesmen and suffered a severe wound to his thigh. Philip recovered from this wound after a few weeks, and was able to get back to Macedonia in late summer of 339 having added all of Thrace to his kingdom and ended the Thracian threat to Macedonia for several generations.

4. Settling Relations with the Southern Greeks

Macedonia's relationship with its southern Greek countrymen had always been highly problematic. The developing city-states of southern Greece saw in Macedonia and the Macedonians a backward region and a people at best half-Greek, but blessed with rich natural resources of timber and metals that the southern Greeks coveted. As a result, southern Greeks had freely interfered in Macedonia throughout its history, from the settlement of southern Greek colonies along the coast— Methone, Pydna, and Therme, for example—to the interventions by Athenians, Spartans, and Thebans in the fifth and early fourth centuries. It was Philip's aim to end the relative subordination of Macedonia, and make it instead the leader of the Greek world, with the southern Greeks following Macedonian commands rather than the other way about.

His first task in this regard was to win control of the southern Greek colonies on the Macedonian coast itself. These were the ports of Macedonia, and controlling them meant controlling Macedonia's imports and exports. The first to be seized was Amphipolis at the mouth of the Strymon, besieged and captured by storm in the winter of 357/6. Later in the year 356 Pydna to fell to Philip's siege: in both cases Demosthenes (1.5) hints at co-operation by pro-Macedonian elements within the cities, which makes sense. As the ports of the Macedonian territory, their future would be more secure as part of Macedonia proper. The same may be said of Apollonia, Galepsus, and Oisyme, on the coast between Amphipolis and the Pangaeum region, which were taken by Philip in late 356 to early 355. Methone took longer: it was not until the winter of 355 that Philip was ready to besiege it, and not until the spring of 354 that the town was forced to capitulate. During the siege, Philip was hit in the right eye by an enemy arrow, losing the sight of that eye. When the town finally surrendered, the people of Methone were permitted to depart freely with one garment each; the city was re-populated with Macedonian settlers. At some indeterminate date Therme too came under Macedonian control—it was later re-founded with the name Thessalonice by Alexander's successor Cassander—and with that Macedonian control of its own coast and harbors was complete.

Beyond the coast of Macedonia, and far more troubling to Philip as ruler of Macedonia, lay the great three-pronged Chalcidice peninsula, home to numerous southern Greek colonies. On their own, these colonies were each no threat; but banded together under the leadership of the largest and most powerful of them, Olynthus, they had posed a very real threat to Macedonian security, most recently during the reign of Philip's father Amyntas III. The obvious solution was to incorporate the Chalcidice into Macedonia, but that would be no easy task. Philip's first move in this direction, in fact, was to assure the Olynthians and their allies of his friendship, securing a treaty with them in early 356. The Chalcidice would have to wait while Philip built his strength. But the Chalcidice was not fully united behind Olynthus: the key city of Potidaea at the neck of the Pallene peninsula—the westernmost of the three peninsulas making up the southern Chalcidice—was hostile to Olynthus. Here Philip offered to demonstrate his friendship to his new allies. He helped them besiege Potidaea, captured the place in the summer of 356, and handed it over to the Chalcidian League. That secured a friendly peace with the Olynthians and other Chalcidians for several years.

Of course, this peace could not last: the ambitions of Philip and Olynthus were essentially at odds with each other. The first crack appeared after Philip's unexpected defeat in Thessaly in 353 (discussed below), when the Olynthians made an offer of alliance to Philip's enemies the Athenians. For the moment this came to nothing, but it was clear to Philip that the Olynthians were at best fair-weather friends. Two years later, in 351, Philip found occasion to deliver a stern warning to the leaders of Olynthus, as Theopompus reveals. What the issue was exactly is not made clear in our sources, but it is evident that an anti-

Macedonian faction existed and was strong at Olynthus; and it was perhaps at this time that Olynthus gave shelter to Philip's two half-brothers (and rivals) Menelaus and Arrhidaeus, and maybe also Derdas of Elimea. All three were in Olynthus a few years later, at any rate. In 349 outright war broke out between Philip and the Olynthian League. The immediate cause, we are told, was that Philip demanded the Olynthians hand over to him his two half-brothers, and they refused. It seems evident that the Olynthians were permitting, perhaps even encouraging Menelaus and Arrhidaeus to intrigue against Philip in Macedonia from their shelter at Olynthus. Philip decided that the time had come to annex the Chalcidice to Macedonia once and for all. The war was fought in two phases, in fall 349 and in 348, with a break for operations in Thessaly in the winter of 349 to 348.

Towards the end of summer in 349 Philip marched his army south of Lake Bolbe in the north-eastern Chalcidice and invested the key city of Stageira (famous in history as the home town of the great philosopher Aristotle). The siege did not take long, and when Stageira was captured the city was razed to the ground. The lesson was not lost on the neighboring cities, which capitulated to Philip in short order—the likes of Arethousa, Stratonice, and Acanthus at the neck of the Athos peninsula. With the eastern part of the Chalcidice under his control, Philip could feel that a good start had been made. In spring of 348 he again invaded the Chalcidice, this time concentrating on the western side of the great peninsula down to the Pallene peninsula, the cities there apparently surrendering without much resistance, no doubt mindful of the fate of Stageira. The Olynthians appealed to Athens for help, and the Athenians—prompted by Demosthenes—ordered their general at the Hellespont, Charidemos, to intervene with eighteen triremes and four thousand mercenary peltasts (a special kind of "medium" infantry; see Glossary). This aid arrived too late: Philip had marched past Olynthus to the south and captured the Olynthian port city of Mecyberna, and then proceeded into the Sithone peninsula (the middle of the three Chalcidian peninsulas) where the key city of Torone likewise capitulated. That left Olynthus, at its inland location north of the Sithone peninsula, isolated and exposed to Philip's siege, which began about mid-summer of 348 after two defeats in major skirmishes had confined the Olynthians behind their city walls.

The siege lasted several months, but was concluded around the beginning of September by the capture of the city. Olynthus was destroyed as being too dangerous to Macedonian security, and the bulk of the population was sold into slavery, an atrocity Philip evidently felt was necessary to secure Macedonia's hold over the Chalcidice. Macedonian settlers were introduced into the Chalcidice, especially to the rich lands south of Lake Bolbe, around Apollonia and Arethousa, and to the territory of Olynthus and the western Chalcidic coast. After a generation or so, the Chalcidice was thoroughly Macedonianized and an integral part of the Macedonian realm. This represented a huge expansion of Macedonia, not only in territory but in wealth. The Chalcidice was home to a number of thriving cities, and had significant natural resources of timber and mines, as noted in Chapter 1. The capture and integration of the Chalcidice rounded off the establishment of a Macedonian homeland that now ran from the Pindus mountains and Lake Ohrid in the west to the River Nestus in the east, and from Mount Olympos and the Aegean Sea in the south to the Messapion range and even beyond to Mount Orbelus in the north.

Two other major regions of Greece bordered on Macedonia to the south and south-west, of unequal importance: to the south was the rich and important territory of Thessaly; to the south-west the poor and mountainous region of Epirus. Relations with Epirus were relatively easily managed. Around the end of 358 or beginning of 357 the Epirote ruler Neoptolemus the Molossian died, leaving three children: two teenage daughters and a son named Alexander, around five years old. It was, consequently, Neoptolemus' younger brother Arrybas who became ruler, marrying the older of his two nieces, Troas, and becoming guardian of his nephew Alexander. It was easy for Philip, fresh from his great victory over Bardylis, to establish an alliance with the new ruler Arrybas, cemented by Philip marrying Arrybas' younger niece Olympias, who thus became Philip's fourth wife, after Phila of Elimea (m. ca. 360), Audata the Illyrian (m. 359), and Philinna of Larissa (m. 358, see below). That alliance and marriage settled relations between Philip and Arrybas for seven years, until Philip felt the need to re-visit the relationship in 350. The cause is not clear—perhaps Arrybas had become too friendly with the Molossian ruling family's traditional allies, the Athenians—but Philip intervened in Epirus and took custody of his young brother-in-law Alexander, now about twelve years old, carrying him off to Pella to be educated under Philip's eye. It seems likely that some borderlands, Atintania and Parauaea bordering on the upper Macedonian canton of Tymphaea, were now added to Macedonia. Young Alexander was educated in Philip's school at Pella, and in time became one of Philip's *paides* (see Chapter 4 section 6), learning to be a good leader and loyal to Philip. In the winter of 343/2, finally, when Alexander was about twenty, Philip again invaded Epirus and completed his settlement of the region as a subordinate ally of Macedonia by removing the ruler Arrybas and setting young Alexander on the throne. Almost Philip's last act was to further secure his relationship with Alexander, in 336, by marrying his daughter by Olympias, Cleopatra, to her uncle Alexander, making the latter his son-in-law as well as his brother-in-law.

Thessaly was a more difficult region to manage. Thanks to its large agricultural plain, the largest in Greece, well-watered by the perennially flowing River Peneius and its tributaries, Thessaly was the largest grain-growing region of Greece, and the only region that regularly had a large surplus of grain for export. That made Thessaly wealthy and important. Like Macedonia, Thessaly was a region of landowning aristocrats dominating and exploiting a large serf population—the *penestai*—and lacking in significant cities: only Larissa in the north, Pharsalus in the south, and Pherae on the coast were major urban settlements. The various regions of Thessaly were dominated by great aristocratic clans, the most important at this time being the Aleuadae of Larissa, and the family of the tyrant Jason and his nephew Alexander in Pherae. The Aleuadae, as we saw in Chapter 2, had long-standing friendly relations with the ruling Argead clan of Macedonia. In the late 370s the tyrant Jason of Pherae had made himself ruler of all Thessaly. After his death in 370, the power of Pherae declined, but in the later 360s Jason's nephew Alexander sought to rebuild his uncle's power. Alexander was assassinated in 358 by his brothers-in-law Lycophron and Tisiphonus, and this upheaval provided the occasion for the Aleuadae to try to break Pheraean power. Too weak, as it turned out, to do this on their own, they turned to the recently victorious Philip for help, which Philip was glad to give. He entered Thessaly with his army, established the independence of northern Thessaly under the Aleuadae, and married a woman of Larissa named Philinna. Though some sources demean

Philinna as a mere "flute-girl," in truth she was doubtless a member of the Aleuad clan, married by Philip in order to cement his alliance with the Aleuadae. Within a year, it seems, Philinna bore Philip his first son, named Arrhidaeus after Philip's grandfather. Sadly, as the lad grew up, it became apparent that he suffered from some form of mental deficiency.

His alliance with the Aleuadae settled his relationship with Thessaly for several years, in Philip's estimation, as he was busy with northern affairs. Only a brief interventions by a small force was needed in early 355 to keep the Aleuad control of northern Thessaly secure. This situation changed as a result of the so-called Third Sacred War, fought from 356 until 347 between the Phocians and the Boeotians with various allies on both sides. In order to prosecute this war the Phocian leaders—at first Philomelus and then Onomarchus and Phayllus—laid hands on the wealth of Apollo's oracle at Delphi, using this money to enroll large mercenary armies that temporarily made Phocis a major power in the Greek world. The Oracle of Apollo at Delphi played a very important role in Greek religion and international relations. It was standard for every Greek state, and for many private individuals too, to consult the Oracle before any major undertaking. Control of the Oracle was thus of importance to every Greek, and especially to every Greek state; and the wealth of the Oracle represented the accumulated gifts of Greeks of all sorts over centuries. Seizing control of the Oracle and its wealth was thus a hugely controversial move by the Phocians, and one that aligned the Greek world into pro- and anti-Phocian camps.

Inevitably, therefore, the "Sacred" war impacted on Thessaly, especially as the Thessalians had long played a major role in the organization—called the Amphictyonic League—that oversaw the Oracle. In the event, the Aleuadae and their regional associates in the Thessalian *koinon* (league or commonwealth) allied with the Thebans, leading their rival Lycophron of Pherae to ally with the Phocians. In pursuit of this alliance, a Phocian force under Phayllus entered Thessaly in 353 to help Lycophron, causing the Aleuadae once again to appeal to Philip for aid. Having captured Methone, rounding off his control of Macedonia's coast, and having for the time being subdued the Illyrians and Thracians, Philip was ready to settle the troubled affairs of Thessaly.

Besides being large, populous, and wealthy, Thessaly was of great strategic importance to Macedonia because it offered the only good land

routes by which Macedonia might be invaded from the south: the Vale
of Tempe between Mounts Olympus and Ossa, through which the River
Peneius reached the sea, was the best, though more mountainous inland
routes to the west of Olympus or via Elimea were also passable. Philip
therefore naturally wanted to control Thessaly, and the Phocian invasion
offered him all the excuse he needed to make his move. At first his invasion of Thessaly went well. In summer 353 he drove Phayllus and his
mercenaries out of Thessaly, but that success turned out to be merely a
prelude to much more difficult campaigning. Late in the summer the
Phocian commander Onomarchus entered Thessaly with a large army
including, crucially as it turned out, a substantial train of catapults and
stone-throwers. Having accurately assessed the strength of Philip's pike
phalanx, Onomarchus decided to fight him via a stratagem. He found a
valley overlooked by hills on either side, and drew up his army in the
mouth of this valley, his aim apparently being merely to protect his
flanks against Philip's Macedonian and allied Thessalian cavalry. Se-
cretly, however, he had stationed his catapults and stone-throwers just
out of sight on the reverse slopes of the overlooking hills on either side.
For once, Philip's scouts failed him: they did not notice and report the
enemy artillery on either side, allowing Philip to be drawn into Onomarchus' trap. When Philip's army advanced to the attack, Onomarchus
had his men retreat in feigned flight, drawing Philip's forces into the valley. At a signal, the artillery on either side crested the hills and rained
down a withering fire of bolts and stones onto Philip's troops. The effect
was devastating. Though Philip managed to extract his army, it had suffered heavy losses in this defeat, and morale plummeted. For the only
time in his career, Philip nearly lost control of his Macedonian soldiery;
and the effects of his defeat were to be felt elsewhere among his many
enemies, who were emboldened to renew resistance to him, as we have
seen. For the moment, Philip could only pull his army back out of Thessaly, to the reassurance of winter quarters in Macedonia, where their
obedience and morale were restored by gifts and rest.

Philip had no notion of giving up, however. He had learned a hard
lesson, but he withdrew from Thessaly, as he said, like a ram, only to butt
harder the next time. Philip realized that he had underestimated the Phocians and their Pheraean allies, and had not committed sufficient forces
to the campaign. He spent the winter of 353 to 352 building up a larger

army and reassuring his allies in Thessaly. In spring 352 he entered Thessaly again at the head of a fully restored army, ready to take up the fight again. At a meeting with his allies in the Thessalian League, they elected Philip, in order to bolster his position, *Archon* (ruler) of the Thessalian *koinon*, a title he held for the rest of his life. Together with the Thessalian forces, he now had an army of more than twenty thousand infantry and three thousand cavalry. To boost morale, Philip formally declared that he was fighting in defense of the god Apollo and his oracle against the sacrilege of the Phocians, and had his men wear crowns of laurel leaves (Apollo's sacred plant) to symbolize this. Alerted by Lycophron of Pherae, Onomarchus too re-entered Thessaly with his mercenary army, and his allies the Athenians sent a substantial fleet into the Thessalian Gulf of Pagasae to co-operate with Onomarchus. Moving fast, Philip bypassed Pherae and attacked its port city of Pagasae, capturing it before Onomarchus could reach the scene. He then moved south to confront Onomarchus, entering the broad coastal plain to the south of Pherae known as the Field of Crocuses, where he could deploy his cavalry to full effect.

It was on the Field of Crocuses, then, that the two armies confronted each other. Onomarchus' army likely matched Philip's in infantry, but had far fewer cavalry. The exact course of the battle is not preserved in any source, but Diodorus does report that Philip's superiority in cavalry was decisive (16.35.5). Most likely Philip used his pike phalanx to pin Onomarchus' mercenary phalanx in place, while his cavalry carried out a flanking maneuver and attacked Onomarchus from behind. That the bulk of the cavalry was stationed on Philip's right, attacking thus from the west, is made likely by the fact that Onomarchus' fleeing soldiers ran east, towards the beaches of the Gulf of Pagasae. There the Athenian fleet under the general Chares was patrolling: thousands of fleeing Phocian troops stripped off their armor and tried to swim to the safety of the Athenian ships. By no means all succeeded: reportedly six thousand Phocians and mercenaries died in the fighting and three thousand more drowned afterwards, among them the commander Onomarchus himself. Philip's victory was total. Left without allies, the Pheraean tyrant Lycophron offered to surrender his city in return for a safe-conduct for himself, his family, and two thousand mercenaries. Philip accepted, and Lycophron and his two thousand men fled south to Phocis to join the surviving Phocian commander Phayllus.

With Pherae in his power, Philip's control of Thessaly was complete, and he spent some time regularizing that control.

Philip's position as *Archon* of the Thessalian League gave a legal basis to his rule over Thessaly, making Thessaly as it were a second kingdom of his besides Macedonia. He kept Pagasae, the harbor of Thessaly, for himself, having captured it that summer. The harbor and market dues from the Thessalian grain trade were a large addition to his revenues. The border region of Perrhaebia between Macedonia and Thessaly, traditionally a dependency of the Thessalians, was annexed to Macedonia, as was Magnesia, the mountainous region between Thessaly and the Aegean Sea, dominated by Mounts Ossa and Pelium. Philip was married for the fifth time this summer, to a lady from a prominent Pheraean family named Nicesipolis: he sought to make friends of the leading families of Pherae. Finally, he established Macedonian colonies at Gonni, at the Thessalian end of the Vale of Tempe, and at Oloosson, commanding the Thessalian end of the route into Macedonia via the western flank of Olympus. His control over Thessaly was only briefly interrupted twice hereafter: in the winter of 349, between his two Chalcidian campaigns, he had to re-enter Thessaly to drive out the Pheraean tyrant family which had returned; and in 344 he had to put down a further revolt at Pherae, finally despairing of gaining Pherae's friendship and garrisoning the place. Late in 352, Philip marched south to Thermopylae, it seems with the aim of entering central Greece to end the Sacred War, but he found the pass there strongly held by Athenian forces, and turned back north. He was not ready for war in southern Greece: the Sacred War could wait.

In principle, indeed, Philip could have ignored the Third Sacred War entirely. With Thessaly safely in his power, and Epirus tied to a firm alliance, Macedonia looked fairly secure from the south, and as of 351 he had the Chalcidice still to deal with. But there were reasons for him still to be concerned about southern Greece. Within living memory three southern Greek states had intervened militarily in Macedonia— the Spartans, the Athenians, and the Thebans—and there was no guarantee they might not do so again. Sparta indeed, since her defeat at Leuctra in 371 and Epaminondas' campaign in the Peloponnesos, was greatly weakened and seemed unlikely to pose a threat in the foreseeable future. Epaminondas had ringed Sparta with three intrinsically hostile states, each holding territory once controlled by the Spartans: Messene, Megalopolis, and Argos. These states made it their business to keep Sparta weak and occupied at home. As for the Thebans, they had hugely miscalculated in starting the Third Sacred War against Phocis, and had suffered greatly in the course of that war. But if they should find a way to win it, they could recover their position as the dominant power in central Greece and pose a threat to Philip's hold over Thessaly, if nothing more. The Athenians, too, had suffered serious losses as Philip had taken control of their former allies, the north Aegean port cities, and the Macedonian seizure of Amphipolis in particular rankled. Though the Athenians had suffered a significant diminishment of their power in the Social War fought between the Athenians and disaffected allies from 357 to 355, the Athenians had been down before and recovered their Aegean sea power. Athens still had to be seen as a possible threat.

The truth was that these southern Greek city-states regarded the Macedonians with disdain, as semi-barbarous if not outright barbarians. Southern Greek citizens had for centuries cultivated a refined urban culture built around exercising at the gymnasium, meeting each other for political debates in the *agora* (town square), attending plays and musical performances at the theater, entertaining each other with songs and talk at *symposia* (drinking parties) where the wine was well watered and drunkenness looked down on, and conducting homoerotic love affairs in which an older man (in principle at least) mentored a younger beloved as much as enjoying sex with him. The Macedonian delight in riding, hunting, and fighting struck southern Greeks as old fashioned and uncouth; though they too held *symposia,* the Macedonians' insistence on drinking their wine unwatered, with consequent boisterousness and drunkenness, seemed positively uncivilized; and even their homoerotic adventures seemed barbarous, as fully grown bearded men engaged each other in amorous sport. As the historian Theopompus, who spent years at Philip's court, complained, the Macedonians at their parties behaved more like *hetairai* (high-class prostitutes) than *hetairoi* (upper-class companions) in their erotic grapplings with each other (according to Polybius 8.9, purporting to quote Theopompus' actual words). All of this made it hard for southern Greeks such as the Athenians to take the Macedonians seriously. In truth, Philip would have liked nothing better, it seems, than to reach an accord with Athens: he had no fleet worth mentioning and no ambition to seek sea power, and did not see why Macedonian land power and Athenian sea power could not co-operate. He admired Athenian culture and was busy importing it to Macedonia. He invited actors and playwrights to perform in Macedonia; he found room at his court for the philosopher Aristotle and the historian Theopompus; he cultivated good relations with Speusippus, Plato's successor at the Academy, and the great rhetorician Isocrates; he patronized the best Greek artists and musicians.

For several years after 352, Philip was preoccupied with matters elsewhere, but after 347 he was ready to turn his attention back to southern Greece, with two basic aims: to secure, if possible, a mutually beneficial peace treaty with the Athenians, since as he saw it their interests no longer clashed; and to bring an end to the Sacred War in a way that would not restore Boeotian power and dominance in central Greece. This is the part of Philip's career on which we are best informed, thanks to the surviving speeches of the anti-Macedonian Athenian orator and politician Demosthenes, especially his three Olynthiac and four Philippic orations, and his speeches "On the False Embassy" and "On the Crown." It needs, of course, to be borne in mind that Demosthenes was anything but an impartial witness in his assessment of Philip and his policies. In 347 and 346 there were extensive negotiations between Philip and the Athenians, including two embassies despatched by the Athenians to Philip. These resulted in the peace agreement known as the Peace of Philocrates, after the Athenian politician who most strongly advocated it. The peace involved Athenian acceptance of Philip's control over Amphipolis and the other north Aegean ports, while Philip guaranteed Athenian control over the Thracian Chersonnese, vital to Athens' grain supply route from the Crimea. The two sides agreed to mutual friendship and co-operation; and Philip had succeeded in persuading important Athenian leaders such as Philocrates and Aeschines of his genuine good will. Demosthenes, however, though initially favoring peace, was not fully persuaded, and did what he could to undermine the implementation of the peace from the moment it was formally agreed.

Meanwhile, Philip had received pleas from various states in central Greece, including the Thebans, to intervene once more as Apollo's champion in the seemingly interminable Third Sacred War. Thanks to the support of the Thebans and eastern Locrians, and to the preoccupation of the Athenians with debating and voting on the peace agreement, Philip and his army were able to march through the Pass of Thermopylae unopposed in the summer of 346. The pass was nominally fortified by a Phocian mercenary force commanded by Phalaecus, son of Onomarchus; but he decided that discretion was the better part of valor and handed over control of the pass to Philip in return for a guarantee of freedom to go where they pleased for himself and his mercenaries. Phalaecus turned to a career as a roving mercenary captain for hire, and Philip proceeded into central Greece to end the Sacred War once and for all. He sent messages to the Athenians to send allied forces to co-operate with him and join him in establishing peace in central Greece and a new and better management of the Oracle at Delphi, but the Athenians declined to act. Not in the least troubled, Philip then settled the Sacred War himself. The Phocians surrendered without a fight, realizing they had no hope of holding out in the face of Philip's forces. At a meeting of the Amphictyonic Council, which formally oversaw the Delphic Oracle, the Phocians were stripped of their votes in the council and these were given to Philip instead. Since he also controlled the votes of the Thessalians, he now had a powerful say in the affairs of the Oracle. In the fall, he was able to preside over a successful Pythian Games festival, with the Athenians staying away. Under pressure from the Amphictyons, however, the Athenians finally assented to Philip's reorganization of the Oracle's management, and Greece seemed at peace.

The roots of further conflict were, however, present in the situation. Though formally allied to the Thebans, Philip had deeply angered them by rejecting their demands that the Phocians be brutally punished for despoiling the Oracle of Apollo. At Philip's insistence, the Phocians were granted humane terms in the peace settlement. They had to destroy the fortifications around their towns, and they had to pay reparations to the Oracle; but Philip guaranteed their safety and the reparations were set at a reasonable level to be paid in affordable annual installments. Thus relations between Philip and the Thebans were soured from the start, and neither side trusted the other. Prompted by Demosthenes and others, moreover, the Athenians dragged their feet in implementing the Peace of Philocrates, and in fact showed more hostility than friendship towards Philip. Again, neither side really trusted the other. This was a pity, since Philip really had no further designs on subjecting the southern Greek states. Prompted by several open letters from the Athenian intellectual Isocrates, who had for decades been calling for a united Greek war against the Persians to punish the Persians for their interventions in Greece and, more importantly, to open up western Asia to Greek colonization as a way of relieving overpopulation and social problems in Greece, Philip had now turned his thoughts to war with Persia. He would much rather have had the Athenians, and especially their fleet, as allies in this effort than as continued opponents.

Nevertheless, tensions continued to rise. The pro-Macedonian Athenian politician Philocrates was attacked and driven into exile. Philip's campaigns in eastern Thrace were portrayed as a threat to Athenian control of the Thracian Chersonnese, and used as an excuse to justify naval operations against Philip. An offer of a Common Peace settlement by Philip in 343, with all disagreements to be fairly settled, was rejected by Athens. In the end, tensions were ratcheted up to the point that, in 340, the Athenians declared war on Philip. In 339 at a meeting of the Amphictyonic Council the people of Amphissa in western Locris were accused of sacrilege in cultivating land sacred to Apollo. This resulted, in autumn 339, in a declaration of Sacred War against Amphissa and, with the Athenians refusing to act, the council turned to Philip and elected him *Hegemon* (leader) for the war. Philip was ready to oblige, and once again led his army through the Pass of Thermopylae and into central Greece. Instead of moving against Amphissa at once, however, he occupied the Phocian town of Elatea, on the main road from central Greece into Boeotia and on to Attica, and began to fortify it. News of Philip's presence at Elatea, not much more than a day's march from the frontier of Attica, caused a panic at Athens. Prompted by Demosthenes, again, the Athenians decided to seek an alliance with the Thebans with the purpose of fighting against Philip. Despite protestations of friendship by Philip's envoys, the Thebans were persuaded by Demosthenes and allied with the Athenians, preparing for war against Philip.

This is the war that culminated in the Battle of Chaeroneia in 338, described in detail in Chapter 4 section 7 below, at which Philip decisively defeated the combined armies of the Athenians and the Thebans, and established himself as the leader of all the Greeks. In the aftermath of his great victory, Philip held a raucous celebration which included a festive dance around the assembled Athenian captives. At the height of this dance, the Athenian orator Demades, one of the captives, reportedly called out: "Philip, are you not ashamed, when fate has cast you in the role of Agamemnon, to appear instead in the guise of Thersites!" This was a reference to the famous Trojan War, in which Agamemnon was the leader of the pan-Greek expedition, while Thersites was remembered as the buffoon of the Greek army. Demades' point was that Philip was now in a position to unite all of the Greeks behind him for an expedition into Asia against the Persian Empire, and he should act the part. Philip at once ended the celebration, called Demades into a meeting, and initiated negotiations for a peace with the Athenians. Athens was treated leniently: her democracy was respected, the Athenian prisoners from the battle were released, and the Athenians merely had to tie themselves to a treaty with Philip in which they agreed to follow his lead. The Thebans were dealt with more harshly: prisoners had to be ransomed, and a Macedonian garrison was installed on the acropolis of Thebes, the Cadmeia.

In the fall of 338, Philip summoned representatives from all Greek states to a meeting at Corinth, symbolically chosen as the place where Greek representatives had met to debate and agree on Greek resistance to the Persian invasion in 481. At this meeting a Common Peace for all Greek states was agreed upon, with Philip as its overseer and guarantor. At a follow-up meeting in spring 337 a common alliance to go to war against Persia was agreed, and Philip was, inevitably, selected as the *Hegemon* of the alliance. All Greek states agreed, at Philip's demand, to send allied contingents to join Philip's Macedonian forces in an invasion of the Persian Empire, to take place in summer 336. Only the Spartans held aloof, insisting that only they could properly lead the Greeks in such an undertaking. Philip left them to their own devices, deeming them insufficiently important to bother with. With this agreement, Philip had arrived at the summit of his power, and had achieved all he set out to achieve as a young man taking over the rule of his country. Macedonia was the dominant power in the Greek and Balkan world and he himself was the acknowledged leader of the Greeks. In the next chapter we shall look in detail at the military reforms by which Philip accomplished all this.

CHAPTER 4

Philip's New Model Army and New Model State

"Prussia is not a state with an army, but an army with a state."
—COMTE DE MIRABEAU

"Prussia is not a country with an army, but an army with a country."
—FREIHERR VON SCHROETTER

"Whereas some states possess an army, the Prussian army possesses a state."
—VOLTAIRE

T HIS REFLECTION ON THE NATURE OF THE KINGDOM OF PRUSSIA IN THE eighteenth century, whichever writer/thinker one should properly attribute it to, provides an interesting comparison to the Macedonia of Philip II. A succession of remarkable rulers of the Hohenzollern dynasty—from the "Great Elector" Frederick William (1640–1688) to King Frederick "the Great" (1740–1786)—created one of the most disciplined and feared armies of early modern Europe and used it to transform a mish-mash of inherited lands in northern and eastern Germany and north-central Europe into the tightly knit and tightly controlled kingdom of Prussia, which thanks to its remarkable army and officer corps became one of the great powers of Europe. It was the centrality of the army to constructing, uniting, and controlling Prussia that gave rise to the above reflections.

Similarly, it was the creation of his remarkable new army, military system, and officer corps which enabled Philip to transform the disunited, weak, and backward territories making up the Macedonian lands into a united kingdom, tightly controlled by the king, and the strongest military power in the eastern Mediterranean region. Like early modern Prussia, therefore, Macedonia under Philip and Alexander was truly "an army with a state," and a careful study of the creation and nature of the Macedonian army under and by Philip is, therefore, at the same time a revelation of the nature of the Macedonian state built by Philip. During his remarkable twenty-four-year reign, almost every element of the Macedonian army was fundamentally reformed by Philip, creating a new and innovative style of warfare which was highly demanding of the skills of the commander and officers of the army, but virtually unbeatable by any contemporary force or military system. The three most crucial elements of Philip's new army were a completely new heavy infantry force, a specialized elite force of versatile infantry who were Philip's main strike force and personal guard in battle, and a reformed and strengthened strike force of heavily armed cavalry. In addition, Philip developed specialized forces of mobile light infantry and light cavalry, which each played important roles in the overall military system; and he developed one of the first truly effective siege trains in Greek warfare, so that his military campaigns would not be stymied by fortifications. Finally, all these reformed and specialized military elements needed highly trained officers to lead them effectively and enable them to operate together on the field of battle under a coherent military plan. We must examine each of these elements of Philip's "new model army" in turn, and then observe how the whole system functioned together in warfare and battle.

1. THE NEW MACEDONIAN PHALANX

In the words of Diodorus, writing about the first year of Philip's rule: "he (Philip) first established the Macedonian phalanx" (16.3.2). That statement seems clear and determinative, but is in fact highly controversial. Diodorus wrote between about 60 and 30 BCE, some three hundred years after Philip's day. The quality of his information depends on the source he was deriving it from, and we cannot be sure who that was. Meanwhile, we have another statement about the Macedonian army that seems at odds with Diodorus' statement, and this other statement comes from a writer contemporary with Philip and Alexander, named Anaximenes of Lampsacus. The late antique lexicographer Harpocration preserves the following fragment of Anaximenes' work:

Anaximenes in book 1 of the "Philippica," speaking of Alexander, says:

"Afterwards, accustoming the most notable to serve as cavalry, he called them *hetairoi* (companions); and dividing the masses and infantry into companies and tens and other commands he named them *pezetairoi* (foot companions); so that both sharing in the royal *hetaireia* (companionship), they should remain most devoted."

The sense is that a ruler named Alexander established both the cavalry and the infantry and named them his companions. Here it must be noted that in the campaigns of Alexander the Great, the phalanx of Macedonian infantry are named *pezetairoi* in our sources. Evidently, therefore, the Alexander of Anaximenes' passage is being credited with organizing the Macedonian infantry phalanx; and since the passage comes from the first book of the *Philippica* (history of Philip), it is often assumed that one of the two kings named Alexander before Philip's time must be meant. That is to say, the Macedonian phalanx would have been established by either Alexander I or Alexander II.

There are problems with either identification. If the Alexander of Anaximenes is taken to be Alexander I, then why is there no sign of a Macedonian infantry phalanx in the campaigns of Perdiccas II in the 420s as described by Thucydides, or in the campaigns of Amyntas III in the 380s/70s described by Xenophon? Neither of these contemporary and well-informed historians knows of any Macedonian infantry phalanx, though if it existed it must have played a part in the wars they describe. For this reason, most historians reject the notion that Alexander I could have established the Macedonian phalanx. That leaves us with Alexander II, but the problem with this ruler is that he ruled only just over a year before being assassinated, and it is not easy to see when he would have had the time or authority to do the work described by Anaximenes. Though one or two notable historians, such as A. B. Bosworth, insist that Alexander II must have been meant, it seems in fact highly improbable that any such radical change to the Macedonian military could have been made by this brief and unsuccessful ruler. But what, then, are we to make of this evidence? Well, the point of Anaximenes' testimony seems to have been the *naming* of the Macedonian cavalry and infantry, their inclusion in the royal *hetaireia*. And indeed, our sources do reveal that under Alexander III (the Great) the Macedonian heavy cavalry were referred to as *hetairoi*, and the infantry of the phalanx as *pezetairoi*. Under Philip, conversely, the name *pezetairoi* was used, as we shall see below, for an elite unit who functioned as the king's personal guard in battle; while the *hetairoi* were the king's personal entourage of elite Macedonian and Greek companions (e.g. Theopompus as quoted by Polybius 8.9: "those who were called Philip's friends and companions," about eight hundred in number according to Athenaeus 6.77, who draws on the same passage of Theopompus). Several historians, consequently, have suggested, rightly in my view, that Anaximenes was actually speaking of *the* Alexander—Alexander the Great—in a forward-looking digression. This will be discussed further in Chapter 5.

In sum, before Philip, we simply find no indication that any Macedonian phalanx existed, and we should therefore accept Diodorus' statement that Philip first established it. Why was there no Macedonian phalanx before Philip, and how did he go about creating one? As we have seen in Chapter 1, what had prevented Macedonia from developing a hoplite phalanx like those of the southern Greek city-states was the fact that hoplite warfare was a citizen militia style of warfare: the warrior was responsible for arming himself. This was not a problem for the well-to-do "middling" elements in the Greek city-states, but Macedonia lacked such a well-to-do middle class, and for Macedonia's poorer herders and farmers, let alone for the serfs, the expense of hoplite armor and weapons was prohibitive. Nor could Macedonian rulers, including Philip, afford the expense of providing ten thousand or more sets of hoplite equipment to poor Macedonians so as to enable them to fight as hoplites. That posed a serious quandary for Philip: he could recruit men, and he could no doubt organize and train them, but they would inevitably be lightly armored—lacking the expensive cuirasses, helmets, and shields of the hoplite warriors—and so, though they might put up a good fight against Illyrians or Thracians if well led and motivated, they could never make a stand against a southern Greek hoplite force. Philip was not content to have an army equal to the Illyrians and Thracians: he wanted outright superiority, and he wanted to match any hoplite phalanx in battle too.

The solution Philip found to this quandary was as simple and elegant as it was effective. Since there was no way to armor his men in a manner equivalent to southern Greek hoplites, he found an alternative

8. Re-enactors show reach advantage of Macedonian *sarissa* over southern Greek hoplite spear   (*Wikimedia Commons public domain image by Jones*)

to defensive armor which gave his men a much cheaper form of defense that was at the same time a potent form of offense. He adopted a kind of pike, some sixteen to eighteen feet in length (about five to six meters), called the *sarissa* (or sometimes *sarisa*). Probably deriving from the long spears used to hunt boar, a traditional pastime of the Macedonian aristocracy, it was first developed for military use (so far as we know) by Philip, presumably making its debut in the winter of 359/8. The advantages of this weapon were clear. Macedonia was, as noted in Chapter 1, a heavily forested region, and by tradition the ruler of Macedonia controlled the extraction of timber. Philip could thus easily provide as many wooden pike shafts as required at just the cost of cutting the wood. Another resource Macedonia enjoyed was mines: iron and copper were available to make steel spear heads and bronze butt spikes. As with the forests, the mines were a royal preserve, enabling Philip to acquire the necessary metal at low cost. This ready and cheap availability was a huge advantage, enabling Philip to equip thousands of men with this weapon quickly and easily. The second great advantage was the weapon's reach: since a *sarissa*, at about seventeen feet in length, was double the length of the hoplite's eight-foot *doru* (spear), a band of men equipped with *sarissas* could hold off a band of hoplites well out of reach of the hoplites' weapons (see ill. 8), meaning that the Macedonian *sarissa* men had much less need of defensive body armor: the *sarissa* served as both offensive and defensive weapon.

The shaft of the *sarissa*, normally three to four centimeters thick, was fashioned from ash or cornel wood, which provided straight shafts with a tough grain. Since shafts about fifteen feet in length (minus the

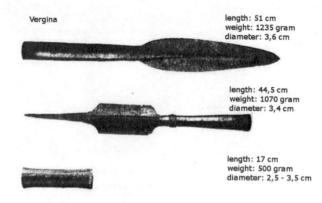

Vergina

length: 51 cm
weight: 1235 gram
diameter: 3,6 cm

length: 44,5 cm
weight: 1070 gram
diameter: 3,4 cm

length: 17 cm
weight: 500 gram
diameter: 2,5 - 3,5 cm

9. Head, butt-spike, and cuff of a Macedonian *sarissa* from the Vergina Museum
(*Wikimedia Commons public domain image*)

length of the metal spear heads and butt spikes) were relatively hard to find and very awkward for soldiers to carry, the *sarissa* shafts were fashioned in two pieces which were carried separately and joined together by a metal cuff just before battle (see ill. 9). The spear heads were leaf shaped, forty to fifty centimeters long (including the shaft attachment: see ill. 9), and made of steel strong enough to penetrate armor with a powerful thrust. At the rear end, the *sarissa* was fitted with a butt spike which served three purposes. In the first place, it enabled the pike to be firmly fixed in the ground, either when not in use, or to anchor it to face a charging enemy. Because it was often driven into the ground, the butt spike was made of non-corrosive bronze rather than steel. In the second place, should the shaft of the *sarissa* break in action, the butt end remaining with the soldier could be reversed and, with its spike, would still make a formidable weapon. Thirdly, the butt spike counter-balanced the *sarissa* by adding weight at the back. The soldier would not want to hold the *sarissa* in its middle section, where the natural balance point would be, but towards its rear, so that as much as possible of the shaft would project out in front of the bearer: that length was, after all, the point of the weapon. A heavy butt spike would shift the balance point of the *sarissa* well back along the shaft, and make it much easier to hold the weapon leveled with most of its length projecting, without the weight of all that projecting wood and metal (the spear head) weighing on the soldier's forward hand and arm and tending to make the spear head droop to the ground.

Wielded two-handed and projecting out some twelve feet in front

10. Macedonian open face helmet from Muzeul de Istorie din Chisinau (Moldova)
(*Wikimedia Commons photo by Cristian Chirita*)

of the warrior holding it, the *sarissa* presented a dire threat to an enemy approaching from in front, and at the same time held that enemy well back from being able to harm the *sarissa* wielder with anything but a missile weapon. On the other hand, the *sarissa* man was vulnerable to arrows, javelins, or sling bullets; and the unwieldy seventeen-foot pike made him clumsy and slow to turn, so that he was easy prey to an enemy coming from the side or from behind. For protection against missile weapons, some kind of armor was needed; but the poor Macedonians recruited as pikemen could not afford extensive armor: else they would be hoplites. Since the *sarissa* occupied the left hand as well as the right, holding one of the large, convex, heavy hoplite shields with its double grip—one for the arm, the other for the hand (see ill. 3)—was out of the question even if it could have been afforded. Philip equipped his pikemen with small wooden shields, about two feet in diameter, that were strapped to the left arm leaving the hand free, and controlled by a neck strap. Much smaller and lighter than the hoplite shield, with its one-meter (about forty inches) diameter, the Macedonian shield (ill. 2) nevertheless covered much of the wielder's torso against arrows and sling shot, and even javelins at a pinch. To protect the head, the Macedonian *sarissa* men wore relatively light, open-faced helmets of the Phrygian or Chalkidian type (see ill. 10), much cheaper than the full-head Corinthian helmet favored by southern Greek hoplites. Beyond this, the pikeman might wear a padded jacket or corslet of boiled leather or reinforced linen; and if he could afford them, some greaves (shin-protectors).

Still, a pikeman operating on his own was slow and easy prey; but the *sarissa* was not a weapon designed to be used in isolation. The point was to create a dense mass of pikemen, standing in close-order lines one behind the other, presenting to an enemy force a serried mass of pikes like a bristling porcupine. To ensure effective co-operation and co-ordination, the Macedonian pike phalanx was carefully organized and drilled to operate as a unit. The basic organizing sub-unit of the phalanx was the file of men standing one behind the other, each man belonging to a different line of the phalanx. The file of men in the phalanx was called a *dekas*: literally a group of ten, though the term could be used more generally to refer to a "company" of men (see the Greek Lexicon of Liddell and Scott, s.v.). In the case of the Macedonian phalanx, it seems the *dekas* was actually made up of eight men, with the front man of the file being the file commander—a position similar to being a corporal in a modern army—and the rear-most man, called the *ouragos*, also having a kind of "non-commissioned officer" status. Directly behind the file commander, in the second and third places in the file, were two experienced and trustworthy "double pay" soldiers, who would have to step forward to command the file if the front man were to be killed or incapacitated. Thus four of the eight men in the *dekas* were ordinary rankers, two were essentially (in modern terms) non-commissioned officers in charge of the file, and two were trusted veterans who could take over from the file commander at need. The responsibility of the file commander was to lead the file forward; by maintaining his place in the front line of the phalanx to ensure that the men behind him also occupied their places in their respective lines; and no doubt to call the order to lower or raise the pikes as needed to fight or march. The *ouragos'* responsibility was to hold his position and keep the men of the file in front of him, ensuring that they did not turn to flight.

With a file (*dekas*) of eight men, it is clear that a standard phalanx depth of eight lines was envisioned; this was also the standard depth of the southern Greek hoplite phalanx. However, there is much evidence to indicate that the Macedonian pike phalanx was in practice often a significantly deeper formation. It was common for two, three, or even four files to be drawn up one behind the other, giving a phalanx of six-teen, twenty-four, or thirty-two lines of men. The number of lines pre-ferred would of course be determined by the equipment and formation of the enemy, the number of pikemen present and the number of men in the enemy formation, and the nature of the terrain. When con-fronting lightly armed Balkan (Illyrian, Thracian, and so on) infantry formations, a pike phalanx only eight lines deep might well be consid-ered perfectly adequate unless the numbers of pikemen and nature of the terrain dictated a deeper formation; but when encountering the heavily armored southern Greek hoplite phalanx, it seems that a deeper pike phalanx of sixteen or thirty-two lines was definitely preferred.

In addition to the file or *dekas*, the pikemen were also organized into *lochoi* (companies) of several hundred men—the exact details are obscure—each with its officer known as the *lochagos*. The most impor-tant unit of the pike soldiers, however, was the *taxis* or battalion, about fifteen hundred men strong. Each *taxis* had its own organization and commander, and formed essentially an independent phalanx; for a pha-lanx is a formation, not a unit, and the infantry phalanx as a whole was made up of the individual fifteen-hundred-man-strong *taxeis* drawn up next to each other. Each *taxis* was recruited locally in the various regions of Macedonia: we know of *taxeis* from the regions of Tymphaia and Orestis, for example, and Arrian (3.16.11) reveals that when new Macedonian recruits reached Alexander at Susa they were assigned to the infantry *taxeis* "according to their *ethnos*," that is, according to the region of Macedonia they came from. In the army with which Alexan-der crossed to Asia in 334, which was the army he had inherited from Philip two years earlier, there were twelve thousand Macedonian heavy infantry, while an equal number were left to serve as the Macedonian home army under the regent Antipater. The twelve thousand with Alexander consisted of six *taxeis* (a total of nine thousand men) plus the three thousand *hypaspistai* (on whom see section 2 of this chapter, below). This means that eight *taxeis* of pikemen were left with Antipa-ter (8 x 1500 = 12,000), showing that in Philip's army there were four-teen *taxeis* of pikemen altogether.

Our best account of the superb training and discipline of the *sarissa*-wielding infantry in their *taxeis* in phalanx formation comes from the first year of the rule of Alexander, when his army was—let it be said again—the army he had just inherited from Philip, recruited, organized, and trained by Philip. Arrian tells of Alexander's campaign in Illyria in 335, and of a situation where Alexander's army was hemmed into a narrow valley overlooked by wooded hills occupied by enemy forces. His account of how Alexander maneuvered the pike phalanx to overawe and defeat the Illyrians runs as follows (*Anabasis* 1.6):

> In this situation Alexander drew up his army with the phalanx 120 lines deep. Posting 200 cavalry on each flank, he ordered his men to be silent and swiftly obey the word of command. At first the infantry warriors were signaled to hold their pikes upright, then at the signal to lower them for the charge, and to swing the serried mass of their pikes first to the right, then to the left. He moved the phalanx itself forward quickly, bringing it round first to one side then the other. Thus in a short time he maneuvered the *taxeis* through many and varied formations, and finally making the phalanx into a kind of wedge facing left, he led it against the enemy. They were already amazed seeing the speed and order of the maneuvering, and they did not await the attack of Alexander's men, but abandoned the first hills.

The superb order and discipline instilled into his pikemen by Philip is evident here, as the soldiers alternately raise and lower their pikes, swinging them to the right then the left, marching and counter-marching, and finally charging in a wedge. Noteworthy is the depth of the formation: 120 lines means fifteen files (*dekades*) one behind the other. One can understand the amazement and fear this extraordinary army of pikemen instilled in the enemy, and how it ruled the battlefields under Philip's and later Alexander's command.

2. The Elite *Pezetairoi*

When the US army in World War II decided to have military historians accompany their forces in battle, to be able to record with the greatest immediacy and accuracy the history of the engagements and battles each unit fought in, they opened up a new era in military history and in our understanding of the nature of warfare. To their great surprise, these battlefield historians discovered that most soldiers, no matter how well trained, are in fact distinctly passive when in battle. They found that only about one of every four soldiers even discharge their weapons in battle, thereby doing the actual fighting, the rest basically hunkering down and trying to survive, offering at best vocal support to their more aggressive colleagues. Battle is an exceptionally frightening and stressful environment. We are all familiar with the "fight or flight" response of animals, including humans, when placed in great fear or stress; but this dichotomy overlooks an equally popular third option: that of simply hunkering down and doing nothing, giving in to the paralyzing tendency of fear and/or stress. We are familiar with this response in the animal world, which gives us such sayings as "playing possum" (pretending to be already dead to escape notice) or "burying one's head in the sand" (from the ostrich's supposed habit of lowering its head so as not to see the enemy, in the hope that the enemy will then bypass it). The plain truth is that rigorous training and discipline will make men hold their ground and stay in formation under the fear and stress of battle, but it cannot make them fight aggressively.

This passivity of most soldiers in the stress of battle was in fact well known to ancient war leaders. The most successful ancient warrior peoples found a way to cope with it: concentrating the most aggressive warriors in elite formations which were tasked with the most crucial roles in battle, requiring the most active and committed soldiers—the tasks which would directly lead to victory if carried out aggressively and well. For example, a Spartan army very rarely had more than a smallish percentage (usually perhaps ten to forty percent, depending on the occasion) of actual "Spartiates" (the true Spartan warriors) in it. The true Spartans—perhaps two thousand strong in an army of, say, twelve thousand—would be stationed on the right wing. When battle began, they would advance faster and with greater determination than their allies, would engage the enemy opposed to them first, and would invariably drive their direct opponents backward and away and then turn to the left to engage the rest of the enemy from the side. The Spartans' allies were there to make up numbers and hold their ground; victory depended on the better trained, better disciplined, more aggressive, elite Spartiates; and for two hundred years or so this system enabled the Spartans to dominate the battlefields of Greece. In the second quarter of the fourth century, when for a generation the Thebans dominated Greek warfare, they relied on an elite force called "the Sacred Band" to spearhead their army in battle and by their determined and disciplined aggression to lead the army to victory.

Philip, who had spent a key part of his adolescence at Thebes at the height of Theban power, understood this principle as well as any war leader; and he made sure from the start of his career as ruler and military commander to develop one of the great elite forces in the history of pre-modern warfare. This elite unit dominated the battlefields of the near east under Philip, his son Alexander, and Alexander's immediate successors. Philip called this unit his *pezetairoi* or "foot companions." Alexander changed the name of the unit, at first to *hypaspistai* or "shield bearers," and late in his reign again to *argyraspides* or "silver shields." Under this final name the unit, three thousand men strong, played a dominant role in several battles in the wars of the succession, until the victorious general Antigonus the One-Eyed broke the unit up as having too much power and unpredictability. Recounting one of the battles this elite unit dominated, in 316, Plutarch gave eloquent testimony to the unit's quality: he described the soldiers of this unit as athletes of war, who had fought in all the campaigns of Philip and Alexander, and had never suffered a reverse (Plutarch *Life of Eumenes* 16)

At his first great battle, against Bardylis and his Illyrians, Diodorus tells us (16.4.5) that Philip personally commanded the right wing of his army, having alongside him "the best" (*aristous*) of the Macedonians fighting with him; and he describes Philip with these "best men" as fighting heroically and forcing the Illyrians to flee. This suggests that Philip had already at that early stage begun to develop the elite unit we later hear of. The contemporary historian Theopompus of Chios, one of the greatest and most widely admired of the classic Greek historians, who spent years at Philip's court, reports that: "from all of the Macedonians the largest and strongest were selected and formed the bodyguard of the king (Philip), and they were called *pezetairoi*" (Theopompos in *Brill's New Jacoby* 115 F 348). Another contemporary of Philip, his Athenian opponent Demosthenes, also refers to the *pezetairoi* in his second Olynthiac Oration (at 17), mentioning their reputation as "marvelous" (*thaumastoi*) warriors who were outstandingly experienced in warfare. Three late antique lexical sources offer explanations for the term *pezetairoi* in Demosthenes' speech here: they agree that the term refers to Philip's personal guard, whom they characterize as "strong" (*ischuroi*) and faithful (*pistoi*). One of these sources, the

Etymologicum Magnum, quotes as illustration a historical fragment (perhaps from Theopompus): "and taking of the Macedonians the so-called *pezetairoi*, who were picked men (*apolektous*), he (Philip) invaded Illyria." Theopompus and Demosthenes thus agree that the *pezetairoi* were an elite unit of selected men who formed Philip's personal guard in battle, and who enjoyed a reputation as outstanding and "marvelous" warriors. It seems certain, finally, that when Diodorus reports (16.86.1) that Philip fought his final battle, the battle of Chaeroneia in 338, in command of "selected men" (*epilektous*) who were certainly infantry (see Polyaenus 4.2.2), this means that Philip was as usual fighting surrounded by his elite *pezetairoi*.

Unfortunately our inadequate sources for Philip's reign offer us no further insight into the development, organization, and use of this elite force. But under Alexander, we see this unit, under its new name as *hypaspistai*, functioning as the elite personal infantry guard of the king and spearhead of his army, as Philip had trained it to be. The *pezetairoi/hypaspistai* (later also called *argyraspides*, as noted above) usually fought as part of the phalanx, wielding the *sarissa* and other equipment of the Macedonian pikeman, and normally stationed on the right wing of the phalanx. But they were also trained to use other equipment when needed: on several occasions Alexander had them equipped as light infantry for operations requiring more speed and mobility: pursuit of enemy forces, fighting in mountainous territory, fighting alongside cavalry, and so on. It seems that they could also, if called upon to do so, adopt the heavier equipment of the southern Greek hoplite and fight as a hoplite phalanx; on one occasion Alexander had them mounted on horseback for an operation requiring particular speed of movement. They were, that is to say, superbly trained and versatile warriors, equally capable of fighting with any equipment and in any style they were called upon to adopt. As light infantry they were swift and tireless; as heavy infantry they spearheaded the phalanx in attack from their post on the right and were frequently chiefly responsible for victory; in any style or formation, they were the "marvelous" warriors of their reputation. They truly were the undefeated "athletes of war" that Plutarch called them, many of them continuing to fight and dominate the field of battle into their fifties and even sixties, until the unit was finally broken up by Antigonus in 316.

By the end of Philip's reign, as indicated above, the *pezetairoi* numbered three thousand men: this is made evident from the sources for the first few years of Alexander's reign, when the unit—now re-named *hypaspistai*—numbered three thousand and was commanded by Parmenio's son Nicanor. The regiment, so to speak, of the *pezetairoi* was divided into three battalions (*chiliades*) of a thousand, each with its own sub-commander. One of the three was the particular personal bodyguard of the king, known as the infantry *agema*, units of which protected the king at all times, and which formed his personal guard in battle when he fought on foot. Philip often chose to fight at the head of his infantry, surrounded by his infantry *agema* and the rest of the *pezetairoi*, as he did at his first great battle against Bardylis, and again at the end of his reign at the Battle of Chaeroneia. Alexander, by con-trast, preferred to lead the Macedonian cavalry in his major battles, though in other operations he frequently employed the *pezetairoi/hy-paspistai* as his special force for all purposes, as already noted. The unit is probably best known to military history in its final avatar as the Silver Shields who dominated several battles in the wars of Alexander's Suc-cessors, but they were more properly Philip's elite infantry unit, organ-ized and trained by him, and instrumental in helping him to turn Macedonia from the weak backwater Philip inherited into the greatest military power in the ancient world.

3. The Reformed Cavalry Strike Force

Cavalry had always, as far back as our sources reach, been the strong suit of the Macedonians militarily, as explained in Chapter 1. The broad plains and plateaus of Macedonia were good horse-rearing country, and the aristocracy which dominated Macedonia socially and economically were enthusiastic horse breeders and riders. This is attested, as we have seen, by the popularity of personal names built on the Greek word *hippos* (horse): *Philippos, Hipponikos, Hippolochos, Hippostratos, Hippias, Hippalos, Hipparchos, Hippodamas, Hippokles, Kratippos,* and many others. In view of this it is particularly surprising to read Anaximenes (quoted above) suggesting that a ruler named Alexander had to "accustom the most notable to serve as cavalry" (the Greek verb for "serve as cavalry" is *hippeuein* which could also, even more uncon-vincingly, mean "to ride horses"). The truth is rather that the Macedonian aristocracy, as enthusiastic horse owners and riders, fought naturally from horse-back; and the Macedonian army from early times was made up predominantly of aristocrats and their retainers riding in at the ruler's call to serve him as cavalry. The problem for Philip was that this cavalry force, though potentially excellent, was unreliable—because the commitment of the aristocrats making it up was unreliable—and incapable of directly and effectively engaging well armed infantry forces prepared to stand their ground in the face of cavalry charges.

What Philip wanted and needed was a cavalry force that was truly at his beck and call and loyal without question; and one that could be used effectively as a strike force even against well disciplined and heavily armored infantry forces. We have already seen in Chapter 3 the steps that Philip took to make the aristocracy, and thereby their retainers too, self-interestedly loyal to him as ruler, using the time-honored "carrot and stick" approach. The carrot was the granting of estates on newly conquered royal land, estates which could be repossessed if the grantee showed insufficient loyalty; the stick was the threat of destruction of disloyal aristocrats by Philip's great infantry army, and the royal school at Pella where sons of the aristocracy, while being educated free of charge, also served as hostages for their fathers' good behavior. Still, a cavalry made up largely of aristocrats and their retainers remained only contingently Philip's to use. It is clear that he enormously expanded the cavalry by hugely increasing the part of the Macedonian cavalry made up of his own loyal retainers.

It will be recalled that at the start of his reign, Philip could call upon just six hundred or so cavalry for his crucial campaign against the Illyrians under Bardylis. Similar sized cavalry forces are attested as being commanded by earlier Macedonian kings such as Amyntas III and Perdiccas II. Evidently this is the kind of force, in terms of numbers, that could be raised by a traditional Macedonian ruler from his own retainers and his most loyal aristocratic *hetairoi*. By the end of Philip's reign, he had available to him a Macedonian heavy cavalry force numbering at least 3,300: an enormous expansion of the Macedonian cavalry (and this doesn't even count special forces of lightly equipped cavalry, some of whom were also Macedonians, discussed below in section 4 of this chapter). Evidently, as Philip conquered border territories and incorporated them into Macedonia, he settled many hundreds, eventually several thousand, men on large land allotments (small estates in effect) on condition that they maintained horses on part of their granted lands and served in the army as cavalry. We hear, for example, early in Alexander's reign (when his army was still in all respects that created by Philip) of cavalry squadrons from several regions annexed to Macedonia by Philip: Amphipolis on the River Strymon, taken by Philip in 357; Anthemous in the north-west Chalcidice, a territory annexed to Macedonia at some point in the 350s or early 340s; and Apollonia in the north-east of the Chalcidice. Evidently several hundred men had been settled in each of these regions on substantial land allotments—so-called cavalry allotments—enabling them to be called up as cavalry whenever needed. These men were self-interestedly loyal to Philip because he had granted them their lands and raised them to the status of cavalrymen; the condition of keeping their allotments (which were revocable), and the status that went with them, was loyal service to Philip. We may reasonably estimate that as many as 2,000 of the 3,300 cavalry available to Philip at the end of his reign were men of this type: men raised to cavalry status by Philip, via revocable land allotments granted by Philip, who therefore were loyal retainers of Philip. With such a force of loyal retainers, Philip could overwhelm the following of even the greatest aristocrats if they should show disloyalty. This made the cavalry truly Philip's cavalry, able to be called up and used by him as he saw fit without needing to pander to the whims of the great aristocrats.

Even such a truly loyal cavalry force, though, still retained the inherent weakness in battle that Macedonian (and other ancient) cavalry had always had up to this time. A horse will not willingly charge into an obstacle it sees no way to get over or through. Consequently, when cavalry charged a densely packed formation of infantry who did not turn to flight but stood their ground and maintained their formation in the face of charging cavalry, the cavalry horses would slow down and eventually pull up when they got close. The cavalry would be reduced to riding to and fro in front of the infantry formation, hurling missile weapons (which well equipped infantry would catch on or deflect with their shields) and insults. If and when the infantry force began to march forward in formation, the cavalry would be obliged to give ground before them, and eventually to flee. Cavalry, that is to say, were excellent against poorly organized and indisciplined infantry, which broke and ran when attacked by cavalry, enabling the cavalrymen to get among them and run them through from behind with spears or hack at them with swords. Pursuing and killing fleeing infantry was indeed what cavalry were best at and had most fun doing. A commander who was unwise enough to draw up his infantry with inadequate protection for their flanks would see enemy cavalry charge around to attack the infantry from the side or the rear; but that was a rarity as even minimally competent commanders confronting cavalry would know to keep their flanks protected. Beyond this, cavalry were useful for scouting and skirmishing before battle. To defeat well organized and disciplined infantry was beyond traditional cavalry forces.

In addition to all of this, cavalry forces were very hard to lead and command effectively. Traditionally, cavalry forces, like infantry forces, were drawn up in square or rectangular formations made up of lines of cavalrymen one behind the other. The commander would be stationed in the post of honor, on the far right of the front rank. From there, he could survey the field and enemy forces and decide when and where he wanted to charge. The signal to charge would be given by a trumpeter stationed with the commander, and the unit of cavalry would move forward, initially at a walking pace, in the direction the commander indicated. As they drew towards the enemy force they were attacking, the cavalry would speed up to a slow trot, and then go faster, trying to intimidate the enemy with their speed and hoping to break his morale and get him to flee. As the force moved faster, the lines of horsemen would inevitably become ragged, the thunder of hooves would drown out other sounds, and all but the few men closest to him would therefore lose touch with the commander, unable to hear or see, and so unable to follow, any other commands he might try to give. The commander, therefore, only truly had control of his force up to the initial charge; after that, it was largely every cavalryman for himself. If well trained and disciplined they would certainly try to remain as much as possible together and in formation; but it was effectively impossible for the commander to lead them in any complex or changing maneuvers.

This was unsatisfactory to Philip. He wanted to use his cavalry as a variable and effective weapon on the field of battle. He wanted the cavalry to be able to maneuver effectively under their commanders' directions, and to attack enemy formations in an effective and destructive

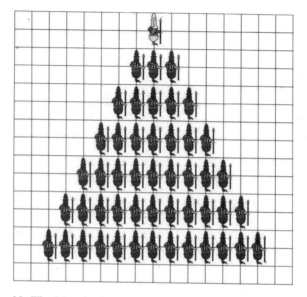

11. The Macedonian cavalry wedge

(Public domain image: Quora—A.L. Chaisiri)

manner. Careful thought led him to conclude that the ineffectiveness of cavalry in battle was largely due to the formation in which cavalry was drawn up to fight: cavalry, to be effective, needed to get in among the enemy infantry, and they needed to be able to follow their commander and respond to his wishes as battle developed. The square or rectangular formation was well adapted to neither of these needs. Instead, Philip drew up his cavalry, and trained them to fight, in wedge-shaped formations (see ill. 11). The formation commander would ride at the apex of the wedge, with his second and third in command immediately behind him, ready to take his place if he was killed or incapacitated. In a wedge with the commander at the apex, the cavalry force rode wherever the commander rode, and so was able to follow him through whatever maneuvers and/or changes in direction he might undertake. In addition, with the front of the wedge only a few horses wide (the commander at the very front, two men behind him, three behind them, and so on), it would need only a small gap to open in an enemy formation for the cavalry wedge to charge at it, the first few horsemen pushing into the small gap. Once inside the enemy formation, the first cavalrymen in could "lever" the formation open by striking down at the enemy to either side, causing them to give way and thus widening the gap to allow more and more of the cavalry wedge to press in and eventually through the enemy formation. This would most often cause the enemy to turn and flee; failing that, the cavalry themselves would turn to attack the enemy from the side and rear. In this way, the cavalry could potentially be used as a genuine strike force in battle, even against well organized infantry.

Thanks to this simple yet elegant and brilliant change in formation, Philip's cavalry became indeed a fearsome strike force in his army and battles, best illustrated (as we shall see) in the battles the Macedonian army fought under Alexander's leadership after Philip's untimely death. At Philip's death, when Alexander inherited his army, we learn that there were some 3,300 Macedonian heavy cavalry: Alexander took eighteen hundred with him when he crossed to Asia, and he left fifteen hundred behind as part of the home army under the regent Antipater. We know from various accounts of Alexander's cavalry force in action that the Macedonian cavalry at this time were organized into squadrons (*ilai*) of about two hundred men led by officers named *ilarchs*, each of which was sub-divided into two sub-units of around a hundred. When we consider Antipater's force of fifteen hundred cavalry in his home army, this creates a problem: fifteen hundred does not easily divide into squadrons of two hundred men. The solution is likely that the number two hundred is a rounded approximation: seven squadrons of 214 cavalrymen would total 1,498 men. It seems likely, therefore, that Antipater had seven squadrons of the Macedonian cavalry; and that another seven squadrons went with Alexander.

Of course Alexander had eighteen hundred cavalrymen, not fifteen hundred: what about the extra three hundred men? A key part of Alexander's cavalry force was a special squadron named the *ile basilike* or "royal squadron," commanded at the start of Alexander's reign by an officer named Cleitus "the Black." This is the cavalry force at the head of which Alexander was accustomed to station himself in battle, and which formed his cavalry bodyguard (*agema*) in battle, being thus the cavalry equivalent of the elite infantry *agema*, the *pezetairoi/hypaspistai*. It will be recalled that this elite infantry unit was stronger in numbers than a regular phalanx battalion (*taxis*), being three thousand strong instead of fifteen hundred. It seems certain that the royal squadron of the cavalry was likewise a larger formation than the regular cavalry squadron: three hundred men instead of around two hundred.

The cavalry at the end of Philip's reign and beginning of Alexander's would, therefore, have been made up of fourteen regular squadrons of cavalry, each a little over two hundred strong; plus the special royal squadron of about three hundred men; for a total of fifteen squadrons in all. We saw above that the Macedonian infantry was organized likewise into fourteen *taxeis* of about fifteen hundred each, plus the elite *pezetairoi/hypaspistai* at three thousand strong. The organization of infantry and cavalry thus matched: fourteen *taxeis* of infantry recruited by region and fourteen *ilai* of cavalry likewise regionally recruited; plus two extra-strength elite selected units, the infantry *pezetairoi/hypaspistai* and the cavalry *ile basilike*.

The standard equipment of the Macedonian "heavy" cavalry is fortunately well attested. Thucydides already mentions that the Macedonian cavalry were "excellent horsemen and armed with breastplates" when telling of a campaign in 429/8 (Thucydides 2.100). But rather than literary descriptions, we can get a sense of the Macedonian heavy cavalry from two excellent depictions in art of Alexander's time: the "Alexander Mosaic" in the Archaeological Museum at Naples (ill. 13), and the "Alexander Sarcophagus" in the Archaeological Museum of Istanbul (see ill. 5). Besides the breastplates mentioned by Thucydides, Macedonian heavily armed cavalry wore kilts reinforced with leather strips, open-faced helmets, and short cloaks. Their main armament was a heavy thrusting spear some ten feet in length (about three meters) which might be wielded either overarm, as does the Macedonian cavalryman on the Alexander Sarcophagus (perhaps Antigonus the One-Eyed), or underarm as Alexander does in the Alexander Mosaic depiction. As secondary arms, the cavalry carried short (around two feet) thrusting swords carried under the left arm by a strap over the right shoulder. No shields were carried, as the cavalry relied on their breastplates for protection against missiles or thrusts from enemy weapons, while using the long thrusting spears to keep enemy warriors at a distance, and speed of movement to enhance their safety. Lacking saddles or stirrups, the cavalryman had need to be an excellent rider, as Thucydides attested Macedonian cavalry were. With the equipment mentioned and the training and discipline instilled by Philip in his new wedge formation, the Macedonian heavy cavalry came, along with the pike infantry, to dominate the battlefields of the near east.

4. THE SPECIALIZED LIGHT INFANTRY AND CAVALRY FORCES

The set-piece battle was the acme of ancient warfare, the event that ultimately decided the fate of a war. And with his powerful pike phalanx, usually spearheaded by his elite *pezetairoi*, and his vastly improved heavy cavalry strike force, Philip had created the crucial units that could win his battles for him. But warfare is not only about fighting battles; battles are not only characterized by the clashes of the "heavy" infantry and cavalry; and the great difference in mobility and speed of movement between infantry phalanx and cavalry could cause gaps in one's battle formation that a swift-thinking enemy might exploit. Philip realized that he needed a variety of specialized forces to carry out peripheral but important tasks in his campaigns.

When an army sets out to undertake a campaign against an enemy force, especially if the campaign is to be conducted in enemy territory, it is of fundamental importance to the commander that he receive regular and reliable intelligence reports about the terrain to be traversed and, most crucially, about the whereabouts of the enemy force(s) and their number and make-up. Providing these intelligence reports was the task, in ancient warfare, of scouts: highly mobile and fast-moving soldiers who were sent out ahead and to the sides of the main army to spy out the lay of the land, look for enemy forces, capture and/or question enemy scouts or local civilians, and report back regularly on what they discovered. Such scouts were usually lightly equipped cavalry, mounted on horses with the qualities of speed and stamina. Heavy armor and weapons were not required by men whose job was not to fight so much as to see, hear, and report. Cavalry scouts wore only the lightest protection—padded jackets and light "target" shields strapped to the left forearm—and typically carried light missile weapons, mostly javelins, along with slashing swords for close in-fighting when necessary. In the Macedonian army of Philip and Alexander, units of light cavalry scouts, called *prodromoi*, are well attested: there were at least nine hundred of them in the army inherited from Philip with which Alexander invaded Asia in 334, for example, many of them recruited from Paeonia and Thrace.

Another crucial activity of soldiers on campaign is foraging for food supplies, i.e. stealing food by force from enemy lands and settlements. This necessity is dictated by the nature of overland transport in antiquity. Bulk goods such as large supplies of foodstuffs could only be carried in very slow-moving ox-drawn carts or mule pack-trains. These would slow down an army's movement dramatically, and besides being very expensive such supply trains would also be vulnerable to enemy attack and need guarding. Philip wanted to be able to move fast, and preferred to keep his baggage-train as light as possible. The solution, adopted by all ancient armies, was that of "living off the land," which means taking food from the indigenous population by force. This too required specialized soldiers. One could, certainly, in theory have the heavy infantry, in Philip's case his pikemen, lay down their pikes and other equipment to go out foraging; but that would be a huge risk, if the enemy were to be able to pull off a surprise attack. The men of the phalanx had to stay in formation, whether it be column of march or line of battle, leaving the business of foraging to more mobile and less crucial troops. It was in fact the business of lightly equipped and hence fast-moving infantry, guarded during the actual foraging by mobile cavalry. Units of lightly armored javelineers, archers, and slingers would be sent out to do the foraging, covered and protected by the light cavalry *prodromoi* and other units of lightly equipped cavalry.

If and when the enemy was sighted and the decision was taken to fight a battle, battle was not joined instantaneously: it took time to shift the heavy infantry and cavalry from their encampment, or from the column of march, into a proper line of battle ready to fight. In the lead-up to battle, as the precise plan of battle was decided and the units of the army were drawn up in corresponding formation, there occurred a preliminary form of fighting known as skirmishing. Thousands of lightly equipped and highly mobile light infantrymen and cavalry would be sent forward to occupy space on the battlefield, to harass the enemy forces, to spy out the exact nature of the terrain on which the battle would be fought and the formation the enemy was adopting and report back on these, and to cover and protect the maneuvering of their own army into battle formation. This role of skirmishing is frequently referred to in ancient accounts of battles, but even more frequently simply passed over in silence as unimportant. It most certainly was not unimportant, however, and Philip had well organized and trained units of specialized light infantry equipped with missile weapons—archers, slingers, and javelineers—to carry out this role of skirmishing along with the lightly equipped cavalry. These special light infantry were often foreign troops recruited as allies or mercenaries. Archers, for example, often came from the island of Crete, since Cretans had long specialized in archery; and in the campaigns of Alexander (and so probably of Philip too) the best javelineers came from a tribe living just north of Macedonia proper, the Agrianians. Skirmishing was also a role played by the *prodromoi*, the cavalry scouts, and in addition we hear of a light cavalry unit named *sarissophoroi* or "lancers": evidently very lightly armored cavalry who carried the same pikes as the heavy infantry to attack enemy infantry and cavalry skirmishers. In some cases it seems that the *prodromoi* and the *sarissophoroi* may have been the same soldiers, employed in different roles.

Finally, when battle was joined, the skirmishers would retreat to join the line of battle formed by the phalanx and the heavy cavalry, but their role in battle was not ended. There remained, in fact, three crucial roles for them to play. In battle, the phalanx, weighed down by their heavy and unwieldy pikes, moved very slowly. The heavy cavalry kept pace with the phalanx until an opening or disruption in the enemy line offered them a point of attack, at which they would then charge. It was the role of cavalry skirmishers and missile-firing infantry to harass the enemy line of battle as the phalanx moved slowly forward, to try to create such an opening or disruption, as several of Alexander's battles reveal. When the heavy cavalry did charge, their swift advance would create a gap between them and the slowly moving phalanx. It was important not to allow an enemy force to move through this gap to attack the phalanx from the side and/or rear: light infantry units had the task of occupying this gap and protecting the phalanx from such an attack. Finally, units of light cavalry were routinely stationed out on the army's flanks to harass and hold off any enemy force attempting an outflanking maneuver, unless the field of battle offered a natural barrier—a ravine, a wood, a hill—providing natural flank protection. In sum, in addition to their important roles during the campaign preliminary to battle, light infantry and cavalry units also played important, if secondary, roles during battle. These light forces might not actually win the battles, but they contributed in important ways to making victory possible. Finally, energetic pursuit of the defeated and fleeing enemy was crucial to make a victory decisive. Here too, the squadrons of light cavalry, especially the lancers (*sarissophoroi*), had an important role to play. Ensuring that he always had such lightly equipped units—infantry archers, slingers, and javelineers, and cavalry *prodromoi* and *sarissophoroi*, as we have seen—in sufficient numbers and in a high state of training and preparedness, was therefore crucial to Philip's advanced form of warfare.

As indicated above, these specialized light infantry and cavalry forces were by no means always Macedonian. Philip recruited and used troops from a variety of sources for this purpose: Paeonians and Thracians are attested as light cavalry *prodromoi*, Cretans as archers, and Agrianians and other Thracians and Triballians as javelineers, for example. In the army Alexander inherited from Philip, we hear of seven thousand light infantry from the Balkan peoples, as well as one thousand Agrianian javelineers. But in addition to all these specialized light infantry and cavalry forces, we should also note an important source of specialized heavy infantry troops: mercenaries drawn from southern Greece. The world of the Greek city-states suffered from severe over-population in the fourth century, at least according to intellectuals such as the pamphleteer and educator Isocrates. Certainly southern Greece seemed to provide an almost inexhaustible supply of rootless young men willing to serve as soldiers for pay in this period. For Philip's purposes, mercenaries, equipped as heavy infantry hoplites or at times as more mobile peltasts—soldiers who carried a lighter shield and had less body armor than the hoplites—had an enormous advantage: they were relatively much more expendable than his Macedonian troops. Losses in mercenary troops could always be replaced by fresh recruitment; and thanks to his enormous income in gold and silver from his mining operations, Philip could afford to employ thousands of mercenaries as he saw fit. These men supplemented his phalanx, easing the burden on native Macedonians for military services, and could be used for dangerous operations where losses might be higher than usual. Highly experienced and versatile, mercenary peltasts could also be used in all sorts of operations in which Philip might prefer not to exhaust his native military manpower.

5. The Siege Train

When ancient peoples did not dare to come out to confront an enemy army in battle, they often took refuge behind strong defensive walls built around their important settlement(s). Southern Greek hoplite forces had never shown much ability to cope with fortifications. Since such hoplites were citizen militia soldiers, who as citizens elected their generals before a campaign, and sat in judgement on them afterwards, southern Greek generals could not just command their soldiers however they saw fit. A general who suffered heavy losses, or treated his soldiers in a way they disliked, would face severe consequences after his term of office was over. Since taking fortifications by storm involved either operations that carried a high risk of sustaining heavy casualties (rushing up siege ladders to capture the enemy wall), or operations calling for heavy manual labor (constructing a siege ramp, or undermining the fortification walls) which Greek citizen warriors deemed work fit only for slaves, the reality was that armies of Greek hoplites confronted by well defended fortifications were reduced to camping around the enemy city and attempting to starve the enemy into surrender, which could take many months or even several years. Mostly Greek armies simply gave up in the face of well defended fortifications, unless they could find a way to get inside help: traitors, that is, to open a city gate.

Philip was well versed in using all the arts of persuasion, including bribery, to get his forces into enemy cities without needing to fight. But when inside traitors were not available to let his forces into an enemy city, Philip was not willing to see his military operations bogged down every time he was confronted with well defended enemy fortifications. He wanted to be able to capture enemy cities quickly. He had the advantage that, as king, he was much less dependent on his soldiers' good will than were the generals of southern Greek city-state forces. Philip could order his men to take risks and perform labors that a city-state commander could not contemplate. In addition, since Philip employed many thousands of non-Macedonian troops—Thracians, Illyrians, mercenaries from southern Greece—who were relatively expendable, he could contemplate sustaining fairly high casualties with relative equanimity. Still, he would not want to sustain excessive losses, which would damage morale in his army. To attack fortifications effectively, the defenders on the wall had to be "softened up" first and/or the walls or gates needed to be breached, and that called for a specialized siege train.

Great advances in siege technology had been made in the Greek world early in the fourth century, especially in the forces of the Sicilian tyrant Dionysius of Syracuse. The key was the invention of the torsion principle: using ropes made of hair and/or animal guts which would be twisted with great force to create enormous dynamic tension. The sudden release of that tension could propel missiles—bolts of various sorts from smaller catapults; rocks and the like from larger ones—that could be used to force enemy soldiers on walls to duck down behind the walls for cover, enabling siege ladders to be raised against the walls and scaled; or else to batter the walls and/or gates in the hope of breaking holes in them. In the former task groups of highly trained archers firing at the tops of the enemy walls would help. In the latter task it would help to send forward, under cover, sappers who could dig under the walls, undermining and weakening them. In addition, more elaborate siege engines came to be developed. Mantlets covered with raw or wet ox-hides could provide cover for groups of specialists to drag battering-rams up to the gates and try to smash them open. Siege towers on wheels could be moved up to the walls and provide a platform for one's soldiers to engage the enemy soldiers on the wall, attempting to cross over and win control of the wall. All of this siegecraft was still in development in Philip's day: it was not until the very end of the fourth century and the early third century, in the army of Demetrius the Besieger, that Greek siegecraft reached its height. But Philip made sure to have the best siege technicians and machinery available in his day, and thanks to them his siege operations were mostly very successful.

With this siege technology and the highly trained and disciplined soldiers of his army, Philip captured a string of well fortified cities with relative ease and quickness: Amphipolis in 357, Pydna and Potidaea in 356, Abdera, Maroneia, and Methone in 354, Heraeon Teichos in 352, Olynthos in 348, to name a few. The list is a long one, and one might add Alexander's capture of Thebes in 335, the year after Philip's death. Not all of Philip's sieges were successful: he failed to capture Perinthus and Byzantium in 340 thanks to the arrival of significant outside help for those cities' defenses. But the principle is clear. As in every aspect of his warfare, Philip gave careful attention to his siege train, made it the most up-to-date and effective it could be, and achieved startling successes in his sieges as a result, enabling him to conquer territories and spread his control without being constantly stymied by strongly fortified cities and guard posts.

6. THE OFFICER CORPS

The point of all of the above was the creation of a new style of warfare: more elaborate, more disciplined, based on more thorough and effective training, aimed at creating swift and decisive successes through the controlled use of varied kinds of soldiers, with different armaments and specialties, operating together in a unified scheme of campaign and battle that not only won victories, but made them decisive, and not only occupied territories, but conquered them thoroughly and brought them firmly under control. But this kind of warfare, in which different specialized units of soldiers had to co-operate together in complex schemes of campaign and battle, was demanding. It did not only require a highly skilled commander who understood the potentialities of different types of soldiers and varieties of terrain, and could create and bring into effect plans that made the most of them. For varied units to co-operate together effectively in war, and especially in battle, each unit had to be led by a unit commander who understood the overall plan of campaign and battle, grasped the precise role of his own unit in it and its relation to other units, and could lead his unit in a disciplined way within the plan of battle, while having enough initiative to adapt his orders to the vagaries of battle and still stay within the overall battle plan. Where to find such skilled officers? Such officers are, of course, not so much found as trained. And in the course of his twenty-four-year rule, Philip trained one of the great officer corps in the annals of warfare, without whom Philip could not have achieved half of what he did achieve; and without whom Alexander—himself trained in the art of war by Philip—could not have conquered the vast empire he did conquer.

The full ability and expertise of this officer corps trained by Philip became apparent after the death of Alexander when, given free rein to operate on their own behalf, many of them carved out empires for themselves in two decades of extraordinary warfare (see Chapter 6 below). Men like Antigonus the One-Eyed, Eumenes of Cardia, Craterus and Perdiccas, Ptolemy and Cassander, Seleucus and Lysimachus, all in various ways showed military skills and leadership abilities of a very high order, in the case of Antigonus and Seleucus perhaps the highest. These skills and abilities did not come out of nowhere: they were developed and honed in decades of training and service under Philip, and then further honed assisting Alexander in conquering western Asia. The noted Hellenistic historian William Tarn, in the third chapter of his very adulatory biography of Alexander the Great (1948), says of these men:

> Here was an assembly of kings, with passions, ambitions, abilities beyond those of most men; and, while he (Alexander) lived, all we see is that Perdiccas and Ptolemy were good brigade leaders, Antigonus an obedient satrap, Lysimachus and Peithon little-noticed members of the staff . . .

It seems to me that Tarn draws entirely the wrong lesson. The real point is not that Alexander dominated these men; it is that Alexander had, thanks to his father's work, officers of such outstanding quality to work with. Alexander did not conquer the Persian Empire on his own. He had a group of brilliantly trained and highly professional officers to carry out and make effective his plans of battle, to co-operate with him in his campaigns and smooth out any problems, to carry out independent operations on his behalf when needed. Men who thoroughly understood the business of warfare and military leadership because they had learned their business in the same school as Alexander: Philip's school.

Philip did not create his new army and officer corps on his own; he was fortunate enough to find two older men of outstanding ability to co-operate with him: Parmenio and Antipater. Both born a year or two either side of the year 400, they were around twenty years older than Philip, in their mid-forties already when he came to rule Macedonia at the age of twenty-four. It says a great deal for Philip that he very quickly identified these two men to be his key aides and supporters, and that he gained their loyalty and held it throughout his reign. Their importance to Philip is well illustrated by a couple of anecdotes recorded by Plutarch which show how they were viewed. Parmenio was throughout Philip's career, and indeed most of the reign of Alexander, the senior officer after the ruler himself, in effect second-in-command of the Macedonian army and often trusted with independent commands: it was Parmenio, for example, who commanded a Macedonian army against the Illyrians under Grabus, and won a notable victory in 356. Of him Plutarch reports (*Moralia* 177C): "He (Philip) said that he counted the Athenians fortunate indeed, in that every year they could find ten men to select as generals (*strategoi*); for he himself in many years had only ever found one general, Parmenio." The point being that the ten *strategoi* whom the Athenians elected every year were magistrates, who often had little real military skill; whereas Parmenio was a superb general on whom Philip could and did wholly rely. Antipater was also a very competent general, often trusted by Philip and Alexander with important commands; but he was above all the officer on whom Philip relied in diplomatic and administrative matters, usually serving as regent of Macedonia when the king was away on campaign. Plutarch reports (*Moralia* 179B): "Once having slept very late while on a campaign, he (Philip) said upon awaking 'I slept safely, for Antipater was awake'." In Antipater, that is to say, as in Parmenio, Philip had a senior officer in whom he reposed complete trust to be able and to do whatever was right and needed in his own absence.

These two, then, were the right-hand men who stood at the apex of Philip's officer corps, considerably older than Philip himself and presumably assisting him in the recruitment and training of the rest of his officers. It may well be suggested, indeed, that they were to some degree co-inventors of the new army and military system with Philip, and so co-creators of Philip's new Macedonian state. Besides these two very senior and crucial officers, there were also a number of important officers who were more or less Philip's contemporaries, Antigonus the One-Eyed and Polyperchon being the best known of them. These men presumably learned Philip's system of warfare by serving with and under Philip, as Philip himself created it and instituted it. They learned by doing, under Philip's command; and perhaps also had some input into the process of developing the new army and military system. Most significant, however, in terms of numbers were the younger officers who were trained up by Philip from the inception of their military careers: such men as Craterus, Perdiccas, Philotas, Ptolemy, Leonnatus, Cassander, Lysimachus, Seleucus, Hephaestion, and—most crucially—Alexander himself. The ancient Greek term for education and training is *paideia*, and the young men, in their late teens, who were being trained by Philip in the business of warfare and officering, were known as his *paides*—often translated into English, via a medieval metaphor, as Philip's "pages," but in effect his trainees.

The *paides* of Macedonia have been assumed at times to be an old and traditional part of the Macedonian monarchy, a way for the sons of the king's *hetairoi* to learn and show loyalty to the ruler, as noted in Chapter 1. But they are first attested under Philip, and seem more likely—as some scholars note—to be one of Philip's many innovations. Young men in their late teens, around seventeen to nineteen years old, from the *hetairos* class would be taken into Philip's service to learn to be a man, a Macedonian, and a leader. They attended the king at all times: at court, in the hunt, at the symposium, and on campaign, fighting as part of his entourage in battle. At court and at the symposium, they served as guards, messengers, and servers of food and wine. They learned the etiquette of the court and the symposium, and the business of the ruler. At the hunt, they served the king, ensured as best they could his safety, and participated in the stalking and killing of game while deferring to the king as principal hunter. Most importantly, on campaign and in battle they guarded the king and his tent, witnessing in that capacity the planning of marches and battles and the giving of orders. They might serve as messengers from the king to various units of the army and their officers, and they fought around the king in battle. In this way, they learned by observing and participating all the business of the army and the state, of leadership and command, of organizing and fighting. When they "graduated" from this *paideia*, the young men of whom the king approved might be appointed to the command of sub-units within the army, whether infantry or cavalry, and gradually progress into the command of larger units: *taxeis* of pikemen, *ilai* of cavalry, or specialized units of more lightly equipped soldiers, whether Macedonian, allied, or mercenary.

The result was that by the end of his reign, Philip had an officer corps of men who had thoroughly learned the structure of the army and its units, the system of warfare Philip had devised, and the business of commanding units of the army in accordance with the overall structure of the army and the plans of campaign and battle. Having been trained and selected by Philip himself, with the aid of his most senior officers as noted above, the king reposed full confidence in their ability to do what was required of them and their units in any military contingency, and they displayed their outstanding quality and capacities in the campaigns and battles of Alexander, and especially in the wars of the succession which followed on Alexander's untimely death. It was officers of Philip who eventually took control of the lands conquered by the Macedonians under Philip and Alexander, and organized those lands into the great Hellenistic empires which dominated the near east for two centuries, and provided the setting for the establishment of Hellenistic civilization and culture.

7. THE SYSTEM OF BATTLE

Key to the success of the warfare of Philip and especially of Alexander was an advanced system of battle, invented by Philip, which used an army of combined arms in a smooth interlocking process to pin the enemy forces down, force them into battle, create disruptions in the enemy formation, and then exploit those disruptions to bring about victory, driving the enemy into flight and pursuing vigorously to make the victory decisive. Unfortunately our sources on Philip's battles are for the most part completely inadequate, merely reporting the battles and Philip's victories rather than describing them. But it is possible to reconstruct Philip's last and most important battle and victory: the Battle of Chaeroneia in 338, whereby Philip secured his position as leader of the Greek world and set the groundwork in motion for the Macedonian invasion of western Asia. This battle illustrates Philip's system of battle in its fully developed form, and was the model, I shall argue, for the great battles and victories of Alexander.

The Battle of Chaeroneia was fought in northern Boeotia, where the small town of Chaeroneia sits in a rather narrow pass between the River Cephisus and Lake Copais to the east and the foothills of Mounts Parnassus and Helicon to the west, athwart the main road from Phocis into Boeotia and beyond. Philip commanded a large Macedonian force of some thirty thousand infantry and two thousand cavalry. Opposing him was a combined southern Greek force made up of large contingents from Thebes and Athens, along with smaller allied forces from a number of other Greek states (Achaea, Corinth, Chalcis, Megara, Epidaurus, and Troizen). The allied southern Greek force had most likely about the same number of men as Philip, though Justin (9.3) suggested that the southern Greeks had far more men. Stationed astride the road facing north, the southern Greeks deployed with the Thebans on the right, their flank protected by the River Cephisus, and the Athenians on the left with their flank resting against the slopes of Mount Thurion, a projection from Mount Parnassus. Philip placed his *pezetairoi* on his right opposite the Athenians, with himself in command. Opposite the Thebans on Philip's left were several phalanx battalions with, most likely, Parmenio in overall command, having Alexander with him sharing in the command in some way. We can only assume that the other southern Greek forces, unmentioned in actual accounts of the battle, were stationed in the center of the southern Greek line, between the Thebans and the Athenians.

Establishing exactly what happened during the Battle of Chaeroneia is not easy. Our main source, Diodorus the Sicilian (16.86.1–6), recounts the battle in a distinctly Homeric manner, focusing on the individual bravery of Philip himself and his son Alexander, and presenting the battle as a rivalry between the two of them to attain the victory by their personal efforts. What we can take from his account is that Alexander held an important command on one wing of the battle, facing the Theban contingent of the opposing army, while Philip commanded the other wing opposite the Athenians. On Alexander's wing were stationed also "the most worthy commanders," which must certainly include Parmenio. A force led by Alexander first succeeded in breaking through the enemy line, leading to a rout of the Thebans. Philip at that point, with his "picked men" (that is, his *pezetairoi*) around him, forced back the Athenians and routed them, over a thousand Athenians being killed and more than two thousand captured, which secured the victory. Thus far Diodorus' account, which offers little detail on troop dispositions or the actual course of the fighting, while giving the impression that Philip and Alexander fought like Ajax and Achilles of old.

A number of other sources supplement Diodorus' inadequate account, adding important details that flesh out what really happened. The second-century CE compiler of military "stratagems" Polyaenus tells us that Philip and his troops withdrew from the Athenians in a staged retreat, drawing the Athenians forward (Polyaenus 4.2.2); and that when the relatively raw Athenians grew tired, Philip had his more seasoned men attack and drive the Athenians back in rout (Polyaenus 4.2.7; also Frontinus *Stratagems* 2.1.9). Plutarch in his *Life of Pelopidas* (18) says that the Theban Sacred Band (an elite unit of three hundred soldiers), stationed on the far right of the Theban line, met the Macedonian phalanx face on and died heroically; in his *Life of Alexander* (9) Plutarch reports that Alexander was the first to "break the line of" the Sacred Band. The widely known story that the 300 men of the Sacred Band all died where they stood, which Plutarch affirms, surely in-

12. The Lion Monument at Chaeronea
(*Wikimedia Commons photo by Philipp Pilhofer)*

dicates that this famous unit was surrounded. It's worth noting here that the famous "lion of Chaeroneia" (ill. 12) which traditionally marked the grave of the Sacred Band has been excavated, and under it were found 254 corpses, which seems to confirm that the Sacred Band was indeed surrounded and annihilated.

Putting all of this together, the most widely accepted account of the battle goes as follows. In Philip's system of battle it was the heavy cavalry who were the strike force charged with penetrating through gaps in the enemy line to attack the enemy from the rear. Though our inadequate accounts don't specifically mention cavalry in the battle, it seems likely that Alexander—who first broke through the enemy line followed by companions (*parastatai*)—was in command of the bulk of Philip's cavalry, evidently stationed on the left. Philip's problem in this battle was that both flanks of the opposing army were protected by natural obstacles—the River Cephisus on his left, Mount Thurion on his right—and so could not be out-flanked. In order to break through the enemy formation, it would be necessary to create a significant gap, therefore. The disparate units making up the opposing line of battle offered an opportunity. By staging a retreat on his right, with his highly disciplined and reliable *pezetairoi*, Philip drew the Athenians forward. As the allied troops in the southern Greek center strove to maintain contact with the advancing Athenians, and the troops on the left of the Theban force moved forward to maintain contact with the Greek center, the southern Greek line became stretched. Since the main Theban force, confronted by the unmoving Macedonian pike phalanx under Parmenio, could not advance, a gap eventually opened in the Theban line. This was the moment Alexander had been ordered to exploit: when he saw the gap, he and his cavalry charged through it and turned to attack the Theban right wing from behind. Most of the Theban force fled, while the surrounded Sacred Band made their heroic stand and died. When Philip saw that his stratagem had worked and that the southern Greek right was in flight, he stopped the retreat of his forces and led them in a relentless attack on the tired Athenians, which routed them and secured the Macedonian victory.

The system of battle thus revealed is a classic example of what is known as "sword and shield" tactics. The phalanx—large, formidable, and relatively slow moving—functioned as the "shield" in battle. It formed a massive front which the enemy had to confront, since they could not risk exposing their flank or rear to the Macedonian pikes, and thus it pinned the enemy in place. Special units, under special tactical plans, operated to try to disrupt the enemy line and create a gap. The heavy cavalry functioned as the "sword", driving through the gap created in the enemy line and turning to overwhelm the enemy, under concerted attack by the pike phalanx in front, by striking them from the side and from behind. The battalions of the phalanx had to operate together in unison, maintaining a solid front and asserting pressure on the enemy line at the opportune moment. Units detailed with special roles in the battle had to carry out those roles effectively and at the right time, to cause the disruptions in the enemy formation that the cavalry needed. And the cavalry, finally, had to charge at the right moment, when a suitable gap in the enemy formation had appeared; and having charged, it had to remember not to over pursue, but to turn against the main enemy formation from behind and secure the victory. This is a complex but highly effective system of battle, that relied above all on the different units and specialists in the army carrying out their different roles efficiently and with the right timing; that is, it relied on the commanders of the various units understanding the plan and ensuring that their units fulfilled their assigned tasks.

When we examine the battles of Alexander, we see that he followed his father's system of battle in each case. At the Granicus in 334, at Issus in 333, and at Gaugamela in 331, though with special adjustments to meet the needs of each location and occasion, Alexander's army operated according to Philip's design. The pike phalanx confronted the enemy and forced them to maintain their line opposed to the phalanx. Specialized units swept forward and harassed the enemy line, seeking to create disruptions and gaps in it between enemy units. And when such a gap had occurred, Alexander in command of the Macedonian cavalry would charge forward and through the gap, to turn and roll up the enemy line from the flank and rear. Alexander's battles thus confirm what we learn from our inadequate sources about Philip's system of battle, and illustrate the crucial importance of Philip's training system both for his soldiers and for their officers. It was Philip's army and officers which conquered the Persian Empire, though Alexander provided the charismatic leadership that was required to make the system work.

8. THE MACEDONIAN ARMY AND THE MACEDONIAN STATE

At the beginning of this chapter I asserted that the Macedonian army in effect owned or *was* the Macedonian state, and that Philip's army-building was therefore at the same time a state-building endeavor. It used to be widely believed, as noted in Chapter 1 and contrary to this, that there was a definable Macedonian state before the time of Philip, with a similarly definable constitution, of sorts. The idea was that the Macedonian state consisted of a "people under arms," that is that "the Macedonians" meant all the men of military age and status (capable of arming themselves and functioning as warriors); and that this "people under arms" functioned constitutionally as the selectors of their rulers via a process of assembly and acclamation, and as a kind of "supreme court," trying and adjudicating cases of high treason prosecuted by the king. Over the past few decades this notion of a Macedonian constitution before the time of Philip has been subjected to devastating critiques, and few historians now accept it. The plain fact is that there is no evidence of any Macedonian ruler being selected by his "people under arms" through a process of acclamation: the nearest example is the establishment of Alexander's half-brother Arrhidaeus as titular king in 323, with the throne name Philip after his father; but that happened under unique circumstances. In fact several Macedonian rulers came to power by violent usurpation, as we have seen. Nor is there any documented example of the "people under arms" trying cases of treason: the nearest example here is of Alexander the Great conducting several treason trials of very highly placed and popular officers before the assembled army, as a way of assuring the army of their guilt.

For the Macedonian people to function in some constitutional manner by assembling under arms, there had to be a unified Macedonian people with a common sense of identity and purpose; and there had to be a large mass of men who had arms and functioned as warriors; that is, there had to be a Macedonian army. As shown in Chapters 1 and 2, neither of these things existed before Philip: it was Philip who, as ruler, created a true Macedonian army including a disciplined infantry force, and it was Philip who unified Macedonia and created a strong sense of common identity and unity of purpose. In short, Philip created the Macedonian state.

Of course, there was before the time of Philip a Macedonian identity, a population who were referred to as Macedonians and who in some sense identified themselves as Macedonians; but that does not mean there was a Macedonian state. One might think of the German and Italian peoples before the mid-nineteenth century and their respective unifications into nation states; one might think of the Kurdish people today, sharing a common identity and language but divided up between four different states. Who exactly thought of themselves as Macedonians and/or were thought of as such by outsiders is very unclear before Philip's time, such was the disunity of Macedonia and its proneness to subdivision into multiple entities—e.g. Lyncus, Orestis, or Elimea as separate and independent entities—and such was Macedonia's openness to invasion by neighboring powers who occupied slices of what had been Macedonian territory. Macedonian identity was therefor mutable and insubstantial. There was a region called Macedonia whose exact extent varied considerably over time; and there were people called Macedonians at one time but not at another, and whose sense of Macedonian identity was not expressed by the kind of common social and political institutions that would permit us to refer to a Macedonian state.

Philip changed all this by creating the first large, well organized, well trained and disciplined, and thus truly effective Macedonian in-

fantry army. It is from Philip's time on that there was a distinctly Macedonian armament—the small Macedonian shield and the long Macedonian *sarissa*—and a distinctly Macedonian style of warfare that went
with it. And it was thus from Philip's time on that the Macedonian
shield and *sarissa* became symbols of Macedonian identity and pride.
Philip, that is, created the Macedonian "people under arms" in the act
of creating the Macedonian pike phalanx. It was successful service, year
after year, in Philip's phalanx that fostered in the Macedonian warrior
class developed by Philip a sense of unity, identity, and common purpose sufficient to form the basis of a national state. In addition his improvement and enlargement of the Macedonian cavalry made that
cavalry for the first time a truly Macedonian force, rather than an agglomeration of personal followings of landed aristocrats. Finally, it was
of course the victories won by this national Macedonian army that finally established a secure Macedonian territory, fully unified and able
to form the territorial basis of a Macedonian state.

The institutions and governing systems of the Macedonian state
were military. The districts of Macedonia were military recruitment districts; Macedonian citizenship was expressed through military service;
the Macedonian ruler was a military monarch who expressed his leadership above all through successful command of the army; and the elite
class of the new Macedonian state, the old aristocracy and the new
members added by Philip, was an officer class trained through an education system (*paideia*) that emphasized military and leadership skills
and loyalty to the military monarch. Under Philip and his successors
then, just as with Prussia under its Hohenzollern rulers, Macedonia was
an army that had a state, rather than a state that had an army.

A Byzantine encyclopedia of sorts, known as the *Suda*, preserves
a definition of *basileia* (kingship), clearly taken from a late fourth- or
early third-century BCE source, which is often quoted in reference to
Alexander's Successors:

> It is not descent (*phusis*) or legitimacy (*to dikaion*) which makes a king;
> it is the ability to lead armies well and handle affairs competently; this
> is seen by the examples of Philip and Alexander's Successors.

Oddly, though this passage directly references Philip, it is too rarely
brought up in connection with him. As the passage indicates, it was by

creating and leading an army successfully that Philip established his kingship and his claim to the loyalty of the Macedonian people, a people to whom he gave unity, stability, security, and prosperity by creating for them a successful military state. This is why, at Alexander's feast in Samarkand at the height of his power and success, the older officers like Cleitus the Black insisted that Philip was a greater ruler than his son; this is why, after Alexander's death, the Macedonian soldiery insisted on having Philip's other son Arrhidaeus, mentally deficient though he was, as their new king, and on re-naming him Philip to remind them of his great father. Philip was truly the father of his country.

CHAPTER 5

The Reign of Alexander

IN SPRING 336, PHILIP WAS AT THE HEIGHT OF HIS POWER AND SUCCESS. Everything he had hoped and planned for at the start of his rule in the winter of 360/59 had been achieved, and more. Macedonia was strong, stable, prosperous, and greatly enlarged; cities were growing, the Macedonian people were thriving, and the economy had developed greatly under his rule. The Balkan peninsula and its peoples, south of the River Danube, were either directly subordinated to Macedonian rule, or effectively under Macedonian domination, thus posing no threat to Macedonian security. And the cities and peoples of northern, central, and southern Greece had either been brought under Macedonian rule (Chalcidians and Thessalians), or brought into a grand alliance system with Macedonia as the dominant partner and Philip as acknowledged *Hegemon* (leader). The Macedonian army, through which all of this had been achieved, was larger and stronger than ever: the largest army by far in all of the Balkan and Greek world, and the most effectively armed, trained, and led. Philip was ready to transition to a new and even grander set of goals, a new phase of his career as ruler: he was ready to take on the Persian Empire and seek to expand Macedonian power and the Greek culture and language into western Asia. At the beginning of the spring, an advance force of some ten thousand men, predominantly mercenaries and commanded by Parmenio, had crossed the Hellespont into north-western Asia Minor and begun the process of establishing a bridgehead there for the crossing of the main Macedonian army led by Philip himself, planned to take place early enough in the summer to give Philip a sufficient campaigning season in Asia Minor.

While Parmenio was campaigning, winning the allegiance of the Greek coastal cities in Asia Minor as far south as Ephesus, Philip marked the success of his endeavors and transition to a new field of operations with a grand festival at the old Macedonian capital of Aegae, centered around the marriage of his and Olympias' daughter Cleopatra to the girl's uncle Alexander of Molossia. Part of the ceremony was a grand procession of part of Philip's army and statues of the gods to the theater of Aegae, where celebratory performances were to be staged. Philip marched at the end of the procession, flanked by his son Alexander and new son-in-law (and brother-in-law) Alexander. At the entrance to the theater, the two Alexanders preceded Philip inside, so the latter could make a splendid solo entrance as the leader and champion of the entire Greek world. Famously, as Philip finally moved forward alone, a disgruntled officer in his royal bodyguard named Pausanias, in pursuit of a personal grievance against Philip, dashed forward and stabbed him to death. So died Philip, the greatest ruler Macedonia had seen, at the very peak of his powers and at the relatively young age of about forty-seven (born around 383, died in early July 336). The assassin Pausanias was immediately pursued by others of Philip's royal guard, caught, and killed, making it impossible to learn whether he had acted alone or had confederates in some sort of conspiracy.

Naturally, conspiracy theories swirled around this abrupt assassination, and have continued to swirl ever since. The apparently official account—retailed by the historian Diodorus and in a more abbreviated version by Aristotle—is of a rather sordid homoerotic intrigue between Philip and two young men in his entourage, both named Pausanias. The story is, perhaps, a little too detailed and sordid to convince. Not unsurprisingly, since Alexander benefited by becoming king, rumors arose suggesting that he and/or his mother Olympias were behind Pausanias. On the other hand, Alexander himself arrested and executed two scions of the dynastic house of Lyncus—Arrhabaeus and Heromenes—as conspirators; but he may simply have been using the charge of complicity in Philip's death as an excuse to rid himself of two over-powerful aristocrats. The truth is, despite rivers of ink spilled discussing the issue, we shall never know more about Philip's death than that Pausanias killed him. With that we must rest content.

1. THE SUCCESSION OF ALEXANDER

In the chaotic upset at the great ruler's assassination, one man conspicuously kept his head: Philip's senior officer and right-hand man Antipater. He immediately grasped that the succession to the throne was now the most important matter and, gathering up Philip's bodyguards, he placed them protectively around Alexander and had him escorted to the safety of the nearby palace. There he summoned the chief Macedonian aristocrats who were present and presided over a meeting at which they proclaimed Alexander as the new ruler. Letters were despatched to Parmenio in Asia Minor, alerting him to the news, and Parmenio responded endorsing Alexander's succession to the throne. Thus, at the age of twenty, Alexander became the ruler of the Macedonians in succession to his great father Philip. This can have come as no surprise to anyone: Philip had been visibly and publicly grooming Alexander for the succession for at least the past seven years. When Alexander was thirteen, Philip hired the great philosopher Aristotle to come to Macedonia and undertake the education of Alexander and a chosen group of companions of Alexander's age; the princely sum Aristotle received for this three-year task enabled him to return to Athens and set up his famous school, the Lyceum (*Lykeion*) there. At sixteen, in 340, Alexander was appointed regent of Macedonia and placed in charge of the royal seal (that is, empowered to make official decisions) while Philip and his senior officers were absent campaigning at the Hellespont and Bosporus. In 338, when Alexander was eighteen, he was placed in command of the crucial Macedonian heavy cavalry at the battle of Chaeroneia, which cemented Philip's leadership of Greece: it was the charge of the Macedonian heavy cavalry led by Alexander which secured victory in this battle, as argued in Chapter 4 above. And at the great ceremony in 336 at which Philip was assassinated, finally, it was Alexander who—along with Philip's new son-in-law Alexander of Molossia—walked beside Philip in the grand procession, as we have just seen. All of this designated Alexander as Philip's chosen heir beyond question.

There had, it is true, beeen tensions between Philip and Alexander in the years leading up to 336. Our sources love to play up these tensions, usually to Alexander's credit and with a great deal of circumstantial detail that, if anything, undermines the credibility of the stories rather than enhancing it. These tensions first appeared, we are told, when Philip decided late in 338 to take a new young wife, his seventh. Unlike his previous six wives, all non-Macedonian ladies married to cement alliances of various sorts, this new wife—named either Cleopatra or Eurydice, in different sources—was a native Macedonian from the high aristocracy: her uncle and guardian was one of Philip's senior officers named Attalus. Romantic stories insist that the marriage was a love match between the aging king (he was in fact only about forty-five) and a pretty young girl. At the wedding feast there was a great deal of drinking, as was usual at Macedonian feasts, and at some point Attalus offered a toast wishing that the new bride might bear Philip legitimate children. Alexander apparently took exception to this toast and attempted to assault Attalus, with others including Philip drunkenly intervening.

A great deal has been made by some scholars of this event. Supposedly the Macedonian aristocracy despised Alexander for his half-Epirote birth (through his Molossian mother Olympias) and regarded only an heir born of a Macedonian mother as well as father as legitimate. This notion, however, runs foul of the fact that Philip himself was only half Macedonian: his mother Eurydice had been of Illyrian birth. Exactly how did Attalus and his aristocratic friends explain to Philip that only a prince of Macedonian birth on both sides could be a legitimate heir? This is nonsense. Others have suggested that Attalus was literally impugning Alexander's legitimacy: suggesting that Philip was not truly his father, Olympias having been unfaithful. But if that were so, why was Philip so visibly grooming Alexander for the succession? One must in fact recall what marriage in antiquity was about: not love and romance, but the begetting of children. As an anonymous Athenian orator famously put it (Ps. Demosthenes 59.122): "we keep courtesans (*hetairai*) for pleasure, concubines to take care of our daily physical needs, and wives to bear us legitimate children." Expressing the wish that the bride would bear her husband legitimate children was a completely normal and standard part of ancient Greek weddings: it was the wife's primary role. Philip had only two sons: Alexander himself and the mentally deficient Arrhidaeus. About to embark on a dangerous military campaign in which he himself and/or Alexander might easily die, Philip could certainly have used another son or two to help secure a legitimate line of succession.

The problem, that is to say, lay not with Attalus' toast, but with Alexander's reception of it. Exactly why Alexander flew into a violent rage at Attalus' words can only be conjectured: no doubt excessive drinking was in part to blame. Alexander was well known, like his father and the Macedonian aristocracy generally, for heavy drinking at *symposia*. And Alexander was extremely touchy about his personal honor, and prone to fly into violent rages if he felt slighted. The most infamous example of this came at a feast held at Samarkand in 327: a senior officer named Cleitus the Black, who had saved Alexander's life at the Battle of the Granicus, made some remarks to the effect that Philip was a greater ruler than Alexander, at which Alexander became so enraged that he snatched a spear from one of his bodyguards and murdered Cleitus with it on the spot. In the present case Alexander, doubtless very drunk, perceived some slight in Attalus' perfectly standard toast and flew at him; Philip understandably intervened to protect Attalus; and at this Alexander became so furious that he took his mother Olympias and decamped with her from Macedonia altogether. After a few weeks, or perhaps months, calmer heads prevailed: Alexander and Olympias were invited back to Macedonia, and Alexander's position as Philip's heir apparent was not affected.

He remained touchy, however, and renewed tensions quickly arose over a proposed marriage alliance later in 337. Pixodarus, the local dynast of Caria, who was at the same time recognized as governor of Caria by the Persian king, knew of Philip's plans to invade western Asia and made overtures to marry his daughter to a son of Philip, suggesting that he might be willing to switch sides and ally with Philip when the time came. Philip proposed that his son Arrhidaeus could marry Pixodarus' daughter, and when Alexander learned of this he again felt slighted and became furious. Through intermediaries, he instead offered himself to Pixodarus as a better match for his daughter; but when Philip heard about this he put a stop to the proposed match. The angry king explained to Alexander that he had no plan to marry his heir presumptive to the daughter of a mere Carian dynast, and instructed him to think things through before acting. A few of Alexander's friends, who had acted as intermediaries, were banished from Macedonia, and a chastened Alexander had to accept his father's criticism for spoiling a potentially useful alliance: Pixodarus now chose to marry his daughter to a Persian grandee instead. The point of both of these upsets is that they were born of Alexander's touchy and impetuous nature, and from the natural frictions between two very dominant personalities. Friction between fathers and teenage sons is in general a common phenomenon, even when the two men concerned do not have quite such outsize egos as Philip and Alexander. Far too much has in general been made of these upsets: at the end of the day Alexander was Philip's publicly ac-knowledged and groomed heir apparent, and he succeeded to the throne of Macedonia at once when Philip died, thanks to the immediate support of Philip's right-hand men Antipater and Parmenio, who knew quite well what Philip's plans and intentions were.

It is appropriate here to point up the contrast between the situations faced by Philip and Alexander when they each became ruler at very young ages: twenty-three or twenty-four in Philip's case, twenty in the case of Alexander. Philip took over in the aftermath of a terrible military disaster in which the Macedonian army had been largely wiped out; he had to deal with a Macedonia that had been chronically weak and disunited for decades at least, and which was at his succession under attack from all sides and seemingly on the verge of complete dissolution. Alexander, by contrast, inherited a strong and unified state, a loyal and obedient aris-tocracy and people, the best and largest army in the eastern Mediter-ranean region with an outstandingly trained officer corps, and a two-decade tradition of unbroken and unparalleled Macedonian success. In addition, Philip came to the throne unexpectedly, the youngest of three brothers with no particular preparation or training for a task of ruling he was never likely to have to take up; Alexander had the best training and grooming for the role of commanding and ruling that the ancient world could provide, at the hands of Aristotle, of Philip's right-hand men Antipater and Parmenio, and most crucially from Philip himself.

This is not to say that Alexander faced no difficulties in taking up the rule of his father's empire. Philip's nephew Amyntas, the son of his older brother and predecessor as Macedonian ruler Perdiccas III, was still alive and aged around thirty. He had been carefully raised by Philip almost as another son: after all, for the first ten or twelve years of his reign, until Alexander began to grow up and show his abilities, Amyntas was Philip's most natural successor should he die. At some point a few years before he died, Philip had married Amyntas to his oldest daughter Cynnane, from his Illyrian wife Audata; which meant that Amyntas' children would not only be Philip's great-nephews or nieces, but also his grandchildren. Amyntas, that is to say, was still very much part of the potential line of succession. As the son of a previous ruler and ap-parently impatient at his subordination, Amyntas decided not to wait. He challenged Alexander's claim to the succession, but received virtually no backing from the Macedonian aristocracy, who understandably followed Philip's intentions and Antipatros' lead in accepting Alexander as the new ruler. Amyntas was quickly hunted down and executed.

More serious challenges to Alexander's power came from outside, from non-Macedonian peoples. To the north of Macedonia the Balkan peoples had only been subordinated by long, arduous, and repeated campaigning under Philip. With Philip dead and Alexander a largely unknown quantity, it is no surprise that peoples like the Triballians and some of the Illyrians saw the chance to recover complete freedom. Alexander reacted swiftly. He led his army on an armed march through Thrace, cowing the Thracians, and into Triballian territory along the Danube. The Triballians were forced to submit, and Alexander crossed the Danube on ships that had sailed up the river from the Black Sea to join him, in order to stage a military demonstration among the Scythian tribes north of the great river. Re-crossing to the southern side, he swiftly marched west into Illyrian lands, where the demonstration of Macedonian military efficiency quoted in the previous chapter, along with some small-scale fighting, taught the Illyrians to accept the new ruler and keep quiet.

In southern Greece, meanwhile, embassies had flown to and fro debating the wisdom of a rebellion against Macedonian domination. The Thebans were all for it, but sensibly preferred not to act alone; they wanted other Greek city-states to join them, especially the Athenians. The lesson of Chaeroneia was too recent, however: the Athenians preferred to watch and wait, with even the anti-Macedonian Demosthenes counseling caution. In the event, the Thebans acted alone, spurred on by false rumors that the Macedonians had suffered a reverse in Illyria and Alexander was dead. In spring of 335, Alexander moved south through Thessaly at the head of a large army and invaded Boeotia. The Thebans preferred not to try battle against a greatly superior force; they pulled their population behind the defensive walls of the city of Thebes and prepared to withstand a siege. Unfortunately for the Thebans, the siege did not last long: an unwise sortie by Theban forces was repelled and, in the confusion, Macedonian infantry commanded by the phalanx officer Perdiccas forced their way through an open gate and into the city along with the fleeing Thebans. Thebes was captured, and Alexander decided to make an example of the city: he wanted no more trouble from southern Greece during his planned eastern campaigns. The men of Thebes were slaughtered, and the women and children were sold into slavery. The city was destroyed and its lands parceled out among the other cities of Boeotia. Thebes, one of the oldest and most famous cities of Greece, ceased to exist. Thoroughly cowed by this act of terror, the other southern Greek states, meeting at Corinth, accepted Alexander as their leader in succession to his father Philip, and renewed their commitment to join the Macedonians in war against the Persians. The story of Alexander's war to conquer the Persian Empire has been written up in every way, from the sober to the fantastical, from the adulatory to the debunking, and everything in between. In view of the dozens of recent full-length accounts on offer, it can be treated relatively briefly here.

2. Alexander's Conquests

Alexander is remembered, indeed world-famous, as one of history's great conquerors. In his rather brief reign of thirteen years—from 336 until his early death in 323—he conquered all of western Asia from the Mediterranean Sea to the Hindu Kush mountains and the Indus River valley, and from the southern shores of the Black and Caspian seas to the Indian Ocean and the Persian Gulf, and also forayed into north Africa to add Egypt to his conquests. That sounds very impressive, but there is another way to put it which sounds a bit less so. In a grand ten-year campaign Alexander *and his army* took control of the Persian Empire away from the traditionally ruling Achaemenid royal family and Persian elite, and extended the empire a little in the region of modern-day Pakistan. This is, I suggest, the truer way of stating Alexander's achievement. He could have done nothing without the magnificent army he inherited from his father, and it was that army as much as or more than Alexander which did the conquering. And if you want to conquer an empire, the easiest way to do so is to find an existing empire and take it over: the hard work of subjecting varied peoples by military force and making them accept their subordination and fiscal exploitation has already been done. All you need to do is defeat the army or armies of the governing power; the subject peoples of the empire will by and large accept the change of rulers, because it makes little difference to them who receives their taxes or gives the orders, so long as the taxes do not go up and the orders are not too onerous.

In the spring of 334, Alexander crossed over from the European to the Asian shore of the Hellespont (Dardanelles) at the head of a large invasion force, some forty thousand strong. About half of this army was Macedonian; the rest was a mix of southern Greek allies and mercenaries, and forces drawn from the Balkan peoples to the north and east of Macedonia. After Alexander himself, the most important leaders in the army were Parmenio, who was the second-in-command of the expedition; and Parmenio's sons Philotas and Nicanor who commanded, respectively, the Macedonian heavy cavalry (eighteen hundred strong) and the elite infantry guard formerly named the *pezetairoi*, now renamed the *hypaspistai* (three thousand strong). At some time before crossing into Asia, Alexander had renamed his key Macedonian forces in a ploy intended to boost morale and loyalty to himself. The evidence is a passage preserved from the history of Anaximenes of Lampsacus, quoted in Chapter 4: whereas under Philip the term *hetairoi* (companions) referred to the closest associates of the king, about eight hundred in number, Alexander extended the term to refer to all of the Macedonian heavy cavalry; and whereas *pezetairoi* (foot companions) had been the name of the elite royal infantry guard unit, Alexander extended that name to all soldiers of the Macedonian pike phalanx (though we also later hear of some battalions using the mysterious name *asthetairoi*). The aim, specifically cited by Anaximenes, was that "sharing in the royal companionship (*hetaireia*), they should remain most devoted."

The main part of the goal of winning control of the Persian Empire was accomplished in three great battles fought in a four-year span: the Battle of the Granicus, fought in north-western Asia Minor in the early summer of 334; the Battle of Issus, fought in north-west Syria in the late summer of 333; and the Battle of Gaugamela, fought in northern Mesopotamia (Iraq) in the summer of 331. In addition to these three great battles, Alexander also conducted a few sieges, particularly the siege of Halicarnassus in south-west Asia Minor in the summer of 334, and the epic seven-month siege of Tyre in Phoenicia (modern Lebanon) in late 333. He also invaded Egypt in 332 and received its surrender: the Egyptians hated the Persians, who had only reconquered Egypt in 343 after more than fifty years of Egyptian independence, and they welcomed Alexander as a savior. After 331, the bulk of the Persian Empire accepted Alexander as its ruler. It took a couple of years of campaigning in Bactria and Sogdia (modern Afghanistan) to bring the eastern part of the Persian Empire under his control. He then passed through the Khyber Pass in 327 and entered north-west India (modern Pakistan) where he defeated the armies of the local rulers, especially that of Porus. The battle of the Hydaspes against the army of Porus ranks as the fourth of Alexander's great battles. In 325, under pressure from his army, Alexander reluctantly left India and turned back westwards, returning to Iran in 324, and Mesopotamia in 323, where he died at Babylon in mid-summer.

In order to bolster his position as the new ruler of Macedonia, Alexander spent lavishly on gifts for the Macedonian elite and soldiery, and we hear as a result that when he crossed into Asia Minor in 334 his treasury was nearly empty and he had with him only a month's pay for his army. This meant that he urgently needed to win control of territory in Asia Minor from which he could obtain funds and supplies to keep his army going. Even if substantial funds and supplies had been available in Macedonia for his use, they could not easily have been forwarded to him: bulk transport in antiquity went overwhelmingly by sea, and a large Persian fleet controlled the sea and its shipping lanes. As a result, Alexander needed to fight and win a battle as soon as possible to give him control of territory. Initial opposition to Alexander's invasion was in the hands of the local Persian governors of Asia Minor, who had concentrated their regional forces into a united army near the Hellespont, on the east bank of the small River Granicus. To aid in seeing off Alexander's invasion, the Persian king Darius III had sent to join the satraps (governors) a substantial force of Greek mercenary hoplites (reputedly twenty thousand men, though the number seems exaggerated) under an excellent Greek general—Memnon of Rhodes—who was to act as military advisor to the Persian satraps.

Memnon understood the reality of Alexander's situation—his need to fight a battle soon to win territory and booty—and advised the Persians to avoid battle at all costs, adopting instead a "scorched earth" strategy. The Persian force should leave the Granicus and march inland, into the interior of Asia Minor, drawing Alexander and his army after them. As they marched, the Persians should remove all supplies, burn farms and settlements, and poison wells and springs, leaving so far as possible nothing for Alexander's army to eat and drink. Meanwhile light and highly mobile cavalry and infantry forces should harass Alexander's column of march, and any foraging parties he sent out to seek supplies. After a month or so of this treatment, Memnon suggested, it might be time to engage Alexander's exhausted and demoralized army in battle, on suitably advantageous ground. The response of the Persian grandees was to the effect that the Persians were not in the habit of fleeing from their enemies, of avoiding a fight, of destroying their own lands. As a proud conquering people, the Persians were determined to fight, and believed in their ability to win. Thus Alexander got exactly what he wanted and needed: as he approached the River Granicus from the west, he found the army of regional Persian forces there awaiting him. Victory over this one force, since it was made up of the collected security forces of the provinces of Asia Minor, would effectively open all of Asia Minor up to his occupation.

The battle was a rather straightforward affair. The Persians drew up their forces on the eastern bank of the river, challenging Alexander and his men to attack through and across the stream bed, a potentially tricky undertaking. But the Persians made a fundamental error in the disposition of their forces, which greatly eased Alexander's task. Distrusting Memnon and his Greek mercenaries, they stationed them as a kind of reserve well to the rear of the line of battle; and in order to attack Alexander's army as it struggled up, in considerable disarray as they hoped, from the stream bed, they stationed their best troops—their cavalry—right on the eastern bank of the river. But holding ground and fighting an enemy force from a standing position is what heavily armed infantry are good at; cavalry fight best in motion, charging at or around the enemy. The Persian disposition of forces was thus exactly the opposite of what it should have been: the Greek mercenary hoplites should have held the river bank and disputed the crossing, with cavalry stationed to the rear to charge at any enemy forces who broke through or got around the infantry. Commanding the Macedonian heavy cavalry on the right, Alexander instructed the battalion commanders of his phalanx to lead their troops across the stream as best they could, covered on the left flank by allied Thessalian cavalry under Parmenio. Meanwhile detachments of light cavalry, and of archers and slingers, made their way across the stream in front of Alexander to harass the enemy line. As Alexander surveyed the situation, he noticed a gravel slope that made a part of the river bank easy to mount, and concentrated his harassing forces there. Before long, they succeeded in disrupting the enemy line at that point enough to make a cavalry charge feasible, and Alexander led a charge across the river, up the gravel slope, and into the enemy line, where he turned in towards the enemy center and began to roll up their line of battle.

In this way a crushing victory was achieved by Alexander's forces in short order. As the Persian line of battle fell into disorder under Alexander's attack, the phalanx battalions and supporting Thessalian cavalry got across the stream, up the bank, and began to support Alexander and the Macedonian cavalry. The only moment of anxiety came when Alexander was hit on the head by a sword blow from a Persian cavalryman. Though his helmet saved his life, part of it was sheared off by the heavy blow and, as Alexander killed the cavalryman who had attacked him, another Persian darted forward to strike Alexander's now unprotected head. Alexander was saved from near certain death by the swift action of the commander of his royal cavalry squadron, Cleitus the Black, who intervened in the nick of time, hacking at the arm of the Persian and sending his blow awry. The Persian cavalry, attacked from the side by Alexander's cavalry and from in front by the pike phalanx, broke and fled; and the Greek mercenaries in the rear were surrounded and for the most part killed. Memnon got away with a few Persian leaders and some thousands of men, and fled south, eventually occupying the well fortified Greek city of Halicarnassus and making a stand there, hoping to hold out until Persian reinforcements could reach him. All of Asia Minor was open to Alexander. He pursued Memnon and his forces down the Aegean coast, sending detachments of troops out to receive the surrender of local cities and communities, Greek and non-Greek, until he reached Halicarnassus, which he besieged and captured after heavy fighting. Alexander then spent the autumn and winter months marching in a grand arcing campaign through southern and central Asia Minor, doing only minor fighting but receiving the surrender of the local communities and territories. In spring of 333 he reached Cilicia, the region of Asia Minor bordering Syria, having left behind the senior commander Antigonus the One-Eyed in charge of central Asia Minor (Phrygia) with orders to complete the pacification of the region.

In Cilicia Alexander learned that the Persian king Darius III was approaching through Syria with a large army, the Persian royal army,

13. The Alexander Mosaic in the Archaeological Museum, Naples
(*Wikimedia Commons photo by Magrippa at the English language Wikipedia*)

intending to engage the Macedonian forces and drive them back out of
Asia. Darius brought with him his entire household, including his principal wife, children, and concubines, and a great treasure, all of which
he stationed at Damascus. From there he marched north to confront
Alexander and succeeded in slipping past Alexander and his army,
cutting him off from his lines of communication back to Asia Minor.
Forced to turn about and face north, Alexander confronted Darius' significantly larger army near the small town of Issus, at the River Pinarus
(most likely the modern Payas, near Iskenderun in southern Turkey).
Like the Persian commanders at the Granicus, Darius drew up his forces
on the bank of the stream, challenging Alexander and his army to attack across and through the stream bed. Alexander, again, accepted the
challenge. As the pike phalanx fought its way up the opposing bank of
the stream against stiff opposition, especially from Darius' Greek mercenaries, Alexander himself—stationed as ever on the right at the head
of the Macedonian heavy cavalry—charged into the enemy line and
turned inward, driving towards the Persian center where Darius himself
was stationed. Darius had acquired a reputation as a bold and valiant
warrior during campaigns he had fought in Bactria, when he was just
a distant cousin of the ruling king; he now put that reputation to shame
by fleeing precipitately at the sight of Alexander's charge towards him.
The scene is likely depicted in the famous Alexander Mosaic (ill. 13).
Though the battle in general was not going so badly for the Persians,

the king's flight changed everything: the Persian center collapsed and followed their fleeing king, and the battle was lost.

The aftermath of the battle was striking in two ways. In pursuing Darius, Alexander and his cavalry prevented the king from returning to Damascus and instead reached that city themselves, there finding and becoming masters of the Persian royal treasury and harem. The capture of Darius' family, including his mother, principal wife, and children, was a striking coup for Alexander. We hear of a remarkable scene in which Alexander, apprised of the presence of the royal family, went to visit Darius' ladies accompanied by his longtime friend and lover Hephaestion. Since Alexander at this time still dressed and comported himself in the casual, everyday style of a Macedonian ruler, it was not immediately clear to Darius' mother Sisygambis which of the two Macedonian officers she saw before her was Alexander. Making an understandable mistake, the old lady bowed to the taller and more striking Hephaestion, rather than to the short and boyish Alexander. He took this error in good part, reassuring the mortified queen that the trusted and beloved Hephaestion was "Alexander too."

More significantly, since the two armies had, before the battle, bypassed each other and fought facing towards their own territories, when the bulk of the Persian army turned to flight after the collapse of their center, they fled backward into Asia Minor, the region just conquered by Alexander, rather than into the heart of the Persian Empire. Gathering in large numbers in Cappadocia, which Alexander had not entered let alone conquered, these Persian forces decided to stage a counter-attack into central and western Asia Minor, to re-conquer the region and, perhaps, link up with the Persian fleet on the Aegean coast, which was staging its own counter-attacking operations in the Aegean. That created a very dangerous and difficult situation for Alexander's governor on the spot, Antigonus the One-Eyed, who had to find a way to cope with this counter-attack by greatly superior forces. Despite his inadequate forces, Antigonus succeeded—in a campaign of swift movement and maneuver—in taking on and defeating the enemy piecemeal, in three separate victorious battles. It seems the Persians helped him out by dividing their force into three, invading along three routes to overwhelm the enemy, but giving Antigonus the chance to beat them in detail. Alexander's trust in him was vindicated.

The Persian fleet in the Aegean remained a problem, as sea-borne communications with Macedonia became more necessary the further Alexander advanced south. Though Alexander had no fleet to engage the Persian fleet, there was a solution open to him, and he took it. The bulk of the Persian fleet came from the ancient maritime cities of Phoenicia, on the coast of modern Lebanon. Alexander reasoned that by capturing these cities, the home bases of the Persian fleet, he would oblige the fleet to become his, and that is in fact what happened. Of the great Phoenician cities, only Tyre offered serious resistance: the city was located on an offshore island, and its inhabitants evidently supposed that without ships Alexander could not harm them. Over the course of seven months in late 333 to early 332, Alexander had a causeway built connecting Tyre to the mainland. Once it was complete, his army attacked Tyre like any other city, and captured it. With Phoenicia his, the Persian fleet become Alexander's too. He seems to have decommissioned most of it for the time being. His own much smaller Macedonian fleet, along with southern Greek allied contingents, was more reliable and quite sufficient for his purposes in overseeing the Aegean and the shipping lanes back to Macedonia. Meanwhile, Alexander had other business: he marched on south, capturing Gaza after a siege, and entering Egypt to add it to his empire. As noted above, the great unpopularity of the Persians in Egypt meant that Alexander had no difficulty in taking over there, being welcomed as something of a savior and readily acknowledged as pharaoh. He left behind a local Greek, Cleomenes from the old Greek port city of Naucratis on the Canopic mouth of the Nile, to oversee Egypt and the gathering of the tribute monies from that wealthy country.

With his army, Alexander returned to Syria, where he received an embassy from Darius. The Persian king was much struck by the two defeats his armies had undergone, and concerned about the fate of his family and harem. He reputedly offered Alexander peace terms: if Alexander would return to Darius the royal harem unharmed, Darius would acknowledge Alexander as ruler of all lands west of the Euphrates—that is, he would accept the loss of the lands Alexander had already conquered and make peace on the basis of the *status quo*. We are told that Parmenio, Philip's old marshal and Alexander's second-in-command, strongly advised him to accept these terms, saying that he would do so if he were Alexander. The point here is that Asia Minor, Syria/Palestine, and Egypt together constituted very large, populous, and wealthy lands that needed to be carefully organized and administered to form an empire under Macedonian control. Opened up to Greek colonization, they could become home to dozens if not hundreds of new Greek cities, relieving population stress in the southern Balkan region and being fully integrated economically, culturally, and militarily into an empire of the eastern Mediterranean region that made sound strategic, logistical, and fiscal sense. Parmenio's advice may well represent the plan of empire that animated Philip's projected conquering mission in western Asia, as has often been noted. But Alexander's reply was to the effect that if he were Parmenio he would accept too (this was meant disparagingly), but as Alexander nothing less than the entire Persian Empire was sufficient to his conquering spirit. Darius' terms were rejected, and Alexander prepared his army for the invasion of Mesopotamia and Iran.

Darius had not counted on his peace offer being accepted, and was himself preparing the largest army his resources could muster. The two armies came together near the city of Arbela (Arbil) in northern Mesopotamia, on the east bank of the River Tigris. By the village of Gaugamela there lay a vast flat plain, dusty and salty, where Darius decided to make his stand, not far from the modern city of Mosul. He would no longer rely on stream beds or other natural obstacles as defenses against Alexander's attack: he proposed to overwhelm Alexander's army by sheer numbers in a place that offered no chance of tactical tricks or stratagems. He had gathered the forces of the eastern half of the Persian Empire—the Iranian and Bactrian lands—to create a great army whose main strength was in cavalry. Numbers given by our sources are so exaggerated that any modern estimate is hypothetical; but it is clear from the course of the battle that his army outnumbered Alexander's very considerably, perhaps by fifty percent or more. As was the Persian custom, Darius himself was stationed in the center of his army with the royal guard around him, bolstered by his remaining Greek mercenaries. To either side were vast contingents of cavalry: on his right Syrian and Mesopotamian troops along with Medians and Parthians; on his left his best cavalry, drawn from Bactria and Sogdia, along with Sacas, Massagetae, and others. In front of his line Darius stationed two hundred scythed chariots: his hope was that charges by these chariots could create gaps in Alexander's formation which his cavalry could charge at and exploit for victory.

When Alexander arrived at Gaugamela and surveyed Darius' army, he realized that in the battle to come his army was bound to be out-flanked: the enemy numbers were so great that he could only have matched the length of their front by thinning out his own formations dangerously. Instead of doing this, he drew up his best troops, the phalanx of Macedonian pikemen and *hypaspistai*, the Macedonian heavy cavalry, and the Thessalian cavalry, in the usual formation: the phalanx in the center with the Macedonian cavalry on the right and the Thessalians on the left. To counteract the effect of possible out-flanking and resultant attack from the rear, he drew up a second phalanx behind his Macedonian phalanx: the southern Greek hoplites, allied and mercenary, with instructions to be prepared to about-face and make a front to the rear if necessary. Specialized light infantry forces were stationed in echelon between the two phalanxes, covering the gap between them, and light cavalry forces screened the flanks of the heavy cavalry on either side. When drawn up, Alexander's right wing was initially out-flanked by the Bactrian and other cavalry on the Persian left, with the Macedonian cavalry facing Darius' center head on. This was not Alexander's plan, however: he wanted to confront the Persian left, create a gap between it and the Persian center, and exploit that gap. He preferred that his army should be out-flanked on the left, where the Thessalian cavalry under Philip son of Menelaus and phalanx battalions led by Craterus and Simmias were stationed under the overall command of Parmenio. As he marched his army forward, therefore, Alexander moved it diagonally to the right, until Bactrian and Saca cavalry moved forward to prevent him out-flanking them. Parmenio and his forces on the Macedonian left confronted a massive out-flanking Persian force: they were to hold their ground as long as they could, while Alexander won the battle.

The battle began with the charge of Darius' scythed chariots, which utterly failed to achieve anything: a screen of Agrianian javelineers drawn up in advance of Alexander's line succeeded in killing most of the horses and immobilizing the chariots. Light cavalry units charged on the right, engaging the cavalry on the far left of the Persian line.

Alexander gradually fed more light cavalry into this fight, which caused more and more of the Bactrian cavalry to move left to join in the fight too. As a result, a gap opened between the Persian left and center, into which Alexander charged with his heavy cavalry, turning in towards the Persian center and fighting his way towards Darius. As at Issus, when Darius saw the Macedonian heavy cavalry under Alexander moving inexorably towards where he was stationed in his royal chariot, his nerve broke and he turned to flight, causing the collapse of the Persian center. Alexander was eager to engage Darius in person, to kill or capture him, and pursued enthusiastically, considering victory his. But meanwhile his own left wing under Parmenio was under extreme pressure. Drastically out-flanked by vastly superior forces, Parmenio had drawn the Thessalian cavalry and supporting phalanx battalions into a defensive mass and worked to hold them steady. The Persian commander on the right, Mazaeus, sent forces around Parmenio's troops to attack Alexander's camp, and to attack Alexander's phalanx from behind. They were thwarted there by Alexander's reserve phalanx of Greek hoplites, but the situation on the left grew desperate. After holding out as long as he could, Parmenio observed the collapse of the Persian center and sent a messenger to Alexander, to remind him of the need to relieve his left wing. That message turned Alexander back from his pursuit of Darius, to attack the Persian right wing from behind and force them into flight, cementing his victory.

Our sources insist on Alexander's desire to catch up with Darius, his frustration at Parmenio's message calling him back, and suggest that Parmenio was over-cautious and irresolute in not handling the fight on the left on his own. That is clearly a libel on the old marshal. The truth is that Parmenio and his men had performed marvelously, tasked with the most difficult and dangerous part of the battle by far. Had they failed to hold out, Alexander's victory in the center would have been negated by Persian victory on his left, and the undefeated Bactrian cavalry on the Persian left might even have tipped the scale of battle Persia's way. As it was, Parmenio did hold out long enough, and his message to Alexander reminded the king just in time that victory depended on driving off the Persian right and saving his own left wing, not on confronting Darius in person. Darius thus escaped, pausing at his base at Arbela only long enough to change into traveling gear and obtain a fast horse. The Bactrian cavalry on the Persian left retreated from the battle under Darius' cousin Bessus, the satrap of Bactria, undefeated so far as their own fight was concerned, and furious at Darius for causing the Persian defeat. They caught up with the king in his flight and placed him under arrest, Bessus assuming the kingship in his place. Many of the troops on the Persian right also escaped unscathed under their commander Mazaeus. He led them around Alexander's army and south to the relative safety of Babylon. Alexander and his army remained victorious on the field of battle, a victory for which Parmenio, it must be said, deserves as much credit as Alexander himself.

After the battle Alexander and his army marched south. Mazaeus and his forces at Babylon represented the most proximate threat, and taking over southern Mesopotamia would strengthen his position. Mazaeus surrendered without a fight, offering his services to Alexander as the new king. This was to set a trend: the elites of the empire, including the Persian elite, could see the writing on the wall. Alexander and his Macedonian army now ruled western Asia, and the only prospect for any sort of comfortable future was to make terms with that new reality. Mazaeus' offer of service was accepted: when Alexander left Babylon in the fall of 331, Mazaeus remained as satrap of Babylonia, though with Macedonian military commanders to support and supervise him. Alexander proceeded onward to the great capital of the Persian Empire at Susa, with its immense treasuries that must be secured: an officer named Philoxenus had been sent on ahead and had already secured the co-operation of the Persian governor there. On his way to Susa Alexander received a mass of fresh recruits from Macedonia to replace his losses in the campaigning so far, and he then moved on into Persia itself, to the ancient Persian capital of Persepolis.

While Alexander was thus engaged, trouble had arisen back in Europe: the governor of Thrace, Memnon, rebelled against the regent Antipater; and in southern Greece the Spartan ruler Agis III organized a rebellion against the Macedonians by many of the Peloponnesian states. Antipater had little difficulty bringing Memnon to heel; the southern Greek rebellion was a more serious matter, especially since Antipater had recently despatched around fifteen thousand soldiers as reinforcements to Alexander. Nevertheless Antipater managed to raise an army of some forty thousand men, and in 330 he entered the Peloponnese and brought the much smaller army of Agis—a little over twenty thousand it seems—to battle at Megalopolis. Though the Spartans fought heroically, the outcome was not in doubt: Antipater's army won a complete victory, and the numerous Spartan dead represented a crushing blow to Sparta from which it was not to recover for a century. Alexander had sent some three thousand talents from the Persian treasury to help Antipater, which was no doubt welcome though it arrived only after the fighting was over: money was always welcome to assist in the post-war resettlement of Greece. When told of Antipater's victory, Alexander snidely dismissed it as "a battle of mice." The ever touchy king could not stand to have any comparison to his own victories. The reference was no doubt to Homer: whereas Alexander's own victories were truly epic and reminiscent of the *Iliad*, Antipater's resembled the mock-epic *Batrachomyomachia* (battle of the frogs and mice) also attributed to Homer.

Alexander's forces seem to have entered Persis at the high pass known as the Tang-i Mohammed Reza, where a large force of Persians awaited him: the Persians were not going to surrender their homeland without a fight. Local prisoners, however, apprised Alexander of an alternative route by which he was able to lead forces on a flanking maneuver and attack the Persians from two sides. His victory was overwhelming, and the Persians put up no further fight, Persepolis opening its gates to him peacefully. The reality was that, though the Persians were splendid fighters, their equipment and system of warfare made them no match for the Macedonian pike phalanx and heavy cavalry designed by Philip. The army stayed in Persis for the winter, waiting for the spring thawing of the mountain passes. At some point during the winter, after getting thoroughly drunk at a feast, Alexander led a party of revelers in the burning and looting of the royal palaces at Persepolis, an action he reputedly regretted in the sober light of dawn. The vast royal treasure at Persepolis was collected on wagons and sent off to be stored and/or distributed elsewhere, for a variety of purposes.

Darius had wintered in the old Median capital of Ecbatana in northern Iran, along with Bessus and the forces from the eastern satrapies. When news arrived in spring 330 that Alexander was moving north to confront them, they fled eastwards towards Bactria. Learning on his march that Bessus and Darius had fled eastward with the royal treasure from Ecbatana, Alexander ignored the Median capital, sending Parmenio to occupy it, and set off in swift pursuit with his most mobile forces, including the *hypaspistai* and the Agrianians. Among the Persians there was dissension: the eastern satraps acknowledged Bessus as the new ruler; a few loyalists, most notably the western satrap Artabazus and some Greek mercenaries who had remained with the king, still clung to Darius. Many of the soldiers in the small force simply defected as they learned of Alexander's inescapable pursuit. Darius was first placed in chains; then news of Alexander's approach with a large force of cavalry led the eastern satraps to mortally stab the ex-king, and flee onward to Bactria with Bessus as their new king. Artabazus and the Greek mercenaries split away north-westward toward the El-burz region. Alexander caught up with Darius at last only shortly after the king had expired. The chase was over. Of the Persian Empire only the eastern satrapies, Bactria being by far the largest and most important, remained as yet unconquered. Parmenio's position in Media was regularized: he was made its governor with oversight of the Iranian lands, and he never saw Alexander again. Freed of the perhaps somewhat oppressive presence of his father's old marshal, Alexander promoted Craterus to be effectively his military second-in-command, and decided he could not rest until the entire Persian Empire was his. Despite the reluctance expressed by many of his soldiers in a near rebellion, Alexander insisted that the campaign must continue until at least Bactria was conquered. And so the army moved further east.

The conquest of Bactria and the surrounding satrapies proved no easy matter. It had taken Alexander four years to conquer the western and central portions of the empire; it took almost as long to conquer the lands that now make up Afghanistan: 330 to 327. Bessus and the other eastern leaders realized it would be folly to engage Alexander's army in battle. Instead they turned to what today would be called guerrilla tactics. Alexander was obliged to divide and re-divide his forces to take the Bactrian lands valley by valley, often having to double back to re-take a previously conquered valley that rebelled as soon as his forces moved on. It was hard, dangerous, exhausting work, and the Macedonian losses were relatively heavy. But Alexander was relentless. It was during this Afghan campaign that two of Alexander's most notorious crimes occurred, which illustrated his increasing tendency to cruelty and autocracy. A minor conspiracy of officers supposedly hoping to assassinate Alexander was brought to light, and it was alleged that Parmenio's son Philotas—Craterus' chief rival in the army now Parmenio himself had been left behind—had known about it but failed to report it. Details are obscured by the fact that our sources are all visibly tainted by anti-Philotas prejudice. At any rate, Craterus persuaded Alexander to arrest Philotas and torture him. After a show trial in front of a few thousand gathered Macedonian soldiers, the broken Philotas was stoned to death. Swift riders were sent to Media to order the execution (murder in effect) of the wholly innocent Parmenio too: he could not be allowed to live on after his son's execution. As Antipater is said to have muttered when news of Parmenio's death reached Macedonia: "If Parmenio was disloyal, then who can be trusted? If he was not, then what is to be done?" Every senior Macedonian leader had to wonder about his own safety now. To drive the point home, Alexander the survivor of the three Lyncestian brothers—it will be recalled that the elder two were executed by Alexander at the start of his reign—was now also summarily executed. Alexander had never trusted him.

The second great crime has already been mentioned: the murder of Cleitus the Black, commander of the royal squadron of the Companion Cavalry, who had saved Alexander's life at the battle of the Granicus. Alexander was drunk again, during a great feast at Marakanda (Samarkand) in eastern Bactria, when this murder occurred, the occasion being Cleitus' defiant defense of Philip as a greater ruler than Alexander. Some may see drunkenness as some sort of excuse; but though intoxication lowers the inhibitions, it surely only reveals what is in a man's character when the normal civilized restraints are off. From this point on Alexander became increasingly intolerant and harsh. He adopted elements of Persian royal dress and ceremony, demanding that all who approached him must perform the ritual obeisance of *proskynesis* (bowing to the ground), which Macedonians and other Greeks found deeply humiliating. In the end, opposition led by Callisthenes forced Alexander to relent on this, but he never forgave Callisthenes, who was later arrested at the time of the "conspiracy of the *paides*" and caused to disappear. Stories of his fate vary, but most agree that he died a cruel and lingering death.

Eventually, of course, opposition to Alexander's rule over Bactria was overcome. Bessus was captured and brutally executed, and Alexander was left as acknowledged ruler over the entire Persian Empire. To cement the good will of the now pacified Bactrian barons, Alexander married the daughter of one of the most powerful of them: Roxane, daughter of Oxyartes. By the spring of 327 Alexander was ready to move on, but he did not turn back westward, as the army hoped. Instead he passed south through the Khyber Pass to continue conquering in north India, even beyond the Persian Empire. It was apparently Alexander's aim to conquer all of Asia to the great surrounding ocean: little did he know of the huge interior spaces of central Asia, and the vast Chinese lands beyond. In north India, in the valley of the River Indus, Alexander found a group of principalities at war with each other. The greatest of them, around the rivers Hydaspes and Hyphasis, was ruled by a king named Porus. Nearer to the Khyber Pass a group of smaller rulers had allied together under one Taxiles, who saw in Alexander's army an opportunity to break the power of Porus. Taxiles surrendered to Alexander, agreed to become a governor under him, and provided him with crucial intelligence about Porus and his forces.

Alerted concerning Alexander's approach, Porus had gathered his army on the south-east bank of the River Hydaspes, which was in full flood as it was the rainy season. Since the numbers in our sources are unreliable, we cannot say exactly how large Porus' army was, but it was a considerable one, and he had eighty-five war elephants, the first such force Alexander had encountered. Alexander faced two problems: how to get his army across the river safely, and how to deal with the elephants. The Hydaspes was not, in its flood, a river that could be forded in the face of enemy opposition. If Alexander had been willing to wait a few months, until the dry season, the river would have become fordable; but waiting was not his style. Alexander split his forces, and for a week or two had units march by night to different spots along the river bank and stage noisy demonstrations, causing Porus to send forces to confront what seemed to be an attempt to cross. No attempt to cross was made, and inevitably Porus' forces wearied of these pointless night marches. When Alexander judged that the enemy was sufficiently softened up, he split his army into three. The main force—hypaspists, several phalanx battalions, and the heavy cavalry—he led quietly to a spot where several

14. Coin of Alexander showing the king on horseback attacking Porus on an elephant
(*Wikimedia Commons public domain image from PHGCOM*)

islands in the stream covered his actions, and there embarked his forces on river boats and got them safely across. A large force of mercenaries staged a diversion elsewhere along the bank. Craterus, with a mixed force of pike battalions and cavalry, stayed at the camp with orders to cross if/when Porus' army moved away and he heard a battle starting. This worked perfectly: Alexander got his main force across under cover of night and advanced to engage Porus' army, and Craterus crossed to attack Porus' army from behind once the battle had started.

As to the elephants, Alexander had already learned about these beasts and their military weaknesses. Unlike a horse, which can be mounted and ridden by any competent rider, an elephant can only be controlled by a human it has bonded with, known in Hindi as its *mahout*. Kill or incapacitate the *mahout*, and the elephant becomes uncontrollable. Consequently, Alexander's men had been prepared in advance not to be terrified of the elephants: they were to stab upwards with their pikes at the *mahout* on the elephant's neck, and/or at the faces of the elephants. Javelineers and archers were to concentrate their fire on the same targets. Once the *mahout* was gone, the elephant—fearful of the noises and smells of battle, and with long pikes jabbing at its face and eyes—would turn to flight, trampling its own people in its urge to get away. In this way Porus' elephant corps was rendered useless. Attacked from in front by Alexander's pike phalanx and heavy cavalry wedges, the Indians proved no more of a match in equipment and fighting style for the army designed by Philip than the Persians had been. Craterus' attack from the rear only confirmed and made more decisive the victory already won by Alexander's main force. Porus was captured alive and treated well by Alexander, who left him in command of his realm as a subordinate king, under Macedonian oversight.

Alexander now learned of another great river, equal to the Indus, with a flourishing civilization and multiple kingdoms along its course: the Ganges, which he understood flowed down to the encircling ocean at last. His aim, consequently, was to advance into the Ganges valley and conquer it, thereby completing his conquest of the eastern part of the world as he saw it. At the bank of the River Hyphasis, however, the army mutinied and refused to cross. The soldiers found the heat and humidity of India in the monsoon season deeply dispiriting, and they had no appetite for further conquest. The Persian Empire was theirs, and even lands beyond it in the Indus valley. It was enough: they wished to turn west and begin the march back home. They had glory enough, they had booty to last a lifetime, they longed for the familiar climate and lifestyle of the Mediterranean and home. After ranting ineffectively at the soldiers for their disloyalty and sulking in his tent for days in the hope of making them change their mind, Alexander had to face the hard truth: the army would go no further, and therefore he had no choice but to turn back. Being Alexander, he could not just accept this gracefully and take the easy route: he insisted on making things hard for the army and for himself. First, the army, accompanied by a fleet of river boats, would march down the River Indus to the ocean, so that he could claim to have reached "the end of the earth" after all. From there, he would lead the army along the shore of the Persian Gulf back to Mesopotamia, while a large fleet of ships accompanied it with ample supplies. That sounded fairly simple in theory, but proved to be anything but that in practice.

In the first place, Alexander insisted on conquering all lands and peoples along the march down the Indus valley. Some of those peoples, naturally resenting being conquered, put up a stiff resistance; and the army had little appetite for conquering people who had, after all, little or nothing to offer that the army wanted. At the town of a people the Greeks called the Malli, things came to a head. Alexander insisted the town must be captured; the soldiers showed little inclination to risk life and limb on this quite unnecessary project. Irritated and headstrong, Alexander decided to show his men how it should be done: with a handful of companions he stormed up a siege ladder onto the enemy wall and called to his soldiers to follow him. It is not a general's business, of course, to be the first up onto an enemy wall. Anxious for their leader's safety, the Macedonian soldiery thronged the siege ladders, which broke under the strain, leaving Alexander himself isolated on the wall with only three companions. He promptly jumped down *into* the enemy town, followed by his three companions. In a desperate fight there, one of his companions was killed, and Alexander himself was struck in the chest by an arrow which pierced his lung. He collapsed, and his companion Leonnatus was also wounded, leaving only one remaining companion, Peucestas, to cover the wounded Alexander with his shield and somehow fight off the enemy soldiers. Amazingly, Peucestas succeeded. Somehow, when the frenzied Macedonians broke down the city gate and streamed in, they found Peucestas still standing over the body of Alexander, protecting the apparently dying king with his shield and fighting off a crowd of enemies. The Macedonians went wild: every living creature in the town was killed.

Alexander was placed on a shield and carried to his tent, where it was found that he was still alive but in a very bad way. The camp doctors, summoned to attend the king, concurred that the arrow would have to be extracted from Alexander's chest, but none was willing to perform the operation: there was a very clear risk that, once the arrow was drawn from the wound, Alexander would suffer a fatal hemorrhage. No doctor wanted to be the man charged with having killed Alexander. It was the senior officer present, Perdiccas, who finally extracted the arrow. Alexander fainted away from the loss of blood that followed, but the doctors were able to stanch the flow and save Alexander's life. After he had been patched up somewhat and revived, there was the condition of the army to be considered. The soldiery were in a panic, with the rumor spreading that Alexander was dead: they saw themselves cut off at the ends of the earth with no commander to control things and lead them home. Messages assuring them that Alexander yet lived did not still the panic and despondency, as they were not believed. Eventually Alexander had to have himself carried onto a river barge and placed as upright as possible on a large bed, and so rowed past the encampments of his soldiers, displaying himself to them and waving to assure them he was alive and on the mend. The men were appeased; but Alexander's senior officers rightly upbraided him severely for running such unnecessary risks, putting the whole expedition in danger by behaving more like a common soldier than a general.

When Alexander and the army reached the mouth of the Indus, the expedition was divided for the return westwards. A substantial part of the army, including the heavy baggage and older veterans, was placed under the command of Craterus with orders to march west along a safe, well-populated route inland. A large fleet of warships and supply ships was placed under Nearchus' command with orders to sail up the Persian Gulf, stopping at set intervals to rendezvous with a military expedition marching by land. This last expedition, commanded by Alexander himself, would march along the coast of the Gulf through the Makran desert (ancient Gedrosia), meeting with the ships to receive supplies. Supposedly no previous conqueror had managed to traverse the Makran, so Alexander would outdo them all. Things went wrong very quickly. Alexander's army and the fleet lost touch with each other almost at once, and the planned meetings never occurred. The army suffered horrendously on its march through the Makran, and in the end Alexander was quite fortunate to reach ancient Carmania in fall of 325 with more than half his force still intact. As to the fleet, it finally arrived at the head of the Persian Gulf weeks late, having suffered from storms, navigational problems, and encounters with whales. Alexander, having feared it was lost for good, was just glad to see it arrive at all. Once again, in pursuit of his own yearning to achieve more than anyone before him (or as some would say, in pursuit of his megalomania), Alexander had exposed many thousands of his soldiers and sailors to danger and suffering for no good reason at all: just to show that he could do it. Not surprisingly, the men of the expedition were now growing more and more fed up with Alexander's style of leadership: the more arrogant and demanding he became, the more they suffered.

After meeting up with Craterus' force, which had made its march perfectly safely, Alexander proceeded through Persia to the great Persian capital of Susa. There he had the governor put to death for supposedly exceeding his power, and indeed conducted a veritable purge of his western governors, discussed further in section 3 of this chapter. Also while at Susa Alexander held a grand wedding ceremony, at which he himself married two Persian princesses and he obliged the Persian and Median aristocracies to produce some eighty of their young daughters to be married off to selected Macedonian officers: a neat symbolism of Macedonian supremacy in the new empire. Many of his soldiers had already, during the years of conquest, taken Asian wives for themselves and had children by them: Alexander now regularized these unions, gave the soldiers wedding gifts, paid off any debts they had, and promised to see to the proper education of the mixed ethnicity children of his soldiers' Asian unions. All of this was doubtless to bolster a popularity among the men that he must have perceived he had damaged by his actions.

If that was his aim, he failed to achieve it. After Alexander had moved on in spring 324 from Susa to Opis, the army mutinied: the second great mutiny Alexander had to face. The Macedonians had long been angered by Alexander's increasing affectation of Persian customs and dress, and his appointment of Persians to positions in the army and administration. The arrival of, reputedly, thirty thousand Asian youths who had been equipped and trained to fight in the Macedonian fashion, coinciding with Alexander's decision to send thousands of Macedonians back home, made the soldiers feel that Alexander had no further use for them. The result was that all Macedonians demanded to return home, jeering that Alexander could continue his conquests without them. Alexander was furious, and had thirteen men he regarded as ringleaders of the mutiny immediately executed. The stand off between Alexander and his army lasted several days until the soldiers begged Alexander's forgiveness, which he was pleased to give. Ten thousand veteran pikemen and fifteen hundred cavalry were deputed to return to Macedonia under Craterus' leadership. They were to be replaced by an equal number of new Macedonian replacement soldiers, whom Antipater was to bring. It seems Alexander no longer trusted Antipater to be his regent in Macedonia. When news of this reached Antipater he, mindful of the fate meted out to Parmenio, declined to obey, sending his son Cassander instead to find out what Alexander's intentions were.

Alexander moved on to Ecbatana, the old Median capital in northern Iran, where a series of parties and entertainments were held. During these, Alexander's long-time lover Hephaestion fell ill and, neglecting his doctor's advice to rest and abstain from alcohol, essentially drank himself to death. Alexander's grief was as extravagant as everything he did. Sequestering himself for days without food and drink, when he emerged he ordered fantastically expensive funeral rites and gave instructions that Hephaestion was in future to be worshipped as a hero. The end was now nigh for Alexander himself. Once somewhat recovered from his grief, he resumed his round of parties and excessive drinking. The court and army moved down from Ecbatana to Babylon, where Alexander received embassies from all around the Mediterranean world and began plans for an expedition to conquer Arabia. He reputedly sent orders around his empire, and particularly to Greece, that he was now to be worshipped as a god. But, un-godlike, he fell ill after several all-night drinking parties and developed a high fever. After several days of fever and illness, he felt sufficiently better to attend another all-night drinking party given by his Thessalian friend Medeius. There, after particularly heavy drinking, he fell ill again and had to be carried to his bed. The illness and fever did not abate. When it was clear the king was dying, the senior officers present surrounded his bed and attempted to ask his instructions for the future. The soldiery insisted on seeing their king, and for hours Alexander was propped up in his bed as soldiers filed by, essentially saying farewell. After this exertion, Alexander was much weakened. His last act, reputedly, was to take off his royal seal ring and hand it to Perdiccas, the senior officer present. When Perdiccas asked to whom Alexander left his power, he is said to have murmured "to the strongest." He then slipped into a coma from which he did not emerge. He breathed his last on 13 June 323 BCE, just short of his thirty-third birthday.

Inevitably, given his youth, rumors swirled alleging poisoning or other nefarious action causing his death. The most elaborate version has Aristotle, seeking revenge for the death of his son-in-law Callisthenes, going to the River Styx, boundary between this world and the underworld, and collecting its highly poisonous and corrosive water in a hollowed out ass's hoof, the only vessel that could contain this water. The noxious liquid was given to Antipater, who had his son Cassander convey it to Babylon, where another son named Iolaus—being the king's cup-bearer—slipped it into Alexander's drink. This arrant nonsense is indicative of the basic reality that there is no good evidence for any murderous plot against Alexander. The young king had recklessly abused his body by physical exertion, courting danger, and heavy drinking throughout his adult life. He had followed the near fatal wound at the Mallian town by the near fatal desert march through the Makran. Instead of taking care of his body, he had indulged in reckless binge drinking, not even deterred when that lifestyle caused Hephaestion's death. The fatal illness that took Alexander has long been debated. The most plausible candidate is malaria, which was an endemic disease in much of the ancient world. His body weakened by wounds, overexertion, and excessive drinking, Alexander was simply unable to fight off a particularly virulent attack of the disease. He died, that is to say, as he had lived: in the midst of extravagance, and giving little thought for the future.

3. ALEXANDER'S PERSONALITY AND IDEAS

One thing that is clear about Alexander is that he had a dominant personality and large ego. Short in stature and boyish in appearance, he made up for what he lacked in physical impressiveness by his force of will and charisma. He more than held his own among a group of high Macedonian officers many of whom were not only talented and dominant persons themselves, but also physically big and powerful: the likes of Seleucus, Lysimachus, and Hephaestion, for instance. Here Philip's grooming of Alexander for power no doubt stood him in good stead, as well as his own natural abilities. Like everything else about him, Alexander's personality has attracted attention, and been judged in very different ways. William Tarn saw him as a collection of virtues, explaining away all evidence that suggested a darker side; Ernst Badian by contrast emphasized the evidence of a darker, more selfish, and cruel Alexander. On the whole, recent historians have tended more towards the Badian view, and with good reason.

That Alexander was a generous man, giving freely from the vast wealth his conquests won him to friends and associates, is not in dispute. Nor is it disputed that he was capable of, even fond of chivalric and at times almost quixotic gestures. He treated the family of Darius with great generosity and respect, seeing to their safety and comfort with such concern that Darius' mother Sisygambis reputedly came to consider Alexander almost as another son. Though Darius' principal wife was reputed to be of extraordinary beauty, Alexander declined so much as to look at her as being his rival king's wife. When a drinking companion named Proteas somehow angered Alexander, he was soon persuaded by friends to give up his anger and instantly made Proteas the princely gift of five talents to show he bore no ill will. Famously, at the sack of Thebes a lady named Timocleia was brought to him for judgement, having killed one of his soldiers. When she told him the soldier in question had raped her, he released her and her children, as having rightly fought for her honor. These kinds of gestures certainly look good, and are often quoted as signs of Alexander's good nature and high personal code of honor. But more than ten thousand Theban women were captured at that city's sack. Are we to suppose none of them were raped, either during the sack itself or afterwards, when they were sold into slavery and were no longer considered to have any right of refusal? Alexander cared nothing about the rape of captive women: he merely enjoyed making a quixotic gesture on behalf of a lady who personally impressed him. In contrast to Proteas, who won Alexander's forgiveness, we might place Callisthenes, who angered the king by refusing to bow down before him, and suffered a lingering and cruel death by Alexander's orders. And if the story of his sexual liaison with the Persian lady Barsine is true—he reputedly had a son by her named Heracles—then his careful observation of the sanctity of marriage is undermined, as she was married to Memnon of Rhodes.

That Alexander was a heavy, often indeed excessive drinker should not be in doubt, though Plutarch offered the excuse that Alexander liked to linger over his wine for the sake of conversation, rather than heavy drinking (Plutarch *Alexander* 23). But the stories of his deep drinking are too many to shrug off; in the last years of his reign it is reported that he quite frequently drank all night and spent the following day in bed recuperating. When drunk he could become very violent, as at the feast at Samarkand in 327 when he murdered his officer Cleitus the Black in a drunken rage. But worse than his violence when drunk is the excessive distrust and cruelty he often showed when sober. The most egregious example of this is his treatment of Parmenio and his son Philotas. There is little doubt that Philotas was unwise: he apparently had a habit of boasting that his father and he were as responsible for Macedonian successes as was Alexander himself, if not more so. One can understand Alexander being annoyed when he heard this, not least because it was essentially true. When an insignificant character named Dimnus supposedly tried to start a plot against Alexander, and this was reported to Philotas by a certain Cebalinus, he twice ignored the information. Obviously he would have done better to pass it along, but Alexander was never remotely in danger. On this basis Philotas was arrested and tortured, even though torture was not normally used against free men, certainly not free men of Philotas' standing. Under torture, Philotas reportedly made some damaging statements which later, placed on trial in front of the Macedonian soldiers, he retracted. Nevertheless Alexander had him executed, and immediately sent assassins to murder Parmenio for the crime of being Philotas' father.

It is of course well known that most people, when tortured, will say whatever they think their questioners want to hear in order to make the torture stop: this is why torture is not used in most societies, not because people are too squeamish but because it is a highly unreliable way of getting at the truth. And even if there was some excuse for executing Philotas (it was at best an exceedingly flimsy one), the murder of Parmenio was carried out for purely prudential reasons: after killing Parmenio's son, Alexander was afraid of what the old man might do. There was not the slightest suggestion that Parmenio was guilty of any disloyalty or crime. The deaths of these two highly placed Macedonian aristocrats, among the most important three or four leaders of the Macedonian expedition after Alexander himself, had a chilling effect on the Macedonian leadership. If Parmenio and Philotas and Cleitus could be murdered, tortured, and/or executed like this, who could consider himself safe from Alexander? Plenty of others suffered from what Badian, exaggerating slightly perhaps, judged to be Alexander's paranoia. Among them were the court historian Callisthenes, a group of the royal *paides* led by Hermolaus, and the officers Cleander and Sitalces who had facilitated the murder of Parmenio on Alexander's behalf: indeed in the last years of his reign Badian speaks of a virtual "reign of terror" as Alexander's anger and suspicion grew. It is true that there was discontent in the army. After the deaths of the Persian rulers Darius and Bessus, Alexander had taken to adopting elements of Persian royal dress and court ceremony, most infamously the practice of *proskynesis*. This was an act of physical prostration, bowing down to the ground, in obeisance to the king's majesty, and it was considered deeply humiliating by most Macedonians and other Greeks, who bowed down only to the gods. The anger at Alexander's perceived tendency towards despotism, and the profound resistance to the act of *proskynesis*, only increased Alexander's suspicion that men around him were disloyal: it became a vicious circle.

Another controversial topic regarding Alexander's person is his sexuality. Many modern commentators on Alexander—most notoriously again William Tarn—insist that Alexander was strictly heterosexual. This proceeds essentially from mere prejudice against homosexuality, and involves a profound misinterpretation of ancient Greek sexuality. Not only was there no prejudice in classical Greek society against homoerotic relationships, in upper-class circles, at least, they were considered natural and even desirable. One of the features of Alexander's personality that is so universally attested that we cannot properly doubt it, is that he had relatively little interest in sex. His passions were fighting, hunting, and drinking, not sex. But from boyhood he had an exceedingly close and intimate relationship with his dearest friend and companion Hephaestion; and though no source happens to say explicitly that their relationship was sexual, this is more likely because in the culture of fourth-century Greece it hardly needed saying, than because it was not so. Alexander and Hephaestion, that is to say, were indubitably lovers: Hephaestion's position as Alexander's virtual *alter ego*, attested in numerous anecdotes, and Alexander's crazed grief when Hephaestion died in 324, make that clear. In addition, we are told that Alexander had a passionate sexual attachment to a beautiful Persian youth, a eunuch, named Bagoas. Limited as Alexander's interest in sex was, it seems that his preference was for homoerotic sex. But like most ancient Greeks, that preference was not exclusive. He had a familial duty to marry and produce children, and though he neglected that duty for years, he did eventually marry the Bactrian princess Roxane in 327. Though presented by our sources as a love match, it was rather a prudential arrangement like his father Philip's marriages: Roxane's father was a great Bactrian noble named Oxyartes, and Alexander needed to cultivate the goodwill of the Bactrian nobility in order to cement his hard-won dominance over Bactria. In 324 Alexander married again: two Persian princesses, daughters respectively of Artaxerxes III and Darius III, became his wives. But there was no love here: it was a matter of tying the remnants of the Achaemenid royal family to himself. The only sign of any purely sexual interest in women by Alexander is the reputed affair with Barsine, if there is any truth to that.

The marriage to the two Persian princesses raises another aspect of Alexander that has been much discussed: his supposed idea of promoting cultural/ethnic fusion, or even an ideal of the "unity and brotherhood of mankind." The evidence for these notions consists of Alexander's employment of Persian nobles in his court and administration after 331; his selection of (reputedly) thirty thousand Asian boys to be educated and trained as Macedonian warriors to supplement his army; and the great marriage ceremony at Susa in 324 at which he married his two Persian princesses, and at the same time more than eighty of his officers also married ladies of the Persian aristocracy. Taking the last first, it is very hard to see in this marriage ceremony any sort of ethnic fusion between the Macedonian and Persian aristocracies: for that to be the case, there would have needed to be a similar number of Macedonian ladies brought over to Susa to marry Persian aristocrats. One of the ways in which conquerors throughout history have habitually expressed their dominance is by the sexual appropriation of the womenfolk of the conquered. That was often accomplished by rape, but it could take the form of forced marriage. The Persian elite will hardly have missed the symbolism in being obliged to hand over their daughters for marriage to Macedonian officers. This is not an expression of cultural or ethnic fusion, it is an expression of Macedonian dominance.

The same can essentially be said of turning Persian or other Asian boys into Macedonians: where were the Macedonian boys being trained in Persian customs? How happy can we imagine the fathers of these boys were to be obliged to hand over their sons to strangers, so that they could be trained to learn the strangers' language, customs, way of life? In other words, to see their sons turned into strangers to them? Again, this is not an expression of cultural or ethnic fusion, it is a pure expression of Macedonian supremacy. Alexander needed large numbers of soldiers for his future plans of conquest. In his estimation, soldiers of the type developed by his father—Macedonian pikemen and heavy cavalry—were the best. Taking Persian and other Asian boys and turning them into Macedonians was not the pursuit of some ideal of cultural melding; it was merely the prudential increasing of his pool of Macedonian soldiers. In the armies of Alexander's Successors we meet with large units of *pantodapoi* (men of varied ethnic backgrounds) who were armed and trained in the Macedonian fashion and fought as Macedonian pikemen and cavalry: there were eight thousand *pantodapoi* phalangites and five hundred such cavalry in Antigonus' army at the battle of Paraetacene, while Eumenes' army in the same battle had five thousand *pantodapoi* in his pike phalanx (Diodorus 19.28–29). It is very conceivable that these 13,500 *pantodapoi* altogether originated in the mass of boys Alexander arranged to have taught the Macedonian equipment and system of warfare. As to the employment of Persians as governors and administrators in his empire, they had an expertise, thanks to two hundred years of Persian dominance in and rule over Asia, which Alexander chose to exploit. Again, there is no sign here of cultural melding.

As with most elements of the adulatory version of Alexander's career, the most extreme account of an ideal of ethnic fusion on Alexander's part comes from William Tarn, in his notion of Alexander as a proponent of the "brotherhood and unity" of mankind. It is perhaps already clear from the above that this is an exceptionally unlikely notion: Alexander was not that kind of idealist at all. Stoic philosophers of the generations immediately after Alexander did indeed come up with the idea that all men are "brothers," but only in an idealized way: they did not draw any practical political or social consequences from this. Later writers, building up the legend of Alexander, took this notion and attributed to Alexander the idea of creating a "world state," of transplanting and mixing populations in this "world state," and thereby creating a practical and effective "unity of mankind" under his own rule. Badian already long ago deconstructed the evidence for this and showed how absurd was Tarn's elaboration of it into a fixed ideology pursued by Alexander. At the very best, if Alexander entertained any idea of some sort of "world state," we should see that as an expression of his megalomania, not of some idealistic striving for the brotherhood of all men.

4. Was Alexander Really Great?

Alexander has been universally known as "the Great" for over two thousand years now, and there is no likelihood of this changing. But the automatic nature of adding the honorific qualifier to his name tends to forestall any serious discussion of whether he deserves it, and if he does, what it is that made him great. What is the standard of greatness that is being applied? There are quite a number of rulers in western history who are standardly referred to as "the Great": the Roman emperor Constantine the Great, the Saxon king Alfred the Great, the Franco-German emperor Charles the Great (or Charlemagne as he is often called, the term "the Great" becoming part of his actual name), the Russian rulers Peter the Great and Catherine the Great, and the Prussian monarch Frederick the Great, to name a few. On the other hand, some rulers who were undeniably among the great, even the greatest, are not so called: Caesar, Augustus, and Trajan among Roman emperors; Elizabeth I of England, Louis XIV of France, and Napoleon among modern(ish) European rulers. Arguably the greatest of the Ottoman rulers, too, is known as Suleiman "the Magnificent" rather than "the Great." Perhaps for some, greatness is so evident that it requires no emphasis: to be called "the Great," would that add to or diminish the standing of a Caesar, an Augustus, a Napoleon? Most of the rulers referred to as "the Great" were in part at least men of great military renown and achievement. Though that is not so much true of Peter and Catherine, and though the likes of Constantine, Alfred and Charles certainly had other claims to achievement beyond the military sphere, it does seem that great military success is often a factor in the granting of the epithet "the Great." In Alexander's case, it can be argued that it was the only factor.

What, in effect, did Alexander do? He won battles and conquered. There is little else to be said for him, despite the attempts of some writers to see in him a deep thinker with ideas of human brotherhood far in advance of his time. As we have seen, such notions are as fanciful as they are wrong-headed. More plausibly, Alexander might be viewed as an empire-builder, with administrative and/or organizational talents along with his military talent. The reality is, however, that there is very little evidence to support this. As Alexander conquered the Persian Empire, he moved on through it, not lingering to organize or administer. Early on, his procedure was simply to depose and/or kill or chase away the regional Persian governor and appoint a member of his officer corps as a replacement, leaving the man so appointed to govern his province as best he could. Alexander's main concern seems to have been that tribute moneys be collected and forwarded. After Gaugamela, as the Persian elite surrendered to Alexander and offered him its services, he began to leave suitably subservient Persian governors in place, to continue governing their provinces on Alexander's own behalf. He evidently recognized the value of the accumulated experience and expertise of the Persian elite, which had been governing the empire for two hundred years, and decided to take advantage of it. The corollary is that he had no particular organizing or administrative ideas of his own, but was content to let things go on in the way the Persians had set in place. One change he did make was to separate military command from civil/administrative command: continued Persian governors would typically be stripped of military powers, which would be granted instead to a Macedonian or other Greek *strategos* (general) established as the Persian satrap's second-in-command and (in effect) watchdog. Alexander, that is to say, did not fully trust most Persians; he simply made use of their administrative expertise.

Alexander did create a new central fiscal structure for his empire, with the evident aim of ensuring that the tribute moneys would be properly accounted for and made available to fund future plans and operations. The system can hardly be considered a great success, however. To oversee his central fiscus, established at Babylon, Alexander appointed his boyhood friend Harpalus son of Machatas, from the old ruling family of Elimea. Harpalus used his position for his own enrichment, living a fantastically luxurious lifestyle and otherwise diverting the empire's money to his own purposes. When Alexander's return to Babylon approached, in 325, Harpalus—fearing punishment—fled taking with him the stupendous sum of five thousand talents of Alexander's treasure. He took refuge at Athens, where he was arrested and his treasure confiscated. Eventually, the Athenians let Harpalus go, but kept the money for ostensible return to Alexander. They still had it in 323 when Alexander died, and the bulk of the sum ended up being used to fund the Athenian rebellion against Alexander's Successors. Besides this unsuccessful central fiscal system, there is little or no evidence of Alexander creating any new administration: he was too busy continuing his conquering to give thought to such matters. And if the document purporting to contain his final plans has any truth in it, he intended to continue that way. When Alexander died, he was planning the conquest of Arabia. He supposedly then intended to march through Egypt to conquer the entire north African coast as far as the Atlantic Ocean, taking over the Carthaginian Empire; then he would cross to Europe and conquer Spain, southern France, and Italy on his way back to Macedonia. While the "last plans" document also envisaged some major and expensive building projects, including city foundations, it is clear that Alexander would not be personally overseeing any of this, any more than he oversaw the building of Alexandria in Egypt. He himself would be busy conquering, while others could see to the building projects for which he merely gave orders. Nor did Alexander indicate how anything was to be paid for, other than by coining the vast stored up treasure of the Persian Empire, which was bound to run out given the scale of Alexander's purported projects.

Finally, there is Alexander's reputation as a great founder of cities to be considered. Though our sources vary in the number of cities Alexander is supposed to have founded—up to seventy or more in some accounts—they do all agree that Alexander was a great city founder. The key example giving witness to this was the great city of Alexandria in Egypt (or by Egypt as the Greeks expressed it). By the late third century, a hundred years or so after its foundation, Alexandria was already one of the greatest cities in the ancient world; and at its height it may have attained a population of over a million inhabitants, fed by the huge annual grain surplus of the Nile valley. Undoubtedly Alexander selected an outstanding site for the city he wanted named after him: at the western edge of the Nile delta, with an excellent harbor that could fairly easily be artificially improved, on a substantial spit of land between the sea and a large fresh-water lake (Lake Mareotis), it was extremely well placed to be the chief harbor of Egypt and one of the great ports of the Mediterranean Sea. And its position between two great bodies of water made it defensively very strong and easy to protect from attack. But Alexander did not build Alexandria: he merely ordered that it should be built, and left. It was in fact Ptolemy I and his son Ptolemy II who built the great city of Alexandria that became the most important commercial and cultural hub of the Hellenistic world. This is not untypical of Alexander, ordering that something should be done and leaving it to others to sort out the organization and carry out the work.

Though various sources give Alexander credit for founding or refounding other cities in western Asia, in pretty much all cases the evidence is late and suspect: the rise of Alexander's legend in the third century and later made cities eager to claim Alexander as founder if they could. The most reliable sources only have Alexander founding additional "cities" in inner Asia, east of the River Tigris, primarily in

Bactria/Sogdia (Afghanistan) and north India (Pakistan). Closely examined, however, it is clear that the word "city" is a bit of a misnomer for most of these foundations: they were in fact just garrison colonies, settlements of veteran soldiers (especially Greek mercenaries) intended to secure Alexander's hold on the eastern lands he had found it so hard to conquer. We hear reliably of about a dozen of these garrison colonies, each apparently having a population of around two thousand men. For shortly after Alexander's death the men of these colonies abandoned them and gathered together into an army determined to march and fight their way back home to Greece: they had never had any desire to be settled in inner Asia. Altogether, we are told, about twenty-five thousand men gathered from these abandoned colonies, which gives us the number of about two thousand, just quoted, as the approximate average population of these dozen or so garrison settlements. On their attempted march home, they were met by a Macedonian army despatched to stop them, defeated, and forced to return to their settlements. Their descendants did flourish for nearly two hundred years as an Indo-Bactrian outpost of Hellenistic civilization. The nature of these cities, as some of them did eventually become, was revealed in the 1970s by French archaeologists excavating such a Greek city at Ai Khanoum in Afghanistan. So Alexander does perhaps deserve some credit for making possible the Greek cities of Bactria and north India and their civilization between 300 and 100 BCE. But that is a far more modest record as a city founder than he is often credited with, and in truth the process of founding Greek cities in western Asia was actually carried out by his successors Antigonus and Seleucus, and by Seleucus' son Antiochus I.

Alexander's sole credible claim to fame, then, is as a warrior, a general, a conqueror. That being so, it is relevant to note again that Alexander did not create the army he led, nor invent the military system he used: he inherited both from his father Philip, who was the inventive, creative one. Moreover, Alexander enjoyed the active co-operation of officers of the highest abilities: without Antigonus and his defeat of the Persian counter-attack in Asia Minor, Antipater and his defeat of the Spartan-led rebellion in southern Greece, Parmenio and his brilliant defensive leadership on the left wing at the Battle of Gaugamela, and the numerous and varied efforts of men such as Craterus, Ptolemy, Perdiccas, and others, how successful could Alexander have been? That

Alexander was able to dominate and lead these men has been laid to his credit, and to some extent deservedly so: had Alexander shown weakness, indecisiveness, or lack of ability it does seem likely that one or more of these officers would have found a way to challenge and/or control him. But it should be borne in mind that Philip had instilled a near fanatical loyalty to himself, and by extension to his sons, in the Macedonian soldiery. That is why, after Alexander's death, the soldiery insisted on Arrhidaeus as their king, and on re-naming him Philip after his father. Macedonian officers obeyed Alexander because he was able to command their respect, but also because they had little choice but to do so. The soldiery would not have backed anyone in a rebellion against Alexander, with the possible exception of Parmenio—which is why Alexander had him murdered.

As a general, Alexander's reputation rests, or should rest, primarily on the battles of Gaugamela and the Hydaspes. The Granicus and Issus were very much his father's battles, in the sense that Alexander won them using not just his father's army and officers, but also his father's tactics. At Gaugamela Alexander had to show considerable tactical ingenuity to achieve success, and at the Hydaspes he faced a new problem—how to confront war elephants—and found the successful solution. The withheld left wing and the reserve phalanx with orders to about-face to confront any out-flanking force attacking from behind: these were clever and effective solutions to the problem of fighting a numerically vastly superior army at Gaugamela. The extensive maneuvering Alexander employed in order to find a way to cross the River Hydaspes unopposed showed great strategic insight; and the way he had learned in advance to attack the *mahouts* controlling the elephants in order to render the elephants themselves uncontrollable showed effective use of military intelligence sources. In sum, there is no doubt that Alexander was an extremely daring, effective and (when needed) inventive battle general. He could adapt his battle strategy and tactics to the needs of the situation, while always operating within his father's overall "sword and shield" strategy as described in Chapter 4.

On the other hand, Alexander was not without weaknesses as a general and leader. His grand strategical sense may legitimately be called into question. It simply made no logical, and especially no logistical sense to extend his conquests as far as Bactria and northern India

(Afghanistan and Pakistan), given that his manpower base lay in Greece and the Balkan region. It is no accident that Alexander's Successors gave up the Indian territories within twenty years of Alexander's death, and showed, on the whole, very limited interest in Bactria after the first twenty years. These territories were just too far from the Mediterranean to be securely held by a Mediterranean power. Parmenio had been right in advising Alexander, in 333, to limit his ambitions (in effect, that is) to Syria/Palestine and Asia Minor (and perhaps Egypt): those were the rich and populous lands that could usefully be combined with the southern Balkan region into a viable empire. Moreover, as a battle general he was, as his officers complained, too apt to behave more like a common soldier than a general, needlessly putting himself at risk in battles and at sieges (most infamously the siege of the Mallian town in India), when the expedition could hardly afford to lose their leader. Clearly Alexander hugely enjoyed the thrill of the fight, and especially of the cavalry chase: as we have seen, he was only prevented in the nick of time from carrying his cavalry chase too far at Gaugamela, and thereby losing the battle. Having no one to succeed him if he died, he should have behaved more responsibly in battle, risking himself only if/when absolutely needed. And of course, his refusal until the last few years of his life to give attention to the crucial business of producing an heir is another justified criticism of Alexander's rulership abilities.

On the whole, the term "the Great" seems an exaggerated assessment of Alexander's real abilities and importance. He fulfilled his father's plans, with his father's army; but then went well beyond those plans in ways that, while immediately successful, made little strategic sense. He always found a way to overcome difficulties, but they were often difficulties he should have avoided in the first place. He showed no interest in organizing his conquests into a coherent, functioning empire, merely continuing the Persian system for the sake of convenience. Empire-building, as opposed to conquest, was left to his successors; and he left his successors with a massive problem of how to create a succession, and how to organize the Macedonian conquests. He was a general pure and simple, who seems to have lived for the thrill of the fight and of conquest for its own sake. Even the Prussian king Frederick the Great, the most purely military of later western rulers called "the Great," had more to him than just military success. Why then the enormous admiration, not to say adulation of Alexander over the millennia that have passed since his death?

5. THE LEGEND OF ALEXANDER

Much of the passionate interest in and adulation of Alexander found in novels, films, other popular media, and even in some scholarly histories, can be explained by the romantic nature of Alexander's exploits at such a young age (in his twenties) and his premature death at just short of thirty-three years old. It has also helped that he was capable, as we have seen, of occasional quixotic gestures that contributed to the aura of romance around him. This romantic element, within not much more than a century of his death, found its expression in a novelistic account of his life and exploits that turned him into a legendary figure, one might almost say western civilization's first "super-hero": I refer to the so-called *Alexander Romance*, attributed to Alexander's court historian Callisthenes, and often cited as Pseudo-Callisthenes as a result. This work, originally composed in Greek, was translated/adapted into Latin, Syriac, Armenian, Arabic, old Slavonic, and various other languages, and had a wide impact, especially during the medieval period, on people's image and estimation of Alexander. But the romanticized view of Alexander did not in fact have to wait for the creation of this outright novelistic account: many of the legendary, indeed almost mythical exploits attributed to Alexander in fact go back to stories told in supposedly sober contemporary historical accounts—contemporary to Alexander, that is.

The process began in the first historical account of Alexander's deeds, that of his official court historian Callisthenes. This man, nephew of the philosopher and Alexander's old tutor Aristotle, had made a reputation as a notable and reliable historian by writing a *Hellenika* (an account of general Greek history) covering the years 386 to 357. As Alexander's court historian, specifically employed to record (and amplify?) Alexander's deeds by putting them in the best possible light, Callisthenes changed his historical approach. He was to be Alexander's "Homer" and his history Alexander's *Iliad*. From the beginning, therefore, he did not so much write sober history as the story of a hero loved by the gods. For example, when Alexander and his army passed along the coast of Pamphylia, they reached a place where the road was extremely narrow between some cliffs and the sea. According to Callisthenes, the sea receded at Alexander's approach, paying obeisance to the great king and giving him and his army an easy passage. When Alexander, during his visit to Egypt, decided to visit the Oracle of Ammon at Siwah, an oasis in the Libyan desert, he and his entourage reportedly became lost due to a dust-laden "simoom" wind that covered the road. According to Callisthenes, ravens appeared to guide Alexander to the oasis, taking such care that they even pursued stragglers who got separated from Alexander's party and brought them back to the group. This is the stuff of legend, not history; but Callisthenes' efforts to legendarize Alexander were modest compared to what happened in histories and memoirs written shortly after his death.

One of Alexander's boyhood friends and trusted officers, Ptolemy son of Lagos, played a leading role in the "wars of the succession" and eventually founded the Ptolemaic Empire in Egypt. Late in life he wrote a history of Alexander's reign, taking care to emphasize his own achievements under Alexander; this history was used by our best surviving history of Alexander, written by the Roman era historian Arrian, who trusted Ptolemy because he was an eye-witness and later a king, who would surely not have lied. Ptolemy did indeed object to Callisthenes' magical ravens leading Alexander to Siwah. It was in fact, he reported, speaking snakes that appeared in the desert and led Alexander to his destination. Ptolemy is usually considered one of the more sober and factual historians of Alexander. Are we really to believe in snakes that speak in human voices? The plain fact is that Ptolemy did lie in his history, making Alexander more than a man.

Things only got more legendary from here. A historian named Onesicritus, who served in Alexander's army and commanded a ship (or at any rate served as its steersman) in his Indus river fleet, wrote an account of Alexander. He enjoyed the patronage of Alexander's general and successor Lysimachus, and Plutarch tells of an occasion when, at Lysimachus' court, Onesicritus read aloud to the king a passage from the fourth book of his history. The passage recounted the visit to Alexander's camp in Hyrcania (south of the Caspian Sea) of the queen of the Amazons, with her entourage of Amazon warriors. Reputedly she wished to mate with Alexander: the two greatest warriors in the world, male and female, would surely produce marvelous offspring. Plutarch recounts Lysimachus' humorous response: "I wonder where I was then?" (Plutarch

Alexander 46). The Amazons, let us be clear, belong to Greek mythology, not to history. Yet the legend of Alexander's tryst with the Amazon queen lived on and became a fixed part of the Alexander story.

One could go on, but the point is clear. From the very beginning, even during his lifetime, Alexander was magnified by those who wrote about him into a legendary, heroic figure: no tale was too tall if it was about Alexander. This was undoubtedly due in part to Alexander himself and his image cultivation. He was not satisfied to be the son of Philip and emulate his father's achievements: he was the descendant of Heracles and Achilles, and his achievements were to be measured on that heroic scale. When crossing the Hellespont to start his Asian campaigns, we hear that Alexander first sacrificed, on the European side, at the tomb of Protesilaus who, in the Trojan War myth, was the first Greek warrior to land on Trojan (Asian) soil. He then stood up in the prow of his vessel, the leading vessel of course, as it approached the Asian side of the Hellespont, and heroically/symbolically cast a spear into Asia. Landed in Asia, he had locals point out to him the supposed tomb of Achilles, where he sacrificed to his reputed ancestor while his lover Hephaestion sacrificed at the reputed tomb of Achilles' lover Patroclus. The point: Alexander was the new Achilles, the hero who would defeat the forces of the Asian world. Already at this early stage Alexander had gathered around himself a coterie of literary figures, such as the poets Choerilus, Agis of Argos, and Cleon the Sicilian, who made it their business (or whose business it was?) to compare Alexander to such humans become gods in Greek mythology as Heracles, Dionysus, and the Dioscuri Castor and Polydeuces. Towards the end of his reign, the question of whether Alexander himself was a god was very much in the air, as contemporary sources attest. Historians are divided on the question whether Alexander regarded himself as a god and demanded worship, or whether it was just flatterers who proposed divine honors for him. The former view does seem to fit with Alexander's self-image as attested in many sources. That Alexander really did demand, near the end of his reign, to be worshipped as a god is perhaps supported by a typically laconic remark attributed to a Spartan named Damis: "Since Alexander wishes to be a god, let him be a god" (Plutarch *Moralia* 219E). The point being that if he was a god, he should show it by displaying divine powers, such as immortality.

15. Coin of Alexander depicting the king holding a thunderbolt
(*Wikimedia Commons public domain image from PHGCOM*)

In other words, the legend of Alexander as a superhuman hero was assiduously cultivated by Alexander himself from early on in his reign, and was spread by his court historian Callisthenes and by other eyewitness historians after Alexander's death, as well as by poets employed to write about Alexander in a deliberately heroizing vein. One can add his cultivation of his physical image. Only one painter, Apelles, the greatest painter of Alexander's time, was permitted to produce official portraits of Alexander. Apelles painted Alexander wielding Zeus' thunderbolt, and Alexander authorized coins depicting himself with the thunderbolt (ill. 15). It is hard to think of another ruler who was as assiduous as Alexander at cultivating his own image and making that image superhuman: perhaps the Sun King Louis XIV of France comes closest. It is understandable, given the exaggerated respect shown in premodern sources for the act of military conquest, that Alexander's self-aggrandizing propaganda should have had its effect and been copied and further exaggerated in subsequent writings, almost down to the present day. But there is no need for us, in the twenty-first century, to go along with it. Alexander was an impressive general and an influential conqueror, but no more than that. The legend of Alexander has had its day.

CHAPTER 6

The Wars of the Successors

WHEN ALEXANDER DIED HIS UNTIMELY DEATH IN JUNE 323, HE LEFT A massive void behind him. This was not so much because he himself was so great and indispensable, though he had been a remarkable and successful general and ruler. It was the fact that there was no heir capable of taking over his role and ruling the Macedonians and their empire that created an extremely intractable problem for the Macedonian elite. From the moment Alexander took power in 336, Antipater and Parmenio had urged him to marry and start producing children. Had he done so at once, there might have been a ten- or twelve-year-old boy who could be installed as king and groomed, perhaps by a regency council, to take the reins of power within six or eight years. Instead Alexander resisted this advice for ten years, only finally marrying in 327. At the time of his death, his first wife Roxane was six months pregnant with Alexander's first child; but no one could know whether that pregnancy would be successfully brought to term, and if so whether the baby would be a boy who could potentially become king. Even if both of those outcomes came true, the baby boy could not be expected to take power for about eighteen years. What was to happen in the interim? Thanks to the successful purging of the Argead royal family by Philip and Alexander, to prevent disunity in Macedonia, there were no surviving males of the Argead family other than Alexander's mentally deficient half-brother Arrhidaeus, who survived only because he was incapable of ruling. Alexander had a sister and two half-sisters—Cleopatra, Cynnane, and Thessalonice—and Cynnane had an adolescent daughter by Alexander's cousin Amyntas. That was the sum total of the surviving members of the Argead family; and Macedonia, patriarchal to the core, had no tradition of women being able to assume the rulership. It was, consequently, a very worried group of Macedonian leaders who met together in the palace at Babylon after Alexander's death to discuss the future rule of the empire.

1. THE SETTLEMENT AT BABYLON AND ITS UNRAVELING

One of the problems facing the elite Macedonian officers gathered in conference at Babylon was that not all of the most important Macedonian leaders and power-players were present. Since the death of Parmenio, the two most senior high-level Macedonian commanders were Antipater and Antigonus the One-Eyed, neither of whom was there. Antipater, in his late seventies but still physically strong and active, had been one of Philip's two most trusted officers throughout his reign, as we have seen, and had served as regent of Macedonia throughout Alexander's reign. The Macedonian home army, thanks to its thirteen-year service under Antipater, was essentially his army; and he had led it to independent victories, first over Memnon, the rebellious governor of Thrace, but much more importantly over the southern Greek alliance led by Sparta in 330. With the home army behind him, he was not only by far the most respected Macedonian leader, but also the strongest. Antigonus, an almost exact co-eval of Philip, was about sixty years old at the time of Alexander's death, and had for twelve years been effectively the overseer of Asia Minor west of Cappadocia (that is, the Macedonian-held part of Asia Minor). Formally his satrapy was Phrygia, but he also governed western Pisidia, Lycia, and Pamphylia; he had personally—in defeating the Persian counter-attack in Asia Minor in 331—added Lycaonia by conquest; and the governors of Hellespontine Phrygia, Lydia, and Caria were greatly inferior both in terms of the territory they governed and in status and seniority. As the long-time governor of a huge and strategically important region, with a local security force he had raised himself and led to independent and important victories, he was a leader to be reckoned with.

Just as important as these two, though significantly younger, was Craterus, who after Parmenio's death had been Alexander's most trusted general and—along with Hephaestion—in effect his second-in-command. At the time of Alexander's death, Craterus was in Cilicia in southern Asia Minor in command of a veteran army of ten thousand Macedonian pikemen and fifteen hundred cavalry. He had been instructed in 324 to lead these veterans home to Macedonia, where they were to become the new Macedonian home army and Craterus himself the new regent of Macedonia; Antipater meanwhile was to lead the existing Macedonian home army to Babylon, to join Alexander. Craterus had lingered in Cilicia for some time, for unexplained reasons. He may have been busy in part establishing a royal treasury there for Alexander, at Cyinda. But Antipater had no desire to leave Macedonia and join Alexander: he had in mind the fate of Parmenio, and distrusted Alexander's intentions. He had sent his son Cassander to Babylon to protest against Alexander's orders. We may guess that Craterus had little appetite for a confrontation with the great and revered Antipater and his home army, and lingered in Cilicia hoping for further (and different?) orders from Alexander. Had Craterus been at Babylon, he would undoubtedly have taken the lead in the debates among the senior officers there. But even in Cilicia, he was a powerful and widely admired leader—reputedly his popularity among the soldiery was second only to Alexander's own—and commanded a substantial and highly experienced army. He was the Macedonians' Macedonian: he stuck to the old Macedonian ways, even to going into battle wearing the distinctive Macedonian *kausia* on his head. The soldiers adored him, and the sight of his *kausia* inspired them. He too had to be reckoned with.

The group of officers that met together at Babylon thus did not fully represent the Macedonian high command. The senior officer present was Perdiccas, who had since Craterus' departure and Hephaestion's death been acting as Alexander's second-in-command. After him there was a mix of younger, rising officers, such as Ptolemy, Leonnatus, Seleucus, Peithon son of Crateuas, and Lysimachus; older officers who had never progressed past mid-level commands, such as Aristonous and the phalanx battalion commanders Polyperchon, Attalus, and Meleager; and non-Macedonian Greeks such as Eumenes of Cardia (head of the military secretariat), Nearchus the admiral, and Medeius of Larissa. In the next few weeks and months, it became clear that though Perdiccas saw himself as the future leader of the Macedonian Empire, he was nevertheless rather unsure of himself and his position: he could neither take firm control of events, nor accept a true sharing of power. That was a recipe for conflict. Besides his position as Alexander's acting *chiliarch* (second-in-command) during the last year of the young king's reign, Perdiccas was also strengthened by the fact that one of Alexander's last actions had been to hand his formal seal of state to Perdiccas, which could be seen as ceding power to him. Yet at the council of leading officers, Perdiccas, instead of using the seal of state as a prop to put forward his claim to power, laid it on the table in a way that seemed to symbolize that power was up for grabs.

There was an immediate split in opinion. Some, notably Aristonous, argued that Perdiccas should hold power as Alexander's designated successor. Others argued instead for a regency council: Ptolemy was one of the leaders of this group. Both suggestions left open the question of the kingship: traditionally only an Argead descendant of Alexander I could be king. Perdiccas proposed that the question be postponed until Roxane gave birth to her child: if she produced a son, there would be an heir to the throne. Some of the less prominent infantry officers felt themselves overlooked in this discussion. One of them, the phalanx battalion commander Meleager, remembered Alexander's half-brother Arrhidaeus, and left the council to look for him. Arrhidaeus was about thirty-four or thirty-five years old at this time, and clearly looked like a normal, indeed fairly robust and handsome adult man. That he suffered from some mental deficiency, however, is not in doubt: thrust into prominence by his brother's death, in the next seven years until his own tragic death he was always controlled by one leading officer or another, never able to act independently and take control of events. Meleager quickly coached Arrhidaeus as to the role he must play, then led him out and introduced him to the Macedonian soldiers who were assembled outside the palace, eagerly awaiting news of the succession, as Philip's son who deserved to be the new king. Arrhidaeus evidently resembled his great father and looked the part. The soldiers, wanting nothing more than a strong new king to lead them, hailed Arrhidaeus as their ruler, and to symbolize his claim to the throne his name was changed to Philip, like his father. Meleager's hope clearly was to rule the Macedonian Empire through the good-looking but incapable and pliant Philip Arrhidaeus.

News of this event outside immediately changed the tone of the council meeting. The opposed factions at once united in the face of Meleager's power grab, and civil strife threatened to break out between the council of high officers, led by Perdiccas and backed by the cavalry and most Macedonian officers, and Meleager, backed by most of the infantry. In the event, cooler heads prevailed. The non-Macedonian Greek Eumenes of Cardia, who had been chief military secretary to

Philip and Alexander, and had also functioned as a cavalry commander
under the latter, mediated. The outcome was a compromise that recognized everyone's claims while satisfying no one. Arrhidaeus was recognized as king with the name Philip—Philip III as he is usually
known—but Roxane's child, if it proved to be a boy, as it did, was to
be co-king and take over rule of the empire once he achieved adulthood,
with the name Alexander like his father—Alexander IV, that is. In the
meantime Perdiccas was to actually run the empire on behalf of the
kings with the title *chiliarch*, and Meleager was to be his chief lieu-
tenant. Antipater was continued as viceroy over Macedonia and the
European lands of the empire: there was no possibility, as everyone recognized, of deposing him from that position. Craterus was given a
vague but honorific title as "protector" (*prostates*) of the kings, specific
powers to be worked out as and when became necessary. Most of the
other leading officers were granted governorships of important
provinces: Antigonus was confirmed as governor of his super-satrapy
in Asia Minor; Ptolemy was granted Egypt; Leonnatus got Hellespontine Phrygia (along the Hellespont and Bosporus); Lysimachus was
given Thrace which, thanks to a recent successful rebellion, he would
need to conquer himself in order to govern it; and other provinces were
similarly parceled out. Eumenes of Cardia, in thanks for his successful
mediation, was promised the governorship of Cappadocia, though it
was not actually under Macedonian rule as yet. Antigonus and Leonnatus were instructed to oust the surviving Persian governor there, Ariarathes, and install Eumenes as governor. That would be quite a task,
as Ariarathes had built up a very strong army over the years, reputedly
numbering as much as twenty thousand men.

Perdiccas kept his closest supporters, his brother Alcetas, his
brother-in-law Attalus, and Aristonous, around his own person to support him as ruler of the empire. Another key younger leader, Seleucus,
was made commander of the Macedonian cavalry, a role that traditionally conferred great authority. One of Perdiccas' first acts as official *chiliarch* was to hold a ceremonial rite of purification for the army, after its
brief outbreak of strife. At the height of the ceremony, Meleager and a
few of his chief supporters were suddenly arrested and brutally put to
death, trampled by elephants. Hereby Perdiccas made it clear that despite his initial hesitation, he meant to be ruler of the empire in more

than name. None of the other Macedonian leaders seems to have regretted Meleager's passing: he had made a play for power above his station or abilities. But his fate must surely have made them ponder their own potential vulnerability. Ptolemy hurried to Egypt, and from the moment he took over rule there showed no sign of being ready to accept or obey instructions from the central administration, instead working to make Egypt his own. Antigonus ignored Perdiccas' orders concerning Cappadocia, clearly displeased that a man so much junior to himself was now in a position to give him orders. Craterus can hardly have been delighted with his vague and undefined role. And Leonnatus harbored ambitions well beyond mere governorship of a relatively minor province. The "settlement" of Babylon, that is to say, in truth settled nothing.

News of Alexander's death spread quickly and widely, and created two major problems for the Macedonian rulers. Though the subject peoples of Asia, used to submission through two centuries of Persian rule, stayed quiet, and the Persians themselves had been too recently and thoroughly defeated to think of rebelling, the non-Macedonian Greeks in Alexander's empire did not stay quiet. In southern Greece, the Athenians saw a chance to reassert their independence. Thanks to the disloyalty of Alexander's treasurer Harpalus, the Athenians possessed a fighting fund of some five thousand talents of Alexander's money; and thanks to Alexander's distrust of his regional governors, which had led him to order the disbandment of the mercenary security forces they had recruited to police their provinces, thousands of unemployed mercenaries had gathered to seek employment at the great mercenary fair on Cape Taenarum in the southern Peloponnese. The Athenians mobilized their citizen army and fleet, sent out a call for allies to join them in a war of liberation against the Macedonian oppressor, and despatched their general Leosthenes to Cape Taenarum, amply supplied with funds, to recruit mercenaries. Leosthenes had served as a mercenary commander before and knew these men: he had no difficulty in gathering a large and well-trained army to join the Athenians and greatly strengthen their forces. A number of Greek states responded to their call for allies, most importantly the Aetolians and the Thessalians: Aetolia provided thousands of highly motivated and disciplined light infantry, and the Thessalian cavalry was of as good quality as the Macedonian. Antipater in Macedonia found himself with a formidable war on his hands.

Meanwhile, at the opposite end of the empire in what is today Afghanistan, trouble was brewing too. Alexander had established a dozen or more garrison colonies there, as we have seen, many (most?) of whose inhabitants were Greek mercenary soldiers. However willingly or unwillingly Alexander had settled them in their colonies, at news of Alexander's death they began sending messages to and fro and before long many thousands of them left their settlements and gathered into a large army, some twenty-five thousand strong. Life in inner Asia did not suit them; their desire was to return home to the Mediterranean and Greece, and they elected leaders and began to march west. This presented a major problem to Perdiccas. If large groups of soldiers were permitted simply to decide for themselves what they would do and where they would go, the authority in the empire of the Macedonian officer elite would be lost. And if the eastern garrisons were permitted to be abandoned, the eastern part of the empire would be lost too. Perdiccas appointed a senior officer named Peithon son of Crateuas to deal with this situation. Peithon was given a large force and instructions to oblige the settlers to return to their garrison colonies. The two armies met in central Iran, and Peithon was victorious. Our sources allege that Peithon had the "rebellious" settlers massacred, but that cannot be true. In fact they were forced back to their colonies. We know this because they and their descendants established a flourishing Greek civilization there that lasted about two hundred years. Though only a handful of references to it survive in our literary sources, it is known to us from the coinages struck by the local rulers there, some of the most beautiful Greek coins ever minted (see ill. 1 for an example); and from the French excavation, in the 1970s, of one of their cities at a place in Afghanistan called Ai Khanum.

The crisis in the east was thus settled fairly quickly, and with great credit to Peithon and his boss Perdiccas; the situation in Greece proved much more tricky. When Antipater marched south with the home army to deal with the uprising, he was met in north central Greece by an Athenian and mercenary army commanded by Leosthenes, and defeated. Antipater barely managed to disengage his defeated army still intact, and took refuge behind the walls of the nearby city of Lamia, where he was obliged to stand a siege. As a consequence, this conflict is known to modern historians as the Lamian War. Antipater sent desperate messages to Asia Minor, to the Macedonian leaders there, calling for help. Two leaders heeded the call: Leonnatus in Hellespontine Phrygia ignored his orders from Perdiccas to conquer Cappadocia for Eumenes, and instead took the forces Perdiccas had given him for this purpose across the Hellespont into Europe and over into Macedonia. There he recruited additional troops and prepared to go to the rescue of Antipater. In addition Leonnatus established contact with Alexander's full sister Cleopatra, widow of Alexander the Molossian. He proposed to marry her: he came of a princely house himself, and thought that with Cleopatra by his side he could make a play for the Macedonian throne. It all came to nothing when he moved south into Thessaly and was met by the Athenian army and defeated. Leonnatus died of his wounds, and Antipater—relieved from his siege at Lamia by Leonnatus' entry into the fight—managed to collect the remnants of Leonnatus' defeated force and retreat with them and his own army back to the safety of Macedonia.

The other Macedonian leader who heeded Antipater's call for help was Craterus, who was still lingering in Cilicia. He did not move at once because, concerned about Athenian naval power, he stayed to collect a great fleet from Phoenicia, Cyprus, and Cilicia, which he placed under the command of his officer Cleitus the White. Cleitus defeated the Athenian fleet in two great sea battles, at the island of Amorgos and in the Hellespont, ending Athenian naval power once and for all. Craterus was able to ferry his veteran army across to Macedonia safely, and there join up with Antipater. The joint armies of Antipater and Craterus, along with the troops Leonnatus had gathered, represented a great army indeed, and the two leaders prepared for a show-down battle with the Athenians and their allies in the spring of the following year, 322. The battle was fought at Crannon in Thessaly and, thanks to outstanding service from the Thessalian cavalry and the rest of the southern army, was fought to a draw. But a draw was as good as a victory to Antipater and Craterus. Immediately after the battle, allied contingents in the southern Greek army began to peel away and head for home, or even sue for peace on favorable terms. The Athenian coalition melted away, and the Macedonian leaders were able to advance southwards, pacifying the Greek states as they went, until they finally reached Athens in October 322. The Athenian democracy was ended and a pro-Macedonian oligarchic regime installed in its place.

There were still mopping-up operations to be conducted, particularly against the Aetolians, but Antipater and Craterus were victorious, and had established an excellent partnership with each other. This was now cemented by a marriage alliance: Craterus married Antipater's oldest daughter Phila. The two then considered their relations with Perdiccas. The latter had successes of his own to his name: frustrated at the failure of Antigonus and Leonnatus to obey his orders to conquer Cappadocia, he had come to Asia Minor himself, bringing the royal army. He invaded Cappadocia, defeated the forces of Ariarathes, and installed Eumenes as the new governor of the region, as he had planned. He then moved south and invaded eastern Pisidia, which like Cappadocia had not yet come under Macedonian rule. There too he was victorious, and the fall of 322 found him established in winter quarters in Pisidia with a greatly enhanced reputation. Antipater sent representatives to Perdiccas proposing a marriage alliance: Perdiccas would marry a second daughter of Antipater, named Nicaea, and thereby become the brother-in-law of Craterus at the same time. Thus the three great leaders, related by ties of marriage, could in future rule the Macedonian Empire on behalf of the kings as a triumvirate. That was clearly an excellent idea, promising stability to the empire, as no Macedonian leader could hope to stand up to these three and their forces, and Perdiccas promptly agreed ... only to suffer almost immediately a case of buyer's remorse. For at that very time there arrived letters from Olympias and Cleopatra, Alexander's mother and sister, proposing that Perdiccas marry Cleopatra instead. Olympias loathed Antipater. Marriage to Cleopatra would mean a decisive break between Perdiccas and Antipater; but it offered Perdiccas the prospect, as uncle-by-marriage of the young king Alexander IV, of ruling the Macedonian Empire on his own, with Cleopatra and Olympias by his side, in the name of his young nephew.

Here Perdiccas' basic indecisiveness reared its head again. His good friend Eumenes, who was also a long-time friend of Olympias, urged Perdiccas to accept Cleopatra's offer and marry her. But Perdiccas' brother Alcetas, more cautious by nature, urged him to stand true to his agreement with Antipater and Craterus, and marry Nicaea. Unable to quite decide, Perdiccas gave encouragement to both ladies, with the result that both arrived in Asia Minor early in 321 expecting marriage. To complicate matters further, two more royal Macedonian ladies arrived at Ephesus on the coast of Asia Minor around the same time, also in pursuit of a marriage: Philip's oldest daughter Cynnane brought her young daughter Adea with the project of marrying her to the senior king Philip Arrhidaeus, no doubt expecting that as wife of the pliant Philip Adea could take control and rule in his name. Perdiccas sent his brother Alcetas with some troops to arrest these princesses, probably with the idea of sending them back to Macedonia. But Cynnane resisted and was killed in the violence that ensued. Alcetas' own Macedonian soldiers then rebelled against him, horrified that a daughter of the great Philip had been killed. In order to quiet the uprising, Alcetas and Perdiccas were forced to agree to Adea marrying Philip: like her new husband, Adea then changed her name and took on the royal name Eurydice instead. For the moment Perdiccas was able to keep young Adea Eurydice under his control, but the situation was becoming fraught. Still undecided about his own future, Perdiccas established Cleopatra comfortably at Sardis and sent his friend Eumenes to keep her sweet, while himself receiving Nicaea and formally marrying her. It was clear to his entourage, however, that Cleopatra, and the prospects she opened up for him, was the one he really wanted. Things were heading towards a crisis.

The crisis was precipitated by Antigonus and Ptolemy. Perdiccas was still angry at Antigonus' refusal to invade Cappadocia, and summoned him to explain himself. Antigonus had no intention of justifying himself to a more junior officer, and no doubt had Meleager's fate in mind. He collected his relatives, friends, and belongings, and fled to Macedonia on several Athenian ships, taking refuge with his good old friend Antipater. There he complained vociferously about Perdiccas' actions; and he kept tabs via his friend Menander, the governor of Lydia, on Perdiccas' relationship with Cleopatra, on which he reported to Antipater and Craterus. Ptolemy was pursuing an independent policy aimed at making Egypt his own realm. To do this, he played up his own connection to Alexander to portray himself as Alexander's legitimate heir in Egypt: he built up Alexandria, the city which Alexander had formally founded but not waited to build. And when Alexander's funeral cortege, with a lavish coffin and wagon it had taken more than a year to build, passed through Syria on its way to Macedonia, Ptolemy intercepted it with troops and carried it off to Egypt where Alexander was first buried in the old capital of Memphis but eventually moved to a magnificent purpose-built tomb in Alexandria itself. This was a direct affront to Perdiccas, who had intended to bring Alexander "home" to Macedonia for burial at the ancestral Argead tomb complex in Aegae, the old Macedonian capital. Perdiccas reacted by finally being decisive: he repudiated Nicaea and sent Eumenes to Cleopatra again to announce his (Perdiccas') intention to marry her. That meant war with Antipater, Craterus, Antigonus, and Ptolemy. The "settlement" of Babylon was broken.

The first War of the Diadochi (Successors of Alexander) did not last long. It was fought on three fronts, with different outcomes, though the overall winners were undoubtedly Antipater and his allies Antigonus and Ptolemy. Antipater and Craterus gathered their forces to march to and cross the Hellespont into Asia Minor to confront Perdiccas. Antigonus took a detachment of ships and sailed to the coast of Ionia, where he joined up with his friend Menander. He learned there of Perdiccas' definitive decision to marry Cleopatra, and sent word to Antipater to hurry his invasion into Asia Minor. Ptolemy built up the defenses of Egypt along the easternmost Pelusiac branch of the Nile delta, and awaited events. With his usual indecision, Perdiccas summoned a council of his closest advisers to decide what to do: should he march south to punish Ptolemy, or should he march to the Hellespont to confront Antipater and Craterus? Rather typically, he selected the apparently easy option: he would deal with Ptolemy. He left a large force in Asia Minor under his friend Eumenes with orders to guard the Hellespont and not permit Antipater to cross; Alcetas, with another force, was instructed to co-operate with Eumenes, as was another Macedonian officer named Neoptolemus. Aristonous, finally, was sent with a detachment to take control of Cyprus, to deny its resources to his enemies and have it serve instead as an advance staging post for his own operations. And so Perdiccas marched through Syria and Palestine, with a fleet commanded by his brother-in-law Attalus accompanying him.

Perdiccas' confrontation with Ptolemy's forces in Egypt was disastrous. Several attempts to force a crossing of the Nile were repelled with heavy losses, and the soldiers were particularly demoralized when Nile crocodiles collected in large numbers to feast on the bodies of the dead. When it became clear that Perdiccas did not know what to do next, a group of senior officers led by Peithon, Seleucus, and Antigenes, the commander of the Silver Shields (formerly Philip's *pezetairoi* and then Alexander's *hypaspistai*), confronted Perdiccas in his tent at night and assassinated him. When word of this reached him, Ptolemy crossed over the river and addressed the men of the royal army at a meeting. He expressed how sorry he was to have been forced into conflict with them and how much he regretted their losses; and he pledged to provide them with supplies and other aid. The men cheered him, and called for him to take up the regency of the kings now that Perdiccas was dead. Ptolemy, foreseeing conflict with Antipater and Antigonus if he took that post, declined. Two other senior officers—Peithon son of Crateuas and Arrhidaeus (not king Philip III Arrhidaeus but another Macedonian officer of that name)—were nominated to the post instead, for the time being. The remaining adherents of Perdiccas in the camp were seized and killed, including his unfortunate sister, and more than thirty others were condemned to death *in absentia*, including the fleet commander Attalus, Perdiccas' brother Alcetas, and Eumenes. Then the army turned and marched back through Palestine towards Syria for a rendezvous with Antipater.

Meanwhile, Antipater and Craterus had crossed the Hellespont unopposed: the forces that were supposed to prevent the crossing were in conflict with each other. Alcetas, angry at being subordinated to the non-Macedonian Eumenes, refused to co-operate with him and took his forces off to Pisidia in southern Asia Minor. Neoptolemus too resented having been placed under Eumenes and was in contact with Craterus, intending to switch sides. Far from opposing Antipater and Craterus at the Hellespont, therefore, Eumenes was forced to fight against his own supposed ally Neoptolemus, soundly defeating him and taking over his army. When Neoptolemus rode into Antipater's camp with only a few dozen cavalry as escort to announce his defeat, a council of war was held. Antipater and Craterus decided to split their forces. Craterus would take his Macedonian veterans and, guided by Neoptolemus, would confront Eumenes and assure control over Asia Minor for his side. Antipater, meanwhile, would march south with his troops as fast as possible to assist Ptolemy; and Antigonus with his ships and a small force would proceed to Cyprus to seize that island.

Craterus' confrontation with Eumenes did not work out as planned. During the previous two years Eumenes had raised and trained a large force of Cappadocian cavalry, with which he confronted Craterus' cavalry on one wing of the battle with orders to charge hell for leather and not give Craterus the chance to choose his own moment to engage. Eumenes distrusted the loyalty of the Macedonian element among his infantry, if they knew that they were going up against the beloved Craterus. He assured them that their opponent was only Neoptolemus with some new forces, and held his infantry back, determined to try to win with his cavalry. On one wing, Eumenes led part of his cavalry in a charge against enemy cavalry commanded by Neoptolemus. The two commanders met in person, and in a vicious fight Eumenes managed to kill Neoptolemus with his own hands, and emerge victor. On the other wing, Eumenes' cavalry charged Craterus and his Macedonian cavalry and, in the midst of the fighting, Craterus' horse stumbled and he had the misfortune to be thrown and then trampled by the Cappadocian horses. When Eumenes found him after the battle, he was dying: an ignominious death for the most highly regarded of Alexander's officers. Craterus' defeated forces offered to surrender to Eumenes and camped where they were for the time being. In the middle of the night, however, they decamped and marched away at full speed to rejoin Antipater. Antigonus, meanwhile, successfully took control of Cyprus, driving out Aristonous and his force, and then moved on to rejoin Antipater in northern Syria. As a result, Antipater with his own army and Craterus' army, and joined by Antigonus' force too, arrived at a Persian resort spot in northern Syria named Triparadeisus (literally "three gardens") where the royal army under Peithon and Arrhidaeus was awaiting him. It was time for a new council of Macedonian leaders, and a new "settlement."

2. THE SETTLEMENT OF TRIPARADEISUS AND ITS UNRAVELING

With Perdiccas and Craterus, the two younger generals most trusted by Alexander, both dead, a completely new arrangement of power in the Macedonian Empire was called for. There could be only one choice for the regency: Antipater. As by far the most senior commander, right-hand man of Philip, viceroy of Macedonia throughout Alexander's reign, revered by everyone, he had no rival. A brief upset was caused by the young Eurydice asserting her right to rule in her husband Philip's name: many of the soldiers admired her spirit and her royal birth. When Antipater attempted to assert control a riot threatened, but order was quickly restored by the intervention of Antigonus and Seleucus, both

huge and physically imposing men. Antigonus had a squadron of cavalry escort the aged Antipater to safety, and a council of all the main
Macedonian leaders was then summoned in Antipater's camp. Eurydice
was made to understand that as a woman she must stay quiet and obey;
Antipater was formally acknowledged as the regent of the kings and so
ruler of the empire; and a new division of powers was put into effect.

A simplifying factor was that Egypt no longer had to be considered: it belonged to Ptolemy. He had governed it successfully for several
years now, had built up his own army there, and had defended it effectively from Perdiccas' attack. There was no question of trying to interfere with him. One thing Antipater also made clear from the beginning
was that he had no intention of staying in Asia. He would be returning
to Macedonia as soon as possible, and would oversee the empire from
there. This meant that he would need a strong leader to act as his lieu-
tenant in Asia, overseeing the governors and the running of imperial
affairs there. There could be little doubt on whom the choice would fall
for this role: Antigonus was the next most senior leader, he had independent successes to his name, he was a close friend of Antipater, and
he would certainly not tolerate anyone being placed above him. He was,
therefore, appointed general with oversight of the Asian provinces, and
also given the specific task of finishing the war against Perdiccas' surviving supporters, Alcetas and Eumenes, who could not be forgiven for
the death of Craterus. To fulfill this task and these responsibilities,
Antigonus was given command of the royal army most recently led by
Perdiccas, and to keep an eye on him Antipater appointed his own son
Cassander to be Antigonus' second-in-command. Along with the royal
army, Antigonus was also to have personal oversight of the kings, which
meant that he was effectively designated as the aged Antipater's successor in the regency: for so long as Antigonus had the kings, it was
obvious no one but he could take the regency when Antipater died.

Thought was then given to governorships of the provinces. Many
existing governors were simply confirmed, but there were a number of
officers who needed to be rewarded, and a number of close associates of
Perdiccas who needed to be deposed. The two temporary regents, Peithon
and Arrhidaeus, were rewarded with governorships over Media and
Hellespontine Phrygia respectively. Peithon already had experience in the
east, in his victorious campaign against the "rebellious" Greek colonists,

and from the powerful satrapy of Media could exercise oversight of the further east; Hellespontine Phrygia had no governor since the death of Leonnatus. The other two assassins of Perdiccas, Seleucus and Antigenes, were granted the governorships of Babylonia and Susiane. Antigenes, however, remained commander of the Silver Shields for the time being, with a special task of convoying treasure to be deposited at Cynda in Cilicia, meanwhile ruling Susiane through a deputy. With this business settled, Antipater set off with his army to return to Macedonia, and Antigonus with the royal army marched with him, headed for Asia Minor and the war against Eumenes and Alcetas. Along the way, friction arose between Antigonus and Cassander, leading to a revision of some key arrangements. Cassander was clearly not suited to be Antigonus' second-in-command, and he persuaded his father that it would be unwise to leave the kings under Antigonus' charge. Antipater therefore took the kings and a large portion of the royal army, leaving Antigonus eight thousand of his own younger Macedonian soldiers instead. With the kings and Cassander now in his entourage, Antipater crossed over to Europe and returned to Macedonia. Antigonus with his smaller but more manageable and reliable army gave thought to fighting Eumenes.

Antigonus was a huge man with a booming voice, a scarred face where he had lost one eye at the siege of Perinthus in 340, and an abundance of energy. He had had to wait a long time to play a leading role: born about 383/2, he was around sixty-three years old when appointed general over Asia in 320. He was determined to make the most of this delayed opportunity. He spent the fall and winter of 320 to 319 preparing his forces and laying his plans, and made his move in spring of 319, advancing to meet Eumenes with an army about fifteen thousand strong. Eumenes was in his province Cappadocia, where he had collected an army well over twenty thousand strong, based on the troops originally granted him by Perdiccas but with additions from the defeated forces of Neoptolemus and Craterus. His main strength was in cavalry: the excellent Cappadocian cavalry he had himself recruited and trained. The two armies drew together in southern Cappadocia, at a place called Orcynia, where Eumenes was completely out-generaled by Antigonus. By a clever stratagem Antigonus persuaded his opponents that substantial reinforcements had reached him just before the battle, demoralizing them by the belief that far from outnumbering Antigonus'

16. Macedonian ruler (probably Antigonus the One-Eyed) from villa of
P. Fannius Synistor at Boscoreale, now in Metropolitan Museum, New York
(Wikimedia Commons public domain image)

army they were now the smaller of the forces. And Antigonus also succeeded in establishing contact with one of Eumenes' key cavalry commanders, persuading him to switch sides with his squadrons during the
battle. The result was a devastating defeat for Eumenes, from which he
escaped with a few hundred men to take refuge at a small fortress
named Nora, where Antigonus besieged him. Eumenes was a quick
study, however, and learned from his defeat: he was to prove a much
tougher opponent in the next few years.

Antigonus left a small force to besiege Eumenes in Nora, and with
the bulk of his army, now supplemented by most of Eumenes' defeated
army, carried out an astonishing forced march across southern Asia
Minor from Cappadocia to southern Pisidia, where Alcetas and his
army were encamped near the city of Cretopolis. Alcetas and his men
were heedless of any danger, secure in the belief that Antigonus was
hundreds of miles away in Cappadocia. The first they knew of
Antigonus' army being present and about to attack was when they
heard the trumpeting of Antigonus' advancing elephants. With Alcetas'
army taken completely by surprise, the engagement was not so much a

battle as a rout. Most of Alcetas' army and officers surrendered to Antigonus; Alcetas himself fled to the nearby friendly city of Termessus, where he was subsequently killed by citizens seeking to gratify Antigonus. In one swift campaign taking only a couple of months and characterized by boldness, speed of movement, and brilliant improvisation, Antigonus had defeated and incorporated into his own force two rival armies, and ended the war against Perdiccas' supporters. As he marched back towards Cappadocia to finish with Eumenes in late summer of 319, Antigonus received momentous news: the aged Antipater had succumbed to illness, and on his deathbed had nominated the former phalanx battalion commander Polyperchon to succeed him as regent. Antigonus had no intention of obeying the rather mediocre Polyperchon, however; and neither did a number of other Macedonian leaders. Already the "settlement" of Triparadeisus had began to unravel, beginning the second War of the Diadochi.

This renewed war was fought essentially on two fronts. Though the coalition opposing Polyperchon included Ptolemy and Lysimachus in its number, they were in fact fully engaged in securing their own realms of Egypt and surrounding territories, and Thrace, respectively. The fighting occurred in the east, where Antigonus with various allies fought out an extended and remarkable duel with Eumenes and a fractious coalition of allies; and in the west, in Greece and Macedonia, where Antigonus' ally Cassander challenged Polyperchon. Antipater's choice of Polyperchon as regent has always been something of a mystery: in many years of service under Philip and Alexander Polyperchon had never risen above the rank of battalion commander, nor apparently shown much ambition to do so. Antipater, when leaving to attack Perdiccas in Asia, had appointed Polyperchon to oversee Macedonia and Greece, and Polyperchon had done so capably. But it may well be that it was the man's very mediocrity that appealed to Antipater: he wanted, we may suppose, a regent who would have no ambition to supplant the legitimate kings, who would hand over quietly to Alexander IV when the time came. But this choice infuriated Cassander, who had naturally expected to succeed his father as regent; and left men like Antigonus and Ptolemy deeply unimpressed. Cassander promptly fled from Macedonia to start building up forces of his own for a rebellion, and Antigonus and Ptolemy simply ignored Polyperchon as a man of little account.

Sensing his weakness, Polyperchon attempted to shore it up by three main expedients. He wrote to Alexander's mother Olympias inviting her to return to Macedonia from her self-imposed exile in Epirus, to take up oversight of her grandson Alexander IV and his education. He announced to the cities of southern Greece that the oligarchies established by Antipater would be abolished, and that the cities would be free to create their own favored governing systems: in effect Polyperchon feared that the oligarchs would be more loyal to Antipater's son Cassander than to the new regent, and rightly so. And Polyperchon sent letters to Eumenes in Asia, offering him appointment as royal general over Asia, authorizing him to draw upon the royal treasuries in Asia for any necessary funds, and instructing all loyal officers and governors in Asia to obey and co-operate with Eumenes. The effectiveness of these moves varied. Olympias stayed where she was for the time being, lacking confidence in Polyperchon, but she did write to Eumenes urging him to accept Polyperchon's offer and asking for advice. The oligarchic regimes in southern Greece did not give up power: instead they predictably turned to Cassander for help, and bolstered his position as rival to Polyperchon. The latter would have to intervene militarily in southern Greece to achieve real change. The letters to Eumenes had the greatest effect, tying up Antigonus with a major war in Asia and preventing him from intervening against Polyperchon directly. For Eumenes was no longer besieged in the small fortress of Nora in Cappadocia.

Late in 319 Antigonus had learned of Antipater's death from Eumenes' close friend and (probable) relative Hieronymus of Cardia, who was later to become the greatest historian of this period. Taking stock of his situation, Antigonus had decided that he would take no more orders from the central government, despising Polyperchon the new regent, but would operate strictly on his own behalf. He calculated that Eumenes, an old friend from the days they had served Philip together, could be a very useful ally, and sent Hieronymus to him with proposals offering Eumenes a high position as one of his chief officers and advisers. Eumenes pretended to agree and was released from his siege; but instead of joining Antigonus he accepted the position of overseer of Asia offered by Polyperchon, which is to say he became Antigonus' chief rival. He made his way to the royal treasury at Cyinda in Cilicia, where there were ample funds for his purposes guarded by the famous three thousand strong unit called the Silver Shields. As already discussed, these men were the former guard unit of Philip (when they had been known as *pezetairoi*) and Alexander (when they had been known as *hypaspistai*). They were the most experienced and feared military unit in the Macedonian Empire, indeed one of the supreme infantry units in military history, comparable in their discipline, ferocity, and elite status to Caesar's tenth legion or Napoleon's "Old Guard." The Silver Shields, along with a younger unit of three thousand men known as the *hypaspistai* who were being trained as their replacements, accepted the orders in Eumenes' letters from Polyperchon and Olympias, and took service under him. With their help and the funds from Cyinda, Eumenes was in a strong position to make trouble.

Before Antigonus could try to deal with Eumenes, however, he had another troublesome situation to deal with: Craterus' former admiral Cleitus the White appeared in the Propontis (Sea of Marmara) with a great fleet as Polyperchon's ally. Affairs in Greece had not been going well for Polyperchon. To counter his rival Cassander's influence with the oligarchies and garrisons installed in many southern Greek cities by Antipater, Polyperchon had declared all Greek cities free to establish whatever governing system they desired (which in effect meant democracies), but it would take military force to make that declaration effective. Meanwhile, Cassander controlled most of southern Greece through various allies, and also received allied troops from Antigonus and Ptolemy. Since he had control of the Piraeus, the great harbor of Athens, through his friend Nicanor, the commander of the Macedonian garrison there, he was able to mobilize the remnants of the Athenian fleet along with ships gathered from elsewhere in southern Greece to seek control of the sea. Nicanor led this fleet to the Hellespont and Propontis to join up with a flotilla of ships gathered there on Antigonus' behalf, and Polyperchon had persuaded Cleitus to side with him against Cassander and Antigonus, and go in pursuit of Nicanor's fleet. Antigonus hastened to the Propontis to take command of this fleet, but arrived too late. In summer 318 the two fleets met in battle near the entrance to the Bosporus, and Cleitus won a clear victory. The bulk of Nicanor's fleet escaped from the battle to port on the Asian shore intact, but greatly dispirited; while Cleitus and his ships encamped on the European shore to celebrate their victory. Antigonus arrived the night after the battle, immediately took command, and set about redressing the situation.

Realizing that the crews on the ships were demoralized by their defeat, Antigonus had the fleet transport most of his army across the Bosporus to the European shore, while posting detachments of his soldiers on the ships to ensure that they would obey orders and fight. The fleet rowed quietly to lie in wait outside Cleitus' camp, while Antigonus marched the bulk of his army along the shore to spring a surprise night attack. Cleitus' men were indeed taken completely by surprise, sleeping off their victory celebration; and as the sounds of fighting rose in the night air, Antigonus' ships attacked from the sea. Just hours after its seemingly decisive victory, Cleitus' fleet was captured by Antigonus with scarcely a struggle. Cleitus himself managed to escape with a few ships, but was forced to land and there captured and killed by soldiers allied to Antigonus. Nicanor sailed back to Athens victorious, the prows of his ships decorated with victory wreaths, to boost Cassander's already successful operations there. Cassander, in fact, was proving to be more than a match for Polyperchon, who turned out to be the classic officer promoted beyond his abilities. His attempts to win control of Greek cities failed, and an attempted siege of Megalopolis proved disastrous. In 317 Polyperchon was forced to retreat to Macedonia with nothing accomplished, leaving Cassander to consolidate his control over southern Greece and lay plans for invading Macedonia.

Meanwhile, his victory near the Bosporos freed Antigonus to deal with Eumenes. He sent messengers to Cyinda to try to detach the Silver Shields from their allegiance to Eumenes, and divided his forces. He had about sixty thousand soldiers available at this point, and selected the twenty thousand fittest to accompany him to confront Eumenes, leaving the remainder under loyal officers to secure full control of Asia Minor. The messengers he had sent to the Silver Shields, as well as others sent by Ptolemy, had failed to detach them from their loyalty to Eumenes. But the latter did face a problem of disloyalty: it came from the senior Macedonian officers of his troops, who resented being subordinated to a non-Macedonian Greek. This was especially true of Antigenes and Teutamus, the commanders of the Silver Shields and the Hypaspists, respectively. To overcome this, Eumenes pretended to have had a dream in which Alexander himself had appeared to him and instructed him to hold collegial meetings in a leadership conference to be held in his (Alexander's) own tent. Setting up a tent formerly used by Alexander, with suitable furnishings, and sacrificing ritually to Alexander, Eumenes presided over councils of the leading officers in Alexander's name, and found it easy enough to persuade them to see things his way. Learning that Antigonus was approaching with a numerically superior force, Eumenes did not wait for a showdown: he moved his army south into north Syria and Phoenicia, and there learned news from the east that greatly encouraged him.

While Cassander and Polyperchon were fighting it out in Europe, and Eumenes and Antigonus were confronting each other in western Asia, trouble had arisen in the eastern or "upper" satrapies (provinces) of the empire too. The strongest governor in the east was Peithon, son of Crateuas, who had defeated the rebellious Greek colonists in the east on behalf of Perdiccas in 322. As governor of Media now, he sought to assert his domination over all of the eastern satraps. They resisted this, and wisely banded their forces together, led by the governor of Persia, Peucestas. A showdown ensued in which Peucestas and his colleagues defeated Peithon and his army. Forced into flight, Peithon with the remnants of his forces took refuge with Seleucus, the governor of Babylonia and an old friend of Peithon. While they were planning together how to get the best of the "upper" satraps, Eumenes appeared leading his small but potent army eastwards through Mesopotamia. Eumenes had calculated that by combining either or both of the two eastern armies with his own forces, he would be strong enough to confront Antigonus with a good prospect of success. Attempts to negotiate with Seleucus and Peithon failed, however: they were both, as we have seen, deeply implicated in the assassination of Eumenes' good friend and patron the former regent Perdiccas, and they neither trusted nor liked Eumenes. On the other hand, envoys sent to Peucestas and the "upper" satraps received an encouraging welcome: they were seeking support against a renewed attack by Peithon and his ally Seleucus, and were very willing to combine with Eumenes to that end. So Eumenes hurried eastwards to link up with the army of the eastern satraps near Susa. Combining his forces with theirs, he now commanded an army of at least forty-five thousand, including strong cavalry forces and war elephants in addition to his own incomparable Silver Shields.

When Antigonus appeared in Mesopotamia pursuing Eumenes,

he was met by messengers of Seleucus and Peithon warning him of Eumenes' new strength. Realizing that his army of about twenty thousand was no longer adequate, Antigonus encamped in Mesopotamia for the winter while sending for additional forces to come to join him, and also sealing an alliance with Peithon and Seleucus. At the beginning of 316 he crossed the Tigris and marched for Iran with an army in excess of fifty thousand men, including strong and excellent cavalry forces in addition to nearly twenty thousand Macedonian or Macedonian-trained and equipped infantrymen. This led to a remarkable campaign lasting a little over a year between two very evenly matched armies of the same type and composition, and two brilliant and inventive generals, whose skills and efforts to outmaneuver each other remind one of a match between chess grandmasters.

Initially, Eumenes faced difficulties asserting control over the ambitious Macedonian generals and governors commanding the various units of his disparate army. He used a variety of ploys to establish and maintain his leadership. The Alexander command tent made its reappearance, for example; the letters signed by the regent and the kings gave Eumenes access to the royal treasury at Susa, enabling him to pay his troops well and distribute gifts; on the other hand, he borrowed money from some of the governors against a promise of handsome repayment terms once he was victorious; and on one occasion he forged letters from Polyperchon and Olympias reporting that Cassander was defeated and dead, and a large relief army commanded by Polyperchon himself on its way to aid him. By these various stratagems and others, Eumenes did retain control over his army, helped greatly by the fact that the soldiers trusted him more than any other general. He decided, however, that he needed time to prepare his army before facing Antigonus, so leaving Susa and its treasury strongly fortified and guarded by a loyal officer, he marched south into Persia. Arriving at Susa to find Eumenes gone and the city's gates closed to him, Antigonus left Seleucus with several thousand men to besiege the place, and moved south in pursuit of Eumenes' army.

Eumenes had had two years now to reflect on how he had been outwitted and outmaneuvered by Antigonus in the campaign and battle of Orcynia, and proceeded to show that he had learned from his defeat. Arriving at a deep and swift-flowing river in northern Persia called the

Copratas, Antigonus found only enough boats to ferry his men across a
few thousand at a time. That would be very risky, but since the opposite
bank seemed deserted, he took the risk, ordering the first contingent to
start preparing a fortified camp while the rest crossed. However,
Eumenes had a large force concealed nearby, which emerged when only
the first group of Antigonus' troops had crossed and caught them isolated on the south bank, cut off by the deep river from the bulk of
Antigonus' army. More than four thousand of Antigonus' soldiers were
killed or captured, a severe setback which demoralized Antigonus'
troops, who had been forced to watch helplessly the fate of their com-
rades. It was Antigonus' turn to retreat, to find time and space in which
to repair his army's morale. He decided to march north into Media, Peithon's satrapy, to rest and recuperate his army, which suffered from the
summer heat in Persia. In Media he found funds in the royal treasury at
Ecbatana, and was able to supply his men with everything they needed
in abundance, including fresh horses. The move was risky in that it
opened to Eumenes the possibility of marching west to attack Antigonus'
lands in Syria and Asia Minor, but Antigonus rightly calculated that the
eastern governors would refuse to allow their troops to be marched so
far from their provinces while Antigonus and his army were in the east.
So Eumenes in fact marched deeper into Persia, and the two forces spent
the hottest months of summer 316 resting and preparing for the coming
showdown, one in Media and the other in Persia.

In late summer it was Antigonus who made the first move, marching south with his army into a region of central Iran named Paraetacene. Informed of Antigonus' move, Eumenes marched north to meet
him. When the two armies came together, they drew up in strong positions about half a mile apart on either side of a steep ravine, each challenging the other to try an attack at a severe disadvantage. Neither was
inclined to take the risk, and after several days of posturing, supplies
in the area ran short and Antigonus decided to march away by night
into a richly stocked neighboring area named Gabiene. However,
Eumenes learned of this plan from deserters, and sent apparent deserters of his own into Antigonus' camp to warn of an intended night attack
by Eumenes. While Antigonus therefore kept his army under arms
through the night awaiting attack, it was Eumenes who stole away in
the night with his army towards Gabiene. Learning in the morning how

he had been tricked, Antigonus set out in pursuit of Eumenes with his
best cavalry, ordering his infantry to rest awhile and then follow at the
best speed it could manage. Eumenes had just emerged from a range of
hills into a broad flat plain when Antigonus' cavalry appeared on the
crest of the hills behind him. Fearing that Antigonus' entire army was
there, Eumenes had to stop his march and draw up his army for battle.
Meanwhile Antigonus simply kept his cavalry in plain view to hold
Eumenes in place, and waited for the rest of his army to catch up. When
it did, he arranged them in battle formation and marched down into
the open plain to confront Eumenes. Diodorus comments (19.27) on
the awe-inspiring sight Antigonus' army made as it marched down from
the foothills into the plain, making it clear that he was drawing on an
eye-witness report: undoubtedly that of Eumenes' officer, the historian
Hieronymus of Cardia.

The two armies were very evenly matched: each was rather more
than forty-one thousand men strong; each had as its heart units of Macedonian or Macedonian-style heavy infantry twenty thousand or more
strong, along with mercenaries and light infantry. Antigonus had the advantage in cavalry, well over ten thousand to a little more than six thousand; but against this Eumenes had the matchless Silver Shields as the
core of his infantry. The battle was fought very much in the style of
Philip and Alexander: each general stationed his best cavalry on his right
under his own command, withheld his left, and ordered his infantry to
advance steadily to try to drive back the opposition. The aim was to
wait for a suitable opportunity for a decisive cavalry charge on the right.
In the event, the fight did not work out quite as planned, however. Peithon, stationed in command of Antigonus' left with a large force of light
cavalry, decided to try to win the battle himself and charged Eumenes'
right instead of holding back. He was defeated and driven back to take
refuge among the foothills behind Antigonus' army. Meanwhile, the Silver Shields took the initiative and charged at a swift pace into Antigonus'
infantry, who could not withstand their ferocious impetus. Antigonus'
phalanx was driven back, fighting hard, to join Peithon. The battle
threatened to become a disaster for Antigonus, but with typical coolness
and decision he refused to retreat to join the rest of his army but led a
cavalry charge on his right which drove back the cavalry on Eumenes'
left. Keeping his head, Antigonus then turned his cavalry to threaten

Eumenes' infantry from behind, forcing them to break off their pursuit of his (Antigonus') defeated infantry. This enabled officers sent by Antigonus to regroup and reorganize his infantry and left wing cavalry, and bring them forward again to rejoin Antigonus and the right wing cavalry. As Antigonus thus reorganized his army to renew the fight, Eumenes did the same, a few hundred yards separating the two armies. By the time they were ready, however, it was nearly midnight.

Both armies were exhausted after a night of marching and a day of fighting, and both commanders decided against trying to fight again. Eumenes led his army back, intending to occupy the site of the battle— a standard sign of victory; but once it was marching Eumenes' army refused to stop at the site of the fight and insisted on returning all the way to the comforts of their camp. Antigonus had his men better in hand: once he saw that Eumenes' army had withdrawn completely, he led his men forward and encamped on the site of the battle, taking up the dead and wounded. Far more of these were Antigonus' men—nearly eight thousand all told—while Eumenes' casualties amounted to under fifteen hundred. Thus, though both sides claimed victory in this drawn battle, it was clear that Eumenes' side had the advantage. Antigonus buried his dead at dawn, and looked after his wounded and the rest of his army, while informing heralds from Eumenes' army that he would hand over the enemy dead and wounded on the next day. In fact, however, he led his army away under cover of darkness into southern Media, where he put them into winter quarters. Eumenes, after taking care of his own dead and wounded, continued his march into Gabiene and there settled his army too into winter quarters.

The year 316 thus came to a close with no outcome to the contest, and with Antigonus getting impatient to finish it off and return west. Through scouts or other informants he learned that Eumenes had dispersed his army widely into separate camps for the winter, and perceived in this an opportunity for a surprise attack. The standard route from his winter quarters to the region where Eumenes was quartered was more than three weeks' march; but the distance was much shorter as the crow flies: a mere nine days' march through a trackless, waterless desert would bring Antigonus' army into Gabiene. This desert was overlooked by hills on all sides, and in order to keep the element of surprise an army marching through it would have to avoid lighting fires at night.

Just after the winter solstice, as the year changed from 316 to 315, Antigonus announced that he intended to invade Armenia to the northwest and ordered his troops to prepare ten days' water and rations for a swift march. He then set out across the desert towards Gabiene instead, intending to roll up Eumenes' army piecemeal in their scattered winter camps. Unfortunately, the winter nights in the desert were so cold that Antigonus' soldiers disobeyed his orders not to light fires; their fires were observed from the surrounding hills and reported to Eumenes, who realized he was about to be disastrously outmaneuvered. Rising to the occasion, he gathered the troops nearest the desert, several thousand strong, and ordered them to build enough fires on the hills overlooking the desert to suggest an encampment of tens of thousands of men. When these camp fires were, in turn, reported to Antigonus, he assumed that Eumenes had already concentrated his army and at once changed his line of march into inhabited lands to recuperate his army before confronting Eumenes. This of course gave Eumenes time to gather his army, and the two forces drew together for another major confrontation in Gabiene.

The resulting battle, fought early in 315, took place on a broad plain with a saline, dusty topsoil. Antigonus drew up his army as at Paraetacene, with his strongest cavalry on the right, light cavalry in a withdrawn position on his left, and his infantry in between with orders to hold their ground and look for the right wing cavalry to win the battle. Eumenes decided to take his station on his left this time, with his best cavalry, to counter Antigonus' right wing cavalry. He relied on his infantry, with the experienced Silver Shields, to win the battle for him. In front of both armies was a skirmishing line of light infantry interspersed with elephants, and when these engaged each other, they threw up such dust clouds that the battlefield became obscured and the action hard to follow. The Silver Shields nevertheless led a charge of Eumenes' infantry and routed the fearful infantry of Antigonus opposed to them. As Antigonus' infantry fled, pursued by the Silver Shields, however, Antigonus charged Eumenes' left wing with his cavalry and, despite fierce resistance from Eumenes' personal guard, broke through and forced Eumenes' left wing into flight. Eumenes managed to extricate his guard and rode to join his right wing cavalry, which had not yet been engaged. Despite all Eumenes could do, however, when his light cavalry saw Antigonus' heavy cavalry coming at it in clouds of dust, they turned and retreated. That left Antigonus free to attack Eumenes' victorious infantry from behind, abruptly halting their pursuit of his own infantry. Led by the highly disciplined Silver Shields, Eumenes' infantry organized themselves in a square formation and counter-marched to link up with Eumenes and the light cavalry forces of his right wing, commanded by Peucestas, leaving Antigonus and his cavalry in control of the field of battle.

So far, the battle seemed like another draw, just as the one fought at Paraetacene in the previous year. But there was a twist to the tale. When his army had reunited some distance from the original battle site, Eumenes urged his men to reform and renew the fight, arguing that victory was within their grasp thanks to the crushing of Antigonus' infantry. Peucestas and the light cavalry, however, refused to confront Antigonus' heavy cavalry, instead insisting that the army withdraw to their camp to rest and consider their position. That proved to be impossible, however. When Antigonus noted the huge obscuring clouds of dust thrown up by the screens of skirmishers, he had taken advantage of the lack of visibility to send a special detachment of cavalry to ride unobserved around the site of battle and capture Eumenes' camp by surprise. In that camp were the wives, children, and life savings of Eumenes' soldiers. As soon as they learned of this, the Silver Shields decided they had had enough. They sent representatives to negotiate with Antigonus for the return of their families and property. Antigonus was willing enough: all they had to do was switch sides and hand over Eumenes. The unwary Eumenes was suddenly arrested by his own elite soldiers, who carried him off to Antigonus' camp and handed him over, ending this campaign. Antigonus was now the clear winner. The other eastern satraps either made their own peace with Antigonus on the best terms they could, or fled back to their provinces with whatever troops would follow them. A few, most notably the Silver Shields' commander Antigenes, were arrested and killed.

After some deliberation, Antigonus decided that Eumenes could not be trusted and was too dangerous to leave alive. Despite their old friendship, therefore, Eumenes was executed; but many of his friends and subordinates, like Hieronymus and Peucestas, found positions in Antigonus' entourage. Antigonus spent the spring and summer of 315 reorganizing the eastern part of the empire so as to pose no further threat to him, his chief goal being to return to the west as soon as possible. Reliable officers were sent to take over those provinces whose satraps had been killed; the governors who had safely escaped back to their provinces were cowed and offered no further threat. To oversee the eastern provinces Antigonus decided to leave a general with a strong force in Media. For this post he judged that Peithon could not be trusted: he was arrested and executed on charges of disloyalty, and a loyal friend named Nicanor was established in the post instead. Antigonus then took the royal treasure at Ecbatana and moved southwest to Susa. There the gates to the citadel were now open to him, and he took possession of the great royal treasure there too. Having scooped up all the remaining great Persian treasures, Antigonus was able to convoy to the west under his charge the stupendous sum of thirty thousand talents of gold and silver. This, along with his army, formed the secure basis of his power, enabling him to pay armies and administrators, build fleets, establish cities and forts, and bring in colonists and garrisons as he saw fit. Arriving in Babylonia, he decided that Seleucus, like Peithon, was too independent to be trusted, and set about deposing him. More wary than Peithon, Seleucus saw the blow coming and fled with his personal entourage to take refuge with Ptolemy in Egypt.

At the end of 315 Antigonus returned to Syria with all of the Asian empire of the Macedonians, in effect the former Persian Empire, under his complete control, making him the great winner so far of the wars of the succession and the most powerful by far of Alexander's Successors. His armed forces had swollen to in excess of eighty thousand men, with outstanding cavalry and a solid core of Macedonian infantry. His wealth was vast and in addition to his treasure we learn that his annual income from his lands amounted to some eleven thousand talents. But new challenges awaited. In the west, Cassander had defeated Polyperchon and established himself as ruler over Macedonia and most of southern Greece. In late 317 Polyperchon had made the mistake of leaving Macedonia to confront Cassander without taking king Philip Arrhidaeus with him. The young queen Eurydice had promptly taken control of her husband and the government, deposing Polyperchon as regent and siding with Cassander and Antigonus. That prompted Alexander's mother Olympias, concerned for her young grandson

Alexander IV, to leave her self-imposed exile in Epirus and enter Macedonia with an army. Eurydice gathered troops to meet her and there occurred the unique spectacle, in western Macedonia, of two armies confronting each other, each of which was commanded by a woman. In the event Eurydice's Macedonians refused to fight against the mother of Alexander, and the young queen was defeated and captured along with her husband. In control of Macedonia at last, Olympias proceeded to lose all the good will she had by instituting a reign of terror. Eurydice and her husband, the hapless king Philip Arrhidaeus, were brutally executed; relatives and adherents of Cassander were hounded and executed; and even the bones of Cassander's deceased relatives were dug up and their graves desecrated.

When Cassander returned at last to Macedonia at the head of a large army, the Macedonians would not fight for the frightful Olympias, who took refuge in the fortified city of Pydna where she was besieged and starved into surrender. Cassander arranged for the relatives of Olympias' victims to take revenge by killing the old queen, and himself recovered the bodies of Eurydice and Philip Arrhidaeus for royal burial, probably in the famed tomb II at Vergina whose magnificent burial goods are now displayed in the museum built over the tombs. Cassander took charge of the surviving king, the child Alexander IV, and had him placed under "protective custody" with his mother Roxane in Amphipolis, there to be properly educated for his future position as ruler, so he let it be known. Meanwhile, 315 found Cassander in full control of Macedonia and a formidable ruler. Polyperchon had retreated with the remnants of his forces to Aetolia and the western Peloponnese, there to live the life of a minor dynast and mercenary commander.

Ptolemy had used the years of Antigonus' absence in the east to secure his control of Egypt, build up his capital city of Alexandria, seize control of the Cyrenaica in Libya, and extend his power over a buffer zone of Palestine (including Phoenicia) and Cyprus. With Antigonus' return to the west, Ptolemy himself returned to Egypt after establishing strong garrisons in the cities of Phoenicia and Palestine, and prudently removing the fleets of the Phoenician cities to Egypt where he could control them. Ptolemy and Cassander had been in touch with each other, and with another still independent dynast, Lysimachus in Thrace, and decided that Antigonus was so strong that, for the security of all, he must be cut down to size. Along with the refugee Seleucus they had prepared a common ultimatum which was waiting for Antigonus when he arrived in southern Syria. This ultimatum portended future strife and warfare.

3. Creating the Empires of the Hellenistic World

With Polyperchon's brief and failed regency brought to an end, the wars of Alexander's generals had resulted in the division of Alexander's realm into three major "empires": Antigonus ruled over western Asia (essentially the former Persian Empire); Ptolemy controlled Egypt, with its immense wealth and matchless grain resources; and Cassander held Macedonia and its neighboring lands, the source of the Macedonian and Greek manpower without which there could be no empire. This division of lands was to prove permanent, at least until the advent of the Romans in the second and first centuries BCE, though there was still much fighting to be done, and both western Asia and Macedonia changed ruling dynasties before things finally settled down after 272. But it was the organization of empires and systems of rule that was the most crucial feature of the years after 315 down to the 280s and 270s. These are the decades when the governing structures of what we call the Hellenistic World were established, in western Asia by Antigonus and Seleucus, in Egypt by the first two Ptolemies, and in Macedonia by Cassander and Antigonus Gonatas.

In between fighting their numerous wars and battles, in fact, Antigonus, Seleucus, and Ptolemy expended enormous effort in organizing the conquered lands in Asia and Egypt into stable empires based on Greek civilization. They reorganized the old provinces, in many cases dividing them up into smaller more manageable provinces governed by military governors with the title *strategos* (general). They revamped the tribute payment system, establishing sub-provinces called *chiliarchies* (by Antigonus) or *eparchies* (after Seleucus took over), each ruled by a regional sub-governor responsible for local security and tribute collection. They settled tens of thousands of veteran soldiers in military colonies, many named after cities of Macedonia and Greece, such as Pella, Cyrrhus, Europus, or Larissa, where they functioned as local security forces and their sons and grandsons were eventually recruited into the imperial armies. Most important of all, they imported many tens if not hundreds of thousands of Greek (or at least Greek-speaking) colonists into Asia and Egypt who were settled in new Greek cities. Frequently these cities were named after the kings and other members— including female members—of the royal dynasties, and by the second century BCE, instead of Athens, Sparta, and Corinth, the leading cities in the Greek world were Alexandria in Egypt, Antioch (formerly Antigoneia) in Syria, Seleucia on the Tigris, and many other cities with dynastic names such as Ptolemais, Arsinoeia, Laodiceia, Stratoniceia, or Apamea. For some six centuries the near east was dominated by the new urban civilization we call Hellenistic, a melding of classical Greek culture with elements of native Asian and Egyptian cultures. This vast colonization program, organized primarily by Antigonus, Seleucus, and Ptolemy—though built on and continued by their early heirs—was undoubtedly the most important work carried out by Alexander's Successors, and deserves careful investigation.

It needs to be recognized what a vast undertaking the colonization program of the great Successors of Alexander was. In excess of one hundred thousand people were transported across the Aegean and eastern Mediterranean from Greece and other Balkan territories to find new homes in western Asia and Egypt. The human and political geography of western Asia and Egypt were thereby fundamentally changed, as was their culture. Thanks to the city-building enterprises of Antigonus, Seleucus, and Ptolemy, Greek urban life and culture became the dominant way of life and culture, and Greek the universal language. This process required immense organizational skills and a vast expenditure of wealth. Thousands and thousands of people—women and children as well as men—could not simply be told to make their ways from their ancestral homes to new lands, and then parked there to organize themselves into cities and thrive or die as luck dictated. These people had to be transported, they had to be fed and cared for during transportation, they had to be assisted to organize themselves in their new homes, they needed all sorts of assistance to build their new houses and urban infrastructure. That process of building would certainly take years, during which they would continue to need assistance in food and supplies of all sorts, as well as in technical expertise and labor for all of the building that must be done.

Unfortunately, our ancient sources tell us very little about this colonizing process: we only see the result. But from the few sources that do offer some detail, a picture of the process can be reconstructed. We may take as an example the city of Antigoneia on the Orontes, founded around 307 by Antigonus the One-Eyed, and later (after 301) moved a few miles downstream and re-founded as Antioch by Seleucus. The late antique chronicler John Malalas, a native of Antioch, reports in his *Chronographia* at book 8.15 that the population of Antigoneia was mostly made up of Athenians but with some Macedonians, 5,300 men in total. The source of the Macedonians is clear: Antigonus had thousands of Macedonian soldiers in his army, whom he settled as they grew older in numerous cities and garrison colonies all around western Asia. But how did the four thousand or more Athenians, perhaps even as many as five thousand, get to Syria and the banks of the River Orontes? And those numbers just account for the men: we must surely assume that many if not most of these Athenian settlers had wives and children too. At a very conservative guess we can assume that more than ten thousand people had to be transported from Athens to Syria to found this city. To begin with this issue sheds a new light on Antigonus' decision at the beginning of 307, as we shall see below, to send his son Demetrius with a huge expeditionary force to "liberate" Athens from the rule of Cassander and restore the traditional democracy there. That gave Antigonus the ability and popularity to request Athenian settlers for his new foundation. It also gave him the means of transporting them.

Generals like Antigonus were experts in the movement of large groups of people over long distances: as leaders of armies they had to be. When Demetrius unshipped his men, horses, and supplies from his transport vessels (more than two hundred of them) to campaign in Greece, we can be sure that the ships did not just sit idle in port at the Piraeus. It must have been in these transport vessels that the Athenian settlers, with their families and goods, were shipped to the mouth of the River Orontes in Syria: there is no alternative, as passenger ships in antiquity were actually just merchant ships with room for a handful of passengers in addition to cargo. Only military transports will have had the capacity to transport people in the large numbers required for city foundation. Antigonus and Ptolemy, and later Seleucus, had plenty of such transport vessels available to them, in which settlers from Greece and the Balkan region could travel to western Asia and Egypt at the ruler's expense. So the initial movement of settlers from the Balkan region to Asia or Egypt was in essence a military operation, carried out in military transport vessels and, once they had landed, by overland march to the sites of their settlements under military escort for protection, and using the logistical supply systems developed for supplying armies on the march. But before this transport operation could be undertaken, there must have been extensive preparation work at the settlement site; because one could not simply deposit ten thousand or more men, women, and children at an empty site and expect them to survive.

The most obvious advance preparation will have been the stockpiling of several months' worth of food supplies at the settlement site, so that the arriving settlers could eat. In addition there must have been planning for an ongoing supply of food to reach the developing settlement for at least a year or two, until the settlers could begin to be self sustaining. Key here was the designation of a large territory around the settlement site as civic land (*ge politike* in the ancient Greek) belonging—with its native inhabitants engaged in farming—to the new city and responsible for supplying the food requirements of the city once the phase of initial development had passed. In addition, settlers could not just be left to fend for themselves in open fields. The founder will have needed to have a city planner on site to lay out the initial plan of the urban settlement, with a street plan incorporating housing blocks, public spaces, sites for temples, a theater, a gymnasium, and the other basic infrastructure considered necessary to the Greek urban way of life. There will have needed to be hydraulic engineers to locate a safe source of drinking water and arrange to pipe it into the settlement. The settlers will have needed building supplies of all sorts—stone, timber, roof tiles, and so on—to build their homes; and the help of trained architects with this, and to plan the temples and other public buildings, will have been indispensable. During the phase of building, which must have taken many months at a minimum, some kind of temporary housing for the settlers must have been made available, lest they die of exposure. The most obvious solution will no doubt have been again to draw on military experience: tents and bivouacs of the sort used by soldiers (and their hangers-on) on campaign could house the settlers until newly built homes became habitable.

In addition to all of the material supplies and planning necessary to creating a physical settlement, the political and legal arrangements of the settlement had to be taken care of. An inscription informs us that when Antigonus planned to create a new city by joining together the older Greek cities of Teos and Lebedos, it was planned that they should draw up their own laws and political structure jointly, under his overall supervision. But while they were engaged on this, the law code—including the political system—of a mutually agreed third city was borrowed to serve as the temporary legal and political system. In the case of Antigoneia, with its settlers drawn primarily from Athens, it is reasonable to guess that a legal/political code and system based on that of Athens will have been applied. No doubt the settlers could have brought a copy of Athens' laws with them. But Antigonus built, we know, a palace (*basileion*) in Antigoneia, planning to live and rule his empire from there. And the presence of a ruling king was not allowed for in the Athenian system. There must have been suitable adjustments to Antigoneia's law code, which will have required negotiation and the expert advice of Antigonus' legal consultants in his administrative chancellery.

The point of all of this is that founding a new city by bringing in thousands of settlers from elsewhere was a huge, expensive, and demanding undertaking, requiring detailed planning, the commitment of resources of all sorts, and the provision of various kinds of expertise that will have needed to be paid for. In the case of Antigoneia, we know that by the middle of 306 the city was already considerably built up, with a town square (*agora*) and the palace of Antigonus nearby; and by 302 the city was mostly complete, as Antigonus was then planning an international festival to inaugurate the new city. That means the initial settling took about a year, and the major building of the city some five years to bring to a state of reasonable completion. And Antigoneia was just one of more than twenty cities and colonies founded by Antigonus between 314 and 302; the largest no doubt, but we begin to see the scale of the work accomplished in these years by Antigonus and his various military and civil assistants.

After 301 the task of continuing the settlement and urbanization, in the sense of bringing in Greek speakers and establishing Greek-style urban settlements, was continued in western Asia by Seleucus, who founded or re-founded many dozens of larger and smaller cities and colonies over the following twenty years, until 281. In the meantime Ptolemy had been doing the same sort of work in Egypt, building the great city of Alexandria, and also founding cities named Ptolemais after himself and Berenice after his favorite wife. Seleucus' son Antiochus and Ptolemy's son Ptolemy II continued their fathers' work, so that by the middle of the third century BCE there was a thriving network of Greek cities and towns in western Asia and Egypt where the Hellenistic culture that dominated the near east for six centuries developed and grew. But the most important work was undoubtedly done in the first generation, by the Successors of Alexander during the forty years following Alexander's death; and the epic scale of this work, made possible by the opening up of the Persian Empire to Greek control and settlement, the existence of a large under-resourced population in Greece and the Balkan lands willing to move to build a better life for themselves, the monetization of the stored treasures of the two hundred years of Persian rule to fund the colonization program, and the extraordinary leadership and organizational talents of the officers Philip had trained during his years as king, cannot be understated. This colonization program literally changed the near eastern world once and for all.

As so often for this era, Alexander has received far too much of the credit for all this colonizing and city-building. As we saw in the previous chapter, properly scrutinized Alexander's city founding work turns out to have been quite modest. It was the three great Successors, Antigonus, Seleucus, and Ptolemy who did most of this work, though Lysimachus, Antiochus I, and Ptolemy II also deserve some credit. Antigonus I founded some twenty cities that we know of, and our record of his city founding is certainly very defective. Seleucus built on Antigonus' work when he took over Antigonus' empire, refounding most of Antigonus' cities with new names—so Antigoneia on the Orontes became Antioch, and Pella became Apameia on the Orontes—and founding dozens of additional new cities. Ptolemy was the real builder of Alexandria, which had been nominally founded by Alexander, and founded several other cities in Egypt. Since much of the stored-up wealth of the Persian Empire and of Egypt was put to work in this colonizing enterprise, instead of being uselessly held in treasuries, the colonizing also had a positive economic effect in promoting the further generation of wealth through productive industry (building activities of all sorts) and associated trading. Our sources focus overwhelmingly on the warfare of the Successor period, giving the impression that men like Antigonus, Seleucus, and Ptolemy were generals pure and simple who devoted their time and energy to campaigning and fighting battles. That obscures the real and much more important work these great leaders, and others like Lysimachus and Cassander too, were engaged on in these decades: the fundamental re-shaping of their world by one of the great settlement and urbanization programs in western history.

4. FURTHER WARS OF THE SUCCESSION TO 301

In 315, though the basic political geography of the new Hellenistic world had taken shape, the conflicts among the Successors of Alexander were far from over. Antigonus had emerged as by far the strongest leader, and as we have seen the remaining autonomous commanders—Cassander in Macedonia, Ptolemy in Egypt, and Seleucus and Lysimachus who had proved to be very capable generals—decided to work together to cut Antigonus down to size. They jointly sent Antigonus an embassy demanding that he cede moneys and lands to them as their share of the successful wars against Perdiccas, Polyperchon, and Eumenes. The treasures of the Persian kings were to be shared (equally?) among all five dynasts, and Antigonus was to cede Hellespontine Phrygia (along the Hellespont and Propontis) to Lysimachus, Lycia and (probably) Caria to Cassander, Syria to Ptolemy, and Babylonia to Seleucus. Thus shorn of money and lands, Antigonus would be no more powerful than the other dynasts; if anything indeed less so. That Antigonus would tamely agree to these demands was hardly to be expected, and in fact of course he rejected them out of hand. To the ambassadors' warning that if he did not accept there would be war his response was to begin the war by marching into Phoenicia and beginning to expel Ptolemy's garrisons there.

The war begun in 315 lasted four years until 311, and was fought primarily on three fronts: in Phoenicia and Palestine, where Antigonus and Ptolemy competed for control; in southern Greece, where Antigonus sought to drive out Cassander's garrisons and allies; and in the Aegean, where Antigonus and Ptolemy competed for naval dominance. A feature of this period is the gradual receding of Antigonus away from active command of his forces in favor of his nephews and his son Demetrius. Antigonus was nearly seventy at the beginning of 314 and had been pushing himself hard for the past ten years. In the years from 323 to 314, in fact, Antigonus had fought with an energy, skill, daring, and success that mark him as one of the great generals of the ancient world: from his Cyprus campaign in 320, to his crushing victories at Orcynia and Cretopolis in 319 and at the Bosporus in 318, and through his extraordinary duel with Eumenes from 317 to 315 culminating in the showdown battles of Paraetacene and Gabiene, he set a record that only the very greatest generals, such as Alexander and Caesar, could match or beat. It is hardly surprising that in his seventies he preferred to leave as much as possible of the active campaigning to younger men, while himself concentrating more and more on the organization and administration of his empire.

As already noted, Antigonus did not wait for his opponents to initiate hostilities at the beginning of 314, but himself made the first move by invading and occupying Phoenicia and Palestine. Ptolemy had already prudently left these lands for Egypt, leaving only garrisons behind; these garrisons offered little opposition to Antigonus. Only Tyre put up serious resistance. Once again, as in the time of Alexander, Tyre withstood a major and long-lasting siege, only to succumb in the end and be captured after holding out for more than a year. While he was besieging Tyre, Antigonus busied himself with a host of other matters. Learning that forces sent by Cassander were operating in Asia Minor, he sent his nephew Polemaeus with an army of around ten thousand men to eject those forces and secure the coasts of Asia Minor, at the Hellespont and Ionia, against further incursions. To keep Cassander busy at home, Antigonus despatched his close friend Aristodemus to southern Greece with a thousand talents to recruit mercenaries and campaign against Cassander's garrisons. In addition, Aristodemus had orders to get in touch with Polyperchon, who was lurking in the western Peloponnesos with a substantial force: now that he was no longer regent, Polyperchon might prove a useful ally against Cassander.

Unwilling to confront Antigonus and his army directly, Ptolemy instead used the Phoenician fleets he had gathered while in control of Phoenicia. He placed Seleucus in charge of this combined fleet and sent him to harry Antigonus' lands from the sea. After spending the summer attacking the coasts of southern and western Asia Minor, Seleucus retreated to Cyprus for the winter. There too, however, Antigonus had been active: he had sent ambassadors with promises, who managed to detach from Ptolemy the city-kings of Marion, Citium, Lapethus, Cerynia, and Amathous. In response to Seleucus' naval demonstration, Antigonus had taken steps to redress the balance of naval power by setting up a huge naval building program. Timber was cut in Lebanon, Cilicia, and along the south Black Sea shore to supply ship-building yards in the Phoenician cities, along the coast of Cilicia, in the Black Sea ports, and on the island of Rhodes, which was allied to Antigonus at this time. Within two years, Antigonus raised fleets in excess of 240 warships. Fifty of these ships were sent to southern Greece under the command of Antigonus' nephew Telesphorus, to aid the operations against Cassander there; the remainder were placed under the command of another nephew, Dioscurides, to sail around the Aegean expelling Ptolemy's ships and forces, and to organize the Aegean islands as allies of Antigonus in the Nesiotic League, or League of the Islanders.

Seeking to undermine Cassander further in Greece and win the good will of the Greeks, Antigonus issued a great proclamation establishing his policy with respect to the Greek cities. The Proclamation of Tyre in 314 established the principle that all Greek cities should be free, autonomous, ungarrisoned, and free from outside taxation. Antigonus committed himself to enforcing and upholding this principle, and called on all Greek cities and other leaders of good will to join him in securing the promised freedom and autonomy for the Greek cities. Ambassadors were despatched far and wide to publicize this proclamation. Antigonus knew that to secure his empire and govern it effectively he needed Greek manpower on a vast scale: soldiers, administrators, and colonists by the tens of thousands. As the great patron of Greek freedom, Antigonus hoped (rightly) that he could secure a strong footing in the Greek world and succeed in importing Greek manpower into western Asia on the scale needed to establish Macedonian control there over the long term. Antigonus' chief rival Ptolemy, who likewise needed Greek manpower to secure long-term control in Egypt, immediately echoed Antigonus' proclamation with a similar one of his own, also espousing the principle of Greek autonomy. Cassander, who had plenty of Macedonian and other Greek manpower and needed control of southern Greece, resisted it, but increasingly unsuccessfully.

The fighting in Greece in the years 314 to 311 was chaotic, and need not be gone into in detail here. Antigonid forces organized and commanded by Aristodemus and (from 312 on) Polemaeus were able, thanks to the genuine popularity of Antigonus' Tyre proclamation, to detach much of southern and central Greece from loyalty to Cassander, greatly weakening Cassander's grip on southern Greece. Antigonus managed, with minimal expenditure of his own resources, to stir up enough trouble for Lysimachus in Thrace and among the Greek cities of the western Black Sea coast to keep that dynast too busy to intervene against Antigonus in Asia or the Aegean. Thus any threat from these two leaders was effectively neutralized. Minor trouble did arise when the governor of Caria in south-west Asia Minor, an influential Macedonian aristocrat named Asander, decided he wanted to rule his territory independently and sought aid from Cassander and Ptolemy to do so. Antigonus decided to put on a show of force to keep his provincial governors submissive. Leaving his handsome and brilliant son Demetrius, now in his early twenties, in charge of Phoenicia and Palestine with a large force, Antigonus marched with a large army into western Asia Minor and seized control of Caria in a brief campaign demonstrating exactly how to use overwhelming force effectively. While Antigonus himself, with a large army, marched through Caria from north to south receiving the surrender of local cities and forts, he sent additional forces on separate marches westward to secure the cities along the coast: a large force marched down the Maeander valley to occupy Miletus and the cities of the Mycale peninsula; another column under Peucestas was sent to take the cities of the Halicarnassos peninsula; and another force was sent down to the coast at Iasus. Meanwhile a great fleet under Antigonus' admiral Medeius co-operated with the columns attacking the coastal cities and prevented any intervention by Ptolemy. Within a few weeks Caria belonged to Antigonus; Asander was in flight never to be heard of again; and the governors of western Asia understood that it did not pay to rebel against Antigonus.

Only Ptolemy remained to be dealt with. Learning of Antigonus' departure from Palestine, and encouraged by the eager Seleucus, Ptolemy prepared a large army and at the end of 312 invaded Palestine to try his chances in war against the young Demetrius. A great battle was fought near Gaza, in which the experience of Ptolemy and Seleucus told over Demetrius' youth: Demetrius' forces were disastrously defeated with heavy losses, and Ptolemy was able to re-occupy Palestine and Phoenicia. Undismayed, however, Demetrius retreated with strong cavalry forces (having lost most of his infantry) to north Syria and there summoned reinforcements from the garrisons of Syria and Mesopotamia, quickly rebuilding his army and securing Syria against Ptolemy. A large raiding column sent by Ptolemy was ambushed and captured by Demetrius, showing that he knew how to recover from a great setback. Having waited to see how his son would do, Antigonus now, in spring 311, crossed the Taurus mountains into Syria with a large army to redress the situation in Palestine. As before, when he heard of Antigonus' advance against him Ptolemy did not wait to fight, but retreated at once back to Egypt leaving Antigonus to recover control of Phoenicia and Palestine with barely a fight.

In four years of fighting, Antigonus had seriously weakened Cassander in Greece, kept Lysimachus busy in his own province, secured naval dominance with a huge fleet-building program, and shown that Ptolemy simply could not hold Palestine against him. The demands of the dynasts allied together against Antigonus in 314 had proved unenforceable, and Antigonus had fought them to a standstill. In mid-311 Cassander and Lysimachus sued for peace, and when he heard of it Ptolemy quickly joined in. The Peace of the Dynasts concluded in summer 311 effectively acknowledged Antigonus as ruler of Asia and owner of the former Persian treasures. Antigonus in return acknowledged Cassander as ruler of Macedonia, Lysimachus as ruler of Thrace, and Ptolemy as ruler of Egypt. The principle that all Greek cities should be autonomous, as pronounced by Antigonus at Tyre, was accepted by all the dynasts; and this division of powers was to be in effect until the king himself, young Alexander IV, could take power. The peace was a clear triumph for Antigonus, who emerged from it as de facto successor to the Persian kings. But there were some troubling issues which were to undermine it from the beginning.

In the first place, the treaty reminded the world of the existence of a king who formally reigned over the conquests of his father Alexander and grandfather Philip, and who—now aged around thirteen—could be expected to come forward to begin to rule over his empire before too many more years had passed. This was an embarrassment to the great dynasts, who had not struggled and fought and bled for thirteen years just to hand over their power to a youth whose only claim to attention was his parentage. It was in particular an embarrassment to Cassander, under whose protection and guard young Alexander was living and, putatively, being trained to rule. Cassander had, in 315, taken in marriage a daughter of the great Philip named Thessalonice, and had by her three sons, the eldest of whom was named Philip after his maternal grandfather, to remind all Macedonians that he was a grandson of the great king. As a direct descendant of the Argead royal line through his mother, Cassander's son might himself be seen as a candidate for the kingship . . . if only the inconvenient youth Alexander IV would just die. Well, such things could be arranged. As calls began to arise for Alexander to be brought out of his seclusion at Amphipolis and introduced to the Macedonian people over whom he would soon be ruling, Cassander announced in 310 that, sadly, the boy and his mother had unexpectedly fallen ill and died. People were not fooled by this: immediately the rumor spread, almost certainly a well founded one, that Cassander had simply had the wretched young Alexander and his mother assassinated. Once again, the Macedonian realm was left with no king, but there was no power vacuum this time: the question was merely under what formal guise or title the great dynasts would govern their lands in the long term.

A far more significant threat to the peace treaty of 311 was an action undertaken by Ptolemy and Seleucus in the winter of 312/11, immediately after the victorious battle of Gaza. Seleucus had been living for four years as a protégé of Ptolemy, giving valuable assistance and advice, but lacking all power and status of his own. He was not content with this role. Intent on weakening Antigonus, Ptolemy gave Seleucus around fifteen hundred soldiers with whom to launch an attempt to recover control of his former satrapy of Babylonia. Setting out in the dead of winter, Seleucus rode at speed with his small force north-west through the Syrian desert, aiming to cross the Euphrates well upstream where it would be easily fordable. He had some luck: the land of Mesopotamia was largely denuded of troops thanks to Demetrius' ingathering of the garrisons to rebuild his army after his defeat at Gaza, enabling Seleucus to ride without significant opposition through Mesopotamia and down the Tigris valley into Babylonia, where he arrived towards the end of winter in early 311. He had been a popular

17.Portrait bust of Seleucus Nicator from Herculaneum, now in Archaeological Museum, Naples   *(Wikimedia Commons public domain image through Creative Commons; photo by Massimo Finizio)*

governor of Babylonia before being ousted in 315, whereas Antigonus remained largely unknown there. Besides, Seleucus was an active and highly effective general, who deserved the epithet he later acquired: Nicator (the Victor). Within a few months Seleucus had not only recovered control over Babylonia, but set about completely undermining Antigonus' arrangements in the eastern or "upper" satrapies, and reorganizing the east under his own control.

This rapid and unexpected success on Seleucus' part was unknown at the time the Peace of the Dynasts was concluded in mid-311, but it immediately undermined a key provision of that peace, the notion that Antigonus ruled all of the Macedonian lands in Asia. Within a few months it became clear that he did not: the eastern provinces were falling under the control of Seleucus instead, introducing a new power dynamic into the equation of the struggle over the succession to Alexander. Key to the rise of Seleucus in the east was a great victory he won on the eastern bank of the Tigris in late 311. Antigonus had left a trusted officer named Nicanor as governor of Media and overseer of the eastern provinces back in 315, and it fell to this Nicanor to respond to Seleucus' invasion of Babylonia. He gathered a large force near seventeen thousand strong and set out to crush the uprising. But Seleucus, though having fewer than four thousand soldiers with which to oppose this force, managed to take Nicanor's army completely by surprise and win an overwhelming victory. That left the eastern provinces wide open to his attack, and within a few years he had organized for himself an empire stretching from Babylonia (southern Iraq) to Bactria (Afghanistan). In truth, Antigonus did little to prevent this, perhaps in the belief that Greek domination so far east could not last. He had only entered the "upper" satrapies in pursuit of Eumenes, and had left as soon as he could, never to return. When Nicanor failed to deal with Seleucus, Antigonus sent his son Demetrius with a flying column of troops to pillage and loot in Babylonia, and around 308 apparently entered Mesopotamia with an army for a showdown with Seleucus. No longer as quick and energetic as he had been (he was now in his mid-seventies), Antigonus suffered a reverse, and seems to have patched up a truce of sorts ceding control of the east to Seleucus, keeping only northern Mesopotamia east of the Euphrates: his interest was in Palestine, Syria, Asia Minor, and the Greek lands and seas.

In 310, no doubt encouraged by Seleucus' growing power in the east, Ptolemy had broken the peace and begun again to harass Antigonus' lands and forces in the eastern Mediterranean. An expeditionary force sailed to Cilicia and harried the coastal settlements, but more importantly than mere coastal raiding, Ptolemy was making his own play for greater power. He got in touch with Alexander's full sister Cleopatra, who since the failure of her proposed marriage to Perdiccas in 320 had been living a retired life under Antigonus' protection at Sardis. With Cleopatra as his wife, Ptolemy hoped to be able to appeal to Macedonians as a possible new king, it seems. But Antigonus' spies in Cleopatra's circle alerted him to what was happening, and he had Cleopatra killed before she could escape to join Ptolemy. The old Argead royal family was now nearly exhausted even in the female line. Ptolemy's attempts to win favor and power in the Aegean and Greece failed, and he had to sail back to Egypt having done little but stir up Antigonus to anger against him. Antigonus, seeing that Cassander and Ptolemy would not respect the terms of the peace deal they had agreed to, prepared great blows against them. He struck at Cassander first.

Equipping a great fleet of warships and transport vessels, he sent a large army commanded by Demetrius across the Aegean to strip Cassander of all influence in southern Greece once and for all. Demetrius landed at the Piraeus, the great harbor of Athens, early in the summer of 307 and announced that he had come to overthrow Macedonian garrisons and pro-Macedonian tyrants and oligarchies once and for all. In particular, the Athenian democracy, disbanded by Antipater in October 321, was to be restored. In a surge of public rejoicing, the Athenians went over to Demetrius and Cassander's forces and allies at Athens found themselves powerless to resist. The restored democracy hailed Antigonus and Demetrius as saviors and loaded them with honors, even going so far as to address them as kings, though for the time being Antigonus did not take up this title. Demetrius quickly extended his operations into the Peloponnese and central Greece, everywhere driving out Cassander's forces and allies and "liberating" the Greek cities, that is allowing them to set up their own preferred governing systems (usually democracies) which then at once allied with Antigonus and Demetrius. Cassander was unable to match the level of forces Demetrius had at his disposal, and saw his position in southern Greece crumbling without being able to do much about it. But in 306 Antigonus recalled Demetrius from this campaign, leaving it unfinished: it was time to strike at Ptolemy.

For some fifteen years, since 320, Ptolemy's main base for operations against Antigonus and into the Aegean, and the secure mainstay of his naval power, had been the island of Cyprus. Antigonus had frequently sought to undermine the loyalty to Ptolemy of the Cypriot city-kings, with mixed success. But in 311 Ptolemy had put a stop to this by deposing the city-kings once and for all and placing his reliable younger brother Menelaus in charge of Cyprus as the island's governor. Antigonus now ordered Demetrius to lead a great fleet and army to the island of Cyprus to conquer it and bring it under Antigonid power. Demetrius landed successfully, defeated Menelaus, and besieged him in Salamis. In response Ptolemy gathered the largest fleet he could, together with a large relieving military force on a fleet of transports, and sailed for Cyprus, landing at Paphus on the south-west coast. This led to a confrontation between the fleets of Demetrius and Ptolemy, the battle of Salamis, one of the great naval battles of the ancient world. As Ptolemy's fleet approached Salamis along the south coast of the island, pausing at Cition before making the final push to Salamis itself, Demetrius deployed his fleet outside the harbor of Salamis. He decided to use only ten warships, chosen for their size and power, to blockade the harbor of Salamis and keep Menelaos' fleet (sixty warships) inside. He himself confronted Ptolemy with 170 ships to 140, counting on this advantage to defeat Ptolemy before Menelaus could break out and intervene. The main interest of the battle, besides the scale of forces deployed and the outsize personalities of the two commanders, lay in the fact that it was the first known battle in which a new type of ship and naval tactics were deployed.

The standard ancient warships of the late fourth century BCE were oared galleys called triremes, quadriremes, and quinqueremes, so named for the fact that at each oar station they deployed the motive power of three, four, or five oarsmen respectively. The largest of these standard warships, the quinquereme, had two banks of oars, one below the other, with each oar on the lower bank being pulled by two rowers, and each oar on the upper bank by three. Ptolemy's fleet was made up of ships of this type. But Antigonus' naval building program had begun to develop larger, super massive galleys which became a feature of Hellenistic navies. Demetrius' fleet contained "sixes" (*hexereis*) and "sevens" (*heptereis*). The extra wide decks of these massive ships were used as fighting platforms, not just for soldiers who might try to board an enemy vessel, but for artillery: catapults firing bolts and stone-throwers. Demetrius had concentrated his large ships on his right wing, and he went into battle with them, subjecting the ships opposite his squadron to a withering hail of catapult bolts and massive stones which damaged many ships and demoralized the rest. This was the first battle in recorded history in which ship-borne artillery played the decisive role: Demetrius won a crushing victory. Ptolemy was forced to flee having lost more than half of his fleet and transports; Menelaus had to surrender to Demetrius with all his forces, and Cyprus belonged to Antigonus.

The significance of this victory went beyond Demetrius' proof that he could compete with the great generals who had learned under Philip and fought under Alexander, and Antigonus' rounding-off of complete naval domination of the eastern Mediterranean region: it was used by Antigonus as the occasion to elevate himself and his family to royal status. The scene is described in detail by Plutarch in his biography of Demetrius. The official messenger sent by Demetrius to announce news of his victory to his father was Antigonus' old and close friend Aristodemus of Miletus. Antigonus was, at the time of Demetrius' victory, not far away: a few miles inland from the adjacent coast of Syria, Antigonus was supervising the construction of his new capital city of Antigoneia on the River Orontes. Aristodemus sailed across from Cyprus to Syria and up the mouth of the River Orontes to land close to Antigonus' new city. Walking silently and grim-faced from his landing point into the city and to the main town square, where Antigonus was awaiting him surrounded by an anxious crowd, Aristodemus ignored all questions until he stood in front of Antigonus himself, where he suddenly changed his expression from grim to joyful and cried out in a loud voice "Hail king Antigonus, we have won a glorious victory!" That this was all a pre-calculated show is made evident by the fact that Antigonus' entourage, far from being surprised by Aristodemus' news and use of the royal title, immediately produced a royal diadem, tied it around Antigonus' head, and likewise hailed him as king. The title was then taken up amidst rejoicing by the surrounding crowd of soldiers and new citizens of Antigoneia. The effect produced, obviously deliberately, was that Antigonus was having the title of king thrust upon him by his entourage of officers and aides, soldiers, and citizens. He could thus gracefully accept the royal title as something bestowed on him by his people, in acknowledgement of his great successes, rather than seeming to usurp the title himself.

After five years of official power vacuum, the Macedonians finally had a king again: Antigonus the One-Eyed, who immediately emphasized the dynastic importance of his new status by sending a letter accompanied by a royal diadem to his son Demetrius, officially elevating him to the status of co-king as well as successor. In the letter too, Antigonus sent instructions for Demetrius to prepare his fleet for a grand new operation: Antigonus wanted to follow up the crushing defeat inflicted on Ptolemy by attempting to finish off Ptolemy once and for all. He prepared a massive land expedition, totaling up to eighty-eight thousand men we are told, to march for the invasion of Egypt, while Demetrius was to sail along the coast with the army with a grand supporting fleet. Late in the year, the army concentrated at Gaza in southern Palestine and marched from there for Egypt. Demetrius and the fleet sailed a day later, and despite some difficulties with the weather, arrived at the border of Egypt to link up there with Antigonus' army, which encamped about a quarter of a mile from the Pelousiac (easternmost) branch of the Nile. Ptolemy, severely outnumbered by Antigonus' forces, had prepared strong defensive positions on the western banks of the Pelousiac Nile, and challenged Antigonus to attack across the broad and deep stream.

About fifteen years earlier, in 320, the regent Perdiccas had attempted such an attack across the Pelousiac Nile in the face of Ptolemy's strong defenses, and had failed disastrously. Antigonus was not inclined to try the same thing: that is why he had brought the fleet. He ordered Demetrius to sail along the Egyptian coast and land troops well to the rear of Ptolemy's defenses. Attacked by Antigonus' forces from in front and behind, Ptolemy would have been very hard put to it to hold out. But Demetrius failed: two separate attempts to land troops were defeated by determined efforts of Ptolemy's local defense forces, and Demetrius brought the fleet back to Antigonus' camp with nothing accomplished. It must be said that Demetrius seems to have shown a lack of determination and perseverance in this absolutely vital operation. Demetrius was at times quite brilliant; but this sort of inconsistency and lack of perseverance were to prove characteristic of him in subsequent years. In the present circumstances, Demetrius' failure caused Antigonus to call off the whole expedition: he would not risk a frontal assault across the well defended Nile, and his supply situation prevented staying where he was for a prolonged operation. He retreated back to Palestine with nothing accomplished. Ptolemy was hailed as victor by his troops, and used the occasion to have himself proclaimed king just as Antigonus had been. From having no king, the Macedonians now had three. And within a year or two, Seleucus in inner Asia, Lysimachus in Thrace, and Cassander in Macedonia followed suit, making six kings in all including Demetrius, ruling five separate kingdoms carved out of Alexander's realm (see map 4).

After the disappointment of the Egyptian campaign, Antigonus and Demetrius decided to make a strong display in 305. The Rhodians had been long-time allies of Antigonus, but in recent years had been edging closer and closer to Ptolemy, refusing to send assistance to Demetrius' fleet for the campaigns of 306. It was time to teach them a lesson. At the beginning of the year, the Rhodians received an ultimatum: submit to Antigonus or else. They refused, and Demetrius was sent with a huge fleet and army to punish them. The siege of Rhodes was one of the great sieges of antiquity, and it established both Demetrius' reputation as a besieger, and the Rhodians' reputation for fierce resistance and independence. The scale of Demetrius' siege engineering was a sensa-

18. Coin with portrait of Ptolemy I Soter from British Museum
(*Wikimedia Commons public domain image from PHGCOM*)

tion, particularly in the building of huge and innovative siege towers, and yet after attacking Rhodes both from the sea and by land for the better part of a year, the siege still dragged on. In the end Demetrius once again failed: Antigonus did not want this operation to extend into 304 and ordered Demetrius to conclude the siege on the best terms he could. The Rhodians agreed to renew their alliance with Antigonus and furnished a hundred hostages, but they were otherwise left free and self-governing and were explicitly freed from ever providing assistance against Ptolemy. While that was a drawn result, the draw was a triumph for the Rhodians and an undeniable setback for Antigonus and Demetrius.

It had been crucial to end the siege of Rhodes, because Demetrius was needed back in southern Greece. In his absence during the years 306 and 305, Cassander had mounted a strong counter-attack there, in particular pressing hard to recapture Athens and putting the Athenians under severe pressure. The return of Demetrius and his forces at the beginning of spring 304 saved the day. Demetrius, reinvigorated it seems to be back to mobile operations, engaged in a classic whirlwind campaign in which he rapidly and inexorably drove Cassander's forces out of southern and central Greece all the way to the border of Thessaly during the years 304 and 303. As he did so, he also organized the cities of southern Greece into what was intended to be a form of permanent federation, a kind of United States of Greece. With Antigonus and Demetrius and their successors as patrons and guarantors, the city-

states of Greece would co-operate in collective self-governance, primarily for security purposes, via a federal *synedrion* (council) which would
meet regularly at the sites of the pan-Hellenic festivals, and whose per-
sonnel would be drawn proportionately from all member states. Copies
of the foundation document of this ambitious project in federal representative governance were set up throughout Greece: a large portion of
the copy inscribed at Epidaurus in the Argolid peninsula survives to
give a remarkable insight into the project. Unfortunately it came to
nothing, as outside events prevented its long-term implementation.

Concerned about the growing power and success of Antigonus and
Demetrius, in fact, the other kings had been engaged in diplomatic contact
and in 302 arrived at an agreement for common action. While Cassander
did his best to hold off Demetrius in Greece, the armies of Lysimachus,
Seleucus, and Ptolemy were to invade Antigonus' Asian realm from three
directions with the aim of bringing the old king down. In spring of 302
Demetrius marched into Thessaly and was confronted there by Cassander
with a large army. The two maneuvered around each other a fair bit,
but Cassander was reluctant to offer battle, looking to events in western
Asia, and Demetrius failed to force a battle. So the campaign ground
to a stalemate with the two armies watching each other. Meanwhile
Lysimachus crossed over with his army from Thrace into Asia Minor and
began to take territory and detach local leaders and governors from their
loyalty to Antigonus. The latter was at Antigoneia in Syria, busy with
arrangements for a great international festival of sport and music to inaugurate his grand new capital, when he heard of Lysimachus' actions.
Antigonus was not the man he had been: over eighty years old, he had
only recently recovered from a near fatal illness, and had put on a lot
of weight. He no longer had the energy and activity that had characterized him in his sixties. Nevertheless, he at once put the festival plans
on hold and gathered his army to cross the Taurus mountains from
Syria into Asia Minor to confront Lysimachus.

While Cassander and Demetrius were at a stalemate in Thessaly,
and Antigonus was marching to confront Lysimachus, Seleucus was
also making his move. He had recently been campaigning in what is
now Pakistan, at the very eastern edge of the Macedonian Empire.
There a new power was arising: an Indian prince from the Ganges valley named Chandragupta (known to the Greeks as Sandrokottos) was

busy building an empire—the Maurya Empire—that eventually unified virtually all of India. Having brought all the principalities of the Ganges region under his control, he had crossed into the Indus valley to conquer there too, and so came up against the Macedonians. After many months of inconclusive fighting, Seleucus decided that holding on to part of north India was not really worth the trouble. He came to an agreement with Chandragupta whereby he ceded control of the entire Indus valley to the Indian conqueror in exchange for the gift of five hundred trained war elephants. With these elephants added to an army composed primarily of light infantry and highly mobile cavalry, Seleucus was marching westwards to join up with Lysimachus against Antigonus. Lysimachus had successfully refused to fight a battle against the far superior army of Antigonus, waging a campaign of maneuver and distraction against the slower moving old general. Finally, in early autumn of 302, Lysimachus succeeded in slipping away from Antigonus and marching to the Black Sea port city of Heraklea, where he put his army into winter quarters. Giving up the pursuit, Antigonus established winter quarters for his army near Dorylaeum (see map x) in northern Phrygia. Learning that Seleucus had crossed the Taurus Mountains and was wintering with his army in Cappadocia, ready to join up with Lysimachus in the spring, Antigonus sent urgent messages to Demetrius to break off his operations in Greece and sail back to Asia Minor to join his father for the great confrontation that was now bound to happen in the new year. As soon as Demetrius had left, Cassander sent a portion of his army, under his brother Pleistarchus, to join his good friend and ally Lysimachus for the coming showdown.

In early summer 301, the four armies came together near the small town of Ipsus, a little north-east of Synnada (near modern Afyonkarahisar). Antigonus and Demetrius had joined their armies, with Demetrius as the effective commander given Antigonus' age and weakness. Lysimachus, with his allied forces from Cassander added to his army, had likewise joined up with Seleucus marching down the Royal Road from Cappadocia: the two kings apparently shared command, though the ensuing battle plan seems to have owed more to Seleucus. Ptolemy, who was supposed to have brought forces to join his allies, merely invaded Palestine once again and focused on winning control over the Palestinian and Phoenician cities.

The great battle of Ipsus changed the balance of power in the Macedonian Empire. The two armies faced each other quite conventionally, with the phalanx composed mostly of Lysimachus' and Cassander's troops confronting Antigonus' phalanx, where the old and immobile king himself was stationed in command. On their right, Seleucus and Lysimachus stationed a vast mass of Seleucus' light infantry; on the left was their heavy cavalry commanded by Seleucus' son Antiochus. Confronting Antiochus was Demetrius in command of Antigonus' heavy cavalry. As the battle commenced, Demetrius and his cavalry charged Antiochus and drove the enemy cavalry off in real or pretended flight. Demetrius proceeded to commit the worst blunder a cavalry leader can commit: he over-pursued, leaving the main battle well behind, instead of turning to attack the enemy infantry from behind. That the flight of Antiochus' cavalry may have been deliberate is suggested by the aftermath. As soon as Demetrius had disappeared in the distance, Seleucus brought forward four hundred war elephants and placed them as a screen between Demetrius and his path back to the battle: when Demetrius finally did try to return, he found the elephants blocking his way and his terrified horses would not approach the huge gray beasts. Meanwhile Lysimachus' phalanx came to grips with that of Antigonus, and Seleucus led his light cavalry in an outflanking maneuver to attack Antigonus' infantry from behind. Attacked from both sides, Antigonus' phalanx collapsed and turned to flight, and the battle was lost.

Antigonus' attendants urged him to flee while he could, but the old king refused. Clinging to the hope that Demetrius would find a way to get back and save the day, he stood his ground until a great force of enemy cavalry came directly at him. His attendants all fled but for one loyal friend named Thorax, and Antigonus died under a hail of javelins. When he realized that he could not get back to the battle and that all was lost, Demetrius rode off with his cavalry to the coast at Ephesus and took ship on his fleet, becoming for the time being a sea-king only. Meanwhile Seleucus and Lysimachus cleaned up the battle site and divided the spoils. Seleucus arranged for his old friend Antigonus' body to be found and cremated with royal honors, the ashes being forwarded to Demetrius. Antigonus' empire was divided at the Taurus mountain range in southern Asia Minor: the lands of Asia Minor north and west of the range went to Lysimachus, except for an enclave in Caria carved out for Cassander's brother Pleistarchus in thanks for Cassander's aid; the lands south and east—Cilicia, Syria and Palestine, northern Mesopotamia—now belonged to Seleucus, except for an enclave in Cilicia set apart for Pleistarchus. When Seleucus arrived in southern Syria to take possession of Palestine, however, he found Ptolemy already in occupation there. In light of Ptolemy's assistance to him in the past, Seleucus let Ptolemy's control of Palestine and Phoenicia stand for now, while insisting that he did not formally accept it: the matter was left open to be the seed of many future conflicts between Seleucid and Ptolemaic kings.

5. THE FINAL SETTLEMENT OF THE SUCCESSION

The seeming decisiveness of the outcome and settlement of Ipsus was only apparent. In 297 Cassander died of an illness in his mid-fifties. Since taking over Macedonia in 316 he had worked hard and well to secure the legacy of Philip and of his own father Antipater. He was succeeded by his oldest son Philip, grandson through his mother of the great Philip, and all seemed well. But the new king Philip IV died within a year of his father's death, apparently of the same illness. Cassander had two other sons, Antipater and Alexander, and they promptly fell out over who was to succeed. Antipater claimed the kingship as the

19. Façade of royal tomb II at Vergina, Greece; possibly built by Cassander as tomb of Philip III Arrhidaeus
(Wikimedia Commons photo by Sarah Murray, CC BY-SA 2.0?)

older of the two, but their mother Thessalonice favored her youngest son Alexander and encouraged him to claim the throne. A civil war broke out, during which Alexander incautiously invited the still powerful Demetrius to come to his aid. Demetrius was glad to oblige, and no sooner had he joined Alexander than he had the young man assassinated and seized the rule of Macedonia for himself. The line of Antipater and Cassander came to an end, and the line of Antigonus once again had a kingdom to rule . . . for a time.

Demetrius was not a popular ruler of Macedonia. He had left his homeland as a child and grown up in Asia. To the Macedonians he seemed foreign and uninterested in learning true Macedonian customs and traditions. The Macedonians found him distant, arrogant, far more concerned with his own pleasures than with the needs of his people. As a long-time ruler of Asian subjects, Demetrius was not accustomed to the forthright frankness of his Macedonian subjects and their expectations, and could not adapt. His main aim and policy as ruler of Macedonia was to build up a large enough army to attack Lysimachus and Seleucus and win back his father's Asian empire. The Macedonians had no interest in this policy. When Lysimachus, fearful of Demetrius' growing military power, invaded Macedonia in 287, the Macedonians deserted Demetrius and sided with Lysimachus. Demetrius was forced to flee in disguise back to his fleet, and Lysimachus added Macedonia to his kingdom of Thrace and Asia Minor. But inevitably, it seems, the rise in Lysimachus' power led to a final showdown fight between Lysimachus and Seleucus, culminating in a great battle fought between them at Cyroupedium near Sardis in 282. Lysimachus had fallen out with and executed his popular son Agathocles, leading various generals and governors in his Asian lands to invite Seleucus in.

By the time of this battle these two kings were the last survivors of Alexander's Successors. Demetrius, after being ousted from Macedonia, had decided in 286 to launch a last desperate attempt to recover at least part of his father's empire. Invading Asia Minor with whatever forces he could gather, he had been driven off by Lysimachus' son Agathocles and forced south into Cilicia, where Seleucus confronted him and succeeded in capturing him. Seleucus treated him with honor: his own son Antiochus was married to Demetrius' daughter Stratonice. Demetrius was placed under luxurious house arrest in a palatial hunting lodge on an island in the River Orontes. There, over the next two years, he drank himself to death, leaving to his son Antigonus Gonatas the title of king, but only a remnant of the great Antigonid fleet and a few garrisoned islands and coastal cities to support that title. Meanwhile Ptolemy had been distracted by internal family disputes: he had two sons, both confusingly named Ptolemy after their father. The oldest, surnamed Ceraunus (the Thunderbolt), was Ptolemy's son by his first wife Eurydice; the younger, surnamed Philadelphus (the sister lover) was the son of Ptolemy's second and favored wife Berenice. Ptolemy drove his eldest son Ceraunus out of Egypt into exile, where he found refuge with Seleucus. The younger son Philadelphus was established as Ptolemy's heir, and succeeded to the position of king when Ptolemy died peacefully of old age in 283, almost the only man of Alexander's great generals to die in his bed.

The final showdown battle between the last two Diadochi standing was evidently an epic affair, but we are very poorly informed about it. Both generals were in their late seventies, but still hale and vigorous. Seleucus as was his custom won: he was not called Nicator (the Victor) for nothing. Lysimachus died in the battle of Cyroupedium, abandoned (we are told) by everyone except for a faithful dog. Seleucus took about a year to establish his control over Asia Minor, and then early in 280 crossed the Hellespont to Europe, to take over the European possessions of Lysimachus. It was apparently Seleucus' intention to return, after a fifty-four-year absence, to his homeland of Macedonia, there to rule as king for his final years and be buried, perhaps, in his home town of Europus. It was not to be. Seleucus' first stop in Europe was at the capital city of Lysimacheia that Lysimachus had been busy building up in his final years. In his entourage as he inspected the half completed city at the neck of the Thracian Chersonnese (Gallipoli peninsula) was the rogue son of Ptolemy, Ptolemy Ceraunus. This young man evidently felt no gratitude to Seleucus for his refuge, and harbored ambitions far beyond being a mere pensioner at Seleucus' court. He stabbed Seleucus to death and persuaded his army to acknowledge him, Ceraunus, as its commander. Leading the army to Macedonia, he obliged the Macedonians to acknowledge him as their king.

Ptolemy Ceraunus, however, did not last long as king of Macedonia. In 279 a band of Celtic tribesmen, who had been moving around central Europe and the Balkan region for many years, abruptly invaded

Macedonia from the north. The Greeks referred to these Celts as Galatians and feared them greatly. Ceraunus, instead of taking his time to get together a large and well organized army to combat the invasion, rushed impetuously north with whatever troops were to hand and engaged the Galatians in battle, with disastrous results. Ceraunus himself was killed; his army, such as it was, was annihilated; and Macedonia lay wide open to the marauding Celts. For three long years—279 to 277—Macedonia was occupied by the Galatians who looted, pillaged, and killed to their hearts' content. No Macedonian leader or general seemed capable of stopping them. Finally, late in 277, a Macedonian savior appeared from an unexpected quarter.

Ever since his father Demetrius' death, Antigonus Gonatas had been left in a very precarious position. Nominally, he was king in succession to his brilliant grandfather and his mercurial father, but he had no kingdom worth speaking of. He had only a remnant of the great Antigonid fleet, perhaps a few dozen ships, and some islands and coastal cities under his control, as mentioned above. He looked around for lands to seize and base his power on, but had little success. He was not the general his grandfather had been, nor even his inconsistent but at times brilliant father. An attempt to profit from the instability in Asia Minor after Seleucus' assassination proved unsuccessful, as he was easily driven out by forces loyal to Antiochus. He seemed destined to be a king without a kingdom until a lucky chance occurred. In 277 it occurred to him that Lysimachus' kingdom of Thrace was leaderless, and might present an opportunity. He sailed to Lysimacheia, finding the half-finished city largely abandoned, and based himself there. While leading forays out into the Thracian territories to the north, he came across a band of Galatians who, tired of the picked-over and impoverished lands of Macedonia, were heading eastwards in search of fresher lands to plunder. Gonatas succeeded in leading them into an ambush and annihilating them, a rare stroke of military brilliance from an otherwise rather pedestrian general. As news of his success spread, messages began to arrive from Macedonia, pleading with Gonatas to come and save his homeland: if he could just free them from the Galatians, the Macedonians would take him as their king and serve him loyally.

Antigonus Gonatas, born about 319 and a grandson of Antipater through his mother Phila, had lived in Macedonia for seven years from

294 to 287, when his father was king of Macedonia and he himself the heir to the throne. The idea of returning to rule Macedonia had enormous appeal and he wasted no time in transporting his forces there, landing to a hero's welcome from the Macedonians. All they needed was sound leadership and proper organization to be able to defeat the Galatians, and these Antigonus provided. Within a year, the fearsome Galatian threat had been dealt with: many Galatians were killed, most were forced out of Macedonia to look for new opportunities further east (where many of them eventually entered Asia Minor), and some thousands, impressed that Antigonus had shown himself able to beat them, took service with the new Macedonian king as mercenaries and helped to enhance his strength.

Gonatas found an enormous task in front of him: Macedonia lay prostrate from its years of Celtic occupation, and much of the work of Philip in building up Macedonia had been undone. He was not daunted. It turned out that, while he might be a mediocre general, Antigonus Gonatas had a genius for governance and organization. He took on the task of rebuilding Macedonia with relish, and over the course of his more than thirty-five years as king (he ruled until 239) won a devotion from the Macedonians second only to that they felt for Philip. There was one brief blip early on when the military adventurer Pyrrhus of Epirus, having been defeated by the Romans in an attempt to conquer Italy, invaded Macedonia in 275. He defeated Antigonus and took control of the kingdom, but promptly left again to pursue an opportunity in the Peloponnese. Gonatas rallied his forces, recovered control of Macedonia, and led his army south to finish off the nuisance Pyrrhus. The Epirote king died in street fighting in Argos in 272, and from then on Antigonus Gonatas' rule over Macedonia was secure.

And so the former empire of Alexander settled down at last into a fixed new order. As had been essentially established in 315, there were three successor kingdoms. The Antigonid dynasty (the descendants of Antigonus the One-Eyed) ruled Macedonia and Thessaly and dominated southern Greece and much of the Balkan region. The former Persian Empire was now the Seleucid kingdom, ruled by the descendants of Seleucus Nicator. Egypt, finally, and some peripheral territories such as Palestine, Cyprus, and the Cyrenaica, were ruled by the descendants of Ptolemy Soter (the Savior), as he was known after his death. This was not an unfamiliar political geography: in the 350s, some eighty years earlier, the same three kingdoms had dominated the eastern Mediterranean and western Asia. The one great difference made by Alexander's conquests was that all three kingdoms were now ruled by Macedonian dynasties, and in all three Greek was the dominant language and Greek urban civilization and culture were the dominant civilization and culture.

CHAPTER 7

The Hellenistic World and Hellenistic Civilization

THANKS TO THE CONQUESTS OF ALEXANDER AND THE HERCULEAN efforts of his Successors, western Asia, north Africa, and the eastern Mediterranean region generally were home for some six hundred years—300 BCE to 300 CE—to the civilization known as Hellenistic. The Greek language was the common language spoken by the educated elites everywhere, from Samarkand to Sardis and from the Crimea to Assuan. Everywhere a person traveled, there were Greek cities where Greek was spoken and a familiar urban environment, with familiar amenities, services, and entertainments, was to be found. For two centuries this civilization was ruled over by Macedonian kings supported by Macedonian armies; then for four more centuries Roman governors ruled and Roman armies provided security, but the urban Hellenistic civilization remained the same throughout. How remarkable a feat it was to unite the very disparate peoples and cultures living from Iran to the Mediterranean and from the Black Sea to the Sudan into one great civilizational sphere with relative peace, order, and security, and a common language and culture superposed over the vast linguistic and cultural diversity, is not well enough acknowledged. It bears investigating what Hellenistic civilization was, and how it was imposed and maintained.

1. THE KINGS

Discussion of the kings of the Hellenistic world begins appropriately by quoting again the definition of kingship found in the *Suda* and already quoted above in Chapter 4. It clearly derives from an early Hellenistic source, and it neatly sets out the basic qualities expected of Hellenistic kings: competent military leadership and capable administration.

Basileia (kingship): it is not descent or legitimacy which makes a king; it is the ability to lead armies well and handle affairs competently. This is seen by the examples of Philip and of Alexander's Successors.

The great kings of the kingdoms and dynasties described in the previous chapter stood at the apex of Hellenistic civilization for its first two centuries, until the advent of the Romans. It was no easy thing, being a Hellenistic king: one had to try to live up to the example of giants. Philip, Alexander, and the Successors—Antigonus, Seleucus, Ptolemy and the rest—strode across the imaginations of the people of the Hellenistic world, and the kings who succeeded them inevitably were measured against their achievements. Many of the Hellenistic kings failed this test, perhaps to some degree crushed by the burden of expectation. There were the incompetents, such as Seleucus II who liked to be called "Callinicus" (Glorious Victor) to hide his military failures; the pleasure-lovers, such as Ptolemy IV and Ptolemy VIII, the latter known to his detractors as "Physkon" (Pot-belly) as a result of his excesses; and the utter nonentities, such as Antiochus IX or Ptolemy X, scarcely remembered for anything at all. But there were also competent Hellenistic kings who strove to live up to the examples of the Macedonian founders and the responsibilities of their positions, and even a few who genuinely met the challenge and deserve to be remembered as great, in their own ways. Each of the great dynasties produced at least one, and they represent what the Hellenistic kings could be at their best.

Around the year 522 CE a Byzantine traveler and monk named Cosmas Indicopleustes (Cosmas the India-Voyager) visited the port of Adoulis on the coast of Eritrea in east Africa. There he saw and recorded a remarkable Greek inscription:

> King Ptolemy the Great, son of king Ptolemy and queen Arsinoe, the Brother-Sister Gods, who were children of king Ptolemy and queen Berenice the Savior Gods, descended on his father's side from Heracles son of Zeus and on his mother's side from Dionysus son of Zeus, having succeeded his father as ruler of Egypt, Libya, Syria, Phoenicia, Cyprus, Lycia, Caria, and the Cycladic islands, marched into Asia with a force of infantry and cavalry, a fleet, and elephants from the Cave-dwellers (Troglodytes) of

20. Gold coin of Ptolemy III Euergetes
(*Wikimedia Commons public domain image by Jastrow*)

Ethiopia, which his father and he were the first to hunt from these places and which they brought down to Egypt and trained for use in war. He secured control of all the land this side (i.e. west) of the Euphrates, as well as Cilicia, Pamphylia, Ionia, the Hellespont, and Thrace, and of all the forces in those regions and of the Indian elephants; and having brought under his control all the governors of these regions, he crossed the River Euphrates and subdued Mesopotamia, Babylonia, Susiane, Persis, Media and all the remaining territory as far as Bactria; and he sought out the sacred objects that had been removed from Egypt by the Persians and brought them back to Egypt along with other treasure from these regions; and he sent his forces across the canals . . . (Austin *The Hellenistic World* doc. 221 = Dittenberger *OGIS* no. 54).

This is the self-representation of Ptolemy III, known as Euergetes (the Benefactor), and it tells a remarkable tale of this energetic and effective king. In the first place, it must be noted that much of what is claimed here is not true: it is essentially certain that Ptolemy III conquered no lands in Asia Minor or east of the Euphrates as here claimed. But that is to a certain degree beside the point. Ptolemy III was a conqueror like his grandfather the first Ptolemy: he did invade Syria as far as the Seleucid capital of Antioch, and add these lands to the Ptolemaic realm for a time. What is of interest here is the nature of the claims made, the reason for them, and what they tell us of Ptolemy and his conception of himself as king. In the first place, he emphasizes descent: he was the third king of his line, after his father Ptolemy Philadelphus and his grandfather Ptolemy Soter. This descent was clearly crucial to him: it made him who he was, a "great king" in his own right. Interestingly he emphasizes his descent in the female line too: he references queen Arsinoe (who was not in fact his biological mother) and his grandmother queen Berenice. Besides this real descent, to emphasize his glorious genealogy, he alleges further descent: his grandfather was descended from Heracles, and his grandmother from Dionysus. It is the first of these fictitious descents that is significant: the claim to descent from Heracles establishes a connection to the old Macedonian royal line of the Argeads, who were supposed to be descended from Heracles. In other words, Ptolemy here claims that his grandfather was some sort of Argead, and that he himself thus descended from the old royal lineage of Macedonia. There is in fact a known story alleging that the first Ptolemy was an illegitimate son of the great Philip, which may be here hinted at.

Next notice the joint exploits of Ptolemy III and his father Ptolemy Philadelphus: together they invaded the land of the "Troglodytes" and were the first to capture and train African elephants there. The *Troglodytai* or Cave-dwellers of "Ethiopia" were described by Herodotus as a very strange people on the very edge of the known world: "the fastest people of any of whom we have found any report. They eat reptiles such as snakes and lizards, and speak a language different from any other, that sounds like bats screeching" (4.183). It has been suggested that the "bat-like" language refers to the distinctive clicking sounds in the old Khoisan languages of pre-Bantu Africa; and the inhabitants of east Africa are of course famously great runners to this day. Ptolemy is saying that he and his father went beyond the known world, which was the kind of thing done by heroes of Greek myth such as Heracles or Jason and the Argonauts. And in this case the claim is true: Ptolemy III really did penetrate well to the south of Egypt, as the inscription set up in Adulis itself proves, and the Ptolemies (or their hunters) really did capture and train African elephants. Most importantly, note the lands Ptolemy III here claimed to have conquered and the title he gave himself. The lands mentioned, all of Asia from the

Hellespont to Bactria, are of course the lands conquered by Alexander; and Ptolemy calls himself "*Megas*" (the Great), the title given to Alexander alone among previous Greek or Macedonian leaders. Ptolemy III, that is to say, here deliberately and consciously presented himself as a second Alexander, who had conquered the same lands as Alexander had and deserved the same title. To cap the likening of himself to Alexander, there is the claim that he recovered sacred artifacts looted from Egypt by the Persians and returned them to Egypt: Alexander had famously recovered in Persia statues and other sacred objects looted from Athens by the Persians, and returned them to Greece.

The point of these claims, then, is to advertise that Ptolemy Euergetes was not just a descendant of kings, but a worthy one; not just a man who lived up to the examples of his immediate ancestors, but a king who could stand comparison to Alexander "the Great"; not just the heir to the Ptolemaic kingship, but the heir of the Argeads of old. That the claims made are exaggerated did not matter: few who read this, or other inscriptions like it that will doubtless have been set up around his kingdom, will have known enough or cared to quibble. It was that Ptolemy claimed to be and strove to be this kind of king that mattered. He did not take the role of king lightly, he did not give himself over to indulgence: he strove to be a worthy heir to the great rulers of the past, and presented himself as such. And he recognized in doing so that he was a king of Egyptians: Alexander might have returned sacred objects to Greece; Ptolemy here claimed to have restored sacred objects to his own people, the Egyptians. Ptolemy, that is, cultivated the good will of his Egyptian subjects, as well as emphasizing his Greek and Macedonian heritage. And that he won genuine good will by his efforts is attested by another famous inscription, the Canopus decree:

> In the reign of Ptolemy the son of Ptolemy and Arsinoe the Brother-Sister Gods, in the ninth year (238 BCE) . . . [extensive further dating formulas omitted] . . . it was decreed: the high priests, the prophets, those who enter the holy of holies to dress the gods, the wing bearers, the sacred scribes, and the other priests who have assembled from the whole land ... for the birthday and ascension day of the king . . . held a session on that day in the temple of the Benefactor Gods at Canopus and declared: since

king Ptolemy son of Ptolemy and Arsinoe the Brother-Sister Gods,
and queen Berenice his sister and wife, the Benefactor Gods, constantly confer many great benefits on the temples throughout the
land and increase more and more the honors of the gods, and
show constant care for Apis and Mnevis and all the other famous
sacred animals in the land at great expense, and since the king
from a campaign abroad brought back to Egypt the sacred statues
that had been stolen out of the land by the Persians, and restored
them to their proper temples from which they had been taken,
and since he has maintained the land at peace by fighting in its
defense against many nations and rulers, and since they have provided good governance to all those in the land ... (Austin *The Hellenistic World* doc. 222 = Dittenberger *OGIS* no. 56)

The inscription continues at great length listing the good deeds of
Ptolemy and his wife Berenice, praising them, and bestowing honors
on them in gratitude. The point is that the priests of the native Egyptian
gods acknowledged and honored Ptolemy III as a diligent and effective
ruler, and specifically endorsed his claim to have repatriated sacred
Egyptian objects. Ptolemy III was, as kings go, a good king who worked
at being worthy of the position and earning the good will of his people,
both Greek and Egyptian. However exaggerated his own propaganda
may have been, it was based in some genuine reality, and reflected his
real desire to be seen to be a worthy king.

   In the early decades of the twentieth century there lived in the old
Hellenistic city of Alexandria, then still a thriving metropolis under
British rule, a remarkable Greek man. Outwardly he was nothing to at-
tract much notice: during working hours he held a minor position in
the British bureaucracy, fulfilling his duties neither negligently nor with
much zeal. But outside working hours this man, Constantinos Cavafy,
lived a rich life filled with amorous encounters and with imaginings of
the long and glorious past of his people, the Greeks. He was a poet,
and a great poet at that; his imagination lingered in the great era of
Hellenistic civilization, and in a way he could be called the last Hellenistic poet, living two thousand years out of his true time. In one of
his poems, he recreates a scene from the life of a Hellenistic king, the
Macedonian ruler Philip V:

He's lost his former dash, his pluck.
His wearied body, very nearly sick,
will henceforth be his chief concern. The days
that he has left, he'll spend without a care. Or so says
Philip, at least. Tonight he'll play at dice.
He has an urge to enjoy himself. Do place
lots of roses on the table. And what if
Antiochus at Magnesia has come to grief?
They say his glorious army lies mostly ruined.
Perhaps they've overstated: it can't all be true.
Let's hope not. For though they were the enemy, they were kin to us.
Still, one "let's hope not" is enough. Perhaps too much.
Philip of course won't postpone the celebration.
However much his life has become one great exhaustion
a boon remains: he hasn't lost a single memory.
He remembers how they mourned in Syria, the agony
they felt, when Macedonia their motherland was smashed to bits.
Let the feast begin. Slaves: the music, the lights!
(C. P. Cavafy "The Battle of Magnesia" tr. D. Mendelsohn 2009)

Thus the poet imagines the scene when Philip V, Antigonid king of Macedonia, heard of the defeat of his contemporary Antiochus III of the Seleucid Empire at the hands of the Romans. These two kings, who came to the thrones of their respective kingdoms within a year of each other, shared an intertwined fate of near greatness and ultimate fall. In many ways, they were the best of the Hellenistic kings, and yet they had the bad luck to still be ruling when Roman power began to encroach into the Hellenistic world, and both ended their lives in defeat. These ultimate defeats should not detract from the near greatness they showed in their primes.

Philip was the grandson of Antigonus Gonatas, and became king of Macedonia when his cousin and predecessor Antigonus III Doson died unexpectedly in 221. Philip was then about seventeen years old, and ruled for some forty-two years until his own death in 179. Doson had been a very capable king, and had trained Philip well for the role. Philip's reign falls naturally into two phases, pivoting around the year 197. In the early phase he was something of a military adventurer, trying to emulate Alexander but in truth more closely resembling Demetrius the Besieger's occasional brilliance but fundamental inconsistency.

21. Coin with portrait of Philip V of Macedonia from British Museum
(*Wikimedia Commons public domain image from PHGCOM*)

Philip wanted Macedonia to be a great power again: he fought the Aetolian
League in the Social War (220–217); the Romans in the First Macedonian
War (216–206); the Ptolemaic Empire in a war (205–201) in which he
sought to take over Ptolemaic possession in the Aegean islands and eastern
coastal cities; and the Romans again in the Second Macedonian War
(200–197). In these wars he displayed considerable military talent and
scored some brilliant successes, but also put himself and his forces in
positions of great difficulty at times, and suffered some serious setbacks.
What remained clear throughout, however, was his desire to be seen as
a king worthy of the title, worthy of succeeding to Philip II, Alexander,
and Antigonus I, and his desire to keep Macedonia secure and strong.
In this latter context, one must also mention repeated campaigning by
Philip on Macedonia's northern borders, keeping the Illyrians, Dardanians, and Thracians at bay as was the duty of every Macedonian king.

During all these years of military adventuring, Philip made one
irreparable mistake: watching events in the west, and the scale of the
warfare between the Romans and the Carthaginians there in the Hannibalic War (218–201), Philip decided it would be wise to make friends
with the eventual winner; and in 216, after Hannibal's crushing defeat
of the Romans at the Battle of Cannae (216), it looked as if the
Carthaginians were going to win. Philip's alliance with the Carthaginians, forged in that year, brought him into hostilities against the Romans, who of course beat the Carthaginians in the end and never forgot

or forgave Philip for joining their enemies at their (the Romans') lowest point. The first war between Philip and the Romans ended in a stalemate peace in 205; but in the second Philip suffering a crushing defeat at the Battle of Cynoscephalae in Thessaly in 197. This defeat highlighted a problem: the constant warfare of the first twenty years of Philip's reign had seriously depleted Macedonia's military manpower. It was only with great difficulty, and by calling up boys as young as sixteen and men over fifty, that Philip was able to muster eighteen thousand Macedonian pikemen and two thousand cavalry to face the Romans (he also had two thousand more men stationed in garrisons in southern Greece and Asia Minor). After his defeat and its heavy losses, Philip managed to call up six thousand five hundred more men from the cities of Macedonia, but his army was in no condition to fight on. He had to sue for peace and accept the conditions the Romans laid down: the loss of Thessaly and all other territories outside the ancestral Macedonian kingdom proper.

Thus began the second and in many ways more impressive phase of Philip's reign: from 196 until his death in 179 he strove successfully to rebuild the manpower and economic strength of Macedonia, modeling himself more on Philip II and Antigonus Gonatas than on Alexander or Demetrius. By the end of his reign he was able to leave to his successor Perseus an army of over forty thousand men: stronger than Macedonia had been since before the Galatian invasion of 279. How did he achieve this? A hint is given by a letter Philip wrote to the people of Larissa in Thessaly as early as 214:

> King Philip to the magistrates and the city of the Larissans, greeting. I have heard that those who had been enrolled as citizens in accord with my letter and your decree and listed in the records have been removed. If this has indeed happened, those who advised you so have mistaken both the advantage of your country and my judgment. That it would be the best of all things if, as many as possible being citizens, the city were strong and the land not left, as now, disgracefully barren, I think not one of you would disagree. It is indeed possible to observe others employing such enfranchisements, among whom are the Romans, who receive into their citizen body even their slaves when they free them and even allow them to share in the magistracies, and by such means have not only strengthened their country but also sent out colonies to some

seventy places. So now, then, I urge you to consider the matter impartially, and to restore those who were chosen by the citizens to the citizenship; and if some have done something to the harm of the kingdom or the city or are not worthy for some other reason to be listed, concerning these persons make a postponement until I, when I have returned from my present campaign, shall hold a hearing . . . (Austin *The Hellenistic World* doc. 60 = Dittenberger *Syll.* no. 543).

We see here king Philip striving to strengthen the cities of his kingdom (in this case Larissa in Thessaly), by adding new citizens to keep the cities strong and their land cultivated. He showed the same concern during the remainder of his reign, strengthening the cities of Macedonia by bringing in new settlers, often from Thrace or even Illyria, thereby rebuilding the population of Macedonia and strengthening its economic base by bringing more land under cultivation and re-opening mines that had fallen into disuse. He was in sum a king who took the business of ruling seriously, both as a commander and as an administrator, following in this the examples laid down—as already noted—by his grandfather Antigonus Gonatas and above all by his namesake, the great Philip II.

When Philip came to the throne in 221, his close contemporary Antiochus III had already been ruling for over a year, having succeeded his older brother Seleucus III as king in 223. He found the Seleucid kingdom at a low ebb: his father Seleucus II had been a weak and ineffective king, and his older brother Seleucus III had been assassinated within a couple of years of succeeding to the kingship. In the east, the Parthians and the Greek colonists in Bactria pursued largely independent policies, and the Median governor Molon was seeking to establish his own power. In the west, in Asia Minor, local dynasts like the Attalids of Pergamon, the Ziaelids of Bithynia, and the Mithridatids of Pontus were building their own kingdoms, and the local representative of Seleucid power—Antiochus' cousin Achaeus—was aiming at the kingship for himself. The Seleucid Empire seemed headed for collapse. Over the course of rather more than twenty-five years of campaigning, Antiochus III rebuilt the empire, reconquering the east as far as the borders of India, and Asia Minor as far as the Hellespont, and in 201 even succeeding in taking Palestine from the Ptolemies and adding it to the Seleucid realm. In doing all of this, Antiochus III won for himself the epithet "*Megas*" (the

22. Portrait bust of Antiochus III "the Great"
(*Author's photo, taken at Metropolitan Museum, NY*)

Great) and a reputation as a second Alexander, having campaigned and won victories throughout the lands that Alexander had conquered. At the height of his power, in 196, the Seleucid Empire was as extensive as it had been under its founder Seleucus I, and it seemed stronger than ever. Had he died in 196 or 195, Antiochus the Great would be remembered as a glorious ruler, the most successful Seleucid ruler without caveat.

Not all of this was achieved by pure campaigning and military force, though Antiochus was clearly an excellent commander and leader of men. To hold lands he had campaigned in, he needed effective administrative arrangements, calling for organizational skills. We are fortunate to possess numerous documents surviving in inscriptions that show his interactions with key subordinates, with Greek cities, and with native communities. He emerges from them as a careful and thoughtful ruler of his realm and its various peoples, recognizing that the strength of the realm depends on the wellbeing of its people. One such document, which I quote here, is not in an inscription but in a literary source—the Jewish historian Flavius Josephus—and is of particular interest since it deals with a non-Greek population group and shows the king's interest in their contribution to his kingdom, and in making them happy to serve the realm.

King Antiochus to Zeuxis his "father" (honorific term for senior trusted subordinate), greeting. If you are well, that is good. I myself am also well. Hearing that people in Lydia and Phrygia are rebelling, I thought that this required careful attention on my part and, having consulted with my "friends" (that is, high officials) about what should be done, I decided to transfer two thousand households of Jews from Mesopotamia and Babylonia together with their possessions into the forts and the most strategic places. I am sure that they will be loyal guardians of our interests because of their piety towards god, and I know that evidence of their trustworthiness and zeal for what is requested of them has been given to my ancestors. I desire, therefore, although it is difficult, that they may be transferred with the promise that they shall use their own laws. And when you bring them to the places mentioned, you shall give to each of them a plot on which to build his house and land for farming and the growing of vines, and you shall grant them exemption from the tax on the produce of the soil for ten years. In addition, until they harvest crops from the land, let there be measured out for them grain to sustain their servants. Let there also be given enough for those performing military service in order that, meeting with kindness from us, they might also be more zealous for our interests. Take care also for this nation in so far as possible in order that it be disturbed by no one (Josephus *Jewish Antiquities* 12.148–53).

What we see is a king who followed the example of his ancestor Seleucus, and of Seleucus' mentors Philip II and Antigonus the One-Eyed, in building up his realm by creating settlements, establishing prosperity in such settlements, and so securing both the good of his people and his own strength. Like Philip V, Antiochus eventually made the mistake of provoking the Romans, leading to a Roman invasion of Asia Minor in 190 and a devastating defeat for Antiochus in the Battle of Magnesia late in that year. To win peace with the Romans, Antiochus had to surrender control of all the Seleucid lands in Asia Minor, and he died an embittered and disappointed king a few years later. His sons, Seleucus IV and Antiochus IV, managed to maintain and even rebuild Seleucid power somewhat, but after the death of Antiochus IV the kingdom fell into repeated civil wars and decline, until the final Roman takeover in the sixties BCE. As a result, Antiochus III is, like Philip V, mainly remembered for his defeat by the Romans. But he was a strong and successful king until that fateful conflict.

What we see with all three of the kings highlighted here, and with the other successful kings of the three dynasties—kings such as Ptolemy II, Antigonus Doson, Antiochus I, and Antiochus IV—is that they did not see the kingship as some sort of privilege allowing its holder to do as he liked and pursue pleasure, but as a serious duty requiring hard work and some degree of self-sacrifice for the good of the kingdom and the people. As Antigonus Gonatas reputedly expressed it, kingship is an *endoxos douleia*, a glorious servitude. That phrase expresses the best ideal of Hellenistic kingship. The servitude is the hard work for the benefit of the subjects and the realm; the glory is what the king wins by performing this servitude tirelessly and well.

2. THE ARMIES

The Hellenistic kingdoms were empires conquered by the spear and maintained by the threat, and at times the active exercise, of military force. Strong and effective standing armies were, consequently, vital to establishing and sustaining security within these kingdoms: keeping the provinces loyal and quiet and deterring or seeing off threats from the outside. The nature of the armies of the Hellenistic kings was that established by Philip II: his army and military system continued to be the standard followed throughout the Hellenistic world. That is to say that at the core of each army was a mass of pikemen armed with the Macedonian *sarissa* and trained in its use. Many of these pikemen were of Macedonian descent, thanks to the numerous Macedonian military colonies founded by the Successors of Alexander; many more, however, were from the native Asian peoples, equipped and trained as Macedonian-style pikemen after recruitment who, from being originally merely "military Macedonians" eventually came to be considered and treated as Macedonians in every way, just as Philip II had turned Thracians and Illyrians into Macedonians. In addition, the armies had thousands of cavalrymen trained in the Macedonian style of cavalry fighting; units of specialized mobile infantry and cavalry to guard the armies' flanks in battle and do the scouting, skirmishing, and foraging; and there were usually units of native troops fighting in their own equipment and styles as auxiliaries.

Since our historical sources are chiefly interested in warfare, we have plenty of testimony of these armies in action. But for a more detailed look at the organization and discipline of such Hellenistic armies, a remarkable inscription found near the city of Amphipolis provides special insight. It records the military regulations in force in the Macedonian army when on campaign in the time of Philip V, and I quote from its remaining fragments here by way of illustration.

> **Making rounds:** in each regiment night rounds are to be made in turn by the *tetrarchoi* (sergeants) without lights. Anyone sitting down or sleeping on guard duty is to be fined by the *tetrarchoi* for each infraction one drachma (roughly a day's pay) . . .
>
> **Equipment:** those not bearing the weapons assigned to them are to be fined according to regulations: for the stomach-guard, two obols; for the helmet, the same; for the *sarissa*, three obols; for the sword, the same; for the shin-guards, two obols; for the shield, a drachma . . .
>
> **Construction of quarters:** when they have completed the palisade for the king and the other tents have been pitched and a space has been made, they are immediately to prepare the bivouac for the hypaspists (an elite infantry unit) . . .
>
> **Foraging:** if anyone burns grain or cuts down vines or commits some other disorderly act, a reward for information against them is to be paid by the generals . . .
>
> **Passwords:** guards are to receive the password whenever they close or open the passages through the palisade . . .
>
> (Austin *The Hellenistic World* doc. 74 = Moretti *ISE* II.114).

There is a good deal more, but these brief quotations are sufficient to give an idea of the care that went into organizing and regulating the Macedonian army in this era. Soldiers in this military system knew exactly what was required of them, and an exacting military discipline was maintained, with substantial fines for infractions against discipline. Soldiers were responsible for keeping their assigned equipment in good condition, for setting up camp in an orderly way, for maintaining proper discipline while foraging and while on guard duty, and so on. The duties of officers to oversee all of this were laid out in detail. Overall, the regulations establish that a Hellenistic army, at any rate under those kings who paid attention and saw to the maintenance of order, was a well organized and smoothly functioning military machine. The success of such armies in creating and maintaining the Hellenistic kingdoms can be readily understood. It is noteworthy that these particular military regulations come from the reign of the Antigonid king Philip V, whom we have seen above to have been a conscientious ruler and a successful military commander.

There was, of course, in the conquered lands of Asia and Egypt, an inevitable disjunction between the Macedonian armies, which were invasive and drawn from a population of settlers brought from the outside, and the native peoples over whom they ruled and whose submission they guaranteed. This disjunction was most clearly manifested in the case of the use of native troops as auxiliaries in the Macedonian armies. Most of the time, Hellenistic rulers in Asia and Egypt took care to use native forces sparingly, and in restricted and subordinate roles, in order not to give such forces, and the peoples they were drawn from, the idea that they might rival or even challenge the military capabilities of the elite Macedonians and other Greeks. What could happen if these restrictions were not observed is seen in the case of the Ptolemaic army in the late third century, when an emergency situation led king Ptolemy IV to make greater use of, and place more reliance on, Egyptian troops than was wise for a non-Egyptian ruler.

In 218 Ptolemy IV faced an invasion of Palestine, which the Greeks tended to call Coele (Hollow) Syria, by Antiochus III at the head of a great army. While Ptolemy IV mostly concerned himself with the pursuit of pleasure, his ministers Agathocles and Sosibius had been preparing for this invasion for some time, and succeeded in gathering a large army to oppose it. They had pursued every avenue to find troops, not just mobilizing the Macedonian and other Greek manpower resources of Egypt, but sending agents abroad to find allies and mercenaries from Greece and elsewhere. They kept Antiochus occupied with diplomatic missions and negotiations while they prepared their force: the whole tale is recounted in detail by the historian Polybius (5.63–64). In the end, they were able to gather a pike phalanx of some twenty-five thousand men and more than eight thousand mercenaries. In addition there were a little less than six thousand cavalry, of whom some two thousand were mercenaries recruited from Greece. Specialized light infantry forces included three thousand Cretan archers, another three thousand Libyans trained to fight in the Macedonian style, and around six thousand Thracians and Galatians drawn from settlers in Egypt. But altogether these forces were not enough to stand up to the army

Antiochus had mobilized. The army was, therefore, supplemented by native Egyptian infantry: "the Egyptian contingent made up a phalanx of about twenty thousand men, under the command of Sosibius" (Polybius 5.65). When the showdown battle finally occurred, at Raphia in southern Palestine in summer of 217, Antiochus defeated Ptolemy's cavalry and made the classic mistake of over-pursuing. While he was gone, Ptolemy's infantry phalanx defeated that of Antiochus and won the battle, the Egyptians playing a significant role in bringing about this success.

For the moment that was a good outcome: Ptolemaic control of Palestine was assured. But Polybius (5.107) describes the aftermath, a few years later:

> after this Ptolemy became embroiled in a war against the Egyptians. For by arming the Egyptians for the war against Antiochus, this king (Ptolemy IV) made a decision which was acceptable in the short term but a great miscalculation for the future. For the Egyptians were elated by their success at Raphia and could no longer endure to take orders, but sought someone to lead them as they now believed they were able to fend for themselves; and that is what they achieved not long after (in 207/6 BCE).

The war was a disaster for Ptolemaic Egypt, severely weakening Ptolemaic rule and lasting for decades: large parts of upper (i.e. southern) Egypt escaped Ptolemaic control entirely until finally "pacified" around 186. As Polybius later summed it up (14.12): "this war, apart from the savagery and lawlessness each side displayed to the other, involved no regular battle, sea-fight, or siege, nor anything else worth mentioning." That is to say, it was fought in guerrilla style, with extreme brutality on each side: the Egyptians trying to drive out the hated Greek and other settlers, the Ptolemaic forces trying to force the Egyptians back into subjection. The utter reliance of the Hellenistic powers on having a strong standing army with a predominance of Macedonian and other Greek manpower could not be more clearly demonstrated.

What such a standing army looked like, when it was well taken care of, is illustrated by another famous event: a military parade held just outside Antioch, in the suburb of Daphne, by the Seleucid king Antiochus IV. After the Romans had defeated and deposed the Macedonian king Perseus, and forced Antiochus himself to retreat from Egypt when he seemed on the verge of conquering it and adding it to his realm to replace his father's loss of Asia Minor, Antiochus decided to make a grand show of military strength, to let the world know he was still a force to be reckoned with. In 166 a great festival was held at Daphne, with envoys attending from all around the Greek world, and the parade of the Seleucid army was at the heart of the festival. Polybius sets the scene (30.25):

> The public ceremonies began with a procession composed as follows: first came some men armed in the Roman fashion, equipped with corslets of chainmail, five thousand in the prime of life. Next came five thousand Mysians, followed by three thousand Cilicians armed as light infantry, and wearing gold crowns. Next came three thousand Thracians and five thousand Galatians. They were followed by twenty thousand Macedonians, five thousand armed with bronze shields, and the rest with silver shields, who were followed by two hundred and forty pairs of gladiators. Behind these were a thousand Nisaean cavalry and three thousand native horsemen, most of whom had gold plumes and gold crowns, the rest having them of silver. Next to them came the Companion Cavalry, a thousand in number, all with gold ornaments, closely followed by the corps of king's "friends" who were the same in number and equipment; after these came a thousand picked men, next to whom came the *Agema* or guard, which was considered the strongest of the cavalry, and numbered about a thousand. Next came the *cataphract* cavalry, both men and horses acquiring that name from the nature of their armor; they numbered fifteen hundred. All the above men had purple surcoats, in many cases embroidered with gold and heraldic designs. And behind them came a hundred six-horsed, and forty four-horsed chariots; a chariot drawn by four elephants and another by two; and then thirty-six elephants in single file with all their furniture on.

Assuming, as we surely must, that the five thousand men armed in the Roman fashion were "Macedonians" being retrained in the newest style of warfare exemplified by the successful Romans, we can see that even after the massive setback of Antiochus III's defeat at Magnesia, the Seleucid army still mustered some twenty-five thousand Macedonian infantry and four thousand cavalry as its core, supplemented by a variety of forces drawn from other settlers (the Thracians and Galatians) and native peoples, both infantry and cavalry. The military colonies in Syria and Mesopotamia evidently remained strong and continued to produce a steady supply of recruits, and the army headquarters at Apamea-on-the-Orontes was still doing its job of training and equipping a Hellenistic army in the best traditions. That this was no mere parade army is illustrated well by Antiochus' successful invasion of Egypt in 168/7, mentioned above, which failed to conquer Egypt only because of Roman intervention. Strong leadership by Antiochus and his older brother and predecessor Seleucus IV had enabled the Seleucid kingdom to recover well from its loss of Asia Minor. The army still thrived, and but for the civil wars between descendants of Seleucus IV and Antiochus IV, the Seleucid kingdom might have remained a significant power for much longer than it did. But it was not kings and armies that were the heart and soul of Hellenistic civilization: it was Greek cities.

3. THE CITIES

While many political, military, and cultural leaders from ancient Greece are still famed in western civilization, there are others whose fame has undeservedly faded. One of these is Hippodamus of Miletus. His influence is still strongly felt in western and indeed world civilization, though few outside a narrow specialty are likely to have heard of him. Hippodamus was a town planner, the first we know of, and he made his name in the late 490s when he was commissioned by the Athenians to design the new port city they were building at the Piraeus, which is still today the greatest harbor in Greece. The design Hippodamus established for the Piraeus, and which he popularized in a great book he wrote on urban design, was to influence all subsequent Greek city-building, and still influences modern urban planning. Though he did not invent it per se, Hippodamus adopted and popularized the rectangular grid design for cities, which is sometimes known as the Hippodamian plan as a result. Modern people are very familiar with this Hippodamian design from many modern examples, the most famous being perhaps New York City. Establishing a rectangular grid based on broad parallel avenues with narrower cross-streets intersecting them at a ninety degree angle, and siting public spaces, most importantly a main town square, at suitable locations within this grid, made for a city that was easy to live in and readily navigable, as inhabitants of New York and many other modern cities know well. The relevance of Hippodamus and his urban design in the present context is that during the Hellenistic era a vast number of new cities were founded in western Asia and north Africa which almost all, to some degree at least, used the Hippodamian design.

23. Stoa of Attalus in the *agora* at Athens
(Wikimedia Commons photo by Ken Russell Salvador, CC BY 2.0)

Between about 330 and the middle of the second century BCE many dozens, in fact ultimately probably several hundred Greek towns and cities were founded or re-founded and developed in western Asia, from the Mediterranean to the Hindu Kush, and—to a more limited degree—in north Africa, that is in Egypt and Libya. And with very few exceptions, these towns and cities were built up according to the rectangular grid, Hippodamian plan of urban design. The historian Peter Green criticized these cities as showing a "dreary sameness," but I think he misses the point. The Hellenistic towns and cities were designed to give a sense of comforting familiarity, to make the Greek settler, citizen, or traveler feel at home.

Each city would, as a matter of course, have a surrounding wall defining the urban space and marking it off from the *chora*, the countryside. When one entered the city through its main gate, one would find oneself on a broad avenue that would lead one directly to the main town square, or *agora*. Around the *agora* would be several long colonnaded buildings of the type called a *stoa* (see ill. 23). In the colonnades of these buildings, citizens and visitors could meet and/or take their ease, in the open air but protected from the sun or rain. At the back of

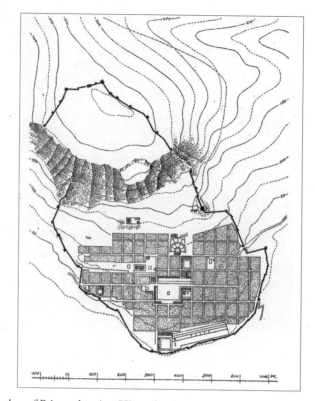

24. Street plan of Priene showing Hippodamian grid design
(*Wikimedia Commons, Wellcome Images, CC BY 4.0*)

these buildings were enclosed rooms that functioned as shops or offices of public officials. Looking out from the *agora*, the city skyline would be dominated by other public buildings: temples of the gods, a theater, a gymnasium. The travel writer Pausanias made it clear that any place that wished to be considered a city must have such buildings, with their associated amenities and services, and archaeological exploration of Hellenistic cities bears him out.

Other than the spaces set aside for public buildings and uses, the city would be divided, by the avenues and cross-streets, into housing blocks where the citizens lived in private houses or, at times in the larger cities, in apartment buildings. In every region of the city there would be a public fountain house, with clean drinking water piped in from a nearby spring or other source, to meet the water needs of the families living in that region. In this way, the Hellenistic cities corresponded to a clear and generally understood and accepted conception of what a

Greek city should be, how it should look, what sort of physical infrastructure and amenities should be present, and therefore what sort of lifestyle was to be pursued there.

Wherever one traveled throughout the Hellenistic world, one would find Greek towns fulfilling this conception of urban life and offering this lifestyle, and in every major region of the Hellenistic world one would find, in addition to the smaller towns and cities where most Greeks lived, also one or more larger cities—regional metropolises—where a wider array of services could be found and a higher level of culture could be sampled. The "sameness" that Peter Green critiqued was planned and desired. It made for a clear sense of belonging and common identity among the Hellenistic cities and their inhabitants.

This sense of common identity is well illustrated by a highly informative inscription surviving from the Macedonian town of Beroea (see map 2), recording a public decree of the people of that town:

> When Hippocrates son of Nicocrates was *strategos* (chief magistrate), on the nineteenth of Apellaeos, at a meeting of the assembly, Zopyros son of Amyntas, the gymnasiarch ... proposed: whereas all the other magistracies are carried out in accordance with the law, and in the other cities in which there are gymnasia and anointing is practiced the laws on gymnasiarchs are deposited in the public archives, it is appropriate that the same should be done among us and that the law which we handed in to the *exetastai* (public auditors) should be inscribed on a stone block and placed on view in the gymnasium, and also deposited in the public archive; for when this is done, the young men will feel a greater sense of shame and be more obedient to their leader, and the revenues will not be wasted away as the gymnasiarchs who are appointed will discharge their office in accordance with the law and will be liable to render accounts. Therefore, the city resolved: that the law on the gymnasiarchy which Zopyros son of Amyntas, the gymnasiarch ... introduced, should be valid and be deposited in the public archive, that the gymnasiarchs should use it, and that the law should be inscribed on stone and set up in the gymnasium. The law was ratified on the first of Peritius (Austin *The Hellenistic World* doc. 118).

The inscription continues with the law proper, regulating the use and oversight of the gymnasium in great detail. What we learn is that, like any self-respecting Hellenistic city, Beroea had a gymnasium, and the citizens of Beroea attended that gymnasium to exercise and bathe. But at the time of this decree, it was brought to the attention of the Beroeans that they had as yet no law regulating the use of the gymnasium, though having such a law was the norm in the Greek cities. This was clearly felt to be a lack: in order for Beroea to "hold its head up" in the community of Greek cities, that lack must be filled. And so a detailed law regulating the use of the gymnasium, and the precise duties and responsibilities of the gymnasiarchs, was offered, adopted, and officially published by being inscribed on stone and publicly displayed. We see here, that is, a clear desire to conform to a recognized standard of what a Greek city should be.

The life lived by the citizens of these cities was on the whole a comfortable and pleasant one. Citizens and visitors were guaranteed an array of amenities and services that made for this pleasant lifestyle. I have already mentioned the public fountain houses around the city that guaranteed a clean and plentiful supply of drinking water. Fouling the public fountains was a serious crime that was harshly punished. There were public granaries where citizens could purchase grain—to be baked into bread—at an affordable price. The religious life of the citizens was taken care of in well maintained temples and sanctuaries with regular festivals that offered enjoyable holidays throughout the year. Social life centered around the *agora* with its stoas where people could meet and shop or take care of public business, and the gymnasium where citizens could exercise and play together, bathe, and enjoy other amenities. Gymnasia often had concert spaces where musical performances, literary readings, or lectures could be attended. And it was common for gymnasia to have dining rooms that could be rented for private parties. Other public entertainments—plays and concerts—were put on throughout the year at the theater, which was free for citizens to attend.

All of these amenities and services required oversight, and the Greek cities had developed an array of magistrates—drawn usually from the wealthy elite—whose job it was to see to the upkeep of the city and its services. The evidence for these civic magistrates is scattered, but altogether it adds up to a good picture of how such cities were run. Cities elected chief magistrates—often called *strategoi* (literally, generals)—to oversee the whole system, along with guardians of the law (*nomophylakes*) to see that the laws and regulations were obeyed. *Astynomoi* or city-

wardens had the task of looking after the city's infrastructure and services, along with a host of more specialized magistrates. There were gymnasiarchs to oversee the gymnasium; *sitophylakes* (grain wardens) to
take care of the public granaries and ensure they were well stocked;
agoranomoi (market wardens) to ensure orderly market squares and see
to it that market stalls and shops functioned legitimately, using proper
coins, weights, and measures; *nuktophylakes* (night guards) to see to
public order during the dark hours of the night (there was no street lighting); *amphodarchai* (street wardens) to see to the upkeep and cleanliness
of streets and drains. To illustrate the functioning of these magistrates,
we are fortunate to have a substantial portion of the municipal administrative code of the city of Pergamon in north-west Asia Minor (see map
5), dating from the late third or early second century BCE.

> [*Concerning the streets*] . . . the *amphodarchai* shall compel those who
> have thrown out rubbish to clean the place up, as the law requires. If
> they fail to do so, the *amphodarchai* shall report them to the *astynomoi*.
> The *astynomoi* shall issue a contract together with the *amphodarchai*
> and shall exact the resulting expense from the offenders immediately and
> shall fine them ten drachmas. If any of the *amphodarchai* fails to carry
> out his written instructions he shall be fined by the *astynomoi* twenty
> drachmas for each offense . . .
>
> *Concerning digging up the streets:* if anyone digs up soil or stones
> on the streets or makes clay or bricks or lays out open drains, the *am-
> phodarchai* shall prevent them. If they do not comply, the *amphodarchai*
> shall report them to the *astynomoi*. They shall fine the offender five
> drachmas for each offense and shall compel him to restore everything to
> its original state, and to build underground drains . . . similarly they shall
> compel already existing drains to be built underground . . .
>
> *Concerning the fountains:* concerning the fountains in the city and
> in the suburbs it shall be required of the *astynomoi* to make sure they
> are clean and that the pipes which bring and remove the water flow
> freely. If any need to be repaired, they shall notify the *strategoi* and the
> superintendent of the sacred revenues, so that contracts (for repair work)
> are issued by these officials. No one shall be allowed to water animals
> at the public fountains nor to wash clothes or implements or anything
> else. Should anyone do any of these things, if he is a free man his animals,
> clothes, and implements shall be confiscated and he shall be fined fifty
> drachmas . . .

> *Concerning the public toilets:* the *astynomoi* shall take care of the
> public toilets and of the sewers which run from them, and any sewers
> which are not covered (shall be covered?) . . . (Austin *The Hellenistic
> World* doc. 216 = Dittenberger *OGIS* no. 483).

This sampling from a much longer and more detailed document makes
clear the care and attention that Hellenistic cities gave to the upkeep
and oversight of their infrastructure and amenities, with careful instructions to the various magistrates regarding their exact duties and how
to carry them out, and fines and other punishments for wrong-doers,
whether citizens or visitors breaking the law or magistrates failing to
carry out their responsibilities. The citizens of these cities cared deeply
about the physical fabric of their cities, the services which they provided
to themselves through this fabric, and the upkeep of the lifestyle that
was thus afforded them. The moneys to pay for all this came from market (i.e. sales) taxes, import and export duties, sacred revenues flowing
into the temples and sanctuaries from gifts and from sacred lands, from
rents on public lands, and—very importantly—from contributions that
the wealthy elite were encouraged (read, pressured) to make in lieu of
taxes. The rich who co-operated and donated were celebrated as public
benefactors and granted an array of honors and privileges that made it
worth their while to be seen to be generous donors to the public good.

Besides all these services, which were a normal and expected part
of Hellenistic civic life, most cities also showed concern for two other
kinds of public service: health and education. It was common in the
Hellenistic cities for funds to be made available, often via donations by
the wealthy, to appoint public doctors whose charge it was to look after
the health of any citizens needing medical attention. The sums paid to
these public doctors as retainers were not always large enough to allow
them to do their work free of charge; but it does seem that they normally tailored their fee structures to the citizens' ability to pay, and there
is evidence to indicate that when necessary they provided some medical
care free of charge. We have an illustrative example known to us from
an honorific decree passed by the people of Samos:

> The council passed a motion to put this matter before the assembly held
> for elections: since Diodoros son of Dioscourides, who took over among
> us the role of public doctor, has for many years in the past time through

his own skill and care looked after and cured many of the citizens and others in the city who had fallen seriously ill and was responsible for their safety, as has been vouched for frequently by many among the people each time when the contracts are renewed; and when the earthquakes happened and many among us suffered painful wounds of every sort because of the unexpectedness of the disaster and were in need of urgent attention, he distributed his services equally to all and assisted them . . . (Austin *The Hellenistic World* doc. 125).

This sort of attention to the public health needs of the citizens is attested by records from other cities too. In particular, an inscription from the city of Teos, regarding tax exemptions granted to new citizens in about 300 BCE, reveals how such public doctors might be paid:

> Those who wish may raise pigs up to (a specified number?) and sheep and they shall be exempt from tax. And they shall be exempt from the other taxes too, except for the tax for the maintenance of doctors (Austin *The Hellenistic World* Doc. 99).

In other words, some cities at least raised a special tax from the citizens to pay for the upkeep of a kind of public health service of doctors whose job it was to accept any citizen in need as a patient, and take care of them.

Regarding education, it is important to note that Hellenistic cities were almost all organized as formal democracies, with the general citizen body sovereign and meeting regularly throughout the year to discuss and vote on matters of public policy and interest. The evidence for this is overwhelming, in the form of numerous publicly voted decrees from cities all around the Hellenistic world. And for the citizens to function democratically, debating public issues in a sensible way, they needed to be informed. That meant, in effect, that they needed to be able to read, since proposals, decrees, and laws were publicized by being written up and exposed publicly in the *agora* and/or other public spaces. Schooling was therefore a public need, and schools at which the sons (and sometimes daughters too) of citizens could learn the basics of literacy are well attested. Though most such schools were private ventures, there was a perceived public interest in making sure that the schoolmasters running these schools knew their job and provided value for the fees they charged. It was not uncommon, consequently, for cities to have a magistrate whose task it was to oversee the schooling of the young: the usual title was *paidonomos* or child-warden. In some cities we happen to know that schooling was provided free of charge: a wealthy citizen might establish a trust fund to pay the fees of teachers whose job would be to educate the children of the citizens. I shall close this section with one such example, from the city of Teos on the west coast of Asia Minor (see map 5):

> So that all the free children may be educated just as Polythrus son of Onesimus in his foresight promised to the people, wishing to establish a most fair memorial of his own love of honor, he made a gift for this purpose of 34,000 drachmas.
>
> Every year at the elections, after the selection of the public secretaries, three schoolmasters are to be appointed, who will teach the boys and the girls. The person appointed to the top class shall be paid 600 drachmas per year; the person appointed to the middle class shall be paid 550 drachmas; and the person appointed to the lowest class shall be paid 500 drachmas. Two physical trainers are also to be appointed, and the salary of each is to be 500 drachmas (Austin *The Hellenistic World* doc. 120 = Dittenberger *Syll.* no. 578).

The inscription goes on to require the appointment of a music teacher and to lay out how exactly the *paidonomos* shall assign children to each of the three classes by age and/or suitability, and to regulate what is to be taught and how and where. The point here is that Teos had, thanks to the generosity of a wealthy citizen, a public trust fund which paid for a free three-year education in literacy and music, as well as some physical training, for all the sons of the citizens, and remarkably their daughters too. This literacy was not just important as a political matter, to enable the citizens to function politically in an informed way. It was also important culturally: because Hellenistic culture was a reading culture, a culture of the book. And this is illustrated by another well known feature of Hellenistic urban civilization: the development of public libraries.

4. THE LIBRARY AND HELLENISTIC CULTURE

In the early decades of the third century BCE, Ptolemy I Soter and his son Ptolemy II Philadelphus established in Alexandria one of the great cultural institutions of western history: the *Mouseion*. This term, the origin of the English word museum, literally means a sanctuary of the

Mousai (Muses), the goddesses who oversaw literature, music, and culture generally in Greek religious thought. But the *Mouseion* at Alexandria was far more than a religious sanctuary: it was a great research institute that offered housing and allowances to writers, philosophers, and scientists of all sorts, who could live at the *Mouseion* free of all the usual cares of life and just concentrate on their writing and/or research. And at the heart of the *Mouseion*, as its greatest resource and research tool, lay the great Library of Alexandria, the first great public library of the western tradition and one of the greatest libraries in western history. Libraries of a sort had already existed in Athens for decades: there were book collections at Plato's Academy and at Aristotle's Lyceum, and the Athenian public archive kept official copies of the tragedies and comedies performed each year at the Dionysia and Lenaea festivals. Not surprisingly, therefore, Ptolemy I brought to Alexandria from Athens a pupil of Aristotle named Demetrius of Phalerum to oversee the establishment of his great institute and library. Demetrius had governed his home city of Athens for ten years (316–307) as a kind of "philosopher-king" on behalf of the Macedonian ruler Cassander; but was seen by pro-democracy Athenians as a tyrant and driven out into exile, so Ptolemy's offer came to him as a godsend. And he was ideal for Ptolemy's purposes: besides his cultural and literary attainments as an Aristotelian philosopher, he had the leadership and organizational skills needed to get the *Mouseion* up and running.

Besides inviting to Alexandria, to stay at the *Mouseion*, leading men in every field of cultural endeavor, one of the key projects in establishing the *Mouseion* was building up its library. The learned Byzantine man of literature Johannes Tzetzes tells us that the aim of Ptolemy and Demetrius was to gather into the library "the books of all the peoples of the world". The Christian heresiologist Epiphanius of Salamis knew of a letter written by Ptolemy to "all the sovereigns on earth" requesting that they have sent to him the writings of authors of every kind: "poets and prose writers, rhetoricians and sophists, doctors and prophets, historians, and all the others also." Stories and legends accrued around this book-collecting. Supposedly the king sent to Athens offering a fantastic sum of money for the right to make copies of the original manuscripts of the great tragic dramatists, stored in the state archive of Athens. The copies were to be made at the *Mouseion* itself, and the story has it that Ptolemy in the end kept the originals for his library and sent the copies back to Athens. There was a law that every ship that put into Alexandria's great harbor was searched by Ptolemaic agents, and any books on board were seized. They were copied by the scribes at the *Mouseion,* and the copies were returned to the ships, while the originals were placed in the library. Supposedly Ptolemy would visit the library regularly to receive updates from Demetrius on how the book-collecting was going. Demetrius would report on how many volumes were present, and on plans to acquire more. The goal, reputedly, was to acquire half a million volumes, at which point Demetrius calculated that every book in the world worth having would be present.

Ptolemy was not content to sit back and wait for books to come or be sent to Alexandria: purchasing agents were sent out around the Hellenistic world to track down and acquire rare books of every sort, whatever the cost. One book collection that eluded Ptolemy's agents, however, was the writings of Aristotle. During his lifetime, Aristotle had published various writings in dialogue form, like those of his old master Plato. But his key writings that formed the basis of his philosophical teaching at his school in Athens, the *Lykeion* (Lyceum), were kept private. Aristotle left them to his pupil and successor Theophrastus, who in turn bequeathed them to the man he expected to succeed him, Neleus of Scepsis. But Neleus did not become head of the Lyceum, and in anger at being passed over he returned to his home town of Scepsis in the Troad, taking Aristotle's writings with him. Ptolemy's agents were alerted and showed up to purchase the writings; and the polymath Athenaeus of Naucratis, writing in the early third century CE, in fact reports the acquisition by the library of "the books of Aristotle and Theophrastus, from Neleus of Scepsis." But whatever Neleus sold Ptolemy's book-buyers, it was not the prized writings of Aristotle himself: those remained buried in a chest in Neleus' ancestral home for nearly two hundred years until an Aristotelian enthusiast of the first century BCE finally tracked them down, enabling the world at last to read Aristotle's true thoughts.

The library was not restricted to Greek texts. A learned Egyptian priest from the temple-city of On-Heliopolis named Manetho made a translation/adaptation of Egyptian chronicles and sacred writings into Greek for his patron Ptolemy II. The sacred writings of the great Iranian prophet Zarathustra—that is the texts sacred to the Zoroastrian religion, whoever their true authors—were reportedly collected and translated into Greek, totaling some two million lines of text. Most famously, there is the legendary story of the translation for the library of the Hebrew scriptures. The early Ptolemies ruled Palestine and it was easy for them, when Demetrius alerted them to the existence of these writings, to have the high priest at Jerusalem send copies of the texts along with religious experts to translate them into Greek. According to the legend, seventy-two translators were sent, who each labored independently for exactly seventy-two days to translate the texts, miraculously producing at the end of the seventy-two days translations that were word for word the same. However it was really produced, a well translated Greek version of the scriptures, known as the Septuagint (from the Latin word for seventy), did come about and is still the standard Greek version of the Old Testament to the present day.

For all the fascination of this acquisition process, the physical accumulation of books is only the first step in the creation of a great library, however, and it is the follow-up stages of analysis, categorization, and evaluation that made the library at Alexandria one of the great cultural institutions and changed Hellenistic culture dramatically. What happened at the *Mouseion* library over the centuries was the creation of library science, of textual scholarship, of literary theory, of new styles of literature that prized erudition as a key component of literary creation, and of a culture of the book as a prized component of a well rounded person's life more generally. The process may be said to have begun with the analysis of multiple copies of Homer's epic poems, the *Iliad* and the *Odyssey*, and with the first formal head of the library per se, Zenodotus of Ephesus.

Copies of Homer's great epics were widely available around the Greek world, and the library acquired a significant number of such copies. When these were analyzed, problems emerged: there were all sorts of differences from one copy to another. Missing or added words, words that made no sense and appeared to have been misspelled, whole lines or passages found in one copy but not in another: what was one to make of such anomalies, and how was one to discover the "true" text of Homer? Zenodotus set himself the task of analyzing the various copies of Homer and solving the problems. In doing so, he began to establish the basic criteria of textual scholarship. Homer's characteristic style and vocabulary were analyzed, and words or passages that did not fit or seemed anachronistic were stigmatized as possible interpolations. Similarly, passages that seemed intrusive to the narrative, or not to fit in terms of Homer's narrative method, were questioned. For example, Zenodotus famously questioned the authenticity of the description of Achilles' shield in *Iliad* 18 as being unique and so un-Homeric. While Zenodotus himself may have been rather cavalier in his method, what came out of this work was true textual scholarship. Eventually Zenodotus' successors produced lexica of the Homeric vocabulary, treatises on Homeric language and style, commentaries on Homer's works explaining obscurities and difficulties, and official cleaned-up texts of the Homeric epics that are the source of all modern texts. And once this process had gotten under way with Homer, the works of other authors of all sorts were naturally subjected to the same analytical investigation.

Besides the work of analyzing and explaining, there was also the business of categorizing and ordering texts, because the texts collected could not just be piled higgledy-piggledy on shelves or in boxes. They had to be arranged in some rational manner, and a key role in this business was played by one of the most remarkable literary figures of the Hellenistic era: the poet Callimachus. Originally a schoolmaster in the city of Cyrene in modern-day Libya, Callimachus was brought to Alexandria to work in the library, and was eventually given the charge of producing a catalogue. After what must surely have been decades of labor and study, Callimachus produced the *Pinakes*, a catalogue of the books in the library ordered by distinct categories of literary work and with some account of each work. This work itself filled 120 book scrolls, and it in Callimachus established eleven different categories of literature, six of poetry and five of prose: lyric and epic poetry, tragic and comic drama, history and philosophy and oratory, and so on. Callimachus—building to be sure on the work of predecessors like Aristotle—established the criteria for these genres and divided the works of Greek literature among them. Eventually this work of classification also came to include judgements of quality, and one began to get lists of the best writers and works in each category. There were the nine lyric poets, the three great tragedians, and the ten orators, for example. Not every genre lent itself to such generally accepted lists: in history there was wide consensus that Herodotus, Thucydides, and Xenophon were at the top, and almost all critics accepted Theopompus of Chios, Philistus of Syracuse, and Ephorus as the next three, but after that lists became more idiosyncratic: whether one should include Timaeus or Polybius or Timagenes were matters of dispute. But what came out of this work was a universally accepted sense that in every genre there were "classic" or "canonical" authors and works which established and illustrated the very best of what could be done in each genre.

Once this process was well underway, it became understood that to be a person of taste and discrimination one had to be familiar with "the classics," and getting access to and reading these classic works was thus expected of every citizen of the Greek cities who prided himself (or herself) on being well educated. The literature written during the Hellenistic era adapted itself to this taste for erudition, and to the existence of a large literate audience. At the top level of culture writers began to produce works which displayed their own erudition. The poet Callimachus, mentioned above, pioneered a new kind of poetry that was highly polished and full of tags from and allusions to the classic works. In order to fully appreciate Callimachus' poems, one needed the near encyclopedic knowledge of classical writings that Callimachus himself had, thanks to his labors in the library. A modern comparandum would be poems of T. S. Eliot—"The Lovesong of J. Alfred Prufrock" or "The Wasteland," for example—which are similarly full of quotations and allusions and require a good commentary to appreciate fully. In a somewhat different way, there is the epic *Argonautica* by Callimachus' rival Apollonius of Rhodes, stuffed full of geographical and ethnic details drawn from the latest historical works such as Nymphis of Heraclea's history of his home town and of the southern Black Sea region generally. In one way or another, erudition was the order of the day for such Hellenistic writers.

Alongside this rather "highbrow" literature, Hellenistic writers also responded to the existence of a wide readership by producing more "popular" works: poetry reflecting rural nostalgia, for example, or humorous mimes and romantic novels. The Syracusan poet Theocritus composed "idylls", many of which were set in an imagined countryside where shepherd lads lazed under spreading oak trees and competed musically with each other for the attention of winsome shepherd lasses.

One can imagine the type of city-dwellers who enjoyed reading or listening to this. Herondas wrote short stories called "mimes" which portrayed humorous (and sometimes erotic) vignettes from everyday life, clearly aimed at readers seeking a break from their perhaps somewhat monotonous existences. And after about 200 BCE the first romantic novels began to appear, starting with the highly fictionalized *Alexander Romance*, and continuing with stories of piracy, kidnappings, magic, travel, and love triumphing in the end in the face of all adversity. Greeks living in fifth- and fourth-century Athens or Corinth or Sparta had plenty of adventure in their lives: real wars, with real battles on land and at sea, real travels, and all too often real adversity. In the safer but more humdrum existence of the Hellenistic citizens, fictional adventures had to take the place of real ones, which was all to the good, of course. The point is that reading material was being created for a wider reading audience than the highly educated elite, making it likely that many citizens were now reading or attending public readings of books. Already in the early fourth century Plato tells us a book could be bought in the *agora* of Athens for a drachma—a day's wage for the average skilled worker. With papyrus production in Ptolemaic Egypt ramping up, the price of books went down, and it was not so unusual for a citizen to own a few books. But as long as books were produced by being copied out by hand, books would remain relatively expensive and relatively rare. And that of course is where libraries came in.

Naturally, the great library of Alexandria did not remain unique. In the late third century BCE Antiochus III sponsored the creation of a great royal library at Antioch in Syria, employing the poet and grammarian Euphorion of Chalkis as chief librarian. The Macedonian kings also collected a royal library at Pella: Plutarch tells us in his biography of the Roman commander Lucius Aemilius Paullus that when he defeated the last Antigonid king Perseus and conquered Macedonia in 169, he kept the books of the royal library as his personal share of the booty, on behalf of his sons. Most famously, the Attalid kings of Pergamon in the early second century created a great library to rival the Ptolemaic library in Alexandria. At its height, we are told that the library of Pergamon held upwards of two hundred thousand book scrolls. The Roman polymath Pliny the Elder tells us that, not wanting to rely on the importation of paper from Egypt, the only place where the papyrus reed was known to grow in abundance, the Attalid kings sponsored the production of an alternative writing material made from animal hides and known today as parchment, a word which derives from the name Pergamon (as may be seen more clearly in the Dutch form of the word parchment—*perkament*). Eventually other cities began to copy these royal libraries by developing libraries of their own, for the use of their citizens: such libraries flourished around the Hellenistic world in the Roman period, as we will see below in section 6 of this chapter. Libraries collected and owned by private citizens also became a thing in that era, as we shall see. Hellenistic culture was truly a culture of the book.

5. THE ROMAN CONQUEST

In 201 BCE the Romans emerged from an epic two-war struggle with the Carthaginians, a struggle that had begun as far back as 264, as masters of the entire western Mediterranean region. They controlled all of Italy, the islands of Sicily, Sardinia and Corsica, and a good portion of Spain—all of Mediterranean Spain in particular. In north Africa, the Carthaginians were thoroughly submissive subject allies, and the kingdom of Numidia (much of modern Algeria) was a client state under their domination. Not surprisingly, the Romans turned their eyes eastward, to the wealthy and highly civilized Hellenistic kingdoms in the eastern Mediterranean. As we have seen, Philip V of Macedonia had made the mistake of allying with the Carthaginians against Rome when it seemed as if the Romans would lose, and vengeance against Macedonia was therefore the first order of business. The Romans were slightly hampered by the peace treaty they had signed with Philip in 205, but they knew ways around the legal niceties of treaties. A roving commission of ambassadors was sent around the Greek world to collect any and all grievances against Philip, who was then given an ultimatum to redress those grievances at once or else the Romans would be "obliged" to make war on him in defense of their "friends" in the Greek world. In Roman eyes, making war in "defense" of these new-found "friends" would be a just war, treaty or no treaty.

Over the course of the next century and a half, the Greeks of the Hellenistic world learned some hard lessons about the Romans: it was never safe for an independent state to have any dealings with the Romans, whether as friends or enemies. Enemies were made war on, defeated, and subjected; but "friends" were expected to show gratitude by being as submissive to Rome as if they had been conquered, and "friends" who failed in such submission soon found themselves being conquered. A series of epic battles early in the second century—the Battle of Cynoscephalae in 197 against Philip V, the Battle of Magnesia in 190 against Antiochus III, and the Battle of Pydna in 168 against Philip's successor Perseus—established Roman dominance over the Hellenistic world. Various follow-up operations were needed to complete full Roman control: there was the Fourth Macedonian War and the Achaean War in 148–147, the subjection of the Pergamene kingdom in 132, and very difficult warfare against Mithridates VI of Pontus in the 80s BCE and again in the late 70s. In the end, it was not until the campaigns of the Roman general Pompeius Magnus in the 60s, and Caesar Octavian (later known as Augustus) annexing Egypt in 30, that full Roman rule over the entire Hellenistic world was rounded off. Thereafter, the Hellenistic world formed the eastern half of the Mediterranean-wide Roman Empire, the former kingdoms now being Roman provinces ruled by Roman governors and secured by Roman armies.

How exactly did the Romans take over the seemingly powerful Hellenistic kingdoms with such apparent ease? The key lies in the very different military systems of the Romans and the Macedonians. The Macedonian-ruled kingdoms, as we have seen, relied for their security on professional standing armies, recruited from a military elite and carefully trained in a complex and demanding system of warfare. These professional soldiers could be complemented by allied "native" troops drawn from the peoples of Asia and/or Egypt, but the Macedonian rulers preferred not to rely heavily on such troops for reasons discussed above (section 2). While there was enough Greco-Macedonian manpower to field large armies of thirty thousand to fifty thousand men when necessary, while keeping thousands more in forts on garrison duty, if the field army were to be defeated with heavy losses the ruler in question would be forced to sue for peace: it would take years to recruit and train replacements and be able to take the field again with a credible army; in the case of Philip V, for example, we have seen that it took around fifteen years for the Macedonian army to recover from Cynoscephalae.

The Romans operated very differently. It was not that Roman soldiers were man for man better than the Macedonians and other Greeks: they were not. It was not that their tactical formations and style of fighting were superior: well led and fighting on the right terrain the Macedonians were very much a match for the Romans. Nor were Roman generals better than the Macedonian kings: not a few Roman generals of this era were in fact distinctly incompetent. It was that rather than using a professional standing army, the Romans relied on a citizen militia army. Every Roman citizen who owned more than a certain minimum amount of property was liable for military service, and was actually required to put in from ten to fifteen years of active service in the legions, at times indeed even more. These citizens were expected to equip themselves, and to some degree see to their own training, but they were in no way disorganized or poorly trained. Constant Roman warfare (the Roman state was in effect never at peace) meant constant military service, and constant military service saw to it that Roman citizens were thoroughly trained, experienced, and battle-hardened soldiers. And there were literally hundreds of thousands of these soldier-citizens. Because the Romans constantly renewed and expanded their citizen body by Romanizing allies and granting them Roman citizenship, the number of Roman citizens by the late third century had reached nearly three hundred thousand. Some two-thirds of these citizens were eligible for military service. In addition, the other Italian peoples, as subject allies of the Romans, were required to send troops to assist the Romans: and these allied Italian troops were as numerous as the Romans, and trained and equipped very similarly. A Roman army of forty thousand men, therefore, would consist of around twenty thousand Roman soldiers and twenty thousand Italian allies.

The upshot was that the Romans simply out-manned their enemies. Defeat a Roman army, as the Macedonian king Perseus did in 171 at the Battle of Callinicus near Larissa, and the Romans would simply send more troops and a different general. But once a Macedonian king—such as Philip V, Antiochus III, and eventually Perseus himself—suffered a defeat he was done for. The Carthaginians had learned this lesson the hard way: numerous major victories over the Romans counted for little when the Romans could simply keep on fighting with more and more soldiers thanks to their seemingly inexhaustible supply

of manpower. The Romans made up heavy losses by enfranchising more
Italians as Romans, and their citizen militia armies just kept on coming.
In the end, no professional standing army could stand up to the pressure: there simply were not enough trained professional soldiers. It was
not any inherent weakness in the Hellenistic world, its kingdoms, and
its armies that saw them crumble under Roman pressure, therefore: it
was simply the extraordinary effectiveness of the Roman citizen militia
system at mobilizing resources of manpower that could not be matched
by Rome's opponents.

Thus it was that Rome took control of the Hellenistic world and
made it part of the Roman Empire. But beyond the switch of Macedonian rulers for Roman ones, little changed. The urban civilization
with its distinctive Hellenistic culture and way of life continued under
new management. Greek remained the dominant language of the eastern Mediterranean and western Asia, and the Greek cities in fact thrived
as never before under the aegis of Roman security: the *pax Romana* or
Roman peace gave the Hellenistic world centuries of security and prosperity. The crucial point here is that the Romans had no high civilization and culture of their own with which to replace Hellenistic culture
and civilization. On the contrary, Roman high culture only developed
in the second century BCE and after, and it developed by copying Hellenistic Greek models. Great Roman poets such as Catullus, Horace,
and Vergil modeled themselves on great Greek poets such as Callimachus, Alcaeus, Sappho, and Homer. Great Roman orators such as
Cicero modeled themselves on Greek orators such as Isocrates and
Demosthenes. Great Roman historians such as Sallust, Livy, or Tacitus
learned from Herodotus and Thucydides. The Romans could and did
crush Hellenistic armies and rule the Hellenistic world, but in the face
of Hellenistic civilization all they could do was accept and imitate. As
the Roman poet Horace famously put it: *Graecia capta ferum victorem*
cepit et artes intulit agresti Latio—conquered Greece captivated her
savage victor and brought her arts to rustic Latium.

6. HELLENISTIC CIVILIZATION UNDER ROMAN RULE

The city of Nicomedia, my lord, has spent 3,329,000 sesterces on an
aqueduct, which was abandoned unfinished and has even been torn
down. Again they spent 200,000 sesterces on another aqueduct which

has also been abandoned. So now, after wasting all that money, they must make a new expenditure in order to have water. I personally have visited a very pure spring from which in my opinion water should be brought on arches, as was tried in the first place, so that it will not reach only the level and low lying parts of the city. A few arches are still standing and some can be erected from the cut stone which was torn down from the previous structure; some part, I think, will have to be built of brick, since that is cheaper and easier. But first of all it is necessary for you to send here an inspector of aqueducts or an engineer, so that what happened before will not occur again. This I am certain of, that the usefulness and beauty of the structure will be entirely worthy of your era (Pliny *Letters* 10.27).

So wrote the Roman governor of Bithynia in north west Asia Minor, Pliny the Younger, a noted man of letters, to his boss the emperor Trajan, who approved of the project. Pliny's letters to Trajan about his activities as governor, along with Trajan's replies, make a fascinating little archive of insider documents about Roman rule in the Hellenistic world. Pliny had more to say about public services in the city of Nicomedia.

While I was touring another part of the province, a great fire at Nicomedia destroyed many private houses and two public buildings—an old men's shelter and the temple of Isis—though they stood on opposite sides of the street. It spread so far first due to the strength of the wind, and secondly due to the inactivity of the people, who evidently stood idle and motionless spectators of this terrible calamity; but in any case the city possessed not a single pump or fire bucket or any equipment at all for fighting fires. These will now be procured, as I have already ordered. Do you, my lord, consider whether you think it right to organize an association of firemen, not to exceed 150 men. I will make sure that only firemen are admitted into it, and that the privileges granted are not abused for other purposes; since they would be few in number, it would not be difficult to keep them under surveillance (Pliny *Letters* 10.26).

In this case, Trajan approved of the provision of firefighting equipment, but—worried that any association of men allowed to hold regular meetings would become political and be tempted to activities outside their remit—disallowed the association of firemen, instructing that propertyowners and the general populace should use the equipment and do the firefighting. The point is that the infrastructure, amenities, and services characteristic of Hellenistic urban life were maintained and even expanded under Roman rule. Not only do we see careful thought given to an adequate drinking water supply; we learn that Nicomedia had a shelter for the elderly maintained at public expense, and that public funds were now also expended on firefighting equipment. That these examples drawn from Pliny's letters are not exceptional is attested by a host of inscriptions from all around the Hellenistic world, documenting the upkeep of the Hellenistic urban way of life as it had existed for centuries before the advent of Roman rule, and even the expansion of certain aspects of it. One is reminded of a famous passage in Monty Python's comic masterpiece *The Life of Brian*, when the Judaean revolutionary leader "Reg" asks rhetorically what the Romans have ever done "for us," only to get some unexpected answers.

> Reg: All right . . . all right . . . but apart from better sanitation and medicine and education and irrigation and public health and roads and a freshwater system and baths and public order . . . what *have* the Romans done for *us*?

But if the Romans as rulers saw to the upkeep and even expansion of public services in the Hellenistic world, what of cultural life? The lifestyle of Greeks did not just revolve around drinking water, public baths, and worship of the gods: it involved watching plays, attending lectures and concerts, and reading books. It is during the period of Roman rule, in fact, that we get clear evidence of the spread of public libraries beyond the old royal centers. Inscriptions inform us of public libraries set up in the cities of Rhodes and Cos, for example. When the emperor Hadrian refurbished the city of Athens, he arranged for a new public library to be established in his new "forum of Hadrian" that expanded the old Athenian *agora*. A wealthy private citizen paid for the creation of a public library at the great *Asklepieion*, the sanctuary of the healing god Asclepius (in effect, a hospital) just outside the city of Pergamon. The most famous public library of this era, though, is no doubt the Library of Celsus at Ephesus, the facade of which was magnificently rebuilt by Austrian archaeologists in the 1970s (see ill. 25). This library, paid for by a wealthy citizen of Ephesus, had space for twelve thousand book scrolls in its great reading room, making it a fabulous addition to the cultural amenities available to Ephesus' citizens. As an interesting sidelight on the urban lifestyle of the educated Greek

25. Façade of the Library of Celcus at Ephesus
(Wikimedia Commons photo by Benh Lieu Song, CC BY-SA 3.0)

citizen, the library also offered an underground passageway leading from the reading room, under the great "Street of Marble" on which the library stood, to a public lavatory (see ill. 26) and a high-class brothel on the other side of the street. When tired of reading, the citizen could unobtrusively take care of other more physical needs.

26. Public toilets, Ephesus
(Wikimedia Commons public domain image by Mykenik~commonswiki)

Like any other era of western culture, the Hellenistic world of the high Roman Empire had its cultural icons and stars. Highly paid public speakers traveled from city to city giving public orations for high fees. Dio Chrysostom (Dio "the golden-tongued") spoke to large audiences of enraptured Greek citizens on topics such as ideal kingship, virtue, the attractions of a life of poverty (which he himself carefully avoided), and so on in the late first century CE. In the next century, Aelius Aristides did likewise, in between visits to the great Asclepius sanctuaries (public hospitals/health spas) to take care of his perpetually failing health. These public orators, and others like them, modeled their style of speaking on the precepts of the fourth-century classical Athenian teacher of rhetoric, Isocrates, and on the example of Isocrates' much younger contemporary, the orator Demosthenes. Scholars of various sorts studied and praised the works, style, and ideas of classical Greek writers: Dionysius of Halicarnassus, for example, wrote essays on the historians Herodotus and Thucydides; Longinus wrote on how to compose literary works in the "sublime" style of the classical greats; Harpocration produced a lexicon of the words used by the "ten great orators" of classical Greece; and so on. The second-century CE historian Arrian wrote a widely read and admired history of, tellingly, Alexander the Great, known as the *Anabasis* and still our best source of knowledge about Alexander. Arrian modeled his language and prose style on the fourth-century BCE Athenian historian Xenophon, going so far as to advertize himself as a second Xenophon.

In other words, the cultural stars of the Hellenistic world in the Roman era went to great lengths to keep alive the cultural works and ideas of the Greek past, to maintain alive the traditions of their fifth-, fourth-, and third-century BCE forebears. The learned man of letters Plutarch, a wealthy Greek from Tanagra in Boeotia who lived in the late first century CE and wrote on almost every topic under the sun, expended a great deal of effort in assuring his Greek and Roman contemporaries that the Greeks were in every way as great as the Romans, if not greater. The project by which he demonstrated this was a huge collection of parallel biographies. Each pair of biographies consisted of a great Roman leader and a comparably great Greek leader: if Rome had its Caesar, the Greeks had their Alexander; for the Roman Cicero, there was the Greek Demosthenes; the great Roman commander Scipio

Africanus was no greater than the Greek general Epaminondas; if the Roman Cato the younger was an example of upright moral fortitude, so was the fourth-century Athenian leader Phocion, and so on. The surviving collection runs to twenty-two sets of biographies, though several are lost, including those of Scipio and Epaminondas just mentioned.

One of the most engaging writers of this Roman era was Lucian, who came from the city of Samosata in northern Mesopotamia (southern Turkey today), near the border of the Roman and Parthian empires. Lucian wrote humorous essays on a wide range of topics. For example, his *True Stories*, parodying the exaggerated accounts of explorers and certain kinds of historians, included narratives of his visits to the Moon and to "Cloudcuckooland." To truly appreciate the latter, the reader needed to be familiar with the play *The Birds* by the fifth-century Athenian comic dramatist Aristophanes, where the notion of Cloud-cuckooland originated. Lucian liked to debunk the self-important, the pompous, and the fakers of contemporary society. He wrote exposés of the false prophet Alexander of Abounoteichus and his splendid new cult of the god Glaucon, and of the pseudo-philosopher and fake Christian prophet Peregrinus. As an admirer of the Athenian philosopher Epicurus, Lucian was highly skeptical of religion in general, and pretensions to sacred revelations struck him as too often merely tools to exploit the gullible, such as the Christian community that funded Peregrinus' lifestyle for several years. For true learning, Lucian had the greatest admiration, and as a man well educated in the Hellenistic manner true learning meant a proper familiarity with and understanding of the writings of the "classical" Greeks.

This is illustrated by a highly characteristic essay of Lucian's called "The Ignorant Book-Collector." In this essay we read of the sort of man who made a display of learning by collecting books and forming a personal library, but without actually having the least notion which books were worth buying and why. Buying books for the look of them is not the mark of an educated man. One must know which authors are worth reading and collecting, and one must know how to read the best works. To aid in understanding the classics, there were commentaries and lexica. The ignorant book-collector knows nothing of all this, but goes by price and look. But the educated reader, reading the right books in the right way, learns how to think and behave and write properly from the great example set by the classic authors of earlier Greek times. But how true to life, how typical of the education and reading habits of Greek citizens of the Roman Empire, were the ideas and outlook of cultural leaders such as Lucian, Plutarch, Arrian, and the others mentioned here? To gauge that we must turn to a provincial Greek city in the heart of Roman Egypt: Oxyrhynchus.

Oxyrhynchus lay at the southern edge of the Fayum district of Egypt, and in Hellenistic and Roman times was the regional metropolis and a fairly substantial city. Still it lay far from the Mediterranean and the center of things: it was no Alexandria or Antioch, but only a provincial center. Yet thanks to the work of modern archaeologists, beginning in 1896 with exploration by the Oxford scholars Grenfell and Hunt, Oxyrhynchus is now in many respects the best known city of the ancient world. During ten years of excavations, from 1896 to 1906, Grenfell and Hunt unearthed the city's rubbish dumps and in them found a vast trove of ancient papyri, waste-paper essentially that had been discarded on the desert fringe of the town and thanks to the arid climate had never decayed. The vast bulk of these papyri, over ninety percent, contain documents of all sorts—letters, wills, petitions, land registers, contracts, and so on—which shed an extraordinary light on the social life, economic life, and administration of Hellenistic and Roman Egypt, giving us unique glimpses into the lives of ordinary people living during these times. But the remaining ten percent or so are of interest here: literary papyri giving us an insight into the reading habits of the citizens of Oxyrhynchus.

Citizens of Oxyrhynchus, to judge by these literary papyri, read widely. There are fragments of religious texts, magical works, novels, rhetorical exercises, essays of various sorts, and in general an array of contemporary writings: contemporary to the readers of Oxyrhynchus, that is. But the bulk of the literary papyri fall into two categories: texts by classical Greek authors—the likes of Homer, Herodotus, Euripides, Plato, Demosthenes, and dozens of others of the sixth to the fourth centuries BCE; and scholarly texts explaining the writings of the classical Greeks to Hellenistic and Roman readers—commentaries, treatises on language and style, lexica, and so on. All of this material has been extensively studied, to give us a clear insight into the reading habits of Roman-era Greek citizens. And in addition to the material from

Oxyrhynchus, papyri from other towns and villages of the Fayum region have been found and studied, showing that Oxyrhynchus was typical in its reading practices. Lucian's picture of the well educated reader is validated: we can discern circles of readers in the Fayum who read together, shared texts and commentaries, and commissioned books that they could go on to read together, very much like modern book clubs in many respects. Hellenistic culture was alive and thriving in the Fayum of Roman times, and this is hardly likely to be unique to that rather provincial region.

One of the most fascinating finds by Grenfell and Hunt was made during their last excavation season, at the beginning of 1906. Excavating one of the dump sites, they found a basket of sorts containing a large collection of fragments of book scrolls. Piecing these together, they found that the basket had contained at least twelve different texts, representing some of the great works of classical Greek literature: writings by Plato, Demosthenes, Thucydides, Pindar, and Euripides, for example. It was clear that they had here a portion of some citizen's personal library, discarded for unknown reasons, but evidence of his literary taste. Thanks to the fact that the most immediately sensational find was a large part of the text of a lost play by Euripides—the *Hypsipyle*—the collection is generally known as the Hypsipyle library or archive. This Oxyrhynchite was, in short, the opposite of Lucian's "ignorant book-collector": we might call him the "discerning book-collector". His collection was not just of original classic works; very characteristically of his time, he also had a commentary on Thucydides and a treatise on literary style. And several of the literary works had extensive annotations by readers in the margins. Hellenistic culture, the culture of the book, could not be better illustrated than by this clear evidence of personal book collections and circles of readers in Roman middle Egypt.

In the end, however, Hellenistic culture in its classic form could not survive. In the same excavation season in which Grenfell and Hunt found the Hypsipyle library, and evidently found in close proximity to it, was a harbinger of the future. Oxyrhynchus papyrus no. 840 is a fragment of a Christian gospel. It is not from one of the canonical gospels: it tells a story of an encounter between Jesus and his disciples and a Jewish priest in the temple of Jerusalem. Jesus and the priest debate the meaning of purity, in a manner similar to debates found in the

Gospel of Mark and elsewhere, but very different in detail. Christianity, that is to say, was on the rise in Roman Egypt by the third century CE, and the triumph of Christianity was to spell the beginning of the end of Hellenistic culture in its fully-fledged form of the years 300 BCE to 300 CE.

CHAPTER 8

Aftermath: the Lingering Impact
of Hellenistic Culture

T HE ADVENT OF CHRISTIANITY AS AT FIRST THE DOMINANT AND THEN
the only permitted religion in the Roman Empire in the fourth century CE, and three centuries later the arrival of Islam as the religion
of most of the peoples of western Asia and north Africa, radically
changed the culture of what had been the Hellenistic world. For instance, the need to remain true to the doctrinal tenets of these overar-
ching religions severely restricted what was open for debate on a variety
of topics, and how any debates were to be conducted. Life centered
around the church and the mosque was not the same as life had been
under the more informal religiosity of ancient "paganism." And the
customs and outlooks that the new religions imported from the Jewish
and Arabic societies and cultures in which they had their roots were
certainly very different from the customs and outlooks of the preceding
Greco-Roman culture. But despite all the changes of focus and outlook,
all the restrictions on debate and lifestyle that accompanied the dominance of the two new religions, the Hellenistic culture of the Greco-
Roman Mediterranean world did not simply die out. However much
that culture might be changed and restricted, its influence was still felt
in the Christian and Islamic cultures of late antique and medieval times.
We must consider how and in what ways the high culture of the Hellenistic world continued to inform aspects of later Christian and Islamic
cultures.

1. A LATE ANTIQUE DIALOGUE AT ALEXANDRIA

When the great Muslim conqueror 'Amr ibn al-'As entered Alexandria
as victor in the year 640 CE, or AH 20 by Muslim reckoning, he found
a city no longer in its glory days, but still a great and bustling metropolis, a hub of trade and culture. 'Amr was by all accounts a cultured
man himself, a member of the old Quraysh aristocracy of Mecca and a

successful trader before his conversion to Islam in 629 (AH 8). As governor of Egypt—at first under the caliph Umar, and later again under the Umayyad caliph Mu'awiyah—he had a reputation as a fair-minded man, a respecter of the Christian faith and church, and an admirer of the culture he found in Egypt. He recommended to the caliph Umar, we are told, that Alexandria—the Hellenistic and Roman capital of Egypt—continue as the capital city of the province. When Umar refused this advice, 'Amr built a new city at the base of the Nile delta, near modern Cairo, called al-Fustat, which became one of the great cities of the medieval world. But he still admired Alexandria, enchanted by the many palaces, public baths, and theaters, and spent much time there. In his wanderings about the ancient and beautifully built city, we hear that he became aware of some old men who went every day to a venerable porticoed building where they spent hours poring over rolls of papyrus. He was intrigued and inquired into the identity of these old men, and the purpose of their activity. He learned that the chief of these men was named John Philoponus, and that he was a scholar, Christian theologian, and philosopher. The building he worked at was what was left of the great library of Alexandria, commissioned and built nine hundred years earlier under the first Ptolemy and his son and heir Philadelphus. 'Amr determined to meet John Philoponus and learn more about him and his activities, and about this mysterious library. And so began, we are told, a most unlikely friendship.

The story of this friendship, and of the fate of the great library, is retailed in a medieval document called the "Dialogues of 'Amr". According to the tradition, 'Amr took to visiting John Philoponus frequently, delighting in the old man's conversation. John was, in the eyes of the orthodox church, a heretic: his arguments concerning the unity implicit in the trinity, and the unity of the conjoined human and divine natures in Jesus, clearly smacked of the notorious monophysite (single-nature) heresy. Such ideas appealed to 'Amr who of course rejected, as a Muslim, the idea of a three-person deity; but to orthodox Christians John's arguments were anathema and still aroused their ire centuries later. In the ninth century the Byzantine patriarch Photios forgot his usually measured language and roundly abused John for his treatise *On the Trinity*:

His arguments are not only blasphemous, but utterly unsound and feeble, and he shows himself unable to give even a superficial coloring of truth to his fallacious arguments against the true faith. Inventing natures, substances and godheads, like the insolent babbler that he is, he pours forth a stream of blasphemy against the Christian faith . . . (Photios *Bibliotheca* 75).

Photios continues in this vein, with words such as puerile, insolent, weak, and silly, and broadens his field of fire to encompass all of John's writings, which he denounces as derivative, falsified, spurious, and degenerate. In contrast to Photios, 'Amr found John a man of wisdom and taste, a man whose conversation was charming and enlightening. But we may guess that they did not discuss Christian theology much; for much more than as a theologian, John Philoponus achieved fame as a philosopher, and especially as a commentator on Aristotle. For John was one of the leaders of the late antique Alexandrian school of Aristotle commentators, including his master Ammonius and his successors, the enigmatic David, Elias, and Stephanus.

John, however, was more than a mere admirer and commentator on Aristotle: he was an inventive thinker in his own right. As a Christian, he could not agree with Aristotle's theory of the eternity of the universe, and wrote extensively arguing against it and in favor of creation. More importantly, he critiqued Aristotle's ideas of dynamics and perspective, arriving at different views that came close to discovering the principle of inertia: his ideas on mass and motion influenced no less a scientist than Galileo. And in his ideas on perspective he conceived of space as an immaterial medium in which material objects exist in three dimensions, influencing later thinkers like Pico della Mirandola and Leon Battista Alberti. It is no wonder, then, that 'Amr reportedly found John fascinating. When their friendship was firmly enough established, John dared to bring forward a topic that was troubling him: the future of the library. He explained to 'Amr the history and nature of the library and its vast collection of books and, while acknowledging that all this now belonged to 'Amr as conqueror, expressed the hope that he and his fellows would be permitted to maintain the library and continue their work. 'Amr, however, decided that making a judgement once and for all on the fate of this collection of non-Islamic material was not for him to do: he referred the matter to the caliph Umar in Mecca. After weeks of anxious waiting, the judgement of Umar arrived:

if what was in these books was also in the Qur'an, then they were un-necessary; if what was in them went against the Qur'an, they were undesirable. Either way, they should be burned. And so, with great reluctance, 'Amr ordered that the books of the library should be used to stoke the fires of the bath-houses of Alexandria; and the friendship between him and John Philoponus came to an end. It was said, according to the learned Muslim historian Ibn al-Kifti, that it took six months to burn all the books.

All this makes a charming and, in its way, rather tragic story; but it is not history. In truth, John Philoponus lived and flourished in the sixth century (he died around 570), not in the seventh, and the meeting and friendship between him and 'Amr is pure legend, as is the burning of the library books on the orders of Umar. But behind the legend lies an interesting truth: the notion of the Muslim leader 'Amr being intrigued by a Greek philosopher like John Philoponus is indicative of a very real fascination the Muslim elites felt for Hellenistic philosophy, science, medicine, and mathematics. Far from burning the books of Hellenistic culture, the Islamic world in fact in many cases preserved them, translated them into Arabic, and used them as the basis for creating an Islamic high culture. John Philoponus' own commentaries on Aristotle were in fact translated into Arabic. In Arabic John is known as Yahya al-Nahwi (John the Grammarian), and his writings among others helped to form the foundation of an Islamic school of philosophy, drawing its inspiration from Aristotle and the Neoplatonists, which flourished between the ninth and the fourteenth centuries. It took a few centuries for Islamic thinkers to translate and absorb the writings of the Hellenistic world they had taken over; and there were areas of Hellenistic culture—drama, poetry, and oratory for example—that held little interest for them. But in the ninth century the great Muslim intellectual al-Kindi founded the study of Greek philosophy as an Islamic pursuit, arguing that rational philosophy and theology are compatible with each other (though theology is to be preferred), promoting the study of Aristotle and Plato, and beginning a long tradition of great Islamic scholars of philosophy and science.

The achievements of Islamic philosophy and science are not as well-known as they should be. Greek mathematics had achieved some very great heights: for example, Archimedes' work on conic sections is foundational to Newton's development of differential calculus, and Euclid's handbook of geometry was still the basic text for learning geometry into the twentieth century. But Greek mathematics had always labored under a very clumsy system of numeration. In taking up Greek mathematics and pondering the ideas and concepts expressed, Islamic mathematicians came up with a number of improvements that changed mathematics for the better: al-Khwarizmi's introduction to the Mediterranean world of the Hindi numbering system, with the zero and the other decimal numbers, for example. More importantly, al-Khwarizmi is widely recognized as one of the founders of the mathematical discipline of algebra. Al-Khwarizmi, who was active early in the ninth century at the great "House of Wisdom" (*Bayt al-Hikma*) established in Baghdad by the Abbasid caliph al-Ma'mun, wrote a book entitled *Kitab al-mukhtasar fi hisab al-jabr w'al-muqabala* (Compendious book on calculation by restoration and balancing). The book proposed the fundamental algebraic method for solving polynomial equations, and the term "algebra" of course comes from *al-jabr*. The Alexandrian Greek mathematician Diophantus had already proposed a theory of equations of sorts, but al-Khwarizmi's work went much further in establishing how to construct and solve equations, both linear and quadratic. Islamic thinkers, that is to say, did not just borrow ideas from Greek culture: they developed and improved them. The same is true in medicine and philosophy. Perhaps the greatest medieval medical expert and writer, for example, was the early eleventh-century Muslim doctor and philosopher Ibn Sina, known in the west mostly by the Latinized form of his name, Avicenna. His *Canon of Medicine*, developed from Greek medical ideas admixed with Indian and Persian medicine and Ibn Sina's own observations and experience, became the standard medical encyclopedia for the Islamic world and, in Latin translation, for western Europe too. But it is above all in philosophy that the influence of Hellenistic culture was felt in the Islamic world.

The example set by al-Kindi was followed by a succession of remarkable Islamic philosophers, of whom only the most important can be noticed here. A foundational figure is al-Kindi's successor, al-Farabi, who came to be known as "the second master" (Aristotle being the first). Born around 873 in the eastern part of the Islamic world, perhaps in modern Kazakhstan, al-Farabi spent the bulk of his active life in

Baghdad, at the "House of Wisdom" that was one of the cultural beacons of the medieval world. Both an influential commentator on Aristotle and a Neoplatonist, al-Farabi strove to gather and develop the ideas of the "two philosophers" (i.e. Plato and Aristotle) for Islamic audiences. Among his most influential works were his commentary on Aristotle's *Metaphysics*, which Ibn Sina credited with having a profound impact on his thought, and his *Al-Madina al-fadila*, a treatise on the ideal state in the manner of Plato's *Republic*. Al-Farabi's work and influence played a major role in ensuring the preservation of the writings of Aristotle and Plato, not just in the Islamic world but in the Christian west too. Thirty years after al-Farabi's death in 951 was born one of the greatest Muslim philosophers, the above mentioned Ibn Sina (Avicenna). Like Farabi, Ibn Sina was born in the eastern, Iranian part of the Islamic world, but unlike Farabi he spent his whole life in that region, in cities such as Bukhara, Balkh, Isfahan, and Hamadan. Making his living primarily as a doctor, Ibn Sina was also one of the most prolific and widely influential Muslim philosophers. His writings on logic, ethics, and metaphysics gave rise to a philosophical movement called "Avicennism" after him, which influenced not only many Islamic philosophers but also such key western thinkers as Albertus Magnus and Thomas Aquinas. He died of a serious illness at the relatively young age of fifty-eight, refusing to moderate his activities until the end, telling his friends that he preferred "a short life with width to a narrow one with length."

Probably the best known of the Islamic philosophers, thanks to his major impact on western Christian philosophers such as Aquinas and the scholastics, was the great Andalusian sage Ibn Rushd, better known in the west as Averroes. Born in 1126 at Cordoba in the Islamic province of al-Andalus in southern Spain, Ibn Rushd represents the western end of the Islamic world and the great cosmopolitan cultural center that Cordoba was in this era. Probably the greatest of the medieval commentators on Aristotle, he was hugely influential via Latin translations of his commentaries in re-introducing Aristotle's works and thought into the Christian world, and helped to spark the so-called twelfth-century Renaissance in medieval Europe. Ibn Rushd was a determined rationalist, and one of his most important works is the *Fasl al-Makal*, the "Decisive Treatise" in which he showed that reason and revelation do not contradict each other, but are merely alternative ways to arrive at the truth. Aquinas was to adapt Ibn Rushd's thought on this into his own defense of rationalism alongside theology. In addition, Ibn Rushd wrote an important work defending philosophy itself, the *Tahafut al-Tahafut* (Incoherence of the Incoherence). The Persian philosopher and mystic al-Ghazali had written, after a spiritual crisis in which he abandoned his career in philosophy to become a Sufi mystic, an attack on philosophy called *Tahafut al-Falasifa* (The Incoherence of Philosophy). Ibn Rushd's defense of philosophy, declaring the incoherence of al-Ghazali's argument, may be his most original work, though it failed in the end effectively to counteract al-Ghazali's influence.

Despite al-Ghazali's assault, however, Muslim philosophy continued, and produced many more notable thinkers. Among the greatest of them, and drawing this brief survey of Greek-inspired Islamic thought to a close, is the fourteenth-century thinker Ibn Khaldun. A north African Arab from Tunis, Ibn Khaldun studied the works of Ibn Sina and Ibn Rushd, among others, but determined to make his own mark as a historian. His universal history, the *Kitab al-'Ibar*, won wide acclaim. The first section (of seven) of this history, the *Muqaddimah* or Introduction, is often read as a book in its own right. In it Ibn Khaldun introduced ideas of social conflict and social cohesion that have had a significant impact in the discipline of sociology, and he was one of the first thinkers to emphasize the importance for a civilization of its political economy, which he described as being composed of value-adding processes carried out by the people. No less a historian than the great Arnold Toynbee, author of the influential multi-volume *Study of History*, praised Ibn Khaldun's work for introducing a "philosophy of history" which is among the greatest of its kind.

In sum, the high culture spread all around the Mediterranean and near east in the Hellenistic era did not vanish in the parts of that world that were conquered by the Muslims. Ibn Khaldun had argued that when desert nomads or other less "civilized" outsiders conquer a great civilization, they inevitably become attracted to its refined literacy and arts, and assimilate and/or adapt aspects of that culture to become their own. In accordance with Ibn Khaldun's principle, under the impact of Hellenistic philosophy and science the Islamic world enjoyed a "Golden Age" of high culture between the ninth and fourteenth centuries, with great cultural centers from Balkh in the east, to Baghdad in the center, to Cordoba in the far west. This era of Islamic culture still influences Muslims to the present day; and the Hellenistic-influenced high culture of the Islamic "Golden Age" in turn influenced the Christian west.

2. A BYZANTINE LIBRARY

Not all of the Hellenistic world was conquered by the Muslims. Despite repeated assaults in the eighth century and later, including several sieges of the city of Constantinople, the Byzantine Empire—comprising Asia Minor (modern Turkey) and the Balkan peninsula as its core lands—held firm for many centuries as an orthodox Christian realm using the Greek language and viewing itself as a continuation of the old Roman Empire: the people we call Byzantines referred to themselves as *Rhomaioi* or Romans. After an era of crisis in the seventh and eighth centuries, involving attacks from outside by the Muslims from the south and Slavic peoples (especially the Bulgars) from the north, and also internal dissensions in the form of the great "iconoclastic" dispute within orthodox Christianity, the Byzantine Empire entered a period of revitalized prosperity and success in the ninth and tenth centuries.

At some time, most likely in the early 850s, an important official in the imperial service in Constantinople named Photios was sent on an embassy to the Abbasid caliph in Baghdad. Preparing himself for this task, Photios decided to undertake a literary work of great importance. We have his own words about it:

> Photios, to his beloved brother Tarasios, in the name of the Lord, greeting. After our appointment as ambassador to Assyria (i.e. Baghdad) had been confirmed . . . and approved by the emperor, you asked to be supplied with summaries of those works which I had read and discussed during your absence. Your idea was to have something to console you for our painful separation, and at the same time to acquire some knowledge, even if vague and imperfect, of the works which you had not yet read in our company . . . Accordingly . . . we engaged a secretary and set down all the summaries we could recollect . . . If during your study of these volumes, any of the summaries should appear to be defective or inaccurate, you must not be surprised. It is no easy matter to undertake to read each individual work, to grasp the subject matter, and to remember and record it . . . Certainly such records will assist you to refresh the memory of what you have read by yourself, to find more readily what you want,

and to acquire more easily the knowledge of what has not as yet been the subject of intelligent reading on your part.

These words introduce Photios' famed work, the *Bibliotheca* (Library). In it he gives more or less concise summaries of some 280 works he had read, works which evidently constituted his personal library. Photios, that is to say, personally owned one of the great libraries of early medieval times, and emerges as one of the most learned men of his era. Photios, in fact, became a great and famous man. In the year 858 the Byzantine emperor Michael III and his uncle and chief minister Caesar Bardas fell out with the Patriarch of Constantinople, Ignatios, and decided to depose and replace him. Their choice fell on the chief secretary of the palace, Photios. In the space of four days, beginning on December 20th, Photios was tonsured as a cleric, successively ordained lector, subdeacon, deacon, and priest, and then on Christmas Day of 858 he was enthroned as Patriarch of Constantinople, that is to say head of the eastern Orthodox church, in succession to Ignatios. This was no doubt the most meteoric ecclesiastical career in history, only paralleled by the fictional Pope Hadrian in Frederick Rolfe's much overlooked novel *Hadrian the Seventh*. Photios served as Patriarch under Michael III until the emperor's assassination in 867, when the new emperor Basil I the Macedonian deposed him and restored Ignatios. But Photios soon ingratiated himself with Basil, and when Ignatios died in 877 it was inevitably Photios who succeeded him, serving again as Patriarch until Basil's death in 886. During his time as Patriarch and his final years in retirement at the monastery of Gordon, he became arguably the most important and influential theologian of the Orthodox tradition, played a key role in the schism between the eastern Orthodox and western Catholic churches, and established the reputation that sees him still today revered as one of the great saints of the Orthodox church.

It is no surprise, then, to find that the library of this man consisted, for rather more than half of its total works, of Christian literature; theological and controversial treatises, homilies, church histories, letters, and other Christian writings of all sorts featured very prominently. But for present purposes, it is the non-Christian segment of Photios' library that is of interest. More than sixty of the works Photios held were non-Christian books. A few of them may nevertheless have been kept for essentially Christian reasons: Flavius Josephus' *Jewish War* and

296 RICHARD A. BILLOWS

Jewish Antiquities, and some of the writings of Philo Judaeus of Alexandria, had long been of interest to Christian scholars as background to the rise of Christianity. But at the core of Photios' non-Christian books was a set of texts that might have formed the personal book collection of any well-to-do and well-educated Hellenistic gentleman of the second or first century BCE: the works of classic historians such as Herodotus, Ctesias, and Theopompus of Chios, and the speeches of the great Attic orators—Antiphon, Andocides, Lysias, Isaeus, Isocrates, Demosthenes, Aeschines, Hyperides, Deinarchus, Lycurgus; supplemented by a few specifically Hellenistic works such as Agatharchides' *Periplous of the Red Sea* and the histories of Diodorus of Sicily and Dionysius of Halicarnassus. The rest of the non-Christian library contains a veritable who's who of the literary culture of the Hellenistic east during the high Roman Empire: Plutarch, Lucian, Galen, Aelius Aristides, Iamblichus, and Philostratus, along with historians such as Arrian, Appian, Herodian, Memnon of Heraclea, Zosimus, and Dio Cassius, and even some less highbrow literature such as the novels of Heliodorus, Achilles Tatius, and Lucius of Patrae. Finally the collection was replete with technical treatises on language and style, including various lexica explaining the obscure words of the Attic orators and philosophers. None of these are works we would be surprised to find being read by any educated man of an eastern Mediterranean city during the second or third centuries CE, as the study of papyri found at the regional metropolis of Oxyrhynchus in Egypt has shown. Leaving aside the specifically Christian works, that is to say, the rest of Photios' library was essentially a collection of works representing the literature and reading habits of the late Hellenistic civilization of the middle Roman Imperial period.

This should be surprising, since Photios did not live during that era, but half a millennium later. Photios' library tells us that the literary culture of the high Byzantine Empire was still very much Hellenistic literary culture, though with a heavy Christian overlay. That is not something that should be taken for granted: half a millennium is plenty of time for an old culture to be forgotten and a new culture to arise. What we find instead is a Byzantine Empire, a Christian Greek state governing the north eastern end of the Mediterranean region for a thousand years between about 450 and 1453, that was not just Christian by religion and Greek in language: it also continued to be Hellenistic in literary culture.

Just one hundred years after Photios' first enthronement as Patriarch of Constantinople, in the year 959, one of the more remarkable men in Byzantine history died at the age of fifty-four. Despite his relatively young age, the emperor Constantine VII Porphyrogenitus had nominally ruled the Byzantine Empire for fifty years, having been elevated to co-emperor by his uncle, the emperor Alexander, when he (Constantine) was only three years old in 908. Alexander died in 913, leaving Constantine as his successor, but having appointed a regency council to govern on his behalf. The dominant figure on this regency council, the Patriarch Nicolaus Mysticus, governed for several years until he was supplanted by Constantine's mother Zoe, who ran the empire on her son's behalf until 919. Due to her failure to deal effectively with the Bulgar threat, however, she was then deposed and replaced by the great admiral and military leader Romanus Lecapenus. He was not content just to rule as regent: in 920 he had himself declared co-emperor with Constantine, regularizing this position by having Constantine marry his daughter Helena Lecapene. And so, until 944, Constantine was emperor in name but the empire was actually ruled by his father-in-law and co-emperor Romanus, who was assisted by his sons Christophorus and Stephanus. It was only in 945 that Constantine, after Romanus had been forced into retirement by his sons in 944, and he and his wife Helena had then succeeded in deposing his ambitious brothers-in-law, was able finally to rule the empire independently, though in truth Helena seems to have played a significant role.

What made Constantine remarkable was what he did during all those years, two decades in fact, when he was grown up and nominally emperor, but in fact was not permitted to rule. Rulers are often flattered by their entourages as men of learning and culture, though few really deserve the flattery. Constantine was one who did. From an early age he showed a passionate interest in reading and books. He encouraged and patronized writers, scholars, and artists of all sorts, and he was himself a writer and scholar of no mean talent. During his reign, the literary revival that had begun under Photios flourished as never before, and Constantine contributed strongly to it. He wrote works on court ceremonial and how to rule that provide us with unique insights into the governing system of the Byzantine Empire; he wrote a biography of his grandfather, the great emperor Basil I; and he was a passionate collector of books and manuscripts of all sorts. Few men did more than Constantine to foster the preservation of Classical and Hellenistic literature and learning at Constantinople and in the Byzantine Empire. Constantine felt, in particular, that the study of history was being neglected in his time, and that the great histories of the Greeks and Romans had much to teach his contemporaries. He decided that the problem was the great length of the works of history written during Classical and Hellenistic times, so he commissioned a series of excerpts that would bring together, under a set of thematic headings (fifty-three altogether, though only six survive), the essential lessons of the great historians of the past. Incidentally, these excerpts reveal how much that is now lost was still available to readers in tenth-century Constantinople. Sadly, Constantine's own project hastened the loss of some notable historical works, as the availability of the excerpts caused the original works to be neglected. But the literary and scholarly activity of Constantine and his contemporaries reveals again how much the Byzantine Empire was still Hellenistic in literary culture, the libraries of Constantinople and other major cities stocked with old Greek texts of which too many no longer survive. But most of what does survive of Classical and Hellenistic literature survives because of the Byzantine interest in and preservation of it.

3. Exiles in Italy

In the summer of 1471 the plague was raging in the city of Florence in northern Italy. In his study at the Florentinum Studium, the university at which many of the great Italian humanists got their education, a man was packing up his books and belongings, preparing to go and seek safety at Rome. He was in his mid-fifties, and this was not the first time he had been forced to pack up his belongings and flee. His name was Ioannis Argyropoulos, and he had been born in Constantinople in 1415, in the declining years of the once great Byzantine Empire. There, in his youth, he had studied theology and philosophy, and eventually became a teacher himself, counting among his pupils the notable scholar Constantinos Laskaris. In 1439 he had been selected to participate in an embassy to Italy, to attend the ecumenical Council of Florence as part of an attempt to heal the great schism between the Catholic and Orthodox churches. He even received a doctorate in theology from the University of Padua in 1444. Argyropoulos seemed set for a brilliant career in scholarship and public service. But in 1453 everything changed: the Ottoman sultan Mehmet the Conqueror captured the city of Constantinople, and the Byzantine Empire was no more. Argyropoulos fled the captured city, taking refuge at first in the Morea (Peloponnese in southern Greece), and then in 1456 moving to Italy. In Italy his career revived. After teaching for a time at Padua, he became head of the Greek department at the Florentinum Studium, where his fame grew. Argyropoulos did not just teach Greek: he played a major role in the revival of Greek literary learning in western Europe, in particular the study of Greek philosophy in the original language, rather than from Latin translations that were themselves often derived from Arabic translations. He was a noted Aristotelian, and was part of a wave of Byzantine scholars who fled to western Europe, especially Italy, at this time, bringing with them Greek texts that had long been unavailable in the Latin west. At the Florentinum Studium, Argyropoulos' lectures were attended by such future luminaries as Lorenzo de Medici (Lorenzo il Magnifico as he was to become) and Poliziano; indeed it has even been suggested that the great Leonardo da Vinci listened to Argyropoulos.

Safely at Rome, Argyropoulos continued his career as a teacher of Greek language and philosophy for years. He finally died in 1487, back in Florence, reputedly from the effects of eating too much watermelon. Lovers of watermelon will agree, I am sure, that there are worse ways to die. Argyropoulos' position as head of the Greek department at the Florentinum Studium did not remain vacant, of course. Within a few years another Byzantine Greek held the position: Demetrios Chalkokondyles. Born in Athens in 1423 to a family of the Athenian nobility, he and his family soon migrated to the Peloponnese, and then in 1447—not waiting for the inevitable end of Byzantine Constantinople —to Italy. At Rome in 1449 the Greek cardinal Bessarion, himself a refugee from the Byzantine Empire (born in the 1390s in Trapezous [Trebizond] on the Black Sea), took Chalkokondyles under his wing. He was able to study with the noted Byzantine humanist Theodore Gaza, established a friendship with Marsilio Ficino, and eventually attained a position teaching at the University of Perugia, where one of his pupils supposedly likened him to Plato to see and hear. From Perugia

Chalkonondyles, following in Argyropoulos' footsteps, moved to Padua in 1463, and then to Florence where he was, by 1479, the head of the Greek department at the Florentinum Studium, enjoying the patronage of the great Lorenzo il Magnifico. Besides teaching the likes of Lorenzo's son, the future pope Leo X, Castiglione, and Giraldi, Chalkokondyles during his time at Florence helped to pioneer a project that changed the future of western education and secured the role of Greek literature as a crucial part of it.

One of the great inventions of the fifteenth century, which in its way had as great an impact on western civilization as the modern invention of the personal computer and the internet, was the printing press. Before the advent of printing, books had to be laboriously copied out by hand, over and over through the generations. One of the major reasons why texts became lost is that no one had a great enough interest to copy them out again, or pay for them to be copied. Without that process, aged manuscripts would simply deteriorate until they crumbled away. Fortunately, many of the more significant works of Classical and Hellenistic Greek culture had continued to be copied until the fifteenth century, but as long as they were dependent on the process of copying by hand, texts were vulnerable to becoming lost; and in addition books were rare and expensive so long as they were handwritten. The printing press changed all of that. The humanists of the fifteenth and sixteenth centuries, with their strong interest in Greek civilization stimulated by the influx of Byzantine refugee scholars with their manuscripts, realized that preserving and spreading the Greek texts they admired would be greatly enhanced by use of printing. Chalkokondyles was one of these humanists, and he helped to set the tone by preparing for printing the first editions of Homer (1488), Isocrates (1493), and the Byzantine encyclopedia known as the *Suda* (1499). These were among the first in a wave of printed editions of ancient Greek texts, securing the preservation of Greek literature once and for all, and establishing its place as a crucial component of western literary culture ever since. In 1492 Chalkokondyles was invited by Ludovico Sforza to move to Milan, where he continued his teaching and editing career until his death in 1511.

Argyropoulos and Chalkokondyles are only two examples of a much wider phenomenon. Dozens of Byzantine Greek scholars visited

Italy or moved entirely to western Europe during the fourteenth and fifteenth centuries, but especially in the fifteenth century when the Byzantine Empire collapsed entirely. The list is too long to offer here, but it includes such notable figures as Maximus Planudes, who introduced the *Greek Anthology* collection of short verse to western Europe; George of Trebizond, famed for his work on Greek rhetorical principles; and George Hermonymos, who taught in Paris, and among whose pupils were influential intellectuals such as Erasmus and Johann Reuchlin. Among the greatest was the aforementioned cardinal Bessarion, who was not only an influential writer on Greek philosophy and defender of Plato, but a great patron and protector of the numerous Greek scholars who fled to Italy, a collector and preserver of manuscripts (his personal library was the foundation of the great library of St Mark's in Venice), and was even a candidate to become pope at one time despite his Greek origin. The term "Renaissance" to refer to fifteenth- and sixteenth-century Europe has been overused and come under criticism in recent times, but it cannot be denied that the fifteenth-century influx of Greek scholars, writers, and teachers and the Greek literary texts they brought with them had a profound influence on western European culture.

4. CONCLUSION

It is clear that Hellenistic civilization did not just die out at the end of antiquity. Its high literary, philosophical, and scientific culture and ideas lived on in the successor civilizations of Islam and Christianity, influencing them until the present day. We have moved a long way in this chapter from that self-confident young man in fourth-century BCE Macedonia who looked disaster in the face in 360 and decided that he would not allow his family and people to pass away, who decided instead that he would build a new and better Macedonia that could dominate the world as he knew it. Philip of course had no inkling, as he built his army and state up from the ruins of defeat, that the effects of his actions would still be felt two millennia later. But if not for Philip's new Macedonia, if not for his unification of Greece, if not for his bold plan to invade and conquer the Persian Empire and spread Greeks, the Greek language, and Greek culture all around the eastern Mediterranean, it is very debatable whether Greek literature and ideas would or could hold the place in western and even Islamic culture that they do. For millennia it has been the custom, if one recognized this phenomenon at all, to give the credit to the romantic young conqueror Alexander. I think the analysis offered in the chapters above shows clearly that Alexander is one of the most overrated figures in world history. The truly great man was Alexander's father Philip; and credit belongs too to the generals—Antigonus, Ptolemy, Seleucus—who took on the role of governing the lands Alexander had merely marched through and fought battles in, and of turning those lands into viable empires with Greek cities and Greek culture. Without their efforts, the history and civilization of the lands and cultures of western Asia, Europe, and north Africa would be very different than they are today.

ACKNOWLEDGMENTS

WHEN WRITING ABOUT ANCIENT MACEDONIA TODAY, ONE STANDS—inevitably—on the shoulders of giants, and it is appropriate here to acknowledge the profound influence on my understanding of ancient Macedonia of two great historians above all else, whose many ground breaking articles and game changing books have established how one should view and think about the ancient Macedonians: I mean Eugene Borza and Miltiades Hatzopoulos, with both of whom I have been privileged to have many personal conversations, and whose work (despite various disagreements) has had a profound influence on my views. I also have to thank, as always, Erich Gruen, under whose tutelage at UC Berkeley I first developed an interest in and understanding of Hellenistic history.

My editors at The Overlook Press, Adam O'Brien and Tracy Carns, deserve great thanks for their patient efforts to speed this work along to its finished form; and I thank Peter Mayer profoundly for his belief in this project. Finally, my wife Clare and daughters Madeline and Colette deserve thanks for putting up with my frequent distraction over the years I have been working on this book.

END NOTES

Sources and Further Reading (in English)

Chapter 1

The archaeological evidence for early Macedonia (before 400 BCE) is well summarized, through the 1960s, in Hammond *A History of Macedonia* vol. I (1972); for subsequent archaeological evidence through the 1980s see Borza *In the Shadow of Olympus* (1990); and for more recent archaeological explorations see Arthur Muller "The Archaeology of Macedonia" in Giannakis (ed.) *Ancient Macedonia: Language, History, Culture* (2012). For Badian's argument against Macedonian as a Greek dialect see his "Greeks and Macedonians" in Barr-Sharrar and Borza (eds) *Macedonia and Greece in Late Classical and Hellenistic Times* (1982) pp. 33–51; but see now the studies by Emilio Crespo and Julian Dosuna in Giannakis (ed.) *Ancient Macedonia: Language, History, Culture* (2012) laying out the evidence for Macedonian as a dialect of Greek. The onomastic studies by Tataki (1988, 1994, 1998) and the epigraphic work of Hatzopoulos (see bibliography below) are of great significance in this regard.

For the early history of Macedonia the evidence comes almost entirely from the passages of Herodotus and Thucydides cited in the text. For modern accounts see, besides the works of Hammond and Borza cited above, Errington *A History of Macedonia* (1986), Hatzopoulos *Macedonian Institutions under the Kings* (2 vols. 1996) esp. vol. 1, and most recently Michael Zahrnt "A History of Macedonia in the Pre-Hellenistic Era" in Giannakis (ed.) *Ancient Macedonia: Language, History, Culture* (2012).

The idea of a Macedonian "constitution" was argued for most explicitly by F. Granier (1931); but see the devastating critiques of Errington (1978) and (1983). Though Hatzopoulos (1996) still tried to uphold it in a limited form, it is no longer accepted by most historians of Macedonia for the reasons outlined in the text. For the importance of drinking and the symposium in Macedonian elite culture, see Borza (1983); and for the southern Greek view of Macedonian symposia see Pownall in Carney and Ogden (eds.) (2010) ch. 6. See also Sawada "Social Customs and Institutions: Aspects of Macedonian Elite Society" in Roisman and Worthington (eds.) (2010) ch. 19. On hunting in ancient Greek (including Macedonian) culture see Anderson *Hunting in the Ancient World* (1985).

The classic exploration of the resources of Macedonia is Borza (1982) and see also Borza (1987) on the importance of Macedonian timber.

Chapter 2

An excellent account of the reigns of Amyntas III and his sons Alexander II and Perdiccas III can be found in Borza (1990) ch. 8. The evidence comes primarily from

Diodorus the Sicilian bks. 14–15 and Xenophon *Hellenica* as cited in the text.

For the practise of polygamy by the Maceodinan rulers see Greenwalt (1989) and Carney (1992).

For the treaty between Amyntas III and Olynthus see Rhodes and Osborne *Greek Historical Inscriptions, 404–323 BC* (2003) no. 12. For Sparta's war with the Olynthian League, see for example ch. 7 of Cartledge *The Spartans* (2002).

On the education of the upper class in early Macedonia see for example Billows (1990) ch. 1, especially on the matter of *syntrophoi* and the relationship between Philip and Antigonus as co-evals.

On hoplite warfare in classical Greece see Hanson (1989), and Kagan and Vigginao (eds.) *Men of Bronze* (2013). On Sparta's defeat at Leuctra and its aftermath see Cartledge (2002) ch. 8; and on the Theban hegemony in Greece see Buckler (1980).

CHAPTER 3

Our main sources for the reign of Philip are Diodorus the Sicilian bk. 16, the only full historical narrative; and the speeches of the Athenian orators Aeschines and Demosthenes, especially the latter's Olynthiac orations, his Philippics, and his speeches "on the Crown," "on the False Embassy," and "on the Peace."

There are a number of full-length modern studies of Philip: Ellis (1976) and Griffith (1979) are foundational; they established the basic chronology and development of Philip's career, and like all subsequent treatments of Philip the present narrative owes much to them. More recent studies of Philip are Worthington (2008) and (2014), and Gabriel (2010); see also Graham's assessment of "The Historical Significance of Philip of Macedon" in Danien (ed.) (1990); and in general Hatzopoulos and Loukopoulos (eds.) (1980) and Carney and Ogden (eds.) (2010).

On Macedonia and the Illyrians, see Greenwalt "Macedonia, Illyria, and Epirus" in Roisman and Worthington (eds.) (2010) ch. 14. On Thrace see Valeva, Nankov and Graninger (eds.) *A Companion to Ancient Thrace* (2015) esp. chs. 4 and 5 on Thrace in the fourth century BCE. On Thessaly see Graninger "Macedonia and Thessaly" in Roisman and Worthington (eds.) (2010) ch. 15. On the importance and role of the Delphic Oracle in Greece the study of Fontenrose *The Delphic Oracle* (1978) is key, and see also Buckler *Philip II and the Third Sacred War* (1989). An excellent study of Philip in relation to the southern Greek world particularly is Cawkwell (1978); in particular Cawkwell's reconstruction of the Battle of Chaironea at pp. 139–48 is crucial.

CHAPTER 4

Besides the standard works on Philip cited in the notes to Chapter 3 above, for Philip's military activity and army see the study by Griffith "Philip as a General and the Macedonian Army" in Hatzopoulos and Loukopoulos (eds.) (1980) 58–77; also Sekunda "The Macedonian Army" in Roisman and Worthington (eds.) (2010) ch. 22.

Bosworth "The Argeads and the Phalanx" in Carney and Ogden (eds.) (2010) ch. 9 still defends the view that the Anaximenes fragment quoted in the

306 RICHARD A. BILLOWS

text refers to Alexander II as establisher of the Macedonian phalanx without really succeeding in dispelling the criticisms of Griffith (1979) 706–9, and see also Borza (1990) 125–26 and 204–6. Borza rightly cites Griffith's discussion in *History of Macedonia* 2 (1979) at 405–49 as the best modern treatment of Philip's military reforms.

For the *sarissa* and related Macedonian military equipment and tactics two studies by Markle remain foundational: "The Macedonian Sarissa, Spear, and Related Armor" (1977) and "Use of the Sarissa by Philip and Alexander of Macedon" (1979); also Hammond (1980). See also on the Macedonian shield Markle (1999) and Liampi (1988). On Macedonian cavalry see the studies by Hammond (1978) and Milns (1981) in addition to Sekunda cited above. The transition of Philip's *pezetairoi* into *hypaspistai* and eventually *argyraspides* was fully laid out by Anson (1981), see also Milns (1971). For the experience of US combat historians revealing that most soldiers remained passive in battle, see S. L. A. Marshall's classic study *Men Against Fire* (1947), and also Keegan *The Face of Battle* (1976) at 71–73. For the development of siege warfare and artillery in the ancient world, the study of Marsden (1969) is still important; see also Campbell (2003) and Ashley (2004) ch. 2 "Siege Operations."

On Philip's officer corps Heckel's study *The Marshals of Alexander's Empire* (1992) is a good survey, since Alexander's marshals were all trained as officers in the army of Philip.

CHAPTER 5

Numerous contemporaries of Alexander "the Great" wrote accounts of his life and activities, all now lost. The indispensable work reviewing these writers and their (mostly scanty) remaining fragments is Pearson *Lost Histories of Alexander the Great* (1960). Four major surviving texts offer more or less full accounts of Alexander; in chronological order they are: Diodoros the Sicilian bk. 17 (ca. 30 BCE), Quintus Curtius *Historiae Alexandri Magni Macedonis* (ca. 55 CE), Plutarch *Life of Alexander* (ca. 100 CE), and Arrian *Anabasis* (ca. 160 CE). The last named, though the latest to write, is generally regarded as the best and most reliable of these historians; he should be read together with Bosworth's excellent historical commentary published in 1980 (vol. 1) and 1995 (vol. 2). Also valuable is *The Landmark Arrian* ed. James Romm (2010). On the "Alexander Romance" often cited as Pseudo-Callisthenes, see Stoneman *The Greek Alexander Romance* (1991).

W. W. Tarn's two-volume *Alexander the Great* (1948) was for many years the most influential English language study; its overly adulatory view of Alexander was, however, debunked in a series of very important studies by Ernst Badian in the 1970s and 1980s, now conveniently available in one volume: *Collected Papers on Alexander the Great* (2012), which are indispensable for the view of Alexander offered here. Modern studies of Alexander are far too numerous to list here; among the most important (in my view) are Lane Fox *Alexander the Great* (1973), Bosworth *Conquest and Empire* (1988), and Heckel *The Conquests of Alexander the Great* (2008).

On Philip's death see chs. 7 and 27 in Badian's *Collected Papers*. On the at times fraught relationship between Philip and Alexander, see e.g. Carney and

Ogden (eds.) (2010) ch. 2 by Victor Troncoso, and ch. 3 by Sabine Mueller; and on the Pixodarus affair see also ch. 1 by Stephen Ruzicka.

On the geography of the Battle of the Granicus I follow the study by Nikolitsis (1974). On Antigonus the One-Eyed's defeat of the Persian counter-attack in Asia Minor see Billows (1990) 43–45. On Antipater's war against the Spartans under Agis III, see Badian *Collected Papers* chs. 11 and 20. On the deaths of Philotas and Parmenio, and other supposed conspiracies against Alexander, see Badian *Collected Papers* chs. 3 and 24; and on the Harpalus affair Badian *Collected Papers* ch. 5. On Alexander's battle at the Hydaspes River in India against Porus, see Possehl "Alexander in India: the Last Great Battle" in Danien (ed.) (1990). On Alexander and the so-called "unity of mankind" see the devastating critique in Badian *Collected Papers* ch. 1; and on Alexander's "reign of terror" towards the end of his life Badian *Collected Papers* ch. 6.

CHAPTER 6

The most important source for the era of Alexander's Successors is Diodorus the Sicilian bks. 18 to 20, who seems to have made extensive use of the relatively excellent contemporary historian Hieronymus of Cardia, see Hornblower (1981). Other valuable ancient sources are Plutarch's biographies of Eumenes of Cardia and Demetrius the Besieger; and for the first few years after Alexander's death the remains of Arrian's mostly lost work *Ta meta Alexandron* ("Events after Alexander") are useful.

There are now a number of good studies of the era of the Successors: Waterfield (2011), Romm (2011), Roisman (2012). In addition there are numerous studies of individual Successors: on Antigonus the One-Eyed see Billows (1990) and Champion (2014); on Eumenes of Cardia see Anson (2004); on Ptolemy I see Ellis (1993); on Lysimachus see Lund (1992); on Seluecus Nicator see Grainger (1990); on Cassander see Adams (1975); on Demetrius the Besieger see Martin (2013); and on Antigonus Gonatas see Gabbert (1997).

For the crucial matter of colonisation and city foundation in the Hellenistic era the most complete and up to date resources are the three volumes by Getzel Cohen: *The Hellenistic Settlements in Europe, the Islands, and Asia Minor* (1995), *The Hellenistic Settlements in Syria, the Red Sea Basin, and North Africa* (2006), and *The Hellenistic Settlements in the East from Armenia and Mesopotamia to Bactria and India* (2013). See also Billows (1990) 292–304 for colonisation by Antigonus the One-Eyed, and Grainger (1990) for city foundation by Seleucus Nicator.

CHAPTER 7

Our historical sources for the Hellenistic era are very fractured, with only Polybius' history surviving in any substantial part. We rely on inscriptions, papyri, and other literary remains to flesh out our picture of Hellenistic society and civilization: a good resource is Austin's sourcebook in translation *The Hellenistic World from Alexander to the Roman Conquest* (1981). There are several good surveys of Hellenistic history: Walbank (1993), Green (1990), and Errington (2008), for example.

A good resource on the reign of Ptolemy III of Egypt is now Clayman (2014); on Philip V see Walbank (1940); on Antiochus III see Ma (1999), Taylor (2013), and Grainger (2015). On Hellenistic kingship more generally see Bilde (ed.) *Aspects of Hellenistic Kingship* (1996).

On Hellenistic armies generally see Baker "Warfare" in Erskine (ed.) (2003), and especially Chaniotis (2005). On the army of the Ptolemies see Fischer-Bovet (2014); on the Seleucid army see Bar Kochva (1976) and Taylor (2013); on the Antigonid army see Hatzopoulos (1996) and Sekunda (2013).

For Hellenistic cities see Billows "Cities" in Erskine (ed.) (2003) ch. 12.

For the great library of Alexandria, see Canfora (1989). On Hellenistic scholarship, Dickey (2007) collects all the known data. On Callimachus see Acosta-Hughes and Stephens (2012).

On the Roman conquest of the Hellenistic world, Harris (1979) and Gruen (1986) have for long been the most influential works; but see now also Harris (2016).

For the Hellenistic world, especially the cities, under Roman rule, a good starting point is Dimitriev (2005); see also Alcock (ed.) 1997.

For literary culture in the Roman Empire, see Johnson (2010); and a useful survey of the key evidence of Oxyrhynchus is Bowman (ed.) *Oxyrhynchus: a City and its Texts* (2007); see also Cribiore (1996) and (2005) on education in the eastern Roman Empire.

Chapter 8

For the supposed dialogue between 'Amr ibn al-'As and John Philoponus see Canfora (1989) ch. 16; the evidence comes from Ibn al-Kifti's *Ta'rikh al-Hukama* ("Chronicle of Wise Men"). On John Philoponus see further e.g. Sorabji (1993); and on his afterlife in Islamic thought as Yahya al-Nahwi see the entry by R. Wisnovsky in *Encyclopaedia of Islam* (2012).

On al-Kindi as "founder" of Muslim philosophy see Abboud (2006); on al-Khwarizmi see Brezina (2006); and on al-Farabi see Majid Fakhry (2002). For ibn Sina/Avicenna a good introduction is McGinnis (2010); for ibn Rushd/Averroes see Majid Fakhry (2001); and for ibn Khaldun see Fromherz (2010), and also Dawood (ed.) (1981) for an accessible edition of his *Muqaddimah* or "Introduction to History."

Despina White (1981) offers a good introduction to Photius and his work; for Constantine Porphyrogenitus, Toynbee (1973) is still worth reading, and see also Treadgold (2013) ch. 5 for Constantine's historical work.

For Cardinal Bessarion and other Byzantine refugees in fifteenth-century Italy, see Monfasani (1995); on Argyropoulos see also Matula (2006); and further on Byzantine emigres Jonathan Harris, *Greek Emigres in the West, 1400–1520* (1995).

GLOSSARY OF GREEK TERMS

agema: the guard unit surrounding the Macedonian king in battle; there was both an infantry *agema*, the first battalion of the *pezetairoi/hypaspistai*, and a cavalry *agema*, the "royal squadron" of the heavy cavalry.

agoge: training, especially referring to the Spartan training system, from the age of seven to eighteen, which turned the Spartan boy into the Spartan citizen-warrior.

agora: originally a public meeting, but in fifth-century and later Greek meaning the central town square where citizens met together for a variety of purposes—political, religious, economic, and social.

andreia: literally manliness (from *aner/andros*, the Greek word for a man as opposed to a woman), this word is commonly used to denote virtue, and especially courage, as expected to be displayed by a man in Greek (and especially Macedonian) society.

archon: literally ruler, this was used as a title for important magistrates in a host of Greek communities, most famously Athens where the *archon* gave his name to the year in which he held office; it was the title under which Philip II assumed the rule of Thessaly in the mid 350s.

argyraspides: the "silver shields," an elite unit of Macedonian heavy infantry so named after their silver-plated shields, originally named by Philip the *pezetairoi* and later (under Alexander) the *hypaspistai*.

asthetairoi: the meaning of this term remains obscure, though it refers to part of Macedonia's heavily armed infantry.

barbaroi: this Greek term essentially means foreigners in the sense of non-Greek speakers; the word is onomatopoeic, the Greek *bar bar* being the equivalent of English "blah blah," signifying incomprehensible speech.

basileus: this word means lord or king, most often the latter; it was frequently used specially to refer to the ruler of the Persian Empire.

chiliarchos: commander of a thousand, the term was used in the Persian Empire and afterwards under Alexander to refer to the senior military officer who functioned in effect as second-in-command of the Empire; later, under Antigonos the One-Eyed, the term referred to a sub-governor of a province in charge of local garrison forces and tribute collection.

dekas: literally a group of ten, the term was used in the Macedonian army from the time of Philip on to refer to the file of men, one stationed behind the other, which formed a kind of platoon unit of the Macedonian pike phalanx; usually the *dekas* in this sense seems in fact to have had only eight men.

doru: spear, usually the ca. eight-foot spear that was the main offensive weapon of the southern Greek hoplite warrior.

ethnos: literally a people, the term could be used to refer to any special sub-group of people united by some characteristic, including geographic origin.

gymnasion: literally the place to be naked (from *gymnos* = naked), this is the structure in Greek cities where citizens went to exercise and bathe, since Greeks exercised naked.

hetaira: literally a female companion, in fact a high-class courtesan, well educated and highly trained, sometimes likened to a Japanese *geisha*.

hetairoi: literally companions; the term refers in Macedonia to the elite supporters of the Macedonian kings until the time of Alexander the Great, when it came to be used to refer to the Macedonian "heavy" (that is, heavily armed) cavalry.

hoplites: literally an armed man (from *hopla* = weapons and/or armor), this term usually refers to the heavily armored southern Greek infantry warrior who equipped himself and fought in a distinctive phalanx formation.

hypaspistai: "shield bearers," an elite unit of Macedonian heavy infantry under Alexander the Great, originally named the *pezetairoi* by Philip, re-named the *argyraspides* towards the end of Alexander's reign.

ile (plural *ilai*): a squadron of cavalry in the Macedonian army usually ca. two hundred men strong; most notably the *ile basilike* or "royal squadron" (three hundred men strong) that formed the king's guard in battle when he chose to fight on horseback.

kausia: a distinctively Macedonian hat, looking somewhat like a modern beret (see ill. 1).

koinon: literally something held in common, this word was used to denote a federation of autonomous or semi-autonomous Greek cities or communities, banded together for various common purposes religious, political, and military; it is often translated into English as "league."

lochos: a sub-unit of the pike battalion (*taxis*), several hundred men strong and each commanded by an officer named the *lochagos*.

ouragos: the rear-most man in a file of the Macedonian phalanx, who served as a sort of non-commissioned officer with the responsibility of seeing that the men of the file held their positions and did not turn to flight.

paides: literally youths; the term referred in the time of Philip and Alexander, if not earlier, to aristocratic Macedonian youths in their late teens who formed part of the entourage of the king, serving him and learning the business of being a Macedonian aristocrat and officer under his tutelage.

paidion (plural *paidia*): refers to a young boy, usually under seven years of age.

pantodapoi: men from all over, referring to men of varied ethnicities trained and equipped to fight, in the armies of Alexander's Successors and later, as Macedonian-style pikemen or heavy cavalry; usually these military "Macedonians" would, upon retirement, be viewed and treated simply as Macedonians.

peltast: a type of (usually mercenary) Greek infantry who were intermediate in role between the heavily armored hoplites and the standard light infantry archers and javelineers; the name came from a distinctive light shield called the *pelta*.

penestai: the oppressed underclass of the north Greek region of Thessaly, who lived in a semi-slave condition under the control of the aristocratic land-owning class; much of Macedonia's rural population were most likely held in a similar semi-slave condition of dependency.

pezetairoi: "foot companions," an elite unit of Macedonian heavy infantry formed by Philip II to be his guard brigade in battle, later re-named under Alexander as *hypaspistai* and then *argyraspides*, while the name *pezetairoi* was used instead to refer to the battalions of Macedonian pikemen making up the phalanx.

phalanx: a formation of heavily armed infantry drawn up in highly disciplined lines and files of men.

phone: literally, speech, in the sense of language or dialect.

prodromoi: "front runners," lightly equipped and highly mobile cavalry who functioned as scouts and skirmishers.

proskynesis: the act of bowing down before the Persian king, touching one's forehead to the ground as a mark of submission and respect.

sarissa: a sixteen- to eighteen-foot pike used as the main offensive weapon by the Macedonian heavy infantry phalanx developed by Philip II.

satrap: derived from a Persian word for governor, this was the title usually used to refer to the governors of the great provinces of the Persian Empire and the empire of Alexander, and was occasionally still used to refer to governors after Alexander's time.

Spartiatai: the full citizens of the city-state of Sparta, who had undergone the rigorous and brutal Spartan education system successfully and dedicated their lives to being outstanding hoplite warriors.

strategos: army commander or general; in many Greek city-states, such as Athens, in fact the title of a magistrate whose duties might or might not be primarily military; later in the Hellenistic Empires often the title of a regional governor.

symposion: often anglicized as symposium, this is the after dinner drinking party that was a key feature of upper-class Greek (and especially Macedonian) social life.

synedrion: the council of state of the Macedonian king, made up of his key *hetairoi* (companions), mostly drawn from the Macedonian aristocracy.

syntrophoi: boys who form the group of close associates of a Macedonian prince, raised and educated along with him as his closest friends and companions; these boys are usually drawn from leading families of the Macedonian aristocracy.

talent: a weight, the exact amount of which varied from one Greek state to another; it most commonly referred to a weight of gold or silver and represented a very large sum of money: since the talent comprised six thousand *drachmai* and the *drachma* was a good day's wage for a skilled craftsman, a family of six or eight people could live comfortably for about twenty years on a fortune of one talent.

taxis: a battalion fifteen hundred men strong of the pike phalanx; each *taxis* was recruited from a particular region of Macedonia and commanded by its own *taxiarchos* or battalion commander.

telesias: a dance for men, usually performed in honor of a god, in which the dancer was armed with weapons and simulated the maneuvers of hand-to-hand combat.

theatron: theatre, a viewing space for dramatic and musical performances, roughly horse-shoe shaped and open to the air.

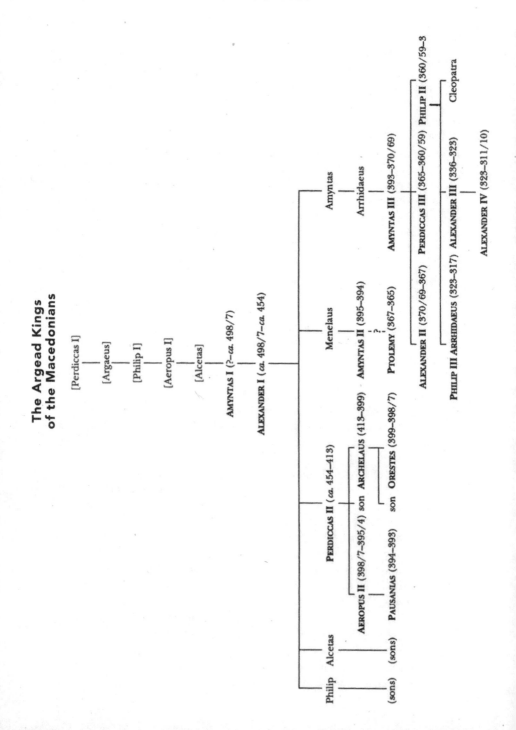

The Argead Kings
of the Macedonians

Philip

Alcetas

(sons)

(sons)

AEROPUS II (398/7–395/4)

PAUSANIAS (394–393)

PERDICCAS II (ca. 454–413)

son ARCHELAUS (413–399)

son ORESTES (399–398/7)

AMYNTAS I (?–ca. 498/7)

ALEXANDER I (ca. 498/7–ca. 454)

Menelaus

AMYNTAS II (395–394)

PTOLEMY (367–365)

ALEXANDER II (370/69–367)

PHILIP III ARRHIDAEUS (323–317)

Amyntas

Arrhidaeus

AMYNTAS III (393–370/69)

PERDICCAS III (365–360/59)

ALEXANDER III (336–323)

PHILIP II (360/59–3)

Cleopatra

ALEXANDER IV (323–311/10)

[Perdiccas I]

[Argaeus]

[Philip I]

[Aeropus I]

[Alcetas]

The Antigonids

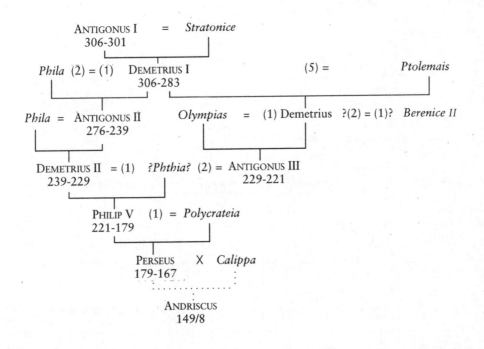

ANTIGONUS I   =   *Stratonice*
306-301

Phila (2) = (1)   DEMETRIUS I   (5) =   *Ptolemais*
306-283

Phila =   ANTIGONUS II   *Olympias*   =   (1) Demetrius   ?(2) = (1)?   *Berenice II*
276-239

DEMETRIUS II   = (1)   *?Phthia?*   (2) =   ANTIGONUS III
239-229   229-221

PHILIP V   (1) = *Polycrateia*
221-179

PERSEUS   X   *Calippa*
179-167

ANDRISCUS
149/8

Ptolemies

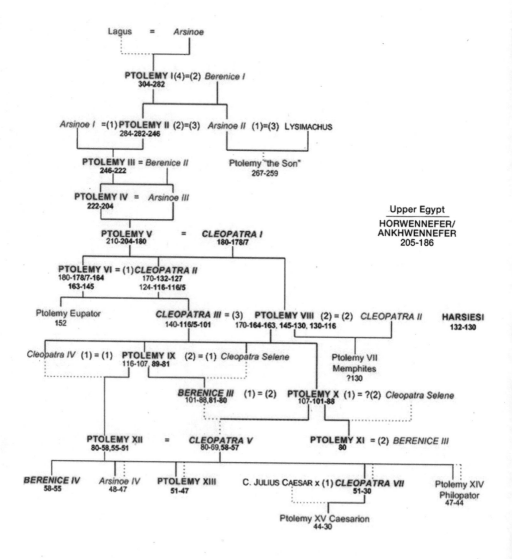

Lagus = Arsinoe

PTOLEMY I (4)=(2) *Berenice I*
304-282

Arsinoe I =(1) PTOLEMY II (2)=(3) *Arsinoe II* (1)=(3) LYSIMACHUS
284-282-246

PTOLEMY III = *Berenice II*   Ptolemy "the Son"
246-222   267-259

PTOLEMY IV = *Arsinoe III*
222-204

Upper Egypt
HORWENNEFER/
ANKHWENNEFER
205-186

PTOLEMY V   =   *CLEOPATRA I*
210-204-180   180-178/7

PTOLEMY VI = (1) *CLEOPATRA II*
180-178/7-164   170-132-127
163-145   124-116-116/5

Ptolemy Eupator   *CLEOPATRA III* = (3) PTOLEMY VIII (2) = (2) *CLEOPATRA II*   HARSIESI
152   140-116/5-101   170-164-163, 145-130, 130-116   132-130

Cleopatra IV (1) = (1) PTOLEMY IX (2) = (1) *Cleopatra Selene*   Ptolemy VII
116-107, 89-81   Memphites
?130

BERENICE III (1) = (2) PTOLEMY X (1) = ?(2) *Cleopatra Selene*
101-88,81-80   107-101-88

PTOLEMY XII = *CLEOPATRA V*   PTOLEMY XI = (2) *BERENICE III*
80-58,55-51   80-69,58-57   80

BERENICE IV *Arsinoe IV* PTOLEMY XIII   C. JULIUS CAESAR x (1) *CLEOPATRA VII*   Ptolemy XIV
58-55   48-47   51-47   51-30   Philopator
                                                                                    47-44

Ptolemy XV Caesarion
44-30

The House of Seleucus

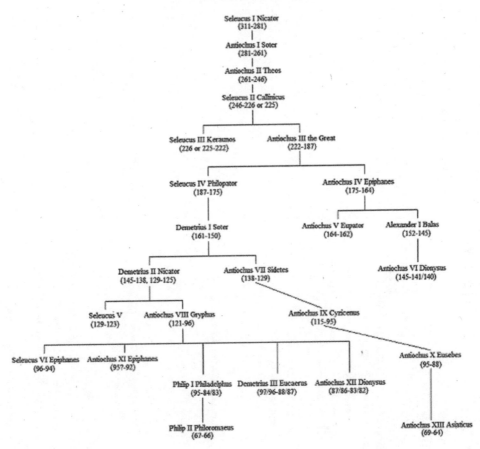

TIMELINE

KEY EVENTS IN GREECE AND WESTERN ASIA

560–530: Cyrus the Great establishes Persian Empire

520–512: Darius extends Persian Empire to Thrace and Macedonia

499–494: Ionian Revolt against Persian power fails; Alexander I of Argead dynasty becomes ruler of Macedonia under Persian domination

490–479: Persian invasions of Greece are defeated by Athenians and Spartans

478–460: in power vacuum after Persian retreat, Alexander I extends his power to west, into "upper Macedonia," and east, to the Strymon valley, establishing the historical Macedonian kingdom

ca. 454: Alexander I dies; his sons vie for power over Macedonia

ca. 450–400: Herodotus and Thucydides develop analytical history writing in Greece, and recount the beginnings of the Macedonian kingdom

ca. 430–413: Perdiccas II rules over Macedonia, holding off Athenian power as best he can

413–399: rule of Archelaus strengthens Macedonia, including foundation of new capital at Pella

399–393: chaotic period in Macedonia with multiple rulers

393–370: insecure and interrupted rule of Amyntas III

ca. 383: births of Philip II and Antigonus the One-Eyed

371: Spartan defeat by Thebans at Battle of Leuctra begins decline of Spartan power

370–368: rule of Alexander II in Macedonia

ca. 369–359: Theban hegemony in Greece

368: Alexander II assassinated; Ptolemy of Aloros rules as regent for Perdiccas III

ca. 366: Ptolemy of Aloros assassinated; Perdiccas III rules Macedonia

360: Perdiccas III defeated and killed in battle against Illyrians led by Bardylis; Philip II becomes ruler of Macedonia

359: Philip II defeats initial opponents and creates new Macedonian pike phalanx

KEY CONTEMPORARY EVENTS IN EAST ASIA

ca. 567: birth of Gautama Buddha in India

ca. 550–500: Confucius (Kongzi), Sun Tzu (Sunzi), and Lao Tzu (Laozi) flourishing in China

481–221: Warring States period in China

372–289: life of Mencius (Mangzi) in China

358: Philip II defeats Bardylis the Illyrian in battle and begins expansion of Macedonian power

356–347: Third Sacred War in Greece damages power of Thebans and Thessalians, and is ended by intervention of Philip II

338: Philip II defeats Athenians and Thebans at Battle of Chaeroneia and becomes Hegemon (leader) of the Greeks

336: Philip II assassinated; Alexander III becomes ruler of Macedonia

334: Macedonians under Alexander III invade Asia and begin conquest of Persian Empire

331: defeat of Darius III at battle of Gaugamela by Alexander III ends Persian Empire; Alexander becomes ruler of western Asia

328–326: Alexander III campaigns in Indus valley and defeats Indian ruler Porus

323: Alexander III dies at Babylon; Perdiccas becomes regent of empire

320: settlement of Triparadisus; Philip III and Alexander IV are co-kings; Antipater is regent; Antigonus the One-Eyed is general over Asia

ca. 313: Chandragupta Maurya begins conquests in Ganges valley, India, that lead to establishment of Maurya Empire

310: death of Alexander IV ends rule of Argead dynasty over Macedonians

306: Antigonus the One-Eyed is named king, and names his son Demetrius co-king

305–304: Ptolemy I becomes king in Egypt and begins to establish Mouseion and Library at Alexandria; Cassander becomes king in Macedonia, Seleucus I in Mesopotamia, and Lysimachus in Thrace

305–303: Chandragupta invades Indus valley; fights Seleucus for control of he region; Seleucus cedes control of Indus valley to Chandragupta and receives 500 war elephants in exchange

301: Antigonus the One-Eyed defeated and killed at Battle of Ipsus by Seleucus I and Lysimachus; Demetrius flees to become sea king

283: Ptolemy I dies and Ptolemy II succeeds him as king, establishing Ptolemaic dynasty in Egypt

281: Seleucus I defeats and kills Lysimachus at Battle of Cyroupedium

280: Seleucus I assassinated; Antiochus I succeeds as king, establishing Seleucid dynasty in western Asia

279: Galatian tribes invade and ravage Macedonia

Key Events in Greece and Western Asia

277: Antigonus Gonatas defeats Galatians and becomes king of Macedonia, ruling until 239 and establishing Antigonid dynasty in Macedonia

247: deaths of Ptolemy II and Antiochos II; Ptolemy III and Seleucus II become rulers

239: death of Antigonus II Gonatas; Demetrius II becomes king

222: Antiochus III becomes king and starts re-establishing Seleucid power throughout western Asia

221: Philip V becomes king of Macedonia and sets out on expansionist policy

218–201: war between Romans and Carthaginians (Hannibalic War) in total Roman victory and Roman domination over western Mediterranean

216: Hannibal's victory over Romans at Cannae leads Philip V to ally with Carthage and make war on Rome, ending in compromise peace in 205

200: Romans declare war on Macedonians (Second Macedonian War) looking for revenge on Philip V

197: Romans defeat Philip V at Battle of Cynoscephalae and deprive Philip of all lands outside of Macedonia proper

194: Antiochus III invades Greece starting war against Romans

190–189: Romans defeat Antiochus III at Battle of Magnesia and, in Peace of Apamea, deprive Seleucid Empire of all of Asia Minor

169: Romans defeat Macedonian king Perseus and end Antigonid kingdom of Macedonia

146: in aftermath of Roman victories over Macedonia and Achaea, Romans establish dominance over all Greek lands

Key Contemporary Events in East Asia

273–232: reign of Maurya Emperor Ashoka brings Maurya Empire to its height; Ashoka converts to Buddhism and sends missionaries to spread the religion, including to the Hellenistic rulers

221–210: Qin ruler Shi Huangti unifies China, becoming first Emperor of all China

ca. 218: Qin Emperor Shi Huangti begins construction of Great Wall

202 BCE–220 CE: after collapse of Qin dynasty, Liu Bang founds Han Dynasty which rules China for over 400 years

187: Maurya Empire collapses in India

ca. 160–55: Greco-Bactrian invasions of Indus valley establish Indo-Greek kingdoms

138–126: Chinese envoy Zhang Qian travels to Afghanistan, witnessing the declining Greco-Bactrian civilization there and learning of Seleucid Empire

66–64: Roman general Pompeius Magnus ends Mithridatid and Seleucid kingdoms, establishing Roman provinces of Pontus and Syria

30: Roman emperor Octavian/Augustus ends Ptolemaic kingdom and completes Roman rule over entire Hellenistic world up to Euphrates River

ca. 6: Jesus of Galilee born

ca. 30 CE: Jesus of Galilee crucified on order of Roman governor Pontius Pilatus

ca. 36–60 CE: missionary voyages of Saul/Paul of Tarsus begin spread of Christianity

98–180: height of the Roman Empire under the "good emperors" Trajan, Hadrian, Antoninus Pius, and Marcus Aurelius

ca. 90: the great Chinese historian Sima Qian publishes his history, recounting China's past up to his own day, including the travels of Zhang Qian

238–270 CE: imperial crisis almost brings about dissolution of Roman Empire

250 CE: persecution of Christians under Emperor Decius

270–305 CE: Roman Empire revived under Aurelian and Diocletian

305 CE: persecution of Christians under Diocletian and Galerius

307–337 CE: reign of Emperor Constantine who re-unites the Roman Empire and legalizes Christianity

402–450 CE: triumph of Christianity under Emperor Theodosius II who ends pagan worship and closes philosophical schools

ca. 476 CE: end of Roman Empire in the west with death of last Emperor Romulus Augustus; eastern Roman Empire continues as Byzantine Empire

632–661 CE: Arab Muslim conquests in Syria/Palestine/Mesopotamia and north Africa permanently divide Mediterranean world between Christian north and Islamic south

ca. 220 CE: collapse of Han Dynasty leaves China disunited

ca. 320–550 CE: Gupta Empire re-unites much of India into great Hindu empire

ca. 495 CE: Buddhism begins to spread in China

581–618 CE: Sui Dynasty re-unites China

712 CE: first Muslim invasion of Sindh in north India begins spread of Islam into north India

BIBLIOGRAPHY

Abboud, T., *Al-Kindi: The Father of Arab Philosophy*, Rosen Central, 2006

Acosta-Hughes, B. & Stephens, S. A., *Callimachus in Context, from Plato to the Augustan Poets*, Cambridge University Press, 2012

Adams, W. L., *Cassander, Macedonia, and the Policy of Coalition, 323–301 BC*, PhD Dissertation, University of Virginia, 1975

Adams, W. L & Borza, E. N. (eds.), *Philip II, Alexander the Great, and the Macedonian Heritage*, Rowman & Littlefield, 1982

Alcock, S. (ed.), *The Early Roman Empire in the East*, Oxbow, 1997

Anderson, J. K., *Hunting in the Ancient World*, University of California Press, 1985

Andronikos, M., *Vergina: The Royal Tombs and the Ancient City*, Ekdotike Athenon, 1984

Anson, E. M., "Alexander's Hypaspists and the Argyraspids," *Historia* 30 (1981), 117–20

Anson, E. M., "Macedonia's Alleged Constitutionalism," *Classical Journal* 80 (1985), 303–16

Anson, E. M., *Eumenes of Cardia: A Greek among Macedonians*, Brill, 2004

Anson, E. M., "Philip II, Amyntas Perdikka, and Macedonian Royal Succession," *Historia* 58 (2009), 276–86

Anson, E. M., *Alexander the Great: Themes and Issues*, Bloomsbury, 2013

Anson, E. M., *Alexander's Heirs: The Age of the Successors*, Wiley-Blackwell, 2014

Archibald, Z. H., *The Odrysian Kingdom of Thrace: Orpheus Unmasked*, Clarendon, 1998

Archibald, Z. H., "Macedonia and Thrace," in Roisman & Worthington (2010), 326–41

Ashley, J. R., *The Macedonian Empire: The Era of Warfare under Philip II and Alexander the Great, 359–323 BC*, McFarland 2004

Austin, M. M., *The Hellenistic World from Alexander to the Roman Conquest*, Cambridge University Press, 1981

Badian, E., "Greeks and Macedonians," in Barr-Sharrar & Borza (1982), 33–51

Badian, E., "Alexander the Great between Two Thrones and Heaven: Variations on an Old Theme," in I. Worthington (ed.), *Alexander the Great: A Reader*, Routledge, 2003, 245–62

Badian, E., *Collected Papers on Alexander the Great*, Routledge, 2012

Baker, P., "Warfare," in Erskine (2003), 373–88

Bar-Kochva, B., *The Seleucid Army: Organisation and Tactics in the Great Campaigns*, Cambridge University Press, 1976

Barr-Sharrar, B. & Borza, E. N. (eds.), *Macedonia and Greece in Late Classical and Early Hellenistic Times*, National Gallery of Art, 1982

Baynham, E., "The Ancient Evidence for Alexander the Great," in J. Roisman (ed.), *Brill's Companion to Alexander the Great*, Brill, 2003, 3–29

Bilde, P. et al. (eds.), *Aspects of Hellenistic Kingship*, Aarhus University Press, 1996

Billows, R. A., *Antigonos the One-Eyed and the Creation of the Hellenistic State*, University of California Press, 1990

Billows, R. A., *Kings and Colonists: Aspects of Macedonian Imperialism*, Brill, 1995

Billows, R. A., "Cities," in A. Erskine (ed.), *A Companion to the Hellenistic World*, Wiley-Blackwell 2003, 196–215

Borza, E. N., "The Natural Resources of Early Macedonia," in Adams & Borza (1982), 1–20

Borza, E. N., "The Symposium at Alexander's Court," *Archaia Makedonia* 3 (1983), 45–55

Borza, E. N., "Timber and Politics in the Ancient World: Macedon and the Greeks," *Proceedings of the American Philosophical Society* 131 (1987), 32–52

Borza, E. N., *In the Shadow of Olympus: The Emergence of Macedon*, Princeton University Press, 1990

Borza, E. N, *Before Alexander. Constructing Early Macedonia*, Regina, 1999

Bosworth, A. B., "Philip II and Upper Macedonia," *Classical Quarterly* 21 (1971), 93–105

Bosworth, A. B., *A Historical Commentary on Arrian's History of Alexander*, 2 vols., Oxford University Press, 1980/1995

Bosworth, A. B., *Conquest and Empire: The Reign of Alexander the Great*, Cambridge University Press, 1988

Bosworth, A. B., *The Legacy of Alexander*, Oxford University Press, 2002

Bosworth, A. B., "The Argeads and the Phalanx," in Carney & Ogden (2010), 91–102

Bowman, A. K., *Oxyrhynchus: a City and its Texts*, Egypt Exploration Society, 2007

Brezina, C., *Al-Khwarizmi: The Inventor of Algebra*, Rosen Central, 2006

Briant, P., *Alexander the Great and his Empire*, Princeton University Press, 2010

Buckler, J., *The Theban Hegemony*, Harvard University Press, 1980

Buckler, J., *Philip II and the Sacred War*, Brill, 1989

Campbell, D. B., *Greek and Roman Siege Machinery, 399 BC–AD 363*, Osprey, 2003

Canfora, L., *The Vanished Library: A Wonder of the Ancient World*, Hutchinson Radius, 1989

Carney, E. D., "Regicide in Macedonia," *La Parola del Passato* 38 (1983), 260–72

Carney, E. D., "The Politics of Polygamy: Olympias, Alexander and the Murder of Philip," *Historia* 41 (1992), 169–89

Carney, E. D., "Macedonians and Mutiny: Discipline and Indiscipline in the Army of Philip and Alexander," *Classical Philology* 91 (1996), 19–44

Carney, E. D., *Women and Monarchy in Macedonia*, University of Oklahoma Press, 2000

Carney, E. D., "Elite Education and High Culture in Macedonia," in W. Heckel & L. A. Tritle (eds.), *Crossroads of History: The Age of Alexander*, Regina, 2003, 47–63

Carney, E. D., "Symposia and the Macedonian Elite: The Unmixed Life," *Syllecta Classica* 18 (2007), 129–80

Carney, E. D. & Ogden, D., *Philip II and Alexander the Great: Father and Son, Lives and Afterlives*, Oxford University Press, 2010

Cartledge, P., *The Spartans, an Epic History*, Macmillan, 2002

Cawkwell, G. L., *Philip of Macedon*, Faber & Faber, 1978

Champion, J., *Antigonus the One-Eyed, Greatest of the Successors*, Pen & Sword, 2014

Chaniotis, A., *War in the Hellenistic World*, Wiley-Blackwell, 2005

Clayman, D. L., *Berenice II and the Golden Age of Ptolemaic Egypt*, Oxford University Press, 2014

Cohen, G., *The Hellenistic Settlements in Europe, the Islands, and Asia Minor*, University of California Press, 1995

Cohen, G., *The Hellenistic Settlements in Syria, the Red Sea Basin, and North Africa*, University of California Press, 2006

Cohen, G., *The Hellenistic Settlements in the East from Armenia and Mesopotamia to Bactria*, University of California Press, 2013

Crespo, E., "Languages and Dialects in Ancient Macedonia," in Giannakis (2012), ch. 3

Cribiore, R., *Writing, Teachers, and Students in Graeco-Roman Egypt*, American Society of Papyrologists, 1996

Cribiore, R., *Gymnastics of the Mind: Greek Education in Hellenistic and Roman Egypt*, Princeton University Press, 2005

Danien, E. (ed.), *The World of Philip and Alexander: A Symposium on Greek Life and Times*, University of Pennsylvania Museum of Archaeology and Anthropology, 1990

Dawood, N. J. (ed.), *The Muqaddimah by ibn Khaldun: an Introduction to History*, Princeton University Press, 1989

Dickey, E., *Ancient Greek Scholarship*, Oxford University Press, 2007

Dimitriev, S., *City Government in Hellenistic and Roman Asia Minor*, Oxford University Press, 2005

Dosuna, J., "Ancient Macedonian as a Greek Dialect: A Critical Survey on Recent Work.", in Giannakis (2012), ch. 4"

Edson, C. F., "Early Macedonia," *Archaia Makedonia* 1 (1970), 17–44

Ellis, J. R., *Philip II and Macedonian Imperialism*, Thames and Hudson, 1976

Ellis, J. R., "The Unification of Macedonia," in Hatzopoulos & Loukopoulos (1981), 36–47

Ellis, J. R., "The First Months of Alexander's Reign," in Barr-Sharrar & Borza (1982), 69–73

Ellis, W. M., *Ptolemy of Egypt*, Routledge, 1993 (2nd edn. 2002)

Errington, R. M., "The Nature of the Macedonian State under the Monarchy," *Chiron* 8 (1978), 77–133

Errington, R. M., "The Historiographical Origins of Macedonian 'Staatsrecht'," *Archaia Makedonia* 3 (1983), 89–101

Errington, R. M., *A History of Macedonia*, University of California Press, 1990

Errington, R. M., *A History of the Hellenistic World, 323–30 BC*, Wiley-Blackwell, 2008

Erskine, A. (ed.), *A Companion to the Hellenistic World*, Wiley-Blackwell, 2003

Fakhry, M., *Averroes/Ibn Rushd: His Life, Works and Influence*, Oneworld Publications, 2001

Fakhry, M., *Al-Farabi, His Life, Works and Influence*, Oneworld Publications, 2002

Fischer-Bovet, C., *Army and Society in Ptolemaic Egypt*, Cambridge University Press, 2014

Flower, M. A., *Theopompus of Chios*, Oxford University Press, 1997

Fontenrose, J., *The Delphic Oracle*, University of California Press, 1978

Fraser, P. M. & Matthews, E., *A Lexicon of Greek Personal Names. IV: Macedonia, Thrace, Regions of the Black Sea*, Clarendon, 2005

Fromherz, A. J., *Ibn Khaldun, Life and Times*, Edinburgh University Press, 2010

Gabbert, J., *Antigonus II Gonatas: A Political Biography*, Routledge, 1997

Gabriel, R. A., *Philip II of Macedonia: Greater than Alexander*, Potomac, 2010

Giannakis, G. K. (ed.), *Ancient Macedonia: Language, History, Culture*, Centre for the Greek Language, Thessaloniki, 2012

Graham, A. J., "The Historical Significance of Philip of Macedon," in Danien (1990), 1–14

Grainger, J. D., *Seleukos Nikator: Constructing a Hellenistic Kingdom*, Routledge, 1990

Grainger, J. D., *The Cities of Seleukid Syria*, Clarendon, 1990

Grainger, J. D., *The Seleukid Empire of Antiochus III, 223–187 BC*, Pen and Sword, 2015

Granier, F., *Die makedonische Heeresversammlung*, Beck, 1931

Graninger, D., "Macedonia and Thessaly," in Roisman & Worthington (2010), 306–25

Green, P., *Alexander to Actium: The Hellenistic Age*, University of California Press, 1990

Greenwalt, W. S., "The Marriageability Age at the Argead Court: 360–317 BC," *Classical World* 82 (1988), 93–97

Greenwalt, W. S., "Polygamy and Succession in Argead Macedonia," *Arethusa* 22 (1989), 19–43

Greenwalt, W. S., "Macedonia, Illyria, Epirus," in Roisman & Worthington (2010), 279–305

Griffith, G. T., "Philip as a General and the Macedonian Army," in Hatzopoulos & Loukopoulos (1981), 58–77

Gruen, E., *The Hellenistic World and the Coming of Rome*, 2 vols., University of California Press, 1986

Hammond, N. G. L., *A History of Macedonia* I, Clarendon, 1972

Hammond, N. G. L., "A Cavalry Unit in the Army of Antigonus Monophthalmus: *Asthippoi*," *Classical Quarterly* 28 (1978), 128–35

Hammond, N. G. L., "Some Passages in Arian Concerning Alexander," *Classical Quarterly* 30 (1980), 455–76

Hammond, N. G. L., "Royal Pages, Personal Pages and Boys Trained in the Macedonian Manner during the Period of the Temenid Monarchy," *Historia* 39 (1990), 261–90

Hammond, N. G. L. & Griffith, G. T., *A History of Macedonia* II, Clarendon, 1979

Hammond, N. G. L. & Walbank, F. W., *A History of Macedonia* III, Clarendon, 1988

Hanson, V., *The Western Way of War: Infantry Battle in Classical Greece*, University of California Press, 1989

Harris, J., *Greek Emigres in the West, 1400–1520*, Porphyrogenitus, 1995

Harris, W. V., *War and Imperialism in Republican Rome, 327–70 BC*, Oxford University Press, 1979

Harris, W. V., *Roman Power: A Thousand Years of Empire*, Cambridge University Press, 2016

Hatzopoulos, M. B. & Loukopoulos, L. D. (eds.), *Philip of Macedon*, Ekdotike Athenon, 1981

Hatzopoulos, M. B., "Succession and Regency in Classical Macedonia," *Archaia Makedonia* 4 (1986), 272–92

Hatzopoulos, M. B., *Une donation du roi Lysimaque*, De Boccard, 1988

Hatzopoulos, M. B. & Gauthier, Ph., *La loi gymnasiarque de Beroia*, De Boccard, 1993

Hatzopoulos, M. B., *Macedonian Institutions under the Kings*, 2 vols., De Boccard, 1996

Hatzopoulos, M. B. & Juhel, P., "Four Hellenistic Funerary Stelae from Gephyra, Macedonia," *American Journal of Archaeology* 113 (2009), 423–37

Heckel, W., "Marsyas of Pella, Historian of Macedon," *Hermes* 108 (1980), 444–62

Heckel, W., *The Conquests of Alexander the Great*, Cambridge University Press, 2008

Heckel, W., *The Marshals of Alexander's Empire*, 2nd ed. Routledge, 2016

Heckel, W., "Geography and Politics in Argead Macedonia," in Müller (2017), 67–78

Heisserer, A. J., *Alexander and the Greeks: The Epigraphic Evidence*, University of Oklahoma Press, 1980

Holt, F. L., *Alexander the Great and Bactria*, Brill, 1988

Hornblower, J., *Hieronymus of Cardia*, Oxford University Press, 1981

Johnson, W. A., *Readers and Reading Culture in the High Roman Empire: A Study of Elite Communities*, Oxford University Press, 2010

Kagan, D. & Viggiano, G. F. (eds.), *Men of Bronze: Hoplite Warfare in Ancient Greece*, Princeton University Press, 2013

Keegan, J., *The Face of Battle*, Viking, 1976

Lane Fox, R., *Alexander the Great*, Allen Lane, 1973

Liampi, K., *Der makedonische Schild*, Habelt, 1998

Lund, H. S., *Lysimachus: A Study in Hellenistic Kingship*, Routledge, 1992

Ma, J., *Antiochus III and the Cities of Western Asia Minor*, Oxford University Press, 1999

March, D. A., "The Kings of Macedon: 399–369," *Historia* 54 (1995), 257–82

Markle, M. M., "The Macedonian Sarissa, Spear, and Related Armor," *American Journal of Archaeology* 81 (1977), 323–39

Markle, M. M., "The Use of the Sarissa by Philip and Alexander of Macedon," *American Journal of Archaeology* 82 (1978), 483–97

Markle, M. M., "A Shield Monument from Veria and the Chronology of Macedonian Shield Types," *Hesperia* 68 (1999), 219–54

Martin, T. R., "Demetrius 'the Besieger' and Hellenistic Warfare," in B. Campbell & L. A. Tritle (eds.) *The Oxford Handbook of Warfare in the Classical World*, Oxford University Press, 2013, 671–87

Marsden, E., *Greek and Roman Artillery: Historical Development*, Oxford University Press, 1969

Marshall, S. L. A., *Men Against Fire*, William Morrow, 1947

Matula, J., "*John Argyropoulos and his Importance for the Latin West*," *Acta Universitatis Palackianae Olomoucensis*, 2006

McGinnis, J., *Avicenna*, Oxford University Press, 2010

McQueen, E. I., *Diodorus Siculus: The Reign of Philip II*, Bristol Classical Press, 1991

Meiggs, R., *Trees and Timber in the Mediterranean World*, Oxford University Press, 1982

Milns, R. D., "The Hypaspists of Alexander III – Some Problems," *Historia* 20 (1971), 187–88

Milns, R. D., "*Asthippoi* Again," *Classical Quarterly* 31 (1981), 347–54

Monfasani, J., *Byzantine Scholars in Renaissance Italy: Cardinal Bessarion and Other Emigres*, Variorum, 1995

Muller, A., "The Other Greece: The Archaeology of Macedonia," in Giannakis (2012), ch. 2

Müller, S., "Philip II," in Roisman & Worthington (2010), 166–85

Müller, S., "In the Shadow of his Father: Alexander, Hermolaus, and the Legend of Philip," in Carney & Ogden (2010), 25–32

Müller, S. et al. (eds.), *The History of the Argeads – New Perspectives*, Harrassowitz Verlag, 2017

Nikolitsis, N. Th., *The Battle of the Granicus*, Astroms Forlag, 1974

Ogden, D., *Polygamy, Prostitutes and Death: The Hellenistic Dynasties*, Classical Press of Wales, 1999

Ogden, D., *Alexander the Great: Myth, Genesis and Sexuality*, Liverpool University Press, 2011

Olbrycht, M. J., "Curtius Rufus, the Macedonian Mutiny at Opis and Alexander's Iranian Policy," in J. Pigon (ed.), *The Children of Herodotus*, Cambridge Scholars Publishing, 2008, 231–52

Palagia, O., "Archaeological Evidence," in Müller (2017), 151–61

Pearson, L., "The Diary and Letters of Alexander the Great, *Historia* 3 (1954/55), 429–54

Pearson, L., *The Lost Histories of Alexander the Great*, American Philological Association, 1960

Possehl, G., "Alexander in India: The Last Great Battle," in Danien (1990), 99–108

Pownall, F., "The Symposia of Philip II and Alexander III of Macedon," in Carney & Ogden (2010), 55–65

Pownall, F., "The Role of Greek Literature in Intellectual Macedonian Circles," in Müller (2017), 215–29

Price, M. J., *Coins of the Macedonians* I–II, British Museum, 1974

Price, M. J., *The Coinage in the Name of Alexander the Great and Philip Arrhidaeus*, British Museum/Swiss Numismatic Society, 1991

Psoma, S. E., "The Kingdom of Macedonia and the Chalcidean League," in R. Lane Fox (ed.), *Brill's Companion to Ancient Macedon*, Brill, 2011, 113–26

Psoma, S. E., "Innovation or Tradition? Succession to the Kingship in Temenid Macedonia," *Tekmeria* 11 (2012), 73–87

Psoma, S. E., "Athens and the Macedonian Kingdom from Perdikkas II to Philip II," *Revue des etudes anciennes* 116 (2014), 133–44

Roisman, J., "Classical Macedonia to Perdiccas III," in Roisman & Worthington (2010), 145–65

Roisman, J., *Alexander's Veterans and the Early Wars of the Successors*, University of Texas Press, 2013

Roisman, J., "Opposition to Macedonian Kings," in T. Howe et al. (eds.), *Greece, Macedon and Persia*, Oxbow, 2015, 77–86

Roisman, J. & Worthington, I. (eds.), *Blackwell's Companion to Ancient Macedonia*, Wiley-Blackwell, 2010

Romm, J. S. (ed.), *The Landmark Arrian*, Anchor, 2010

Romm, J. S., *Ghost on the Throne: the Death of Alexander the Great and the War for Crown and Empire*, Knopf, 2011

Ruzicka, S., "The 'Pixodarus Affair' Reconsidered Again," in Carney & Ogden (2010), 3–12

Rzepka, J., "How Many Companions Did Philip Have?," *Electrum* 19 (2012), 131–35

Sawada, N., "Social Customs and Institutions: Aspects of Macedonian Elite Society," in Roisman & Worthington (2010), 392–408

Sekunda, N. V., "The Macedonian Army," in Roisman & Worthington (2010), 446–71

Sekunda, N. V., *The Antigonid Army*, Akanthina, 2013

Sorabji, R., *Philoponus and the Rejection of Aristotelian Science*, Cornell University Press, 1993

Stewart, A., *Faces of Power: Alexander's Image and Hellenistic Politics*, University of California Press, 1993

Stewart, A., "Alexander the Great in Greek and Roman Art," in J. Roisman (ed.), *Brill's Companion to Alexander the Great*, Brill, 2003, 31–66

Stoneman, R., *The Greek Alexander Romance*, Penguin Classics, 1991

Stoneman, R., *Alexander the Great: A Life in Legend*, Yale University Press, 2008

Strootman, R., *Courts and Elites in the Hellenistic Empires*, Edinburgh University Press, 2014

Stylianou, P. J., *A Historical Commentary on Diodorus Siculus, Book 15*, Clarendon, 1998

Tarn, W. W., *Alexander the Great*, 2 vols., Beacon Press, 1948

Tataki, A., *Ancient Beroea: Prosopography and Society*, De Boccard, 1988

Tataki, A., *Macedonian Edessa: Prosopography and Onomasticon*, De Boccard, 1994

Tataki, A., *Macedonians Abroad: A Contribution to the Prosopography of Ancient Macedonia*, Centre de Recherches de l'Antiquité Grecque et Romaine, 1998

Taylor, M., *Antiochus the Great*, Pen & Sword, 2013

Toynbee, A., *Constantine Porphyrogenitus and His World*, Oxford University Press, 1973

Treadgold, W., "The Official Histories of Constantine Porphyrogenitus," in *The Middle Byzantine Historians*, Palgrave Macmillan, 2013, 153–96

Troncoso, V. A., "The Bearded King and the Beardless Hero: From Philip II to Alexander the Great," in Carney & Ogden (2010), 13–24

Tronson, A., "Satyrus the Peripatetic and the Marriages of Philip II," *Journal of Hellenic Studies* 104 (1984), 116–26

Valeva, J., Nankov, E., Graninger, D. (eds.), *A Companion to Ancient Thrace*, Wiley-Blackwell, 2015

Walbank, F. W., *Philip V of Macedon*, Cambridge University Press, 1940

Walbank, F. W., *The Hellenistic World*, Harvard University Press, 1993

Waterfield, R., *Dividing the Spoils: The War for Alexander the Great's Empire*, Oxford University Press, 2011

Weber, G., "The Court of Alexander the Great as Social System," in W. Heckel & L. A. Tritle (eds.), *Alexander the Great: A New History*, Wiley-Blackwell, 2009, 83–98

Wheatley, P., "The Diadochi, or Successors to Alexander," in W. Heckel & L. A. Tritle (eds.), *Alexander the Great: A New History*, Wiley-Blackwell, 2009, 53–68

White, D. S., *The Life of Patriarch Photios*, Holy Cross Press, 1981

Wisnovsky, R., "Yahya al-Nahwi," in *Encyclopedia of Islam*, Brill, 2012

Worthington, I., *Philip II of Macedon*, Yale University Press, 2008

Worthington, I., *By the Spear: Philip II, Alexander the Great and the Rise and Fall of the Macedonian Empire*, Oxford University Press, 2014

Zahrnt, M., "A History of Macedonia in the Pre-Hellenistic Era," in Giannakis (2012), ch. 1

Zambrini, A., "The Historians of Alexander the Great," in J. Marincola (ed.), *A Companion to Greek and Roman Historiography* I, Wiley-Blackwell, 2007, 210–20

INDEX